Library of
Davidson College

EARLY JEWISH HERMENEUTIC

IN

PALESTINE

EARLY JEWISH HERMENEUTIC

IN

PALESTINE

by

Daniel Patte

Published by
SOCIETY OF BIBLICAL LITERATURE
and
SCHOLARS PRESS

DISSERTATION SERIES, NUMBER 22

1975

Distributed by

SCHOLARS PRESS
University of Montana
Missoula, Montana 59801

EARLY JEWISH HERMENEUTIC IN PALESTINE

by

Daniel Patte
Vanderbilt University
Nashville, Tennessee 37240

Th. D., 1971
Chicago Theological Seminary

Library of Congress Cataloging in Publication data

Patte, Daniel.
  Early Jewish hermeneutic in Palestine.

  (Dissertation series - Society of Biblical
Literature ; 22)
  Bibliography: p.
  1. Bible. O.T.--Criticism, interpretation,
etc., Jewish--History. 2. Bible. O.T.--Hermeneutics. 3. Apocalyptic literature. 4. Dead Sea scrolls. I. Title. II. Series: Society of Biblical Literature. Dissertation series ; 22.
BS1186.P3   221.6'3   75-22225
ISBN 0-89130-015-5

Copyright © 1975

by

The Society of Biblical Literature

Printed in the United States of America

Printing Department
University of Montana
Missoula, Montana 59801

CONTENTS

PREFACE xiii

INTRODUCTION

PURPOSES AND METHODOLOGY 1

    Exegesis and Hermeneutic
    Our Topic: Early Jewish Hermeneutic

PART I

THE USE OF SCRIPTURE IN CLASSICAL JUDAISM

CHAPTER I. THE PROBLEM OF THE SOURCES 11

    A Foreign Way of Thinking
    Late Date of our Sources
    The Transmission of Halakic Traditions
    The Transmission of Haggadic Traditions

CHAPTER II. THE EXPLICIT DOCTRINE OF SCRIPTURE
              IN CLASSICAL JUDAISM 19

    The Fixation of the "Canon"
    Designations of Holy Scripture
    Torah, Wisdom and Israel
    Remarks on the Availability of the Sacred Text

CHAPTER III. SCRIPTURE IN THE SYNAGOGUE:
              READING CYCLES AND HOMILIES 31

- Origins of the Synagogue
- Cycles for the Reading of Torah
- Seder and Haftarah
- Relationship of the Seder and Haftarah
  with the Halakah and/or the Petihtah
- Concluding Remarks

CHAPTER IV. SCRIPTURE AT THE SYNAGOGUE:
             TARGUM AND LITURGY 49

- Early Date of the Targumic Genre
- Targum and Massoretic Text
- Targumic Methods of Interpretation
- The Targum as Popular interpretation
  of Scripture
- Targum and Tradition (Oral Torah)
- The Doctrine of Scripture implied
  in the Targum
  1) *Everything is meaningful in Scripture*
  2) *Scripture is to be explained by Scripture*
  3) *The synthetic view of Scripture and of Sacred History*
  4) *Theological developments in the Targum*
  5) *The actualization of Scripture in the Targum*
- Liturgical Use of Scripture

CHAPTER V. THE USE OF SCRIPTURE IN THE SCHOOLS:
            WRITTEN AND ORAL TOROTH 87

- Oral Torah, Halakah and Jurisprudence
- Origins of the Oral Torah
- The Authority of the Oral Torah: the Controversy
  between the Sadducees and the Pharisees
- The Oral Torah as living Tradition:
  Cultural Changes and Scripture
  1) *The Gezeroth*
  2) *The Takkanoth*
  3) *The Takkanoth and the Sanctification of the Name*
  4) *Making a fence around Torah*
  5) *The Hermeneutical Rules (middoth) of Hillel*

CHAPTER VI. CLASSICAL JUDAISM AND SCRIPTURE 117

- The Midrash as the "Inquiring of God"
- The Two Functions of Scripture
  in Classical Judaism
- Exegesis, Hermeneutic and the Sadducees
- Exegesis, Hermeneutic and the Pharisees

Part II

The Use of Scripture in Sectarian Judaism

CHAPTER VII. THE PROBLEM OF THE SOURCES 131

    The Sources
    Eschatology and Apocalypticism

CHAPTER VIII. THE USE OF SCRIPTURE IN
APOCALYPTIC LITERATURE 139

    Limitations for our Study

   I. TRADITION, ORAL TORAH, AND APOCALYPTICISM . . . 145

      Similarities with the Targumic Use
      of Scripture
      The "Tables of the Law and of Testimony"
      and the "Heavenly Tables"
      Written and Oral Toroth versus
      Open and Secret Revelations
      Apocalypticism and the "History of
      Cultural Changes"

  II. SCRIPTURE AND HISTORY IN APOCALYPTIC
      LITERATURE: TYPOLOGY 159

      A "Cosmologization" of the Biblical
      Concept of Sacred History
      A Liturgical View of History

  III. THE USE OF BROAD BIBLICAL PATTERNS
      TO STRUCTURE APOCALYPTIC WRITINGS 169

  IV. SCRIPTURE AND PSEUDONYMITY 177

   V. THE VISIONARY TEXTS: ANTHOLOGICAL
      AND STRUCTURAL USES OF SCRIPTURE 181

      Vision as Literary Form and as
      Ecstatic Experience
      The Nature of Apocalyptic Inspiration
      Anthological and Structural Styles
        A. *Sibylline Oracles III:8-91*
        B. *I Enoch 90:13-19*
        C. *I Enoch 1:1-9*
        D. *Assumption of Moses 10:1-10*

VI. VISIONS, INSPIRATION AND SCRIPTURE 201

CONCLUSION 205

CHAPTER IX. THE USE OF SCRIPTURE IN
THE DEAD SEA SCROLLS 209

I. THE ESCHATOLOGICAL COMMUNITY
AND SCRIPTURE 211

The Basis for their Sectarianism: Scripture
The Teacher of Righteousness, Inspired
Interpreter of Scripture
"Hidden Things", "Mysteries", and Scripture
   A. *The "Hidden Things"*
   B. *The "Mysteries"*
The Explicit Quotations of Scripture

II. THE RE-WRITINGS OF SCRIPTURE:
GENESIS APOCRYPHON, BOOK OF JUBILEES
AND SAYINGS OF MOSES 233

III. THE USE OF SCRIPTURE IN THE
ZADOKITE DOCUMENTS 237

   A. The Use of Scripture in
      the Narrative Texts
   B. The Use of Scripture in
      the Exegetical Texts
   C. The Use of Scripture in
      the Juridic Texts

IV. THE USE OF SCRIPTURE IN THE
HODAYOT (1 QH) 247

   A. The Use of Scripture in
      the Hymns of the Community
   B. The Individual Thanksgiving Hymns
      1. *Weak Anthological Style*
      2. *Anthological Style*
      3. *The Structural Use of Scripture
         in the Hodayot*
A Threefold Locus of Revelation:
Scripture, The Community,
The Salient History

V.   THE USE OF SCRIPTURE IN THE
     MANUAL OF DISCIPLINE (1QS) 271

     Explicit Scriptural Quotations
     Halakic Interpretations
     Anthological Use of Scripture
     The Structural Use of Scripture
     The Manual of Discipline:
     a Quasi-Liturgical Text

VI. THE USE OF SCRIPTURE IN THE
     SCROLL OF THE WAR OF THE SONS
     OF LIGHT AGAINST THE SONS OF
     DARKNESS (1QM) 281

     A. Introduction: The Eschatological War
         (col. 1:1-2:14)
     B. The Rule of the War (2:15-14:15)
     C. Description of a Final Phase
         in the War (14:16-19:13)

VII. THE USE OF SCRIPTURE IN THE
     "ANGELIC LITURGY" AND OTHER
     LITURGICAL TEXTS 289

     An Allegorical Interpretation:
     4 Q sl 40
     4 Q Dibre Ham-Me'orot and the Origin
     of Typology

VIII. THE USE OF SCRIPTURE IN 4 Q TESTIMONIA 295

  IX. THE USE OF SCRIPTURE IN 4 Q FLORILEGIUM 297

   X. THE USE OF SCRIPTURE IN THE PESHARIM 299

     "Pesher" as the Interpretation
     of Scripture as Dream
     The Hermeneutical Methods of the Pesher

  XI. CONCLUSIONS: CLASSICAL JUDAISM,
      DEAD SEA COVENANTERS AND SCRIPTURE 309

      Classical Judaism and Scripture
      The Dead Sea Covenanters and Scripture

Postscript

A PROPOSAL FOR THE NORMALIZATION
OF TERMINOLOGY 315

    A. The Basic Terminology for the Uses
        of Scripture in Classical Judaism
    B. The Basic Terminology for the
        Apocalyptic Uses of Scripture

BIBLIOGRAPHY 325

A mes Parents:

    leur vie est un discours qui s'enchaîne
    à celui de l'Ecriture.

A Murielle, David et Chantal:

    qu'ils puissent à leur tour enchaîner de nouveaux
    discours à celui de l'Ecriture.

PREFACE

I want to express here my deep gratitude to all those who contributed to this work in one way or another. My gratitude goes especially:

to those who introduced me and guided me in the field of Jewish Studies: Professors Otto Betz, Andre Lacocque, and Rabbi Judah Roszenthal;

to the officers of the Chicago Theological Seminary for the scholarship they generously awarded me for two years;

to the librarians of the Chicago Theological Seminary, Union Seminary (New York), the Jesuit Seminaries at Chantilly (France) and Lyon (France) for kindly opening the treasures of their libraries.

To all of them goes my deep gratitude. I have still to express my thanks to four persons who contributed more directly to this work:

to Edward McMahon who spent many hours at the computer terminal helping me prepare the camera-ready copy;

to Stephen Langfur and Brian Kovacs. They had the patience to read the entire manuscript in order to help me correct the numerous mistakes due to my inexperience with the English language (yet I hold myself responsible for what is written here);

to my wife, Aline, who had the courage to type three times a far from easy manuscript.

Vanderbilt University   Daniel Patte
Nashville
May 1975

INTRODUCTION

PURPOSES AND METHODOLOGY

The title "Early Jewish Hermeneutic in Palestine" implies at once our goal and the scope of this study. Dealing with early Palestinian Judaism this work aims at exposing an important part of the setting of the New Testament hermeneutic of Scripture. We define Judaism broadly because we shall deal not only with the hermeneutic of classical Judaism (early Rabbinic Judaism), but also with that of sectarian Judaism (mainly represented by the Apocalyptists and the Covenanters of Qumran); these different hermeneutical approaches will be compared with each other.

The use of the term "hermeneutic" focuses our research: we are not directly concerned either with the exegetical methods of early Judaism, or with the results of its use of Scripture (that is, how such or such biblical passages were interpreted). We concentrate rather on early Judaism's *attitude* toward Scripture as evidenced in the principles or axioms which govern its use.

In order to express further the purpose and methodology of this study, let us define briefly what we understand by "hermeneutic"[1] and its relationship to exegesis in the context

---

[1] We limit ourselves to the question of the hermeneutic of a *text*. It should be noted that we use the term "hermeneutic" and not "hermeneutics". We adopt here a distinction similar to that pointed out by James M. Robinson in *New Frontiers in Theology II. The New Hermeneutic*, J. M. Robinson and J. B. Cobb, Jr., eds., New York, 1964, 1-77. Cf. also Robert W. Funk, *Language, Hermeneutic, and Word of God,*

of contemporary scholarship.[2]

EXEGESIS AND HERMENEUTIC

The study of the object of a text, of its *"signifiance"* and of its *"signification"*[3] is the task of exegesis. As a second step, and only as such, the hermeneutical task can take place: it is an attempt to take upon ourselves the meaning (*"sens"*) of the text.

This distinction between exegesis and hermeneutic is necessary in the contemporary theological discussion. Since the 19th century--because of the impact of the *Religionsgeschichtliche Schule*--biblical scholars understood exegesis mainly as a descriptive task, without concern for theological relevance.[4] Thus by means of different approaches (e.g. the historico-critical, the form-critical, the traditio-critical methods) one studies the object of the biblical text in itself--its significance, that is the systems of signs which constitutes it (its language, its forms, its structures, its *Sitz im Leben*, its historical setting) and its "signification", that is, the meaning this biblical text had for the community in which it emerged. This search is undertaken with the constant preoccupation of respecting the text. Thus, for critical biblical scholars since the 19th century exegesis demands the suspension of any concern for apologetic or theological relevance.

New York, 1966, 10ff. "Hermeneutics" (plural) refers to the rules for the interpretation of Scripture what ever may be these rules. In contrast we understand "hermeneutic" (singular) as referring to a specific mode of interpretation to be distinguished from exegesis.

[2] We follow Paul Ricoeur, "Problèmes actuels de l'interprétation", *C.P.E.D.*, Mars 1970, 51-70, and *De l'interprétation*, Paris, 1968.

[3] I use these terms with the specific meaning given to them by the French structuralist school: cf. for instance Roland Barthes, *Le Degré Zéro de l'Ecriture*, Paris, 1968, 79ff.

[4] Cf. K. Stendhal's article, "Contemporary Biblical Theology", *I.D.B.*, I, 418ff.

It is to be noted that this twofold exegetical task (the quest for the "signifiance" and for the "signification") is a *historical* research. It cannot, therefore, pretend to any absolute result:[5] the outcome necessarily depends upon the culture of the exegete.

For the Church and the Church theologian, on the other hand, the same biblical text is Holy Scripture; the relevance of the text becomes important. It becomes the task of hermeneutic--as contrasted with exegesis--to express the meaning of the biblical text for contemporary men. In this way hermeneutic takes upon itself more and more of the work which traditionally belonged to systematic theology.[6]

The distinction between exegesis and hermeneutic is necessary for a discussion of the different contemporary uses of Scripture. This distinction is also necessary for the study of the uses of Scripture in early Palestinian Judaism.

As mentioned above, hermeneutic is a second step in the process of interpretation. It is possible only on the basis of an understanding of the *"signifiance"* and *"signification"* of the text. These are apprehended by means of an exegesis --either an explicit exegesis (in contemporary times) or an implicit exegesis (in former times). Any exegesis is dependant upon the culture of the "exegetes" who have to comply with the demand of their culture.

To say that the hermeneutic of a text is done on the basis of its *"signifiance"* and *"signification"* is to say that the hermeneutical methods are determined by these characteristics of the text. For instance, in order to discover a text's meaning for me or for us, I cannot approach it in the same way if, according to my exegesis, it is a fairy

---

[5] On this debate, see Van A. Harvey, *The Historian and the Believer*, New York, 1965, and our review article of this book: Daniel Patte, "Foi et Histoire", *C.P.E.D.*, June, 1970, I-XIX.

[6] Cf. for instance John Macquarrie, *The Scope of Demythologizing: Bultmann and his Critics*, New York, 1960. Carl Michalson accurately describes the situation even though he deplores it: "New Testament exegesis done as existential hermeneutic bids to make systematic theology superfluous" (cf. his review of Macquarrie's book in *Interpretation* 15, 1961, 496.

tale, or a historical document, or a law of my country. The *"signifiance"* and *"signification"* of a given text will demand a particular hermeneutical method. There is no choice between different kinds of hermeneutic[7] once a specific exegesis of the text has been accepted.

Such a statement is indeed far reaching. We need to explain it briefly. It is actually based on an understanding of the relationship between the text and the reader.[8] This relationship cannot be understood as a dialogue because the text does not "answer": the author is already dead. Thus the text is dead. It is an *"it"* which can be analyzed as in an autopsy. This is why an exegesis is not only possible but legitimate, the text being a system of signs closed upon itself--i.e., it *has* a *"signifiance"* and a *"signification"*. Yet the text is also open: it waits for a reader (again, not an interlocutor) who will not only take upon himself the argument of the text but also add to it a new argument. Thus, the reader prolongs in a new discourse the discourse of the text. His new discourse, i.e., his hermeneutical interpretation, depends upon the discourse of the text.[9] This remark suggests that in the text there is the potentiality of a "taking over"*(reprise)* or, to use Martin Noth's vocabulary, of a "re-presentation". The reader by "taking over" the discourse of the text discovers himself in a new light: the light which the text projects on him. Thus certainly the reading of a text is an appropriation; the text becomes the reader's own, it is meaningful to him. But at the same time the text remains the text. To use an image, the text becomes

---

[7] I am here paraphrasing Martin Noth, who said this about what he calls exegesis as "re-presentation" *(Vergegenwartigung)*, which is the equivalent of what I call "hermeneutic". He opposes this to historico-critical exegesis: "The 'Re-presentation' of the Old Testament in Proclamation" in *Essays on Old Testament Hermeneutics*, Claus Westermann ed., Richmond, Virginia, 1963, 80.

[8] Here again I am following Ricoeur, especially his article "Problèmes actuels de l'interprétation".

[9] Cf. Ricoeur, "Problèmes actuels de l'interprétation", 64, "Lire c'est en tout hypothèse enchaîner un discours nouveau au discours du texte".

a mirror in which I as reader can see myself. In this, reading is similar to dialogue, since my interlocutor is the necessary medium for any apprehension of my self.[10] Yet reading is different in the sense that this mirror is not the "fugitive other" which in his freedom cannot be fully apprehended. To continue the metaphor, when the "fugitive other" is the mirror, I cannot apprehend the mirror's size, shape and form, nor evaluate which part of myself I can expect to see in it and with what kind of distortion. The text, on the contrary, is fixed and therefore the reader has the possibility to apprehend the size, the shape and the form of the mirror in which he can discover himself.

The text is indeed a discourse which I, as reader, can prolong by my own discourse (and by so doing I can express and discover my self). But precisely as a text it is not a fugitive discourse. I have therefore the time to place myself within the perspective of the text. Using another metaphor we could say that I have the time to apprehend the vectors of this discourse by means of the exegesis. In the hermeneutic I shall latter on extend these vectors up to me. This hermeneutic is legitimate if I respect the direction of these vectors as defined by the exegesis.

Thus the hermeneutic of a text requires that the reader sets himself in the perspective of the text—the term "perspective" is used in this statement with a dynamic meaning.[11]

---

[10] Cf. Daniel Patte, *L'athéisme d'un chrétien ou un chrétien à l'écoute de Sartre*, Paris, 1965, 67-97, in which I discuss at length the role of other people for the apprehension of our self.

[11] Cf. Ricoeur, "Problèmes actuels de l'interprétation", 68, "Interpréter le texte c'est se mettre dans le sens du texte".
This being said we are conscious that it is nothing new. We mentioned already that Martin Noth and K. Stendhal are expressing a similar distinction, if in other terms. E. C. Blackman reaches a like conclusion, although from a very different view point, by combining the views of the pietist Bengel with those of the Platonist Jowitt: "Said Bengel: Apply all thy powers to the text, and all its meaning apply to thyself. And Jowitt declared: The true use of interpretation is to get rid of interpretation, and leave us alone in company with the author". *Biblical Interpretation*, London, 1957, 206.

OUR TOPIC: EARLY JEWISH HERMENEUTIC

We can now be more precise on the definition of our topic, by using the preceding distinction between exegesis and hermeneutic. One could object that such a distinction was not made in early Judaism. And it is true indeed. Such a distinction was not made for the very reason that the only conscious use of Scripture was hermeneutical. Even the *middot* of classical Judaism (sometimes called exegetical rules) are according to our definition nothing else than hermeneutical rules: they are describing the "legitimate" way to prolong the discourse of Scripture by a new discourse. Yet our assumption is that these hermeneutical rules as well as the other hermeneutical interpretations are based upon implicit exegeses, that is, on understandings of the "signifiance" and "signification" of the biblical text. We are simply assuming that the Jews of that time had some kind of conception of the biblical text.

That their conception may seem strange and possibly meaningless is another matter: it comes as a reminder that any exegesis is culturally bound. Just as today our exegetical methods are dependant upon our culture, so their culture demanded from the early Jews that they grasp the "signifiance" and "signification" of the biblical text in certain ways. Yet these exegeses were more assumed than practiced: their results were taken as self evident. The primary focus was on hermeneutical interpretations, which were nevertheless built on the results of what we could call implicit exegeses.

We may now re-state the aim of our research. We are concerned neither with showing the process of Jewish exegesis in itself (which would demand extensive speculations), nor with presenting the results of the Jewish hermeneutical interpretations in themselves (this has been done by many

---

In our terms we could put this as follows: "Apply all thy powers to the text": the exegetical task. "All its meaning apply to thyself": hermeneutical task. We take Jowitt's saying to mean that exegesis should lead to and make room for hermeneutic.

scholars necessarily dealing with limited topics). Although we shall need to take both into account, we shall attempt to point out the principles or axioms which govern these hermeneutical interpretations.

One could wonder why we have not simply used the phrase "doctrines of Scripture" to designate these axioms. They are "doctrines of Scripture" indeed, but also more than that. For "doctrines of Scripture" are so concerned with hermeneutical interpretation that the use of this phrase makes us lose sight of some of the results of the exegesis. This danger is all the more real when exegesis is implicit. Our contention is that aside from the explicit doctrines of Scripture, there are implicit axioms which complement them. In our research we shall therefore take these explicit doctrines into account, yet try to grasp their meaning more fully by taking into account the other axioms which governed the uses of Scripture in early Judaism.

For this purpose we shall scrutinize how, in different ways, the various Jewish groups set themselves into the perspective of the texts, i.e., how they prolonged in a new discourse the discourse of the biblical text. This implies further that we shall not only scrutinize their explicit uses of Scripture[12] (as when they quoted biblical passages, or interpreted them explicitly), but also their implicit uses of Scripture.

Our research will necessarily lead to certain considerations about early Jewish conceptions of revelation. Actually, as implied above, any hermeneutic of a text is revelatory: we may anticipate the results of our research by saying that the Jews themselves considered their hermeneutic of Scripture to be revelatory. This is to say that revelation for them was not Scripture considered in itself, but Scripture as prolonged in a new discourse. As we shall see this new discourse extends the vectors of the Scriptural perspective

---

[12] We shall use from now on the phrase "use of Scripture" with a hermeneutical connotation, i.e., as an abbreviation for "hermeneutical use of Scripture". In the same way "to interpret" and "interpretation" are used with a hermeneutical connotation.

different directions, so as to touch upon different components of the life of the Jewish communities. We could say that the revelation occurs in the "tension" between these components and Scripture. Mixing metaphors we shall speak of different "loci of revelation", or different "poles" between which this tension is found. Scripture, then, is a locus of revelation when it is in tension with (or extended to touch upon) one of the components of the life of the Jewish communities; and each such component is itself another locus of revelation.

Besides Scripture itself, we shall point out several loci of revelation. Among them we shall find the contemporary history of the different Jewish communities. We shall be led to make a distinction between two kinds of history,[13] which have to be considered as two different loci of revelation. Thus we shall make a distinction between what we call the *"salient history"* and the *"history of cultural changes"*. A similar distinction is made by the noted historian Page Smith[14] who gives these two kinds of history ambiguous appellations: a) "Existential history", which is made out of "the most dramatic and sharply defined episodes"[15] (which we term "salient history"); b) "symbolic history" which deals with the subtle changes in "modes of existence"[16] (which we term "history of cultural changes", in agreement with Jacques Barzum who calls it "cultural history"[17]).

Having given these definitions of the scope and purpose of our study, having introduced some of the vocabulary that we have been led to use in our research we can now turn to the study of early Jewish hermeneutic in Palestine, first in classical Judaism and later in sectarian Judaism.

---

[13] This term is always intended below to include the present and the future as well as the past.

[14] Page Smith, *The Historian and History*, New York, 1960, 3rd ed., 1966, 200ff., in his chapter entitled "Categories of Historical Reality".

[15] *op. cit.*, 202.

[16] *op. cit.*, 203.

[17] Jacques Barzun, "Cultural History as a Synthesis", in *The Varieties of History*, ed. by Fritz Stern, Cleveland, Ohio, 1956, 387ff.

PART I

THE USE OF SCRIPTURE IN CLASSICAL JUDAISM

CHAPTER I

THE PROBLEM OF THE SOURCES

A Foreign Way of Thinking

When opening the huge literature of classical Judaism--which includes not only the *Mishnah*, the two *Talmudoth* and the *Midrashim* but also the *Targumim*--one cannot but be bewildered. And this bewilderment increases when focusing one's attention upon the uses of Scripture therein. Even noted scholars specialists of this field of study like J. Bonsirven cannot keep themselves from expressing this feeling, by the use of adjectives like "artificial" to qualify this use of Scripture.[1] And this is not only the case with Christian scholars but also with eminent Jewish scholars like Lauterbach.[2]

In this study we shall avoid such qualifications. We are indeed convinced that what we could be tempted to qualify as being artificial, meaningless, etc., appears to us as such only because it derives from a way of thinking foreign to us, but coherent in itself. It is with this basic assumption that we shall investigate this literature; we shall attempt to find

---

[1] Cf. J. Bonsirven, *Exégèse Rabbinique et Exégèse Paulinienne*, Paris, 1939, *passim*.

[2] Cf. J. Z. Lauterbach, "Midrash and Mishnah" in *Rabbinic Essays*, Cincinnati, 1951, 163-256.

the underlying general attitude, the axioms, which could help to overcome this bewilderment, For this purpose we shall try in a first step to make our own the early Jew's way of thinking. In a second step, we shall try to express it in our terms in order that it may make sense for us: for indeed it is only in so far as we shall be able to express it in our own way of thinking that we may claim to understand it. Thus for each point we shall use successively these two steps, passing to the second as soon as we shall have gone far enough in the way of thinking of the early Jews to be able to assume legitimately that we have in our grasp one of its elements. This is to say that in the beginning of our research we shall necessarily dwell a long time on the first step, before passing to the second; then, later on, we shall pass more often from one to the other.

LATE DATE OF OUR SOURCES

As previously mentioned our research is focused on the Palestinian Judaism of the New Testament time (first century B.C. and first century A.D.). We cannot, however, in the case of Pharisaic and early Rabbinic Judaism (which we call classical Judaism)[3] limit ourselves to the sources written down before the end of our period: otherwise we would have to dismiss the discussion on the use of Scripture by the Pharisees.[4] For indeed we shall have to depend upon Rabbinic texts[5] which cannot be dated, in any case, earlier than the second century A.D. The crucial problem is to know how much we can rely on these sources which compiled traditions transmitted orally for decades if not centuries.

This is raising the whole question of the dependability

---

[3] We use this phrase in opposition to "sectarian Judaism" by means of which we will designate the Judaism of the Apocalyptic literature, and of the Dead Sea Scrolls.

[4] As, for example, Annie Jaubert did in her study on the Covenant: *La Notion d'Alliance dans le Judaïsme aux abords de l'Ere Chrétienne*, Paris, 1963.

[5] *The Psalms of Solomon* are another possible source. Josephus' work gives us only indirect information.

of oral tradition. We cannot here enter into this discussion.[6] Suffice it here to say that modern critics often underestimate the accuracy of the transmission of those traditions.[7] Granted that this accuracy varies with their contents and forms, yet in our case it was greatly improved by the very life structure of Palestinian Judaism: the schools and the synagogue.

THE TRANSMISSION OF HALAKIC TRADITIONS

Even if we do not know exactly how the schools were organized in the period before Jabneh, we know that disciples gathered around the great masters in order to learn the tradition "in the teacher's words."[8] As Gerhardson shows,[9] this rule demanding that tradition be quoted in the exact wording in which it has been received was practiced very early: from the time of Hillel and possibly much before. This applies especially to the halakic traditions which by their very character as legal decisions demanded such a precision, and implied a study by rote, a constant *repetition*.[10] This was implemented with the help of aids to

---

[6] Cf. S. Mowinckel, "Oral Tradition", *I.D.B.* IV, 683ff. and mainly for our topic Birger Gerhardsson, *Memory and Manuscript*, Coppenhagen, 1961.

[7] Yet, recently, there has been a strong trend in the opposite direction: cf. below our remarks on the research on the targumic literature. We have to avoid carefully going to either extreme.

[8] M. Ed. I. 3 אדם חייב לומר בלשון רבו

[9] *Op. cit.*, 131.

[10] This is the etymological meaning of the term "mishnah". Cf. J. Z. Lauterbach, "Mishnah", *J.E.*, vol. VIII, 609ff.; Mielziner, *Introduction to the Talmud*, 6f.; Gerhardsson, *op. cit.*, 134ff. The teachers themselves in order to be sure that their disciples would remember were supposed to repeat several times their teaching: four times (R. Eliezer ben Hyrcanos according to a *baraita* in Erub. 54b) or "until the pupil has learned" (according to R. Akiba, same source but also *Mekilta* on Exod. 21:1, cf. J. Z. Lauterbach's edition, vol. III, 1).

the memory, namely catch-words,[11] that is, formulated phrases which, to use Finkelstein's image, "served as pegs on which the unformulated portion depended." These formulated phrases were later committed to writing in a kind of shorthand notes. In the *Mishnah* we find numerous examples of this style: the biblical proof texts are just alluded to or assumed known and many halakoth are quite laconic. It should be noted, however, that, as far as the halakic teaching is concerned, these shorthand notes did not exist before the end of the first century A.D.[12] Yet since the oral transmission of these halakoth was scrupulously done we can expect a relatively good accuracy. We shall take into account therefore, the halakic teaching of the Sages and Rabbis of our period even if it is to be found only in later Rabbinical writings. But we shall have to do so with caution, for indeed, there is always the risk that the authorship may have been wrongly ascribed, as is clear in the cases in which the same teaching is attributed to different teachers.[13] Furthermore we have to be aware of the phenomenon of pseudonymity which played an important role in the intertestamental Jewish literature.[14] What Russell says about the pseudonymity in Apocalyptical writings can be said *mutatis mutandis* about the Rabbinical literature. So conscious were the disciples of their indebtness to their master or to the founder of their school that they regarded themselves not as formulators of new halakoth, but simply as inheritors and interpreters of their masters' teaching. We can expect therefore that sayings emanating from a school have been attributed to its founder (according to the case to

---

[11] סימנים. Cf. Louis Finkelstein, "The Transmission of Transmission of the Early Rabbinic Traditions", *H.U.C.A.* 16, 1941, 115-35.

[12] Cf. H. L. Strack, *Introduction to the Talmud and Midrash*, 12ff., where the author discusses the "interdict on writing down".

[13] e.g., *Aboth* IV 7 (9) attributed either to R. Ishmael, or to R. Simon, or to Bar Kappara.

[14] Cf. D. S. Russell, *The Method and Message of Jewish Apocalyptic*, Philadelphia, 1964, 99ff., 127-39, 184ff.

Hillel, Shammai and other famous teachers)[15] just as several times certain teachers designated their *own* teaching as originating with Moses (*"halakah le-Mosheh mi-Sinai"*).[16] To this should be added the constant concern to stress the authority of the different halakoth by pointing at their antiquity. The older the halakah the more authoritative it is.[17] Thus we find the use of phrases like *"halakah le-Moshe mi-Sinai,"*[18] *"Mizwat zekenim,"*[19] *"Qabbalah ha -aboth."* and *"Masoreth ha-abotenu."*[20] Yet it should be noted that this emphasis on the authority of the older halakoth certainly contributed also to their faithful (because respectful) transmission and thus to the correct preservation of the sayings emanating from the period which concerns us. This being said we should neither underestimate the role of pseudonymity nor the constant adaptation of the halakah to new situations. It is precisely this ability to adapt itself which is significant for our study.

Thus despite the later date of our sources we can assume

---

[15] Cf. also this problem in the New Testament about Jesus' teaching and the teaching of the early Church. Of the large literature which attempts to distinguish them since the end of the 19th century let us mention only one of the latest: N. Perrin, *Rediscovering the Teaching of Jesus*, New York, 1967.

[16] As the Talmud recognizes in the cases of halakoth given as "from Moses" by R. Akiba (Niddah 45a), R. Dimi (*Pes.* 110b). Cf. J. Z. Lauterbach, "Sinaitic Commandments", *J.E.*, vol. XI, 383.

[17] Cf. M. *Pe'ah* 2:6, where the halakah is traced back from Rabban Gamaliel to the Zuggoth and finally to Moses.

[18] Yet this phrase is used only three times in the Mishnah: cf. Strack, *op. cit.*, 9. One of these is *Pe'ah* 2:6 (cf. preceding note).

[19] The earliest name for Oral Torah according to J. Z. Lauterbach, "Oral Torah", *J.E.*, vol. IX, 424, found in the Talmud in *Suk.* 46a.

[20] *Meg.* 10b, *Shek.* VI. These phrases are the equivalent of the ἡ παράδοσις τῶν πρεσβυτέρων of the New Testament and of similar phrases in Josephus *Ant.* XIII, 10, 6; 16, 2, as Louis Ginsberg ("Cabala", *J.E.*, III) and D. Daube ("Rabbinic Methods of Interpretation and Hellenistic Rhetoric", *H.U.C.A.* 22, 1949, 242) pointed out rightly.

the presence in halakic teaching of relevant material for the study of our period, namely in the *Mishnah*, *Tosepha* and in the Tannaitic Midrashim (i.e., *Mekilta*, *Sifra* and *Sifre*, in their halakic parts).

THE TRANSMISSION OF THE HAGGADIC TRADITIONS

In the case of the haggadic teaching the existence of shorthand notes is well attested[21] and can even be witnessed in the early midrashim where we can find not only evidences of catch-words common to several midrashim on the same text,[22] but even mere transcription of shorthand notes in the Tannaitic midrashim.[23] Furthermore this haggadic teaching is, generally speaking, related more closely to the biblical text.[24] By this very fact the oral transmission of this teaching was relatively easier: the very words of the biblical text bring to mind by mental association the haggadic teaching drawn from this text.

On the one hand we can say that by its very content and its character the haggadic teaching was not preserved and transmitted as carefully as the authoritative and normative halakic teaching. As is well known haggadic teaching is not binding.[25] Nevertheless it must be studied as well as the halakah.[26] On the other hand the haggadic teaching is not

---

[21] Cf. Strack, *op. cit.*, 13-14.

[22] As L. Finkelstein shows it with several examples, *op. cit.*, 117ff.

[23] Good examples of this from *Sifre* Deut. are given by L. Finkelstein, *op. cit.*, 131ff. He cites parables in syncoped form which are therefore not intelligible for us as long as we are not able to complement them by what is implied.

[24] Cf. Bacher, "The Origin of the word Haggada", *J.Q.R.* 4, 1892.

[25] Cf. G. F. Moore, *Judaism*, vol. I, 162f.

[26] Cf. *Sifre on Deut.* XI, 22, ed. H. S. Horovitz, 113. "So, too, you might perhaps say, I have learnt halkah! This is enough! Therefore it says: 'all this commandment', so you

subjected to the necessity of adapting itself to the new situations in the same way as the halakah: it can be said therefore to be more stable than the halakah.[27] Consequently we can be confident that the haggadic sources which we shall use contain, compiled together with later ones, teaching which originated in the period we are considering if not earlier. As has been demonstrated by G. Vermès[28] it is possible to trace in these sources by means of historico-critical methods the development of the haggadic traditions through the centuries. This is a life long research in which obviously we cannot involve ourselves here inasmuch as it is aiming at the evolution of the *content* of these haggadic traditions. Our topic does not aim at the content but at the hermeneutical principles: we can assume safely that as far as the haggadah is concerned these methods were in use much before the fall of Jerusalem and did not change significantly. This is one of the conclusions we can draw from G. Vermès' study. Furthermore, as we shall see below, the Synagogue which is the *Sitz im Leben* of the haggadah was functioning before the destruction of the second Temple, as well as being one[29] of the factors which allowed Judaism to subsist with the necessary religious continuity after the disaster of A.D. 70.

Thus eventhough we shall have to draw on sources written down after the end of the period we wish to consider, this procedure is a legitimate enterprise because of the nature of the oral transmission of the halakic and haggadic traditions and because of the nature of our topic.

---

must learn Bible (Midrash), Halakoth and Haggadoth". Furthermore , by means of the haggadah, one gets to know the Creator, *ibid.*, 114.

[27]Thus R. Le Déaut,*Liturgie Juive et Nouveau Testament*, Rome, 1965, 15: "L'aggadah est plus stable que la halakah qui par définition devait s'adapter sans cesse. ... Pour l'aggadah on aimait au contraire s'attacher aux explications traditionnelles quitte à y voir se superposer une bonne trouvaille occasionnelle".

[28]Cf. G. Vermès, *Scripture and Tradition in Judaism*, Leiden, 1961.

[29]Together with the increased role of the schools.

CHAPTER II

THE EXPLICIT DOCTRINE OF SCRIPTURE IN CLASSICAL JUDAISM

From the above comments it appears that in classical Judaism we find two types of use of Scripture: the halakic and the haggadic.[1] We shall have to consider them as a whole, as the Sages remind us to do, by associating them in the collocation "Halakoth and haggadoth".[2] Yet before trying to point out the "doctrine of Scripture" implied in this twofold hermeneutic let us indicate briefly the explicit doctrine of Scripture of classical Judaism which can be summarized in the phrase *"Torah min ha-shamayim"* (lit. "Torah from heaven").[3]

THE FIXATION OF THE "CANON"

At the beginning of the Christian era, the collection of Holy Scriptures was already fixed in what we can call, despite the fact that no such designation of the Bible can be found in

---

[1] We include in the second all which is "not halakic", using the term "haggadah" with its traditional meaning (cf. Strack, *op. cit.*, 7), rather than its etymological one, which could include also the halakah (cf. Bacher, "The Origin of the word Haggada", *J.Q.R.* 4, 1892, 419.

[2] Cf. e.g., *Sifre* on Deut. XI, 22, cited above; *Exod. R.* Beshallach XXIII, 10; Mishpatim, XXX, 14; *Tanh* B., Ki Tissa, 58b (quoted by Montefiore & Loewe, *Rabbinic Anthology*, 159-60.

[3] Sanh., X, 1.

early Judaism,[4] the "canon", that is, a body of Scripture which was distinguished from profane literature and to which was ascribed a divine origin. Yet the concept of canon[5] involves the concern to distinguish these writings from other, "extraneous" (חיצונים) books[6] and therefore demands a polemical context. It seems that this attitude appeared only after the fall of Jerusalem (at Jabneh *circa* A.D. 90) or very shortly before (about A.D. 65 if Gratz's theory about an assembly of the Hillelite and Shammaite schools in Jerusalem is correct)[7] that is when the precise extent of Scripture was the subject of debates. Should Ecclesiastes, Canticles (Song of Songs), Esther and also Ezechiel[8] be considered as "defiling the hands" (i.e. holy) or not? Such was the problem the Sages were considering. It is only after that time that the phrase "extraneous" (חיצונים) books came into use in order to designate profane or heretical books, as in R. Akiba's usage.[9] It is only after that time (end of the first century A.D.) that we find references to the number of books in the

---

[4] Cf. Ludwig Blau, "Bible Canon", *J.E.*, vol. III, 140.

[5] With its Greek meaning of "rod" and "norm". Cf. Beyer, "κανών", *T.W.N.T.*, vol. 3, Engl. tr., 596ff.

[6] Cf. R. Akiba's saying in *Sanh.*, X, 1.

[7] Cf. Gratz, *Kohelet*, Leipsic, 1871, 149, quoted by L. Blau, *op. cit.*, 149. Cf. also Nahum N. Glatzer, *Hillel the Elder*, 59ff., based on *Edu.*, V, 3, "Ecclesiastes does not render the hands unclean according to the view of the School of Skammai: but the school of Hillel says, it does render the hands unclean" (cf. also *Shab.* 30b).

[8] This last book was objected to because of its contradictions with the Pentateuch. They were solved exegetically by Hananiah ben Hezekia ben Garon, according to *Hag.*, 13a, cf. K. N. Cornill, "Book of Ezechiel", *J.E.*, col. V, 318.

[9] e.g., *Sanh.* X, 1.

Bible.[10]

Designations of Holy Scripture

This observation, together with the fact that in the Tannaitic literature we find references to biblical books from every part of the canon, shows that if the canon was not fixed in theory it was fixed in actuality. These books were considered as "defiling the hands".[11] Holy books,[12] they were often simply referred to as ספרים[13] or as מקרא ("that which is read")[14]--referring to the custom of the reading of Scripture in Sabbath services --or more frequently as כתוב (Scripture, literally "It is written"). This latter is a kind of shorthand indeed[15] but very significant in itself. There was no need to specify *where* "it is written": it was obvious for everybody![16]

---

[10] In non-Rabbinical literature, IV *Ezra*, XIV:44-46 (24 books) and Josephus, *Contra Apionem*, I, 8 (22 books). The hesitation between 22 and 24 books is found also in later Rabbinical literature and can be explained by the content of the rolls. Cf. L. Blau, *op. cit.*, 142ff.

[11] It is difficult to pinpoint the origin and meaning of the phrase ממטא את-הידים which may have had as *Sitz im Leben* the Temple. Cf. L. Blau, *op. cit.*, 141, for hypotheses and references. It does not seem to have appeared before the assembly of the Hillelite and Shammaite schools in A.D. 65.

[12] Yet the phrase Holy books ספרי הקדש is not found before medieval times, *ibid.*, 140.

[13] Τὰ βιβλία. Cf. already *ben Sirach* (in the introduction).

[14] *Aboth*, 5:21, *inter alias*. Yet cf. *Sifre*, Deut. 317 where Mikra designated only the Prophets and Hagiographa.

[15] As suggested by L. Blau, *op. cit.*, 141.

[16] Cf. Bacher (*Terminologie* I, 92) who points out that with the article הכתוב meant the whole of Scripture by opposition to the plural use without article (כתובים), which designated the third group of biblical books. Cited by Moore, *op. cit.*, vol. III, 64.

This sober way of designating Scripture signifies the absence of polemic about their holy and inspired character. It is only in a polemic setting that a phrase like כתבי הקדש (holy Scripture) appears.[17]

A last, very common designation for the entire Bible is "Torah".[18] This designation[19] is significant for an understanding of the inspiration of Scripture. For indeed the use of the word Torah, which refers first of all to the book of Moses, extends to the rest of Scripture the "canonicity" recognized very early of the Pentateuch.[20] It implies the unity of Scripture: despite a clear distinction between the authority of its three parts (Torah, Prophets and Hagiographa)[21] Scripture as a whole is considered to be inspired by the Holy Spirit.[22] Here we should emphasize that

---

[17] Cf. for instance *B.B.* I, 6: "Scripture should not be divided" ("as the profane books can be", is implied). Cf. also *Shab.* XVI:1 and elsewhere in the Mishnah; and *Tos. Yom Tob* 4:4 (cited by Moore, *ibid.*) where כתבי הקדש is opposed to כתבי הדיוט (profane writings).

[18] Cf. for instance *Mek.* Beshallah, 9, ed. Friedmann, 34b, 40b, cited by L. Blau, *ibid.* This is explicitly expressed in later Rabbinic literature: Midr. Ps. on LXXVIII (Buber's ed. 172b, 1): "Let not a man say, the Psalms are not Torah; they are Torah and the Prophets too are Torah, and the riddles (Proverbs) and the parables are also Torah". Cf. also *Tanh. B.*, Re'eh, 10a, (Montefiore & Loewe, 158); *Bab. M.* 83a (Proverbs as Torah) and *Sanh.* 91b (Psalms as Torah).

[19] We should avoid "Law" as a translation of "Torah". As is well known a better translation would be "instruction", "teaching". Cf. for instance R. Travers Herford, *The Pharisees*, 54, and R. Bloch, "Ecriture et Tradition dans le Judaisme: Aperçus sur l'origine du Midrash", *Cahiers Sioniens*, 1954, 11.

[20] Already at the time of the Samaritan schism in the 4th century.

[21] This difference in authority was particularly felt in the use of these different parts in the Synagogue as we shall see below.

[22] Another explanation could be that this designation has been adopted for the whole of Scripture because Torah was the first part, as a shorthand for "Torah, Nebiim and Ketoubim" (from which the later abbreviation ת/נ/ך). Yet the very fact of the use of this abbreviation implied a comparable inspiration for the three parts.

in Rabbinic theology the Holy Spirit and the spirit of prophecy are considered as identical.[23] Yet inspiration is more commonly expressed by the phrase *Torah min ha-shamayim*.[24] We shall have therefore to take this into account in order to avoid projecting on the early Jewish concept of inspiration, connotations which would be foreign to it. It remains that Scripture was considered beyond any question as "inspired". It was a matter of fact. The "inspiration" of Scripture needed to be mentioned only in polemic passages[25] and the term Torah was practically identical with the term revelation.[26]

TORAH, WISDOM AND ISRAEL

That Torah is the complete, final and immutable[27] revelation is drawn from Deut. 30:11-14.[28] Yet it should not be forgotten that if Torah is used to designate the whole of Scripture it includes the Oral Torah[29] also revealed *"le Moshe*

---

[23] Cf. Ludwig Blau, "Holy Spirit", *J.E.*, vol. VI, 447ff.; cf. also the discussion on the canonicity of Ecclesiastes, Song of Songs, and mainly Esther which are recognized as composed "in" the Holy Spirit, *Meg.* 6b.

[24] Cf. *Sifre* on Deut. 14:7, in a saying by R. Akiba; cf. also *Sanh.* X, 1; *Sanh.* 99a:1; *Y. Pea*16b, etc.

[25] Cf. the passages mentioned in the preceding note.

[26] Cf. Moore, *op. cit.*, vol. I, 263.

[27] In the world to come, God himself cannot do anything but teach it (*Hag.* 14a).

[28] "This commandment . . . is not hidden from thee, neither is it far off. It is not in heaven . . . neither is it beyond the sea". Cf. *Deut. Rab. ad. loc.*: "Nothing is left from it in heaven".

[29] Cf. *Sifra* on Lev. XXVI:46 and *Num. R.* Naso XIV:10 which express it explicitly (Montefiore & Loewe, 159); see below how this unity of Torah (Pentateuch, Prophets, Hagiographa and Oral Law) was expressed in the so-called *"yelamedenu"* homilies.

mi-Sinai" (to Moses on Mt Sinai).[30] We shall come back at length on the relationship between Written Torah and Oral Torah when examining the use of Scripture in the school.

As the possession of God,[31] Torah was identified very early with Wisdom,[32] that is to say, the divine pre-existent Wisdom which was with God at the creation (following Prov. 8:22ff.).[33] From this conviction many later haggadic traditions were drawn. Torah was stored in heaven before the creation of the world.[34] The world has been created for the sake (lit. for the merits) of Torah.[35] Torah is therefore referred to as the "tool of the creation".[36] Even if this haggadic development occurred much later, the identification of Torah with the pre-existent Wisdom can be traced back as we saw to the period we are considering.[37]

The fact that Torah has been given to Israel gave also rise to many haggadic developments on this same line.[38] One

---

[30] Cf. *Sifra, loc. cit.*

[31] Together with Abraham, Israel, Heaven and Earth, and the Temple, *Aboth* 6:10.

[32] The origin of this identification can be found in the Pentateuch itself: Deut. 4:5-6 (where חקים and משפטים are in parallelism with חכמה and בינה); in Proverbs the teaching of the author (תורתי) is parallel (if not identified) with חכמה (cp. Prov. 3:1-4 and Prov. 3:13 and 16; Prov. 6:23-24 and Prov. 7:4-5). This identification is made explicitly in Ben Sirach (1:4-5, 26; 15:1ff.; 21:11; 24:23ff.; 34:8). Cf. also *Letter of Aristeas* 31, and 313; *Wisdom of Solomon* 6:18; *I Baruch* 4:1; in Rabbinic literature: *Gen. R.* 1:1; 17:5.

[33] Proof text of *Aboth* 6:10.

[34] *Zeb.* 116a: for 974 generations; cf. also *Sab.* 88b.

[35] *Gen. R.* XII:2.

[36] *Aboth* 3:14, cf. also *Pes. R.* 95a; *Tanh. Bereshit* 1f., 6b, as quoted by Montefiore & Loewe, *op. cit.*, 170-71.

[37] This kind of theological speculation is at home with a mystico-allegorical interpretation of Scripture (cf. Philo). As we shall see there are reasons to believe that such a trend existed in Palestine at the beginning of our era.

[38] Torah has been created for the glory of Israel, according to a saying of Simeon b. Yohay (A.D. 130-160). (*Sifre* on Deut. XI:21). Torah was offered to all the nations but Israel only accepted it, *Mek.* on Exod. XIX:2, and mainly

of the most important is that in Torah God gave himself to Israel.[39] To study Torah[40] or to recite passages from Torah[41] is to be in the Presence (*Shekinah*) of God. Therefore Torah is a surrogate of the Temple, the place *(makom) par excellence* of the Presence of God,[42] and to take on the yoke of Torah[43] is to take on the yoke of Heaven (God).[44] Accepting the yoke (of Heaven) is identical with accepting Torah and the Covenant.[45] In this line of thought it is not surprising to find that Torah is personified not only in phrases like "Scripture says"[46] but also as an intercessor for Israel before God.[47]

All of these haggadic developments indicate not only the understanding of Torah's inspiration, but also its central place in the life of Israel. The Israelite (the Jew) was created for the purpose of studying Torah.[48] Torah is a Crown[49] for all Israelites and should not be studied and

---

on Exod. XX:2 (Lauterbach ed., vol.II, 234); cf. also *int.al. Sifre* on Deut. XXXIII:2, Bonsirven, *Textes*, 85.

[39] Cf. *Exod. R.* Terumah XXXIII:1, 6, where several parables are used to express this idea.

[40] *Aboth* 3:3

[41] *Viz.* the blessings, *Aboth* 3:4.

[42] Cf. *Sifre* on Deut. XXXII:46, and also *Tanh. B. Ahare Mot* 35a, Montefiore & Loewe, 119.

[43] *Aboth* 3:6.

[44] As is implied in *Aboth* 3:6. Generally one takes on the yoke of Heaven (or of the Kingdom) by the recitation of the *shema*. Cf. Solomon Schechter, *Aspects of Rabbinic Theology*, New York, 1961, 65-115, and Buchler, op.cit., 75-84.

[45] *Y. Pea.* 16b, according to a saying of Abba Saul (A.D. 130-160), both given "without condition" to Israel, *Mek.* on Exod. XVIII:27, Lauterbach ed., vol. II, 190.

[46] Which can be understood as a mere figure of speech.

[47] *Ex. R.* XXIX:4.

[48] *Aboth* 2:9. It is a saying of Johanan b. Zakkai in the name of Hillel and Shammai.

[49] *Aboth* 1:13, cf. also *Sifre* Num. Korah, 119f., 40a Montefiore & Loewe, 129-30.

learned for one's profit but for its own sake.

That Israel was elected for the purpose of studying Torah is expressed in *Sifre* on Deut. 32:9, which comments on the election of Israel with the help of Gen. 25:27. This latter text is interpreted as follows: "And Jacob, a perfect man[50] dwelling in houses of study".[51] The point of this text is that God chose Israel even after her idolatry at Sinai[52] and that the election is not connected with faith (Abraham) but with the study of Torah (Jacob).[53]

Other metaphors used for Torah are very significant.[54] Let us take some of them: Torah is compared with "water" because it is at once gratis, priceless, bringing life, and purifying;[55] with "wine" because it is kept in humble vessels (humble people), it rejoices the heart, and "grows better by keeping" (as a man grows older).[56] Torah is also compared with fire;[57] with the tree of life;[58] with a wife with whom one lives joyfully.[59]

Since Torah rejoices the heart (as wine and wife) it can

---

[50] תם was interpreted as "perfect".

[51] אהלים, tents, being interpreted in this way. Cf. Eugene Mihaly, "A Rabbinic defense of the Election of Israel. An Analysis of Sifre Deuteronomy 32:9 Pisqa 312", *HUCA* 36, 1969, 103-63 (we used his translation of this passage).

[52] Deut. 19:2 is used as proof text.

[53] Yet it is not necessarily a reaction against the Pauline doctrine of the election in Abraham (Rom. 4), as Mihaly contends: in the *Book of Jubilees*, already, Jacob has a predominent role. Cf. below our discussion of the *Book of Jubilees*.

[54] For a convenient list of the most common metaphors see *Cant. R.* I:2, 3, water, wine, oil, honey and milk.

[55] *Sifre* Deut., 'Ekeb 48f., 84a, Montefiore & Loewe, 164.

[56] *ibid.*

[57] *Mek.* on Exod. 19:18, Lauterbach ed., vol. II, 221; *Sifre* on Deut., Berakah 343f., 143a-143b, Montefiore & Loewe, 165.

[58] *Sifre* on Deut. 11:21, Bonsirven, *Textes*, 64.

[59] *Eccles. R.* 9:9, Montefiore & Loewe, 443.

be read during the joyful day of Sabbath.[60] Torah should be fulfilled in deeds[61] as well as learned and studied in the Synagogue and in the School.

In the preceding pages we have sketched the main points of what we have called the explicit doctrine of Scripture in classical Judaism. We have now to put flesh on these dry bones in an attempt to point out how this explicit doctrine of Scripture was actually implemented in the different uses of Scripture made by early Judaism. This is to say that we shall try to grasp the "implicit doctrine" of Scripture of the Midrashim, the Targumim, and the Mishnah. This will allow us to see a dynamism beyond the static understanding of Scripture—the complete and final revelation—which appears as a characteristic of this explicit doctrine of Scripture.

Remarks on the Availability of the Sacred Text

Before going further we need to make a few remarks on the accessibility of the Hebrew Bible to the Jewish people of this period. This should be obvious, but we have the tendency to forget it too easily. It is a fact that the books of the Bible were not as available to the general public as they are now![62]

In the time of Ezra and Nehemiah (Neh. 8:1-8) the people did not have any book. It had the possibility of knowing about the book of the Law only by means of the public reading and explanation (and eventually targumization).[63] Yet in the time of the Maccabees it appears that copies of the "Book of the Covenant"[64] as well as of the "Books of the Law"[65] were

---

[60] *Mek.* on Exod. 15:22, Lauterbach ed., vol. II, 88.

[61] Cf.*Aboth* 3:11, 12, 22, *passim*.

[62] Cf. Le Déaut, *Liturgie juive et Nouveau Testament* Rome, 1965, 9-10.

[63] Cf. also II Chr. 17:7-9.

[64] I Maccabees 1:59-60.

[65] *ibid.*, 56-57.

to be found in private homes. What made up the content of these books remains an open question in spite of the different hypotheses found in the footnotes given by different scholars in their editions of the Apocrypha.[66] There is also mention of a library in Jerusalem[67] gathered by Judas Maccabeus in order to save the books from destruction.

Thus it seems that beside the copies belonging to the Temple and the Synagogues there were a number of copies of Scripture available. Yet they were mainly in the hands of scholars, teachers, Rabbis and their disciples. For most people all that was known from the Bible was what was learned in the School and the Synagogue.

Furthermore the handling of the rolls of Scripture was, as Abram Spiro showed,[68] a very complex operation which, together with the rule "defiled are the hands that touch Scripture",[69] certainly discouraged most of the pious Jews from studying Scripture by themselves.[70] This law, already implemented at the time of the Sadducees and Pharisees,[71] necessitated scrolls with rollers, and the use of a pointer (instead of a finger). Furthermore the very language of the scrolls (Hebrew and not Aramaic), possibly the old script,[72] demanded a training in school for the reader.[73] Abram Spiro

---

[66] Cf. Charles, *ad loc.*, "books of the Law, i.e., rolls of the Pentateuch." Charles seems to identify completly the "books of the Law" and the "Book of the Covenant." F.M. Abel, *Les Livres des Maccabées* (1949) suggests that the Book of the Covenant may be compilations of the Law.

[67] II Maccabees 2:14-15.

[68] *Samaritans, Tobiads and Judahites in Pseudo Philo*, 6ff.

[69] *Yadaim* 3:2-5; 4:5-6; cf. above.

[70] And it discouraged them from checking the accuracy of haggadic tradition over against the Biblical text. This is the point that Spiro wants to make.

[71] *Yadaim* 4:6.

[72] Cf. Spiro, op.cit., 9-11.

[73] Yet recently, i.e., after the discovery of the Dead Sea Scrolls, the scholars are less inclined to think that Hebrew was known only in scholarly circles: cf., e.g., Le Déaut, *Introduction à la littérature Targumique*, Institut Biblique Pontifical, Rome, 1966, 26.

agrees[74] the schools for the children *(Beth ha-Sepher)* existed at least since the second century: this is documented by ben Sirach 51:17 and 23; and *Aboth* 1:1. Yet he warns us: these passages may well refer to the *Beth ha-Midrash* (the Rabbinic School) rather than to the *Beth ha-Sepher*. At any rate only privileged circles frequented such schools. According to the Babylonian Talmud[75] the teaching of children was generalized only when Joshua b. Gamla (*circa* A.D. 63) appointed elementary teachers everywhere in the country. Yet the Palestinian Talmud[76] attributes this organization of the school for children to Simon b. Shatah (*circa* 65 B.C.). (Both Talmuds agree that, previously, the child learned from his father). Spiro[77] considers as fantastic both W. Bacher's and J. Klausner's conclusions on that matter. For W. Bacher, an organized school system existed in Palestine during the second century B.C.: he reached this conclusion after emending the text of the Babylonian Talmud just mentioned to read "Joshuah b. Perahyah" (a Sage living one generation before Simon b. Shatah) instead to reading Joshuah b. Gamla. J. Klausner, on the other hand, accepted the tradition of the Palestinian Talmud and rejected the testimony of the Babylonian Talmud. For Spiro these two positions are "a highly romanticized version of Jewish history". As proof of the fact that there were no extended school systems in Palestine before the end of our period, Spiro points to "the shocking ignorance of the Bible" displayed in the Apocrypha and "the peculiar 'quotations' from the Bible that are found in the New Testament." But such a statement is excessive. It is clear that the Apocrypha, Pseudepigrapha, and New Testament present a quite different use of the Bible from that of the Rabbis in their Schools, but the fact remains that they used the Bible to such an extent that some of their writings are almost a mosaic of Biblical text. Such a performance is difficult to

---

[74] *op.cit., 13.*

[75] *Baba Bathra* 21a.

[76] *Y. Ketuboth* 8, 11, 32c.

[77] op.cit., 13ff.

realize without a tremendous familiarity with Scripture. Yet we have to agree with Spiro that these texts emanated from learned circles. In other words, Spiro's argument about the illiteracy of the great mass of the people[78] and even of some of the leaders (namely the High Priests),[79] is valid. The learned circles were certainly limited in the period under consideration. Yet maybe they were not so limited as Spiro would like to say, for indeed the sects were also learned circles, as we can see in the Qumran scrolls.

---

[78] Which is corroborated by the need for a Targum.

[79] Cf. *Yoma* 1:2-7.

CHAPTER III

SCRIPTURE IN THE SYNAGOGUE: READING CYCLES AND HOMILIES

Let us turn now toward the Synagogue as *Sitz im Leben* of the haggadic use of Scripture in Judaism--yet keeping in mind that the Rabbis, in spite of a quite different use of Scripture in halakic decision,[1] were also present as "leaders" at the Synagogue and often as homilists. Thus we should not forget the unity between the *beth ha-midrash* (the School) and the *beth ha-kenesset* (the Synagogue).[2]

ORIGINS OF THE SYNAGOGUE

The question of the origin of the Synagogue has given rise to many hypotheses. Let us first say that its existence is well attested in the literature of the beginning of our era.[3] In the writings of Philo[4] and Josephus[5] as well as in

---

[1] See below, ch. V.

[2] This unity is visible in the so-called *"Yelammedenu"* homily, as we shall see.

[3] Cf. Philo, *De Vita Mosis*, III, 27; Josephus, *Contra Ap.* II, 17; *Ant.* XIX, 6, 3; *Vita*, 54; *B.J.* II, 14, 4-5; *passim*. Cf. also many passages in the New Testament.

[4] *De Vita Mosis*, III, 27.

[5] *Contra Ap.*, II, 17.

later Rabbinic sources we find statements which attribute immemorial antiquity to the Synagogue (i.e., claiming that Moses was its founder). These are doctrinal statements indeed, but by the very fact that they could be made in the first century A.D., they testify that the Synagogue had been an institution at least for a few generations. Archeological evidences help to fix *a terminus ad quem* for the creation of the Synagogue. At Masada Y. Yadin's expedition discovered the remnants of a synagogue which appears to have been in use before the fall of the stronghold in A.D. 73 (and quite probably already in the time of Herod); this is the first archeological confirmation of the literary testimonies we just mentioned.[6] As for the *terminus a quo*, a very frequent conjecture is that synagogues were first erected in Babylonia during the exile as a substitute for the Temple.[7] Yet as Dembitz notes[8] there is no mention of any destruction of any synagogue during the Maccabean war in I and II Maccabees. This seems a very strong argument as long as we confuse the Synagogue as a building with the Synagogue as an institution.[9] For indeed the different terms which were translated by συναγωγή[10] mean the congregation rather than the place of assembly,[11] which could have been, at first, in any building or even outdoors.[12] Thus in the period of the Maccabean war

---

[6] The excavation of a *Genizah* containing scrolls of the books of Deuteronomy and Ezekiel does not allow any doubt about the function of this building, the earliest synagogue ever discovered: cf. Y. Yadin, *Masada* (French ed., Hachette, 1966), 180-91. We emphasize this to point out the weakness of S. B. Hoenig's contention that the Synagogue as a place of worship did not exist in Judea before the year 70. Cf. S. B. Hoenig, "The Suppositions Temple-Synagogue", *J.Q.R.* 54, 1963.

[7] Thus *inter alios* I. Sonne, *I.D.B.*, vol IV, 478ff.; L. N. Dembitz, "Synagogue", *J.E.*, vol. XI, 619.

[8] Ibid. 620.

[9] Obviously it is the second which interests us here.

[10] עדה (congregation), קהל (assembly) in the LXX; כנסיה (*Aboth* 4:11), (which is a very unusual form) כנסת and in Aramaic כנישתא

[11] As is obvious in the phrase כנסת הגדולה (the Great Synagogue); the building is designated in Rabbinic literature by בית כנסת.

[12] Namely by the rivers (cf. Acts 16:13), or in open doors public places.

the institution could have existed without a special building of its own.

To understand the place of Scripture in the Synagogue it would be useful to know the original purpose of this institution. Unhappily we are reduced to conjectures. Some see the creation of the Synagogue as that of a substitute for the Temple[13] when the latter was not available for the Israelites; others as that of an institution which was developed first parallel, then later in opposition, to the Temple[14] or altogether in opposition to the Temple.[15] Yet precisely this conjecture of a reaction against the Temple worship seems unrealistic to a number of scholars who, on the contrary, see the Synagogue as having developed, through the *ma'a madoth* in connection with the Temple.[16] When a *mishmar* of priests and levites were performing their service in the Temple, the corresponding *ma'amed* assembled wherever they were in Palestine, in order to read passages of Scripture corresponding to the sacrifices taking place in Jerusalem, and in order to pray. It is possible, therefore, that synagogues developed from these "assemblies". If this were so, it would mean that there was from the start a direct connection between the reading of Torah and the Synagogue. We should note that this theory as a whole is actually based on the Mishnah[17] which mentions only readings from the creation story of

---

[13] During the exile, cf. above I. Sonne's opinion.

[14] Thus S. W. Baron, *Histoire d'Israel*, vol. I, French ed., 484. He bases his remarks on the mention of the Egyptian Temple (5th century B.C.) in the *Elephantine Papyri*. This he looks like a link between the Jerusalem Temple and the Synagogue.

[15] For a presentation of these theories, cf. I. Sonne, *op. cit.*, 479.

[16] Thus K. Hruby, "La Synagogue dans la littérature rabbinique", *L'orient syrien*, 1964, 474ff., following S. Krauss, *Synagogale Altertümer*, Berlin, 1922, and I. Elbogen, *Der jüdische Gottesdienst in seiner geschichtichen Entwicklung*, 3rd ed., Frankfurt, 1931; cf. also John Bowker, *The Targums and Rabbinic Literature*, Cambridge, U.S.A., 1969, 9ff.

[17] *Taan.* 4:2, cf. also *Tosephta Taan.* 4:3 (Bonsirven, *Textes*, 264).

Genesis, and this during the week days only.

This is furthermore sustained by the Greek inscription from a synagogue in Jerusalem (probably first century A.D.) which dedicates the synagogue "for the reading of the Law and for the teaching of the commandments".[18]

The scholars generally agree that the synagogue was both a house of prayer[19] and a house of reading and study of the Torah. Yet they disagree concerning which was the predominant trend. Following Hruby[20] it seems that the synagogue, *beth ha-kenesset*, was first of all a house of prayer; this is to say that the reading of Torah was done in a liturgical setting more or less fixed according to the period of the year, as opposed to the study of Torah which was done in the School, *beth ha-midrash*.[21] This is not to say that they were not closely connected: what was learned in the *beth ha-midrash* was obviously used in the Synagogal service.[22] But what we

---

[18] I. Sonne, *op. cit.*, 480. Unhappily the photograph of this inscription was too small to allow the deciphering of the Greek word translated here by *"teaching* of the commandments"; J. Bowker, *op. cit.*, 11, translated it by "*searching* of the commandments"; cf. on this E. L. Sukenik's books, *The Ancient Synagogue of el-Hammed*, Jerusalem, 1935, and *Ancient Synagogues in Palestine and Greece*, Schweich Lectures, 1930.

[19] From the Greek designation.

[20] *Op. cit.*, 481ff. and therefore against Bowker, *op. cit.*, 10, and Michael Friedlander, *Synagoge und Kirche in ihten Anfängen*, Berlin, 1908 (quoted by Hruby). These two scholars consider that before the fall of Jerusalem the Synagogue was mainly a house of study. Here Bowker is not consistent with himself: he is not taking into account for this point the very text of the Mishnah (*Taan.* IV) which he used earlier to point out the origin of the Synagogue. This text not only implies that prayers were said besides the biblical readings but also that there was a liturgical setting for these readings.

[21] Here it may be useful to note that we are not making a distinction between two buildings but between two institutions, which according to the locations and the period may or may not have used the same building. Cf. Hruby, *op. cit.*, 506.

[22] Later (in the period of the Amoraim) the synagogue was the place of the elementary school, the *beth ha-midrash* being the place for more advanced studies. Cf. *Berakhot* 17a; *Giddushim* 30a; *Ber. R.* 52:4, *passim*.

want to stress here is the liturgical setting of the biblical reading and study in the synagogue, this without denying that the Torah had a central place in the Synagogue. As Hruby notes, what is new is the *"détachement du lieu de culte au sens fort"*,[23] that is to say from the Temple. The presence of the holy was sought on Torah-study, rather than on the Temple service alone, even before the fall of Jerusalem: it was by means of Torah that the Presence of God was apprehended.[24] Thus the Synagogal liturgical service was not focused on the sanctity of a place (Temple) or on that of the sacrifices, but on Torah.

In the Synagogue Scripture was used in four ways: a) it was read (seder, haftarah); b) it was preached (homilies as conserved in Midrashim); c) it was translated and made understandable (Targums); d) it was used in prayers (liturgy).[25]

The rest of this chapter will deal with the reading of Scripture and the preaching in the Synagogue. In the next chapter we shall study the use of Scripture in the Targum and the liturgy.

CYCLES FOR THE READING OF TORAH

An examination of the practice of reading Scripture and of the use of Scriptural texts in the homilies will help us progress in our elucidation of the early Jewish hermeneutical principles or axioms in so far as we shall be able to point out what governed the choice of the Scriptural passages which

---

[23] *Op. cit.*, 507.

[24] The Shekinah is at the Synagogue (with the ten persons assembled for the service), at the *beth ha-din* (the three who judge) and even when one studies (Torah), (cf. *Mekilta* on Exod. 20:24, Bonsirven, *Textes*, 33; cf. also *Aboth* 3:3), as it was at the Temple (cf. *Sifra* on Leviticus 9:21, Weiss ed., 44c; Bonsirven, *Textes*, 39).

[25] We shall deal with a) and b) together: we shall see it is not possible to understand them separately.

were read in the worship service and integrated into the homilies.

Like the origin of the Synagogue itself, the origin of the readings from the Bible at Sabbath services[26] is wrapped in obscurity "owing to its very antiquity",[27] but there can be no doubt that it was practiced at the beginning of our era.[28] The question which needs to be raised is: what was read from the Bible?

At first the Torah does not appear to have been read consecutively. Only certain sections of Torah were read in the Synagogue.[29] For instance Deut. 32 was apparently in use in the Jewish liturgy "from an early pre-christian age".[30] There are, then, evidences that during the last centuries B.C. fixed lections were ascribed to specific Sabbath services, as well as to holiday services. Yet we should not conclude from this that already at that time this practice was systematized in a cycle so as to allow the Synagogal reading of the whole Torah.[31] On the other hand, such a cycle for the reading of Torah is well attested for Talmudic period. In contrast with Babylonia and the Diaspora, where an annual cycle was in use, in Palestine the cycle was triennial.[32] It was a fixed series

---

[26] It was also read at festivals: we assumed that our observations on the readings and preaching at the Sabbath services were representative enough.

[27] J. Mann, *The Bible as Read and Preached in the Old Synagogue* vol. I, 1940, vol. II ed. by I. Sonne, Cincinnati, 1966; vol. I, 4.

[28] Cf. what we said on the origin of the Synagogue.

[29] Cf. Moore, *op. cit.*, vol. I, 288ff.

[30] McNamara, *op. cit.*, 112ff. McNamara notes further that it is natural in this case "that those sections of the Torah read in the synagogue would be the first to be provided with a liturgical paraphrase". *Op. cit.*, 113.

[31] Cf. J. Heinemann, "The Triennial Lectionary Cycle", *J.J.S.*, 1968, 41-48.

[32] Cf. Gaster, *Studies and Texts* I, 503ff., "The Biblical Lessons"; Mann, *op. cit.*, 5; Joseph Jacobs, "Triennial Cycle:, *J.E.*, vol. XII; I. Elbogen, "Review of J. Mann's The Bible as Read . . .", *J.Q.R.*, N.S., XXXI, 1940-41 ("It [the existence of the Triennial Cycle in Palestine] is proved by the

of lections from the Torah and the Prophets to be read on the Sabbaths, allowing the reading of the whole Torah in three years.[33] Exactly when this Triennial Cycle was fixed is difficult to determine in spite of the fact that according to Mann[34] we have one instance which testifies to its use in the years just preceding the fall of Jerusalem.[35] Even though we cannot assume that the Triennial Cycle was fixed in the period we are considering,[36] we can assume that it was in formation and even, maybe, that it existed in some kind of flexible form (varying from locality to locality).[37] A study of the inner structure of the Cycle and of its principles is therefore legitimate for our topic as long as we do not attempt to draw

---

Masoretic division as well as by many midrashim"); A. Buchler, "The Reading of the Law in a Triennial Cycle", *J.Q.R.*, V, 1893, 420-68, and VI, 1894, 1-73; A. Guilding, *The Fourth Gospel and the Jewish Worship*, Oxford, 1960, 6-23.

[33] For such lists cf. Joseph Jacobs, *ibid.*, and also I. G. Dibsevagem "Sidra", *J.E.*, vol. XI, list established according to the fragments of the Fustat Genizah, cf. Buchler, *J.Q.R.* V, 420-68; VI, 1-73.

[34] Mann, *op. cit.*, vol. I, 5.

[35] Yet recorded only in the *Midrash Tanhuma* 7, cf. Mann, *op. cit.*, col. I, 105; see below for the discussion of this passage; for other instances before the end of the first century A.D., see 472-73.

[36] With Moore, *op. cit.*, vol. I, 299ff., and with Heinemann, *op. cit.*, but against Thackeray, *The Septuagint and Jewish Worship*, London, 1923, 45, who states as if it were obvious: "The Pentateuch was divided into some 150 sections and was read through once in three years. On this system, which was in vogue in New Testament times . . . I need not dwell", and also against W. O. E. Oesterley, *The Jewish Background of the Christian Liturgy*, Oxford, 1925, 39, who follows Thackeray.

[37] We can agree with Oesterley, *op. cit.*, 38-39 (following I. Elbogen, "Bemerkungen zur alten jüdischen liturgie" in *Studies in Jewish Literature in honor of K. Kohler*, 159) that the reading of the Torah as a fixed, regular institution can be dated "not later than the middle of the 3rd century B.C." provided that this does not imply the existence of the fixed cycle which we find in use in Palestine during the second century A.D. The reading of *haftaroth* can be dated about 200 B.C. yet again as an institution not as a fixed cycle (cf. also Moore, *op. cit.*, 300; M. McNamara, *The New Testament and Palestinian Targum*, 42ff.). Such reading probably lead to the canonization of the books of the Prophets (cf. on this Thackeray, *op. cit.*, 45ff.).

conclusions on the association of such and such specific Torah texts with such and such specific Prophetic texts. Furthermore such a study will prove very fruitful in that it will help us to understand the hermeneutic principles involved in the Jewish homily of the old Synagogue. In such a study we shall follow very closely the *"Opus Magnificum"*[38] of Jacob Mann,[39] which was hailed by the best scholars in this field, in spite of a number of criticism which we shall take into account.[40]

Drawing from a considerable amount of material, from the Midrashim already published as well as from Genizah material (which he published for the first time at the end of each volume), Mann studied the "inner structure" of the homilies corresponding to each *seder*.[41] His attempt was to discern the relationship between this seder and the *haftarah*[42] of the Triennial Cycle of the Genizah, when available;[43] he often tried to discover, as well, what was (or were) the haftarah (or haftaroth) implied in the homiletic texts instead of that found in the Triennial Cycle list. This done, when dealing with a petihtah homily, he attempted to discern what was the relationship of the seder and haftarah with the *petihtah*[44] (or petihtoth) of the homily. If by contrast the homily was a so-called *Yelammedenu* homily (i.e., if it began with a halakic theme introduced by ילמדנו רבינו) he attempted to show the

---

[38] So I. Elbogen, *op. cit.*, 193.

[39] Mann, *op. cit.*

[40] Besides Elbogen's review we shall take particularly into account the remarks made by S. Lieberman (quoted by I. Sonne, Mann, *op. cit.*, vol. II, pp. XXXIIIff.), Sonne's own criticisms, *ibid.*, XXI, XXXVIII and 236-55, and Heinemann's brief remarks, *op. cit.*, 47-48. Henceforth we shall refer to Mann simply by mentioning volume and page.

[41] Passage from the Torah which should be read on a specific Sabbath morning service (plural: sedarim).

[42] Passage from the Prophets for that service (plural: haftaroth).

[43] e.g., there is no haftarah in the Genizah list for seder 96 (Lev. 24:1ff.), cf. vol. II, 120.

[44] Passage generally from the Hagiographa used as starting point for the homily (plural: petihtoth).

relationship of the seder and haftarah with the halakah. From this very careful analysis, using a wide range of midrashim,[45] Mann reached important conclusions revealing for the first time the inner structure of the Jewish homilies.[46] Let us summarize his conclusions.

SEDER AND HAFTARAH

The length of each seder according to the rule expressed in the Mishnah (*Meg.* 4:2-4) must be at least twenty one verses.[47] What are the principles which were followed in the division of the Torah into sedarim? Mann's untimely death prevented him from spelling them out but Sonne attempted to express them.[48] His first remark is that no one principle emerges as *the* characteristic principle. The topical division played a part, but so did a preoccupation with balance (in length, between two consecutive sedarim) and symmetry (inside the seder itself a correspondence was sought between beginning and end, taking into account the topic). There was also a

---

[45] A total of more than 1,400 pages of which 585 of text were published for the first time from the Genizah fragments.

[46] This is contested by Lieberman, "Scholars of the past century have already observed that the Y. (Yelammedenu) homilies were sometimes based on the H. (Haftarah) (see Rapoport Erek Millin, s. v. Aphtara II; Friedmann PR, I note 1)", vol. II, XXII, but it is refuted by Sonne (*ibid*, XXIIIff.) and already by Mann, vol. I, 11ff., where he emphasized that if the *external* form has been already hinted at by these scholars and others, "the *inner* structure has not yet been properly understood" (my italics).

[47] Seven persons were called upon to read from the Torah at least three verses each; yet it can be a little shorter by repeating a few verses, but not shorter than eighteen verses. Mann shows that this is actually the case, in spite of the Triennial Cycle lists and the sigla ס/, סדר of the Massorah, because of the variations of the sedarim from locality to locality. Cf. vol I, 8.

[48] He did so when editing Mann's notes. Cf. vol. II, XXVIII.

preoccupation with avoiding bad endings or bad beginnings.[49] But as we noted above none of these principles was absolute: they were only applied *as far as possible*, that is to say as far as the text allowed. A respect of the Torah text appears quite clearly when we compare the way the Prophetic texts were used.

The haftarah was generally shorter (about ten verses)[50] with a very significant feature which Mann calls, with the Mishnah, the *skipping*.[51] A number of verses were skipped in order to provide a tenth verse with a "happy ending". Thus for instance the haftarah corresponding to seder 15 (Gen. 18:1ff.) begins in Isaiah 33:17 and ends with 35:10. This *parshiyah* (pericope) would be much too long. Yet merely reading ten verses beginning 33:17 would leave the audience with a "sad" ending (34:2):

> "For the Lord is enraged against all the nations,
> and furious against all their host,
> he has doomed them, has given them over
> for slaughter".

Thus the ending was found further in 35:10:

> "And the ransomed of the Lord shall return,
> and come to Zion with singing;
> everlasting joy shall be upon their heads;
> they shall obtain joy and gladness,
> and sorrow and sighing shall flee away".

This provides a happy ending. Thus according to the Genizah fragments the haftarah is 33:17-24 and 35:10.[52]

The haftarah was supposed to bring consolation and encouragement for Israel (נחמות ישראל) by leading down "to a conclusion that was heartening and foretelling the ultimate redemption".[53] This tells much concerning the purpose of the use of the Prophets in the Synagogue.

What is the relationship between the seder and the haftarah? How was the haftarah chosen? Mann answers: by

---

[49]Cf. below the principle governing the ending of the haftaroth.

[50]This applied whenever there was an Aramaic interpretation (Targum) or an accompanying sermon (*Meg.* 23b), otherwise it should be of the same length than the seder (*Meg.* 23a), vol. I, 9.

[51]*Meg.* IV, 4: מדלגין בנביא.

[52]Vol. I, 134. Biblical quotations from R.S.V.

[53]Vol. I, 11. Cf. *Y. Ber.* V, beg. 8d.

means of the principle of *tallying*. That is the seder and the haftarah were connected by *mere linguistic affinity*, and not by a common topic (or at least this is only a secondary factor): it was enough if the haftarah was comforting.[54] This linguistic artificial connection was *always* (according to Mann) between the first verse of the seder and first and/or second verse(s) of the haftarah.

This rule can be illustrated by a few examples. Seder 101 begins by Num. 1:1: "The Lord *spoke* unto Moses *in the wilderness* of Sinai . . ."

וידבר ה/ אל משה במדבר סיני

The haftarah begins in Hosea 2:16: "Therefore, behold, I will allure her, and bring her *into the wilderness and speak tenderly to her*"

לכן הנה אנכי מפתיה והלכתיה המדבר ודברתי על לבה

The haftarah is connected with the seder by the expressions "into the wilderness and speak" ודברתי המדבר (Num. 1:1: "Spoke . . . in the wilderness" וידבר) . . . במדבר). Furthermore there is an allusion to the exodus from Egypt in Hos. 2:17 as in Num. 1:1 (end of the verse).[55] For an example without topical connections we can take seder 82 (Lev. 12:1-2), the haftarah being Isaiah 9:6. In Lev. 12:1-2 we read "(if a woman) bears a male child" וילדה זכר, in Isaiah 9:6, "For to us a child is born, (to us) a son" ילד יולד לנו בן.[56] Although the tallying is made purely on the ground of linguistic affinity, it should be noted that such a choice is pregnant of very meaningful interpretations. The seder dealing with the ritual of purification following the birth of a child is now connected with the birth of the "Prince of Peace". Another example of pure linguistic tallying is that

---

[54] This has been already recognized by Büchler, yet for him originally the haftarah was connected with the seder by a common topic, a rule which had to be abandoned because of the great number of sedarim.

[55] Vil. II, 175. Another typical example would be that of seder 98 (Lev. 25:35) tallied with Isa. 35:3.

[56] Vol. II, 61.

of seder 47 (Exod. 3:1) with Isa. 40:11.[57]

If such a linguistic connection in the first verses is not found, Mann looks for another haftarah (which he finds in the texts used in the homilies). Here Sonne criticizes him rightfully, pointing out that this linguistic connection can be found farther along in the haftarah or even in its immediate context which Sonne calls "the area of the magnetic field".[58]

Furthermore, sometimes we can detect that a given haftarah was itself chosen because of a former homiletic interpretation, the connection being this time between the first verse of the seder and the interpretation of the haftarah. As an example of this we can take seder 103 (Num. 3:1), the haftarah being Isaiah 45:19. There is a weak linguistic connection (דבר), yet the choice of this haftarah has certainly been determined by its homiletic interpretation as found in the Mekilta,[59] according to which this prophetic text refers to the giving of the Torah openly on a mountain of the wilderness of Sinai. Num. 3:1 mentions: "The day when God addressed Moses on Mount Sinai".[60] The choice of such a haftarah is quite significant.[61] This relationship of the seder and the haftarah is found again in the homilies in which are also integrated halakic elements (from the Oral Torah) and texts from the Hagiographa.

---

[57] Vol. I, 365.

[58] Vol. II, XXXVII.

[59] *Yitro, Bahodesh* c. 1 (ed. Horovitz, 205-06): "The Law was given publicly and openly, in a place to which no one had any claim . . . in the wilderness . . .". Then follows a saying of R. Jose quoting Isa. 45:19 and interpreting it in this sense (Montefiore's and Loewe's translation *ad loc.*).

[60] Vol. II, 185.

[61] In the Dead Sea Scrolls we shall find a similar choice of biblical passages to interpret a given text.

Relationship of the Seder and Haftarah with the Halakah and/or the Petihtah

A few general remarks are useful on the elements found in the homilies. The *Yelammedenu* (halakah) and the *petihtah* (Hagiographa), as introductions to different homilies, together with the peroration, have been considered for a long time to be the external (artificial) frame of the homily, containing marvellous little masterpieces but without unity of purpose or ideas.[62] Bacher in his study of the petihtah[63] pointed out that the purpose of the petihtah was to stress the unity between the three parts of the Bible (Torah, Prophets, Hagiographa), i.e., to show "that there is nothing in the Prophets and the Hagiographa that could not be found in the Torah, that all three parts are but one and the same expressed in various forms, various modes of the same substance".[64]

---

[62] Cf. J. W. Bowker, "Speeches in Acts: A Study in Proem and Yelammedenu Form", *N.T.S.* XIV, 1967, 96-111: as Bowker rightly points out the basic method of the homilies was *haruzim* (a term which brings the image of stringing beads together), i.e., "stringing" texts of Scripture together, leading generally from the proem text (petihtah), or from the halakic question, to the *seder* reading. This of course applies to "live homily". As J. Heinemann pointed out in his article "Profile of a Midrash: The Act of Composition in Leviticus Rabba", *J.A.A.R.*, XXXIX, 1971, 141-50, the literary compilations of sermons may be quite logically composed. Such is the case of those presented in Leviticus Rabba. Heinemann's criticism of Mann's argument based on the latter's failure to distinguish between literary compilations and "live sermons" is indeed valid. Literary compilations present the coherent development of a theme. Yet this is not to say that the Midrashim are always literary compositions. Often they merely transcribe, although in a summary form, "live homilies". In this case they fail to present the coherent development characteristic of a literary composition. We shall have to make a similar distinction about the Apocalyptic literature; this shall lead us to point out different hermeneutical structures. In the case of the synagogal homily, although we agree that Mann's argument does not apply to literary compositions, we maintain against Heinemann that it is as a whole valid for "living homilies", object of our study in this chapter.

[63] Bacher, *Die Proömien in der alten Jüd. Homilie*, Leipzig, 1913; cf. Mann, vol. I, 12.

[64] As Sonne expressed it: vol. II, XXXI.

This principle underlying the choice of the petihtah will be shown to be correct by Mann's investigation. Yet for Bacher "the petihtah verse was left entirely to the free choice of the speaker",[65] to his fancy. Mann on the contrary shows the thread which unites the petihtah with the haftarah and the seder, a thread that he discovered first in the *Yelammedenu* homilies.

How was that particular halakah chosen which was used to open the sermon? He answers: "Within the given haftarah the homilist always obtained a suggestion for the choice of the particular halakah".[66] Then from the halakah the speaker went on in a haggadic exposition introducing one petihtah or several (connected to the haftarah by means of linguistic tallying) before concluding in the peroration by returning generally to the seder (often to the first verse of the seder which was connected to the haftarah and the petihtah).

As an example let us take the Yelammedenu sermon of seder 36.[67] The seder is Gen. 39:1. The haftarah of the Genizah list is Isa. 52:3-10 and 53:4-5. Yet it is not the haftarah which is used in the sermon, as we shall see.[68] The Yelammedenu sermon[69] begins as follows: first there is a brief reminder of the seder, "And Joseph was brough down to Egypt" (ויוסף הורד מצרימה) then the formula ילמדנו רבינו, which introduces the halakah based on the Mishnah.[70] What could be the haftarah fitting at once the seder and the halakah? Mann found it in Isa. 55:11. This tallies with the second verse of the seder (Gen. 39:2), which contains מצליח

---

[65] Bacher, *op. cit.*, 7; Mann, vol. I, 12.

[66] Vol. II, 13.

[67] Vol. I, 298ff.

[68] Cf. above on the variations of the haftaroth for the same seder according to the localities.

[69] From *Tanhuma*, *Wayyesheb* 3.

[70] Ber. VIII, 6: "They may not say the Blessing over the light or over the spices of idolaters, nor over the light or over the spices for the dead nor over the light or over the spices of idols. They should not recite the Blessing over a light until one can make use of its light". (Blackmann's translation).

(prosperous). In Isa. 55:11 we found והצלוח (and it shall prosper). The haftarah was probably Isa. 55:11 to 56:7 (ten verses). What was the connection with the halakah? In Isa. 56:3 we find mentioned the *separation* (from the stranger): הבדל. In the halakah we find also להבדיל: the very topic of the halakah is precisely the *Habdalah* (separation) blessing[71] over the light of a non Jew. Then the homilist introduces Isa. 40:17 (in contrast to 56:3); this leads him to a story about Rabbi (Judah), and to Rabbi's remarks about God accomplishing His purpose through small creatures (allusion to Isa. 55:11). "Likewise through the youngest of the tribes God fulfilled His purpose, *viz.* Joseph was sold to Egypt and therefore ultimately Jacob had to go there".[72] At this point the homilist returns to the first verse of the seder (Gen. 39:1).

Another homily (or a continuation of the preceding) introduces Ps. 92:6(5), in which we find מעשיך (thy works), which tallies with the haftarah (Isa. 55:11), where we find עשה (it shall accomplish).[73] Then using Ps. 92:6b(5b), "Thy thoughts are very deep", and applying it to the scheme of bringing down Jacob to Egypt by means of Joseph, the homilist comes back to the seder and also to the haftarah Isa. 56:4 and 6.

This example shows all the speaker's skill in weaving together halakah, haftarah, petihtah and seder. In this case (and Mann presents hundreds of them) it is quite clear that the haftarah is the necessary bridge between the halakah (and

---

[71] We refer to the blessing of separation. This is a benediction over wine, light and spices at the conclusion of the Sabbath. It contains reference to the distinction between Israel and other people: cf. *Pes.* 104a (Mann, vol. I, 300, note 326). The Habdalah benediction reads: "Blessed art Thou, O Lord, our God, King of the Universe! Who hast made a *separation* (habdalah) between what is holy and what is profane; between light and darkness; *between Israel and the nations*; between the seventh day and the six working days. Blessed art Thou who hast separated the holy from the profane" quoted by Kaufmann Kohler, "Habdalah", *J.E.*, vol. VI, 119 (my italics).

[72] *Ibid.*, 301.

[73] There is also a link with 55:8 which forms a unity with 55:11: מחשבותי tallying with מחשבותיך of Ps. 92:6(5).

the petihtah: Ps. 92:6) on the one hand and the seder on the other.[74] It is also clear that the connection is linguistic, as it is between the haftarah and the seder. The structural purpose of this skilful exercise appears also: to demonstrate the union not only of the three parts of the Bible but also of the Oral Torah with the Written Torah.

It is not necessary to say anything more about the petihtah; Mann reaches similar conclusions about its tallying with the seder through the intermediary of the haftarah.

From all this, and the stress put on the role of the haftarah, one may get a false impression which needs to be corrected with the help of Lieberman's and Sonne's remarks. If the role of the haftaroth is certainly important in determining the structure of the homily, it should not be seen as supplanting the seder, that is, the Torah. On the one hand, as we saw above, the respect for the text of the Torah and its authority would not allow the use of strict principles for the division of the Pentateuch into sedarim. On the other hand, as Lieberman shows, many petihtoth and halakoth of yelammedenu homilies are connected with their respective sedarim by their topics and not linguistically.[75] Thus we should allow for more flexibility and permit exceptions to the main principles elaborated by Mann. In this case it means that sometimes the primary connection among seder, haftarah and petihtah (and/or halakah) is the theme, the topic. With this limitation Mann's conclusions remain valid; most of the time the primary connection is linguistic, the topical connection being only secondary in "live homilies" although it may become essential in literary compositions.

Furthermore (and this will help us to understand the actual place of the haftarah) the haftarah does not determine the theme of the homily. "It is only the mainstay, the center of gravitation of the external frame, the structure of the homily. And in order to be able to accomplish this central

---

[74] Yet the ideal, found in many cases but not always realizable, is to have a double tallying of the halakah and/or petihtah with the seder as well as with the haftarah.

[75] Cf. vol. II, XXXIII.

function . . . it has to be separated from its content and used as cement welding together the various elements by artificial joints".[76]

Concluding Remarks

From this research by J. Mann we could already draw several conclusions about the use of Scripture in classical Judaism. By pointing out the mechanics of the use of Scripture in the homilies, J. Mann elucidates some basic axioms which govern it: a) the respective degree of inspiration of Torah, the Prophets and the Hagiographa and their relationship; b) the importance of the very letter of Scripture over against the themes (theological or otherwise) expressed by Scripture; c) the continual interpretation of Scripture by Scripture (which could be interpreted to mean that Scripture was conceived as a "closed system of signs"); d) the close relationship between Written Torah and Oral Torah (the latter being used in the same way as the Hagiographa).

We must, at this point, refrain from drawing any conclusion. The scope of our examination of the phenomenon "use of Scripture" in classical Judaism is still too narrow. Mann is dealing with documents much later than the first century A.D. Furthermore his focus on the relationship of seder, haftarah, petihtah and halakah leaves aside and hides several essential aspects of the use of Scripture in classical Judaism. Thus, keeping in mind the precious insights that he gave us, let us turn toward the use of Scripture as represented by the Targumim.

---

[76]Sonne, in vol. II, XXXV. Cf. also Mann, vol. I, XIff.

CHAPTER IV

SCRIPTURE AT THE SYNAGOGUE: TARGUM AND LITURGY

EARLY DATE OF THE TARGUMIC GENRE

On the basis of our examination of the doctrine of Scripture and of the use of Scripture in the reading cycles and the homilies, we turn toward the study of the actual hermeneutic of Scripture practiced in the Synagogue. Here again our goal is to evaluate the attitude toward Scripture, i.e., the hermeneutical structure rather than to study how specific biblical passages were interpreted. The Targum as a phenomenon imposes itself as the best witness of such a hermeneutic.

Very closely related to the homily (of which the Midrashim are witnesses), the Targum is the Aramaic translation and interpretation of the biblical readings. The traditional view that the origin of the Targum has to be traced back to the days of Ezra[1] is questioned by some modern scholars:[2] it is not certain indeed that an Aramaic

---

[1] Cf. *Meg.* 3a based on Neh. 8:8.

[2] Thus McNamara, *op. cit.*, 39. Yet in favor of the traditional view, cf. K. Hruby, "La survivance de la langue hébraïque pendant la période post-exilienne" in *Mémorial du Cinquantenaire de l'Ecole des langues orientales anciennes de l'Institut Catholique de Paris 1916-1964*, Paris, 1964, 120.

translation was needed at the time of Ezra. Yet it cannot be doubted that the Targum as a phenomenon existed during the period under consideration: it is anterior to the Mishnah. This can be inferred from the casual reference to it in *Meg.* 4:4 and 6.[3] The discovery of fragments of a Targum on Job among the Dead Sea Scrolls[4] confirms this inference.

Since our concern is with the Targum as a phenomenon, i.e., as one of the ways the Hebrew Bible was used in early Judaism, we shall not dwell on the question of the Targumic literature.[5] About the date of the Targumic traditions let us say only that despite late additions and/or late redactions of the Targumic literature, many of these traditions can be dated

---

[3] 4: "He who reads the Torah . . . may not read to the *Meturgeman* more than one verse at a time or three from the Prophets. . . ." 6: "A minor may read the Law and translate (מתרגם) but he may not recite the *shema* . . . one clothed in ragged garments may recite the *shema* and translate but he may not read the Law. . . . A blind person may recite the *shema* and translate". (Cf. Blackman ed., *ad loc.*).

[4] Cf. J. van der Ploeq, "Un Targum du livre de Job: Nouvelle découverte dans le désert de Juda", *Bible et vie chrétienne* 58, 1964, 79-87. See below our remarks on this.

[5] On this see the works by R. Le Déaut: *Introduction à la littérature targumique*, Rome, 1966; *La Nuit Pascale*, Rome, 1963, 1-75; *Liturgie juive et Nouveau Testament*, Rome, 1965; Martin McNamara, *The New Testament and the Palestinian Targum to the Pentateuch*, Rome, 1966, 1-68. For a complete bibliography (up to 1966) see: P. Nickels, *Targum and New Testament*, Rome, 1967. To these should be added: A. Diez Macho, ed., *Ms. Neophyti I*, vol. I, *Genesis*, vol. II, *Exodus*, Barcelone, 1968 and 1970, and John Bowker, *The Targums and Rabbinic Literature*, Cambridge University Press, 1969. The first contains text and translations (Spanish, French, English) of the Palestinian Targum to Genesis and Exodus, recently discovered. The second contains translations of several chapters of Pseudo-Jonathan on Genesis with variants of the Fragmentary Targum and of the Targum Onqelos. For these targumic texts themselves cf. their edition by A. Sperber, *The Bible in Aramaic*, vol. I; *Pentateuch according to Onqelos*, vol. II, III; *The Prophets according to Targum Jonathan*, col. IV; *The Hagiographa*, Leiden, 1959-68.

from the period preceding the fall of Jerusalem.[6] This can be established by following the methodology proposed by Renée Bloch.[7] It is characterized as a comparative study of the traditions found in the Rabbinic literature with other related texts which can be dated (namely the texts of the Hellenistic Judaism, the Apocrypha and Pseudepigrapha, the Pseudo-Philo, Josephus, the Damascus Document and the Dead Sea Scrolls, as well as the New Testament). G. Vermès used this method with success.[8] Furthermore A. Diez Macho,[9] also using her methodology, confirmed the first conclusions of R. Bloch's unfinished researches about the Targum, *viz.* that the Palestinian Targum[10] is the most ancient Rabbinic recension of these haggadic traditions. This is why in order to study the use of the Hebrew Bible in the Synagogue we do not turn first toward the Midrashim but toward the Targumim. With Renée Bloch[11] we think that the Targum is the (oral and literary) genre which was at the origin of the Midrash of the later Rabbinic literature. To use her image the Targum is the

---

[6] Cf. already M. Gaster, *Samaritan Oral Law and Ancient Tradition*, vol. I, London, 1932, 47ff., who has pertinent remarks about the date of the targumic traditions as compared with the Mishnah and Apocrypha and Pseudepigrapha: "we have in the Targumim the oldest deposition of so much of the Oral Law and Traditions as could be brought within the compass of the Written Law".

[7] "Note méthodologique pour l'étude de la littérature rabbinique", *Recherches de Science Religieuse* 43, 1955, 194-227.

[8] G. Vermès, *Scripture and Tradition in Judaism*, Leiden, 1961.

[9] "The Recently Discovered Palestinian Targum. Its Antiquity and Relationship with the other Targums", *Supplements to Vetus Testamentum*, vol. VII, 1959, 222-45.

[10] For her the Palestinian Targum included only the *Targum Pseudo-Jonathan* (Targum of Jerusalem), and the *Fragmentary Palestinian Targum*; the copy of the complete Palestinian Targum to the Pentateuch, the *Ms. Neofiti I* of the Vatican library is known only since 1956 (exactly it was discovered in 1949 but identified only in 1956), the first part of it (Genesis) being at last published in 1968.

[11] Cf. "Moïse dans la Tradition Rabbinique", *Cahiers Sioniens* VIII, 1954, 214-15.

"articulation", the hinge, between Scripture and Midrash. Furthermore, as this specialist of the Midrashic literature also notes, the Targum contains already "all the structure and all the themes" of the Midrash. Therefore a study of the use of Scripture in the Targum will have the double advantage of dealing with a phenomenon which existed without any doubt in the period we are considering and which is well representative of the Synagogal hermeneutic.

This early date of the genre as well as of many traditions found in the Targumic literature is now generally accepted even outside the circles of the specialists in Targumic studies. Yet there are some discussions on the methods used to establish this early date. Such is the discussion on the method that A. Diez Macho used in addition to R. Bloch's.[12] We shall report this discussion because it introduces us to the heart of our topic: the Targumic use of Scripture.

TARGUM AND MASSORETIC TEXT

Diez Macho's method consists in the reconstruction of the Hebrew text which is underlying a Targum in order to compare this reconstructed text with the Massoretic Text, which has been practically uniform since the second century A.D. He discovered that the Palestinian Targum (exactly the Ms. Neofiti I that he was studying) is based on a text somewhat different from the Massoretic Text used by the Targum Onqelos and (usually) by the Targum Pseudo-Jonathan. From this Diez Macho concluded that the Palestinian Targum used a pre-massoretic text which was often in agreement with the LXX and that it "is on the whole a pre-christian version" even if it seems to belong to the first or second century A.D. in its

---

[12] Cf. A. Diez Macho, *op. cit.*, in *Suppl. to Vetus Testamentum*, 233ff.

present recension.[13] These conclusions are regarded as being valid by P. Wernberg-Møller,[14] despite the fact that he objects to the argumentation just mentioned. Wernberg-Møller's remarks against Diez Macho seem particularly significant in that he points out the differences, with the MT, of the *Vorlage* of other manuscripts as well. Furthermore if Diez Macho's argument is indeed correct as a whole, since the existence of a pre-massoretic text is generally accepted,[15] it should be qualified for two reasons. First, the differences between the pre-massoretic text and the Massoretic Text are not as important as was thought: this is shown by the manuscripts of biblical texts discovered at Qumran[16] and at Masada.[17] Second, in the Targum as well as in the Midrash the starting point of the interpretation is not necessarily the text in itself. Often it is the text as traditionally interpreted.[18] In other words, what the Targum is expressing in Aramaic is not Scripture by itself, but Scripture as already interpreted in the Synagogue.

---

[13] Kahle made a similar comment in his new edition of *The Cairo Geniza*, Oxford, 1959, 207. Without contesting that this Targum is "on the whole a pre-christian version" McNamara shows that the present recension of this Targum should be dated "in the talmudic times" rather than in the second century A.D., McNamara, *op. cit.*, 46-63, and especially 62-63.

[14] "An Inquiry into the validity of the text- critical argument for an early dating of the recently discovered Palestinian Targum" in *Vet. Test.* 12, 1962, 312-31.

[15] Cf., for instance, Thackeray, *op. cit.*, 9.

[16] Cf., for instances, M. Cross, *The Ancient Library of Qumran and Modern Biblical Studies*, London, 1958, 126-27, and W. H. Brownlee, *The Meaning of the Qumran Scrolls for the Bible*, New York, 1964.

[17] Cf. Y. Yadin, *op. cit.*, 168ff. and especially 189.

[18] This is precisely the point Thackeray is making about the Septuagint. Cf. Thackeray, *op. cit.*, 40ff.; in the case of the Targum, cf. the remarks of R. Le Déaut, *Liturgie juive. . .*, 8 and 20. Cf. above our remarks on the tallying of Num. 3:1 with Isa. 45:19.

We should add here that if it is clear that the original *Sitz im Leben* of the Targum is the Synagogue,[19] the Targumim (and namely the Palestinian Targum as represented by the Fragmentary Targum, Pseudo-Jonathan and Neofiti I) contain also many halakic developments.[20] Thus the Targumim seem to presuppose not only the haggadic synagogal interpretation, but also the halakic interpretation of the School, and this from a very early period (pre-christian times if we follow Kahle,[21] and A. Diez Macho[22]). Does it mean that the Targum had another *Sitz im Leben* viz. the School?[23] This is not necessarily so, for indeed, as we pointed out, the halakic

---

[19] Cf. *Meg.* 4:4 and 6, quoted above.

[20] This is namely the case of the Targum on the Pentateuch. These halakic developments are found under the form of re-interpretation of the life of the Patriarchs in order to fit the halakic interpretations of the Mosaic Law. Cf. for instance the Targumim on Gen. 14:13: Og discovers Abram on the eve of the day of the Passover making the unleavened bread; cf. also in Pseudo-Jonathan on Lev. 1:4; 4:14; 9:16; 10:16, examples of halakic interpretations which are in opposition to the Mishnah. In the Targum Neofiti I such interpretations are in agreement with the Mishnah. Cf. Le Déaut, *La Nuit Pascale*, 41.

[21] Kahle, *The Cairo Geniza*, ed. 1959, 208 and 272; cf. Le Déaut, *La Nuit Pascale*, 30-31.

[22] Diez Macho, "The Recently Discovered. . .", 222-45; cf. also P. Grelot, *Semitica* X, 1959, 9-89; M. Black, *An Aramaic Approach to the Gospels and Acts*, Oxford, 1954, 13-25.

[23] R. Bloch suggested that the Targum Onqelos should be considered as created in a school situation: ". . . le Targum Onqelos rédigé en Babylonie dans une langue artificielle, est cependant moins une véritable version qu'une adaptation du Pentateuque d'après les discussions des grandes écoles rabbiniques, une sorte de *peshat* interprétation de la Torah d'après la halakhah talmudique, tandis que Tg J lui, se rapproche beaucoup plus du *derash*". "Note méthodologique", 211, n. 29. If this is true of the redaction of the Targum Onqelos it is certainly not true of the origin of the traditions contained in it. It is generally accepted that this Targum is the result of a purging of the older targumic material (cf. Le Déaut, *La Nuit Pascale*, 27ff.). Thus in it we have remnants of a much older tradition which had its origin somewhere else than in the School.

teaching was not foreign to the Synagogue. It could mean on the contrary that something like the *Yelammedenu* homilies existed very early at the Synagogue. This should warn us, once more, against making a clear cut separation between the use of the Bible at the Synagogue and the use of the Bible in the School. We can therefore consider the Synagogue as the *Sitz im Leben* of the Targum[24] if we keep in mind its close relationship with the School.

TARGUMIC METHODS OF INTERPRETATION

Having a liturgical setting, the Targum is therefore not a mere translation but rather an interpretation. The tradition recorded in the Babylonian Talmud (*Meg.* 3a), in spite of its late character, is quite helpful for understanding the nature of the Targum and its method of interpretation.

> "What is meant by the text, *And they read in the book, in the law of God, with an interpretation and they gave the sense, and caused them to understand the reading* (Neh. 8:8), *'And they read in the book, in the law of God'*: this indicates the (Hebrew) text; *'with an interpretation'*: this indicates the Targum; *'and they gave the sense'*: this indicates the verse stops; *'and caused them to understand the reading'*: this indicates the accentuation, or, according to another version, the massoretic notes".[25]

This interpretation of Neh. 8:8 attributed to Rabbi Judah ben Ilai is significant not only because it traces the origin of the Targum to the time of Ezra, but also because it points out two of the Targumic methods: the use of "the verse

---

[24] We use thereupon the term to designate the phenomenon Targum rather than the literary genre, unless otherwise indicated.

[25] I quote from R. I. Epstein's translation, London, 1938, *ad loc.*

stops" and of the punctuation (vocalization) in order to interpret a text. In other words we find here again an exegesis which appears to us as very artificial since it allows a great freedom from what we would call the "meaning of the text in its context".

Thus if one uses different vocalizations for the same consonantal text, he will obtain different meanings. For instance in Gen. 22:14 ("And Abraham called the name of that place the Lord will provide") we find the word שם. Using the vocalization שָׁם the Targum Onqelos interprets: "Abraham worshipped and prayed *there in that place*. . . ." The Targum Pseudo-Jonathan reads: "Abraham gave thanks and prayed there in that place. . ." But whence comes the idea of prayer and worship? From the same text using this time the other vocalization: שֵׁם understood as meaning "The Name" *par excellence*, i.e., God. Since the verb קרא has two meanings, "to call" and "to pray", there is the possible interpretation: "And Abraham worshipped and prayed in the name of the word of the Lord God. . . " which is precisely the text of the Fragmentary Targum.[26] Let us note that in this process another rule of exegesis is used,[27] viz. "playing with homonymous root",[28] or with the different meaning of a same word.[29]

In the same way, according to how one separates the sentences or the words in a sentence, the meaning of the text changes. A good example of this is Gen. 22:8:[30] "And Abraham said, God will provide himself a lamb for a burnt offering, my son". Yet we get another meaning by breaking up the sentence

---

[26] For the texts of the different targumim, cf. Bowker, 225 and 227; cf. also Le Déaut, *Liturgie*. . ., 31.

[27] Namely Rule 28 of the 32 *middoth* of R. Eliezer. Cf. H. L. Strack, *op. cit.*, 97.

[28] According to S. Lieberman, *Hellenism in Jewish Palestine*, New York, 1950, 68.

[29] Another example of this is to be found in Pseudo-Jonathan on Gen. 49:1 where the exclamation "O Israel" of the *shema* is understood as meaning "O Jacob" in the Fragmentary Targum: cf. Bowker, 282.

[30] Cf. Le Déaut, *Liturgie*. . ., 31.

as follows: "God will see;[31] (as for) the lamb of the burnt
offering (it is) my son". Thus the Fragmentary Targum
interprets: "From before the Lord has been prepared the lamb
for a burnt offering; and if not then you are the lamb.

Going farther, one can break one word into two parts, as
in Gen. 41:43 where the difficult word אברך[32] is interpreted
as אב רך, i.e., "father of the King".[33] The substitution of
letters was even possible according to the so-called *Athbash*
alphabet:[34] for instance לב קמי in Jer. 51:1 ("the heart of
my enemies") becomes כשדים[35] the Chaldees. Among other
similar methods which were used in the Targum we find the
Gematria: for instance in Gen. 14:14, Eliezer (אליעזר which
has the numerical value of 318) is understood as being by
himself the 318 servants which went to war with Abram.[36] We
could multiply the examples of this minute exegesis, by means
of which many meanings can be extracted from any text.
Actually these techniques and methods are nothing else than
those contained in the thirty-two *middoth* for haggadic
interpretation, which are ascribed to R. Eliezer ben Jose
ha-Gelily.[37] Therefore many of these *middoth*, even if they

---

[31] Another possible meaning of the verb.

[32] R. V. "Bow the Knee", Dhorme "Attention!" from the
Egyptian which means "to your heart", i.e., "Beware", "Pay
attention to". Cf. Ed. Dhorme ed., *La Bible*, L'Ancien
Testament, Paris, 1956 and 1959.

[33] רך being understood as "Rex".

[34] i.e., א (the first letter) is written instead of ת
(the last letter), ב (the second letter) instead of ש (the one
before the last), etc.

[35] Cf. Targum on Jeremiah (Sperber, vol. III) *ad loc.*;
cf. also Dhorme, *Bible*, *ad loc.* and note.

[36] Cf. Ps. Jonathan, *ad loc.*: "When Abram heard that his
brother was taken captive he armed the young men whom he had
trained for war, having grown up in his house, but they were
unwilling to go with him. So he chose from among them
Eliezer, the son of Mimrod, who was equal in might to all of
them, 318, and pursued as far as Dan". Bowker's translation,
op. cit., 193.

[37] Cf. for their translation H. L. Strack, *Introduction
to the Talmud and Midrash*, 95-98.

THE TARGUM AS POPULAR INTERPRETATION OF SCRIPTURE

To these methods and techniques of interpretation we should add another characteristic of the Targum: its popular origin. We should remember first that the Targumic interpretation could be made by practically anybody, including a minor.[39] No wonder then that the Targum appears often as being simplistic when compared for instance with Philo's schorlarly interpretation. This is easily understandable when we remember the *Sitz im Leben* of the Targum: it was to meet in advance any question anybody in the audience could have when listening to the sacred text. Thus naturally the *meturgeman* (the targumist) gave an explanation for any passages which could be obscure for his listeners. For instance the corrupted text of I Sam. 13:1[40] which reads literally "when one year old Saul became king", becomes "Saul when he began to reign was like a one year old child who has not sinned".[41] In the same way Gen. 20:13, "And it came to pass when God caused me to wander from my father house . . ." is difficult because the verb (התעו) is plural. In spite of the construction of the text God (Elohim in the text) cannot be the subject since by definition he is One (cf. the *Shema*). Furthermore the verb usually means "to err": the sense cannot

---

[38] They are not therefore "much later" than the seven *middoth* of Hillel and the thirteen *middoth* of Ishmael, as Bowker contends, *op. cit.*, 318.

[39] Cf. *Meg.* 4:6 quoted above, note 3.

[40] בן-שנה שאול במלכו.

[41] Quoted by Le Déaut, *La Nuit Pascale*, 61.

be "God caused me to err"! Therefore the text is interpreted as follows, "And it came to pass, when the worshippers of idols tried to lead me astray, I went forth from my father house. . ."[42] or "And it came to pass, when the people went astray after the works of their own hands the Lord brought me to fear him from my father's house".[43] In this last example, we see together with the desire to solve the difficulty of a text, the attempt to avoid what could be shocking for the pious man. This is indeed frequent: we constantly find the Targum trying to avoid what would be irreverent toward God. To take another example in Gen. 6:2, we find the mention of the *"bene elohim"*, which might be understood in too crude a sense as "God's sons". Thus the Targum interprets this as "the sons of the great ones"[44] or the "sons of the judges".[45]

For the same reason the Targum often adds the details which are missing in the texts, for instance the name of an otherwise unnamed personage. Let us take as example Gen. 14:13, "And there came *one* that had escaped. . ." Pseudo-Jonathan supplies his identity "Og".[46] Why? Because of a play of words on "ogoth", the unleavened cakes, which Abraham was making when he came.[47] He was therefore identified with Og, king of Bashan, who was according to Deut. 3:11 the only one who "remained of the remnant of the Giants" and who therefore was understood as having escaped from the

---

[42] Pseudo-Targum Jonathan, *ad loc.* Translation J. Bowker, *op. cit.*, 218.

[43] Targum Onqelos, *ad loc.* Translation: *ibid.*

[44] This alteration is found both in Pseudo-Jonathan and Onqelos, *ibid.*, 151ff.

[45] בני דייניא: Neofiti I, *ad loc.*, Diez Macho ed., 33.

[46] Bowker, *op. cit.*, 193ff.

[47] This is not according to the Hebrew text, but according to its traditional interpretation. It is also an example of another characteristic of the Targum: the Patriarchs are shown as keeping the Law before its promulgation.

flood.[48] Other examples of such identifications are:[49]

- Those who kept the manna in spite of the order given by God are Dathan and Abiron (Num. 16:25), according to Pseudo-Jonathan, *ad loc.*, and a gloss of Targum Neofiti.

- Darius is identified as the son of Esther (T. Esth. 7:2).

- Melchizedek is Sem (Pseudo-Jonathan on Gen. 14:18: "The righteous king, Sem, son of Noah, King of Jerusalem...").[50]

-The chiefs of Pharaoh's magicians are Yannes and Yimbres (cf. Pseudo-Jonathan on Exod. 1:15)[51] who are furthermore identified with the sons of Balaam (cf. Pseudo-Jonathan on Num. 22:22).

- The two young servants of Abraham are identified with Eliezer and Ishmael (Gen. 22:3, Pseudo-Jonathan *ad loc.*).

- Pharaoh's advisers are Balaam, Job and Jethro (Pseudo-Jonathan on Exod. 9:21; cf. also gloss in the Targum Neofiti *ad loc.*).

All the different kinds of amplifications which we just mentioned can be illustrated at once by the Targumim on Exod. 4:24-26. The biblical text reads:

> "At a lodging place on the way
> the Lord met him and sought
> to kill him. Then Zipporah took
> a flint and cut off her son's
> foreskin, and touched Moses'
> feet with it, and said,
> 'Surely you are a bridegroom
> of blood to me!'"

---

[48] This points out another characteristic of targumic method: the telescoping of chronology. Og is understood as living in the time of the Flood and in the time of Abraham.

[49] As listed by Le Déaut, *La Nuit Pascale*, 60.

[50] Cf. also the other Targumim; see R. Le Déaut, "Le Titre de *Summus Sacerdos* donné à Melchisédech est-il d'origine juive?" *Recherches de Science Religieuse* 50, 1962, 224.

[51] Quoted by R. Bloch, "Moïse dans la tradition rabbinique", *Cahiers Sioniens* 8, 1954, 223.

This text is indeed obscure and many questions can be raised, which G. Vermes has summarized as follows: "Whom, for instance, did the Lord seek to kill? Moses or his son? At whose feet was the foreskin thrown: the Lord's, Moses' or his son's? Who was the 'bridegroom of blood': the Lord, Moses, or the child?"[52] To these could be added the question of the identity of Moses' son (he had two sons, Gershom and Eliezer, according to Exod. 18:3). Why is it that only one is mentioned? Doctrinal questions also arise, since the circumcision is a rite reserved to men alone and since it is difficult to admit that either Moses or his son was uncircumcised. Furthermore does the text really mean that the Lord tried to kill Moses?

The different Targumim elaborate more or less extensively on this text, yet all of them follow the same tradition.[53] Let us quote the most representative, Pseudo-Jonathan:[54]

> 4:24 - "And it came to pass on the way, at the lodging place, that the Angel of the Lord met him and sought to kill him because his son Gershom had not been circumcised on account of Jethro, his father-in-law, who did not permit him to circumcise him. But Eliezer had been circumcised by virtue of an agreement they had made between them. (25) And Zipporah took a flint and cut off the foreskin of Gershom her son, and brought what had been severed to the feet of the Destroying Angel, and said: My husband wished to circumcise but his father-in-law prevented him. May now the blood of this circumcision atone for my husband. (26) And the Destroying Angel desisted from him. Then Zipporah gave thanks, and said: how beloved is the blood of this circumcision which has saved my husband from the hand of the Destroying Angel".

---

[52]*Scripture and Tradition in Judaism*, Leiden, 1961, 178.

[53]*Op. cit.*, 183.

[54]We quote the translation given by G. Vermès, *op. cit.*, 182-83.

Thus most of the questions we could ask are answered by the Targum.

Other kinds of amplifications or precisions added to the biblical texts are also to be found. The locations were identified: thus "the mountains of Ararat" (Gen. 8:4) are identified with "the mountains of Qardon";[55] "the sand of Moriah" (Gen. 22:2) is identified with "the land of worship" (Pseudo-Jonathan and Onqelos), that is, "where the Temple was to be built" (Neofiti, marginal note *ad loc.*), thus the location of Solomon's temple.[56] In the same way on Gen. 8:20 ("And Noah builded an altar unto the Lord") the Pseudo-Jonathan has: "And Noah builded the altar before the Lord, the altar which Adam had built at the time when he was cast out of the garden of Eden, and had made an offering on it; and Cain and Abel made their offerings on it. But when the waters of the Flood came down it was destroyed. So Noah rebuilt it. . . ."[57]

Dates corresponding (i.e., exactly to dates of the religious calendar) were also ascribed to events. In the Targumim on Gen. 14:13[58] the date of the event is given as "the eve of the day of Passover".[59] Other examples can be found, for instance, in Pseudo-Jonathan on Gen. 8, which specifies the different dates of the events described in this chapter, giving the names of the months.[60]

---

[55] Pseudo-Jonathan and Onqelos *ad loc.*, Bowker, 197ff.

[56] This identification is already to be found in II Chr. 3: "Then Solomon began to build the house of the Lord at Jerusalem in mount Moriah" and in Josephus (*Ant.* I, 226; with mention of *David*'s (sic) Temple).

[57] Bowker, *op. cit.*, 167-68. For the reference to Adam cf. Pseudo-Jonathan on Gen. 3:23.

[58] See above.

[59] Pseudo-Jonathan *ad loc.*

[60] The same thing occurs in *Neofiti* (marginalia) *ad loc.*; on this specification of dates see also what we say below about the Book of Jubilees.

Targum and Tradition (Oral Torah)

Such haggadic methods and techniques of interpretation give the freedom to do practically what one wants with the text. We could even say that they put the biblical text at the mercy of the interpreter. The Rabbis, aware of this danger, promulgated the rule that nothing can be added to the text.[61] Let us quote this rule *in extenso*:

"R. Judah said: If one translates a verse literally, he is a liar; if he adds thereto, he is a blasphemer and a libeller (*megaddef*). Then what is meant by translation. Our (authorized) translation".[62]

Thus the freedom of the *meturgeman* from the biblical text (Written Torah) is limited by the Tradition. As an example let us take Exod. 24:10a: "And they saw the God of Israel".[63] It would be a lie to translate it literally: man cannot see God. It would be blasphemous to add "angel", a creature, instead of the Creator. Thus the proper rendering: "They saw the Glory of the God of Israel".

Such a rule is certainly to be dated after the end of the period under consideration. Attributed to R. Judah be n Ilai (end of second century A.D.), it seems to be a reaction against the lengthy paraphrases characteristic of the Palestinian Targumim. It implies almost a codification of the oral haggadic tradition: "what is meant by translation? Our (authorized) translation". Furthermore it denies the popular character of the Targumim.[64] Yet this is not to say that the

---

[61] *Kidd.* 49a.

[62] Soncino Edition; cf. also Tosephta *Meg.* 4:41 (quoted by Bonsirven, *Textes*. . ., 271) and McNamara, *op. cit.*, 41.

[63] From the Tosephta *loc. cit.*, quoted by I. Epstein in his notes on B. Talmud, *Kidd.* 49a, and by McNamara, *op. cit.*, 41.

[64] This is precisely the point of the paragraph in *Kidd.* 49a: cf. the preceding sentences: "He must be able to read and translate it. Even if he translates it *according to his own understanding*?" (my italics). Then the rule quoted above is given as an answer to this question.

oral tradition did not have any role in the establishment of the Targumim in the period preceding the fall of Jerusalem. It means rather that this role was certainly of a different nature: the *meturgeman* was borrowing from the oral tradition not because he was compelled to do so by an authoritative codified tradition, but because it was the very way of thinking of the *milieu* in which he was living. He was so much involved in this tradition that he could not understand the biblical text in any other way.[65]

Seeing the biblical text through the colored glasses of the Tradition, the *meturgeman* occasionally went so far as to contradict it directly. For instance he refused to accept what Num. 12:1 repeats twice: *viz.* that Moses "has married an Ethiopian (Kushite) woman:, that is, a woman of another race. Thus the Targum of Onqelos speaks of a "*beautiful* woman"; the Targum Pseudo- Jonathan explains that he was forced to marry the Queen of Ethiopia but that he repudiated her. Other Targumim go so far as to say directly that she was *not* an Ethiopian woman.[66] In the same way[67] in Deut. 28:36 and 64, it is said that Israel "will worship other gods" during the exile. This is read as meaning that they will pay taxes to worshippers of idols.[68]

Is this to say that the biblical text escapes the fancy of the individual *meturgeman* so as to follow the fancy of the Jewish community as a whole? That would be to forget the role of the liturgical setting of the Synagogue. As we saw the traditional interpretation of a biblical text is often understood only in its relationship with texts from the other parts of the Hebrew Bible which are read together with it in

---

[65] Cf. Le Déaut, Liturgie, 26-27.

[66] Cf. Le Déaut, *Liturgie*, 28ff. and G. Vermès, "Moïse au tournant des deux Testaments", *Cahiers Sioniens*, 1954, 187.

[67] Other example given by Le Déaut, *ibid.*

[68] Cf. also the Targumim on Gen. 37:33; Gen. 4:23-24; 4:26; etc.

the Synagogue. As Le Déaut notes,[69] this is also true of the
targumic interpretations: frequently they cannot be
understood as long as one does not recognize their
relationship to other biblical texts. For instance, as C.
Perrot pointed out, [70] the Targum to Isa. 57:19 understands
the biblical text which reads, "I created the fruit of the
lips; Peace, peace to him that is far off; and to him that is
near; saith the Lord; and I will heal him", as referring to
the "Peace" of those who *kept the Torah* or came back to it.
This reference can be easily understood when we know that Isa.
57:19 is the concluding part of the haftarah corresponding to
the seder Exod. 21,[71] a part of the code of the covenant
which expresses a number of prescriptions (*mishpatim*).

THE DOCTRINE OF SCRIPTURE IMPLIED IN THE TARGUM

Out of the limited number of examples which we took, we
see emerging the "doctrine of Scripture" (or hermeneutical
principles) which is implied in the Targum. We shall now
spell out its main characteristics, substantiating them by
other examples.

1) *Everything is meaningful in Scripture*

The basic conviction (or axiom) on which this
hermeneutical use of Scripture in the Targum is built, is
clearly that there is nothing without meaning in the Sacred

---

[69] Le Déaut, *op. cit.*, 20.

[70] "La lecture synagogale d'Exode XXI-XXII", in *A la Rencontre de Dieu. Mémorial Albert Gelin*, Le Puy, 1961, 229.

[71] Cf. J. Mann, *op. cit.*, vol. I, 469: we can assume here that this haftarah corresponds indeed to this seder, yet without implying that it is always the case.

Text words, everything is meaningful and thus must be understood. This is implied in the very fact that the Targum serves the audience in two ways: as a translation and an interpretation of the difficult passages. Such a conviction demands a complete hermeneutic of Scripture, yet it does not give us any hint about the hermeneutical principles themselves. We propose to show that the hermeneutic of the Targum is clearly *not* structured on a theological system (or a philosophical system, for that matter). Rather, the targumic hermeneutic is characterized a) by the phenomenon of the interpretation of Scripture by Scripture, and b) by the concurrent phenomenon of the actualization of Scripture.

2) *Scripture is to be explained by Scripture*

As we suggested earlier one of the major characteristics of several of the hermeneutical techniques is that Scripture was interpreted by Scripture. Yet by its very literary genre the Targum presents only the results of this use of other biblical passages. In a number of cases it is possible to discover which text has been used for the interpretation of a given passage. Examples of this have been given above. To take only one other example, if Tamar is said to be "daughter of a priest" (Pseudo-Jonathan on Gen. 38:6 and 24) it is because only the "daughter of a priest" must be condemned to be "burnt with fire . . . if she profanes herself by playing the whore" (Lev. 21:9).[72]

Yet more often the texts which are used are not as easy to trace, because such use is not the result of a logical process, but rather of the liturgical setting[73] and of the

---

[72] Her father is identified as Sem (Melchizedek) by R. Meir according to *Gen. Rab.* on 38:24. Cf. Le Déaut, *Liturgie*, 23.

[73] Cf. above the influence upon each other of the different texts read on the same Sabbath. We gave above an example of a targumic interpretation of a prophetic text (Isa. 57:19) which is understandable only in the light of the corresponding seder (Exod. 21).

method of "tallying" which we spoke of in connection with the homily.[74] Therefore in the many cases where we cannot understand the reason for a targumic interpretation, we should resist the temptation to conclude that it is the product of the mere fancy either of the targumist or of the community. Indeed the homiletic developments seemed fanciful as long as the role of the haftarah was not pointed out as it was, so masterfully, by J. Mann. On the contrary, we should assume that in most instances the targumic interpretations are the result of an explanation of Scripture by means of Scripture, as was the case for the homily. This assumption is supported by the very close relationship between Targum and Homily.[75] Furthermore we should not forget that our phrase "explanation of Scripture by means of Scripture" can also be heard as meaning "explanation of Torah by means of Torah", and therefore it can involve not only Written Torah but also Oral Torah[76]. . ., a remark which brings us back to the question of the origin of the Oral Torah and its relationship with Scripture. For the present we must continue to postpone the latter problem.

3) *The synthetic view of Scripture and of sacred history*

What is important to emphasize, now, is that such an interpretation of Scripture by Scripture leads to what we can call a synthetic view of Scripture and of sacred history.[77] This is an expression of the unity of Scripture which manifests itself as a *"telescoping"* of all the elements of Scripture around a limited number of locations, dates and

---

[74] As we shall see this method is to be found already in the *middoth* of Hillel.

[75] Cf. R. Bloch, "Note méthodologique", 211ff.; Le Déaut, *Liturgie*, 23.

[76] Cf. Le Déaut, *Liturgie*, 27.

[77] Which is a corollary of the preceding.

personages. This practice has certainly a pedagogical value (it gives the audience a simpler frame of reference, in which it will be less easily lost), but it also has several implications concerning the hermeneutical principles.

About the "telescoping" of locations we do not need to elaborate further. The examples which we have given concerning Moriah, the site of Solomon's Temple, and concerning the location of the altar of Adam, of Cain and Abel, and of Noah are telling enough. We should emphasize nevertheless that it is an attitude already present in the Hebrew Bible (cf. II Chr. 3:1).

The "telescoping" of dates is worth further investigation because of its implications. This principle can be expressed in the phrase: "There is no before and after in Scripture", which is the last of the 32 *middoth* compiled by Eliezer ben Jose Ha-Gelili. This rule which is ascribed to R. Ishmael,[78] goes as follows: "The before comes after in the biblical sections", or "the after comes before in the biblical sections".[79] It is certain that this principle, in òne form or the other, antedates R. Ishmael's time; for it is demanded by the biblical texts themselves, which show many discrepancies which can hardly escape even a cursory reader. Modern scholars explain them by assuming different sources as a result of literary criticism. The targumist as well as the Rabbi used the principle, "There is no before and after in Scripture", in order to solve these discrepancies.[80] Thus

---

[78] Cf. *Mekilta* on Exod. 15:9, Lauterbach ed., vol. II, 151; R. Joshua ben Levi (middle of third century) is also said to have used it: cf. *Cant. Rab.* on 1:2, Soncino ed., vol. IX, 22-23.

[79] Quoted by J. Bonsirven, *Exégèse Rabbinique et Exégèse Paulinienne*, Paris, 1939, 168ff. and D. Daube, *The New Testament and Rabbinic Judaism*, London, 1956, 409.

[80] Cf. the examples which D. Daube took from the *Mekilta* (Exod. 15:9 before Exod. 15:1-8) and *Sifre on Numbers* (on Num. 9:1 and 1:1); cf. D. Daube, *op. cit.*, 408. Cf. also J. Bonsirven, *op. cit.*, and Rabinowitz, "The Study of a Midrash", *J.Q.R.* 58, 1967, 150ff.

chronological order as given by the text should be "turned around" if necessary.[81] It is actually another method of interpretation of R. Ishmael's school: the so-called *seres* or *haplakh*[82] already used by Hillel.[83] This second method of interpretation goes much further than the first: it implicitly draws the conclusion that since "there is no before and after in the Bible", the interpreter can ignore the demands of the chronology when his interpretation would be limited by it.

The latter is precisely the attitude that we find in the Targum: in it there is no any historical perspective. Therefore, as we saw, Melchizedek can be identified with Sem, but also Balaam with Laban,[84] Dinah (Jacob's daughter) with Job's wife,[85] Og, a personage of the period of the Flood, with another of the time of Abraham.[86]

We could multiply the examples. But what we would like to emphasize here is the significance of this attitude, *viz.* that the history is a synthetic unity, and that its different periods are closely interrelated. Because of this understanding of history the meaning of an event is to be understood together with similar events which occurred before and after it. We could express this by saying that such an event is prefigured (or prophesied) by an event of the past and prefigures (or prophesies) events of the future. Yet this is not exactly so. Rather, for the Targum, there is an implicit unity, or better a basic identity between these events. Here the principle that the Bible interprets the Bible is combined with that of historical "telescoping".

---

[81] Such is the case of the vision by Jacob of the ladder reaching to heaven, which is followed by a vow which should be placed before not after (*Gen. Rab.* on 28:20, Sonico ed., vol. I, *ad loc.*), and this for theological reasons. Cf. Daube, *op. cit.*, 411.

[82] Daube, *op. cit.*, 410-12.

[83] Cf. *Aboth* 5:22. It is to be noted that this rule can be used for other than chronological purposes.

[84] Pseudo-Jonathan on Num. 22:5.

[85] According to Le Déaut, *Liturgie*, 24.

[86] Cf. above, p. 60.

Let us take the example that Le Déaut[87] found in Targum Neofiti I on Exod. 12:42, which brings together the four important nights of the history of the world, *viz.* the night of the creation, the night of Abraham (either the night of the Covenant, Gen. 15:13, or that of the *Aqueda*, i.e., "binding" of Isaac on the altar), the night of the Passover, and the eschatological night of the Messianic salvation. The identity of these nights is expressed first by ascribing them to the same calendar day. Thus the Covenant of Abraham with God is put on Nisan 15, that is, on the Passover night.[88] The same thing is done with the *Aqueda*,[89] the night of the creation, and that of the *Eschaton*.[90] furthermore the

---

[87] Text and French translation in Le Déaut, *La Nuit Pascale*, 64-65 (photocopy of the manuscript of this passage, 2-3); cf. also Pseudo-Jonathan on Exod. 12:42: text and French translation in J. J. Brierre-Narbonne, *Exégèse Targumique des prophéties messianiques*, Paris, 1936, 19-21.

[88] Cf. Pseudo-Jonathan, Fragmentary Targum and Neofiti on Exod. 12:42 quoted by Le Déaut, *op. cit.*, 133ff.; cf. also *Mekilta* on Exod. 12:41, Lauterbach ed., vol. I, 113, which is justified by the length of the sojourning in Egypt, exactly 430 years (or 400, Gen. 15:13), ("even the selfsame day", Exod. 12:41) which is counted traditionally from the divine promise. Because of the discrepancy between the two dates it was thought that the 400 years should be counted from the birth of Isaac (cf. D. Daube, *op. cit.*, 410, n. 1), thus also on Nisan 15 (Exod. R. 12:2, Soncino ed.).

[89] Same targumic texts; cf. *Mekilta*, *ibid.*, *Exod. R.*, *ibid.*

[90] Yet in the Rabbinic literature we find another tradition setting all these events on *Tishri* (except Passover for obvious reasons). These conflicting traditions are explained by conflicting calendars which have the year beginning either on Nisan or on Tishri. On this cf. J. van Goudoever, *Biblical Calendars*, Leiden, 1959, mainly 145-48; A. Jaubert, *La date de la Cène*, Paris, 1957, 13-75; Le Déaut, *ibid.*, 218ff.; etc. Let us note that in spite of J. Mann (*op. cit.*, vol. I, VI) we agree with Le Déaut: the Triennial cycle began in Nisan. The following scholars reached the same conclusion: A. Guilding, *The Fourth Gospel and Jewish Worship*, Oxford, 1960, 6-23, and A. Buchler, "The reading of the Law in a Triennial Cycle" in *J.Q.R.* 5, 1893, 420-68 and 6, 1894, 1-73. If this Triennial cycle was seen as beginning in Nisan, then the dating of several events in the Targumim becomes more understandable.

identification of these four nights allows the interpreter to understand each of them in terms of the others. The Exodus is understood in terms of the Creation and the Creation in terms of the Exodus in many targumic and Rabbinic texts.[91] In the same way the *Eschaton* is interpreted in terms of the Exodus (*viz.* as an Exodus from this world to the world to come), as well as in the terms of the Creation (a re-creation and not a renovation).[92] The *Aqueda* is interpreted in terms of, and helps to interpret, the Passover.[93] In the same way Gen. 15 (the covenant with Abraham) is interpreted in terms of the Exodus and of the Eschaton.[94]

Although such an extensive development is rare (even in the Targum Pseudo-Jonathan), nevertheless this passage well represents the synthetic conception of history which we find frequently attested in the Targum. In order to point out more precisely the significance of this view for an understanding of the hermeneutical principles, we could say that the unity or basic identity between these events is to be found in that they are all considered as Act or Word (*dabar* in both cases) of God, the God who is One.[95] This theological perspective, which we see as underlying this attitude toward the history recorded in Scripture, cannot be better expressed that in the words of the Targum itself: on Isa. 43:12,[96] "I have declared *to Abraham your father what would come to pass; I have saved you from Egypt according to the Covenant with him; I have made*

---

[91]Cf. Le Déaut, *op. cit.*, 226ff. and especially 226, 232-33.

[92]*Ibid.*, 248ff.

[93]*Ibid.*, 153ff.

[94]*Ibid.*, 147ff.

[95]Cf. the *Shema*.

[96]"I have declared and have saved and I have made known".

known *to you my Law on the Sinai. . . .*"[97] Thus according to the Targum, this one sentence of the prophet alludes to the actions of God through all the sacred history, or more exactly to the actions of God in a number of selected events. For indeed the result of this synthetic view of history is to reduce the sacred history to a schematic series of privileged events. This is nothing new: such a schematic view of the sacred history is already to be found in the Hebrew Bible.[98] But what is interesting to note is that for the Targum this sacred history is, so to speak, *closed*: everything in the Bible is interpreted as referring to this limited number of sacred events (acts or words of God). Only one element is added: the eschatological event. For the targumist then, Scripture refers exclusively either to the sacred history contained therein or to the eschatological time which is far in the future. There is not reference in the Tarqumim, so far as I know, to *present* events (present to the targumist, that is) which could be considered as having this basic identity with the events of the sacred history. To put it bluntly: it is as if for the targumist God acted[99] (in the past), will act (in the eschatological future) but is not acting in between.[100]

Either the principle of interpreting Scripture by Scripture had the result of closing the sacred history, or it was itself the consequence of a conception of *"closed"* sacred history. This would imply, also, that the whole of revelation was understood to be in Scripture.[101]

---

[97] Cf. P. Churgin, *Targum Jonathan to the Prophets*, New Haven, 1927, *ad loc.*; J. F. Stenning, *The Targum of Isaiah*, Oxford, 1949, *ad loc.*, and Le Déaut, *La Nuit Pascale*, 144. In the quotation the italics represent the targumic interpretation.

[98] Cf. the famous Deut. 26:5-9 and also Deut. 6:21-24; Joshua 24:2ff., etc.

[99] "To act" is to be understood here as referring to revelatory acts of God.

[100] This does not exclude, as we shall see, an actualization of Scripture.

[101] This is indeed *un lieu commun* of the Rabbinical theology, but this will have to be qualified in terms of the implicit doctrine of Scripture that we discover in the different uses of Scripture in classical Judaism.

This telescoping of all elements of Scripture around a limited number of locations and dates (events of sacred history) could be expressed by saying that a given biblical event is prefigured (or prophesied) by an event of the past and prefigures (or prophesies) events of the future (all that is the closed "fence"[102] of Scripture). Therefore, one could conclude with Le Déaut,[103] that this can be considered as a first step toward the typological interpretation which we shall find elsewhere. Nevertheless we should emphasize that this is *not* a typological interpretation: typology acknowledges the identity of biblical events taking place in history beyond the Scriptural sacred history. Here such an interpretation takes place exclusively in the closed "fence" of Scripture (the eschatological event is beyond history).

It is to be noted that we are drawing these conclusions from our examination of the telescoping of biblical locations and dates, leaving purposefully aside a similar telescoping around a third pole of attraction: a limited number of biblical personages, *viz.* the Patriarchs, Adam, Elijah, Moses, David, Solomon, etc.[104] The biblical personages are indeed quite often interpreted in the closed "fence" of Scripture; they belong to the events of the sacred history. Other examples of this can be found in the identifications of unnamed personages that we mentioned earlier. We could multiply the examples of texts interpreted as referring to the biblical personages despite the fact that they do not mention them. To avoid repeating ourselves we shall take only one

---

[102] We are not using this term in its Rabbinical sense here; but the image is appropriate.

[103] Thus Le Déaut, *Liturgie*, 25: "Les innombrables applications historiques que l'on rencontre dans le Targum contiennent une sorte d'ébauche *d'interprétation typologique* . . ." (our italics).

[104] We should note here the relative diversity of the figures on which the tradition has been focused. It is one of the characteristic differences with the Samaritan tradition, which is heavily focused on the figure of Moses. Cf. J. Bowman, "The Exegesis of the Pentateuch among the Samaritans and the Rabbis", *Oud testamentische Studien*, Leiden, 1950, 226, 240, *passim*, and J. MacDonald, *The Theology of the Samaritans*, Philadelphia, 1964, 135.

example, which will lead us to our next point: the Targum Neofiti on Lev. 22:27.[105] The biblical text reads: "Where a bullock or a sheep or a goat is brought forth, then it shall be seven days under his mother". It is interpreted as referring to Abraham (who entertained the angels with a calf of his herd: Gen. 18), to Isaac (bound like a lamb: Gen. 22), and to Jacob (who got the blessing of his father by using the meat and the skins of two kids of the goats: Gen. 27). Thus the interpretation: the sacrifices of thanksgiving made with the calf, lamb and kid will be accepted by God because of the merits of the Fathers. God will remember because of these animals. Such interpretations of the biblical personages reflect the synthetic view of Scripture that we just discussed. Yet these personages are also presented as "moral types" of the faithful Jew. In this latter case the circle of interpretation of Scripture by Scripture is broken. The biblical personages are interpreted in terms of the believer's situation: this is a "moral" typology which is an important characteristic of the actualization of Scripture in the Targum, that we shall discuss below. Yet before this discussion we need to consider the theological development in the Targum.

4) *Theological developments in the Targum*

The fourth characteristic of the Targum is its attitude toward theological developments. Because of the *Sitz im Leben* of the Targum, *viz.* the Synagogue, and because of its homiletic character, these developments cannot be brought together in a "systematic theology". The hermeneutic of the Targum is clearly *not* structured on a theological system (or a philosophical system, for that matter). To be convinced of this it is enough to compare the targumic hermeneutic with

---

[105] Cf. Le Déaut, *La Nuit Pascale*, 171ff., for text and French translation.

Philo's. This is not to say that there is no theological development in the Targum. On the contrary they are quite numerous and they reflect indeed theological problems and discussions of the targumist's time. A good example of this is the Targum Pseudo-Jonathan on Gen. 4:8 that we shall quote and discuss below. Yet these developments are not a "systematic theology". They could be called an "atomistic" theology[106] because their development follows the relatively haphazard character of the biblical text and of its legitimate[107] interpretations. This in itself is noteworthy: for indeed it means that Scripture is given preeminence over any theological development.[108] In other words what is essential is not a correct (orthodox) theological doctrine but an openness to Scripture, a "listening to Scripture". The result is a multiplicity of theological conceptions not necessarily fitting with each other (if not conflicting), which is for our logic a theological *tohu-wabohu*, in which an attempt to attenuate the biblical anthropomorphisms[109] goes

---

[106] Cf. P. Humbert, "Le Messie dans le Targum des prophètes", *Revue de Théologie et de Philosophie* 44, 1911, 5-46; especially 20, where the authors used the word "atomistic" to speak of the targumic exegesis.

[107] i.e., according to the accepted rules.

[108] To say with Le Déaut (*La Nuit Pascale*, 60) that the reason for what we have called an atomistic theology is the fact that Judaism is a "theopraxy" rather than a "theology" is, without being contestable in itself, not to the point when speaking of the Targum and even of the haggadah in general. For even though the "praxy" is present in the haggadah as well as in the halakah, this does not mean that it is the only concern of the former. Otherwise it would be quite difficult to explain most of targumic developments. On the fact that haggadah cannot be equated with "theopraxy", see Henry Slonimsky, "The Philosophy implicit in the Midrash", *Hebrew Union College Annual*, 1956, 235-36.

[109] Cf. the very common rendering of "Yahweh" by the "Memra" or the "Shekinah" (*passim*). Cf. also Targum on Gen. 5:22, "Enoch walked with God. . ." which is transformed in "Enoch worshipped before the Lord" (Pseudo-Jonathan and Onqelos, *ad loc.*). See also the Targumim on Gen. 6:6, "And the Lord repented", 8:21, "The Lord accepted his offering with favor" (Pseudo-Jonathan, *ad loc.*) etc.

hand in hand with the most daring developments.[110] Certainly at the time of the Mishnah some kind of codification took place,[111] but to force the theological doctrines about the Messiah, the world to come, Passover, etc., into a system would be to falsify the very reality of the haggadic tradition which we witness in the Targum.[112] We can conclude therefore, that the targumic hermeneutic was not theological.

5) *The actualization of Scripture in the Targum*

The conviction that everything is meaningful in Scripture leads to an actualization of Scripture:[113] it has to be meaningful for the Jewish community of that place and time. For this purpose the mere translation into its language (Aramaic) was not enough. The text had to be adapted to the cultural situation of the Jewish community. In a community which lived several hundred years after the writing down of Scripture and which had been submitted to the influences of Persian, Hellenistic and even Roman civilizations, we could expect that this process of actualization would be very important. What is striking, on the contrary, is the moderate

---

[110] Cf. for instance Targum on Gen. 5:24, "And Enoch served before the Lord in uprightness, and, behold, he was not with the dwellers on earth, for he was withdrawn and went up to the firmament by the word before the Lord, and his name was called Metatron the Great Scribe" (Pseudo-Jonathan, *ad loc.* Bowker's translation). This is even more striking in the Midrash, where one finds together, on the one hand, the effort to avoid anthropomorphisms and, on the other hand, anthropomorphic haggadic developments. Cf. the introduction to *Lamentations Rab.* depicting God as weeping.

[111] Cf. the "authorized interpretation" about which the Rabbis were speaking. *Kidd.* 49a.

[112] As Le Déaut notes correctly, *La Nuit Pascale*, 60ff.

[113] We borrow the phrase which R. Bloch used in order to characterize the Midrashic genre: cf. her article "Midrash" in *D.B.S.* Yet it is to be noted that we shall refine considerably the meaning of this phrase.

character of this actualization as opposed to the very important actualization (which can be qualified as apologetic) which we find in Hellenistic Judaism from the *Letter of Aristeas* to Philo's writings. In other words even if the influence of the complex cultural *milieu* of that period in Palestine was felt,[114] it appears that these traditions were subordinated to Scripture. This is particularly true of all the passages where the Targum attempts to solve theological difficulties by appeal to a theological way of thinking which emerged from an interpretation of Scripture itself.[115]

Nevertheless the circle of the interpretation of Scripture by Scripture was broken. This Jewish community belonged to a specific culture. The geographical knowledge of the community influenced its interpretation of the geographical biblical references.[116] In the same way concrete conditions of life were read into the biblical text[117] and played also an important role as far as the interpretation of the biblical commandments was concerned. For because of new situations their fulfillment was no longer possible either absolutely or as far as the spirit of the commandment was concerned.[118]

---

[114] Cf. for instance the tendencies to adopt a dualistic view (cf. below what we say about the biblical characters as types of virtues or vices), to spiritualize God (reaction against anthropomorphism), but also to adopt the angelology and the many haggadic stories which were common to Jewish and non Jewish literature of that time: cf. the numerous examples pointed out by S. Lieberman in *Hellenism in Jewish Palestine, passim.*

[115] For examples, cf. above.

[116] We saw above the tendency to identify unknown locations. To this could be added another example: the interpretation of the "valley of Hebron" in Gen. 37:14. Hebron is on a hill. Therefore it is interpreted as "the profound advice (valley) spoken to Abraham in Hebron" (Pseudo-Jonathan *ad loc,* Bowker, 237).

[117] Cf. for instance the description of Pharaoh and the Egyptian armies in terms of the Roman troups: Pseudo-Jonathan on Exod., *passim.*

[118] This will be discussed below in connection with the use of Scripture in the halakah.

Another aspect of this actualization was brought about by the homiletic character of the Targum: the moral teaching it points out in the text. Certainly in the Targum we do not find explicit exhortations as in the Midrashim.[119] This moral teaching is nevertheless frequently implied by making out of the biblical personages either moral types or anti-moral types. We could multiply the examples about each of the main biblical personages. To avoid being too lengthy we shall limit ourselves to one particularly characteristic example:[120] the targumic interpretation of Gen. 4:8 (the murder of Abel introduced by the words "And Cain said to Abel his brother, and it came to pass. . ."). The Targum Pseudo-Jonathan is worth quoting:[121]

> "And Cain said to Abel his brother: 'Come, and let us both go into the field.' So it was that when they had both gone out into the field Cain answered and said to Abel: 'I can see that the world was created in love, but it is not ordered by the issue of good works, because there is partiality in judgement; thus it is that your offering was accepted with favour, but my offering was not accepted with favour'. Abel answered and said: 'Certainly the world was created in love, and by the issue of good works it is ordered and there is no partiality in judgement. But because the issue of my works was better than yours, so my offering has been accepted before yours with favour'. Cain answered and said to Abel: 'There is no judgement and no judge, and no world hereafter; there is no good reward to be given to the righteous, nor any account to

---

[119] Except for the Targum on the Hagiographa which is more midrashic than targumic, as Sperber points out. Cf. his introduction to *The Bible in Aramaic*, vol. IVa. Cf. also P. Grelot, "Remarques sur le second Targum du livre d'Esther", *Revue Biblique*, 1970, 230-39.

[120] For studies on Moses as a type see *inter alias* R. Bloch, "Moïse dans la Tradition Rabbinique", *Cahiers Sioniens*, 1954, where the author relies heavily on the targumic literature; on Abraham, see P. J. de Menasce, "Traditions juives sur Abraham", *Cahiers Sioniens*, 1951, 188-95 (unhappily it is a very sketchy study) and mainly G. Vermès, *Scripture and Tradition*, 67-126; on each of the sons of Jacob as type, cf. the Targumim on Gen. 49.

[121] Bowker, trans. 132ff.

be taken of the wicked'. Abel answered and
said: 'Certainly there is judgement and a
judge and a world hereafter: there is a
good reward to be given to the righteous,
and the wicked will be called to account'.
And because of these words they fell into
a dispute in the open field, and Cain rose
up against Abel his brother, and drove a
stone into his forehead, and slew him".

This gives us an excellent example of the actualization we just spoke about. The theological dispute we have here was a common one in New Testament times and earlier, *viz.* the dispute between Pharisees and Sadducees about the "world hereafter" and consequently about the judgement and the importance of good works.[122] This dispute has been read into the text. At the same time Abel is presented as an example to the Jewish community; he went up to martyrdom rather than deny the doctrine that the world is "ordered by the issue of good works" and that of the judgement. By contrast Cain (who is said to be the son of Sammael--later identified with Satan--and not of Adam)[123] is depicted as an anti-moral example: as an antinomian.[124] As Moore notes, in the biblical personages the Jewish community of that time saw the "divinely revealed descriptions of the two classes into which mankind divides itself":[125] each personage being either considered as a type of the righteous, צדיקים (Abel), or of the wicked, רשעים (Cain). Or as Rabinowitz puts it (speaking of the Midrash): the biblical characters are regarded "as the outstanding prototypes of specific virtues and vices".[126]

As is apparent in the above example these virtues and vices were understood in terms of the value system of the Jewish community rather than in terms of the biblical value system *per se*. This is why we can term this interpretation of

---

[122] Cf. Lauterbach, *Rabbinic Essays*, Cincinnati, 1951, 23-48.

[123] Cf. Pseudo-Jonathan on Gen. 4:1.

[124] For the relationship of this interpretation with the New Testament see McNamara, *op. cit.*, 156ff.

[125] Moore, *op. cit.*, vol. I, 494.

[126] L. I. Rabinowitz, "The Study of a Midrash", *J.Q.R.* 58, 1967, 147.

the biblical personages a *moral typology*. It identified the value system of the community (which is beyond the biblical sacred history) with the biblical value system represented by the biblical personages. The circle of the interpretation of Scripture by Scripture was indeed broken, and yet in the Targum (as well as in the Midrash) this actualization remained quite moderate. Such was the case because of the very *Sitz im Leben* of this hermeneutic: not the Jewish community at large, but the Jewish community as gathered in the Synagogue. This was the Jewish community as "framed" in a liturgy composed of biblical texts, a liturgy which enclosed the people in a "biblical world" (that is in a mode of thinking structured by the Bible). Therefore we find ourselves in a circle: the targumic actualization of the Bible occurred as the function of a community whose life was structured by the Bible as understood through the Tradition which was nothing else than this very actualization.

At least ideally, there was no gap between the Jewish community (as gathered in the Synagogue) and Scripture. Scripture was what gave to the community its identity as Chosen People. As such Scripture was *locus* of revelation: complete and final revelation, Scripture must be interpreted by Scripture. Concurrently the Jewish community (as gathered in the Synagogue) was (or should have been), so to speak, the "incarnation" or "embodiment" of Scripture.[127] As such the community itself became *locus* of revelation. Consequently Scripture was secondary as in the non-biblical liturgical texts. It was the "actualized Scripture", i.e., the "embodied Scripture" which was the *locus* of revelation.

The hermeneutical process could be expressed by two metaphors: on the one hand the worshipping community understood itself *in the framework of Scripture*, and on the other hand it understood itself *as the unfolding of Scripture in new cultural situations*.[128]

---

[127] The first term was used by A. Lacocque in "Tradition dans le Bas-Judaïsme", *R.H.Ph.R.*, 1960, 16. J. Neusner, *The Way of Torah*, Belmont, Cal., 1970, 25ff., speaks of the "embodiment" of Torah in the Jewish community.

[128] This second metaphor avoids the static connotation of the metaphor of a framework.

The first metaphor, the framework, expresses: a) the fact that everything was meaningful in Scripture (nothing could be neglected since it was part of that structure which gave meaning and identity to the community); b) the necessity that Scripture be interpreted by Scripture, since as framework it was a closed system of references. The hermeneutical process as framework was clearly predominant in the Synagogal uses of Scripture. It implied two *loci* of revelation which were kept in balance: Scripture and the worshipping community. This hermeneutical structure was coherent with the doctrine of Scripture.

The second metaphor, the unfolding, expresses that the interpretation of Scripture occurred in tension with the cultural changes which were part of the concrete life of the Jewish community. The hermeneutical process as "unfolding" was present in the Synagogal hermeneutic in the actualizations of Scripture. Yet here it was secondary: these actualizations were quite moderate. We shall see that this second aspect of the hermeneutical process was predominant in, and even characteristic of, the use of Scripture in the School. It implied (in spite of the doctrine of Scripture) a third *locus* of revelation, the cultural changes, which balanced the two other *loci* of revelation. Before spelling out more precisely this complex hermeneutical process we need therefore to examine the uses of Scripture in the liturgy and the School.

LITURGICAL USE OF SCRIPTURE

A few remarks will be sufficient to understand the role of Scripture in the liturgy[129] of the Synagogal services and also for that matter in that of the Temple services. We saw above their close relationship.

Without going into the intricacy of the complete Temple

---

[129] The basic study of Jewish liturgy remains the work of Abraham Levi Idelsohn, *Jewish Liturgy and its Development*, first ed. 1932, second ed. New York, 1967.

service as it is described in Mishnah *Tamid*, we would like to point out the main component of the service (Mishnah *Tamid* 5:1). It reads:

> "Recite one Benediction, and they recited [it] [and then] they read the *Ten commandments*, the *shema*, *And it shall come to pass if ye shall hearken*, and *And . . . spake*. They pronounced [next these] three *Benedictions* with the people: *True and Firm* and *Avodah* and the *Priestly Blessing*".[130]

The introductory benediction was the *Ahabah Rabbah*,[131] which begins by a quotation or quasi-quotation of Jer. 31:3:[132] "with everlasting love, hast Thou loved us, O Lord our God". The text of the benediction is developed and combined with Isa. 63:9, ". . . in his love and in his pity he redeemed them. . ." although the latter is not explicitly quoted. This benediction became the introduction to the *Shema*, but here the *Shema* is preceded by the reciting of the Ten Commandments (Exod. 20).

The *Shema* was then recited. As is well known it is made of the three biblical passages, Deut. 6:4-9, Deut. 11:13-21, and Num. 15:37-41. Yet as is clear in our text, the three passages are not yet considered as forming a unit. The three passages are designated as three different (although successive) elements of the service. Then were recited three blessings:

a) "True and firm" (אמת ויציב), that is, the *Geullah* (redemption): thanksgiving for the redemption of Israel, using the Song of the Sea (Exod. 15) more or less extensively.[133]

---

[130] Blackman's translation *ad loc*.

[131] For the morning service cf. *Ber.* 11b. For the evening service it was the *Ahabat 'Olam* according to *Tos. Ber.* 11b; cf. Kaufmann Kohler, "Ahabah Rabbah", *J.E.*, vol. I, 281.

[132] It was an actual quotation in *Ahabat 'Olam*.

[133] More extensively in the morning service and less in the evening service: cf. *Ber.* 1:4 and 2:2. Jer. 31:10 and Isa. 47:4 were possibly used with Exod. 15: cf. Lewish N. Dembitz, "Geullah", *J.E.* V, 648.

b) The *Abodah* (service) was originally the sixteenth blessing of what later became to be known as the *Shemoneh Esreh*. It can be summarized by quoting its conclusion: "Blessed be He that receiveth the service of His people Israel in favour".[134]

The Priestly Blessing, *viz*. Num. 6:24-26, concluded the service.

These brief comments on *M. Tamid* 5:1 show how the Temple service was structured by means of Scriptural texts. This was certainly valid also for the Synagogue service which, as suggested,[135] was originally created in order to allow the people to associate themselves with the Temple service even if they were not in Jerusalem. The use of biblical texts as liturgical texts once more signifies that Scripture was locus of revelation. Yet this suggests also that the worshipping community which recited these texts "embodied" Scripture. This phenomenon is apparent in the *Shemoneh Esreh* (or *Amida*).

It is doubtful that this prayer actually consisted of eighteen benedictions during the period under consideration. Yet at least six of them were used very early: witness to this is the "psalm" which is included in the Hebrew text of ben Sirach between the verses 12 and 13 of ch. 51.[136] This text contains almost word for word the first, third, seventh, tenth, fourteenth and fifteenth benedictions.[137] Without going into a detailed study of all the benedictions[138] let us examine the use of Scripture in those we can assume to have been used at that time.

---

[134] According to the restitution by Blackman, *ibid*.

[135] Cf. above (ch. III).

[136] Cf. Israel Levi ed., *The Hebrew Text of the Book of Ecclesiasticus*, Leiden, 1904, *ad loc*.

[137] On this cf. Idelsohn, *op. cit.*, 20ff., and Dhorme, *Bible, ad loc*.

[138] Cf. on this the excellent article by Emil G. Hirsch, "Shemoneh Esreh", *J.E.* XI, 270ff. I shall quote his translation.

Although no Scriptural text is explicitly quoted, these benedictions are made out of biblical phrases, and can be said to be almost a mosaic of biblical phrases. To show this it will be enough to give the text of the first, third and seventh benedictions and to include in them references to the main biblical passages from which the phraseology is borrowed.

The first benediction reads:

> "Blessed be Thou, O Lord, our God and God of our fathers, God of Abraham, God of Isaac and God of Jacob (Exod. 3:13) the Great, the mighty and the fearful God (Deut. 10:17). God Most High (Gen. 14:19), who bestowest goodly kindness and art the Creator of all (Gen. 14:19) and rememberest the love of (or for) the Fathers and bringest a redeemer (Isa. 49:20) for their children's children for the sake of Thy name in love. King, helper, Savior and shield. Blessed be Thou, shield of Abraham (Pss. 7:1; 18:3, 36; 84:10; Gen. 15:1)".

The third benediction reads:

> "Thou art holy (Ps. 22:4) and Thy name is holy, and the holy ones (Ps. 16:3) praise thee (a technical term of the "Hallel") every day. Selah (an other technical term of the Psalms). Blessed be Thou, O Lord, the holy God".

The seventh benediction reads:

> "Look upon our affliction (Pss. 9:14; 25:18; 119:153) and fight our fight (Pss. 35:1; 43:1; 74:22) and redeem us (Ps. 119:154, cf. also Lam. 3:58) speedily for the sake of Thy name: for Thou art a strong redeemer. Blessed art Thou, O Lord, the Redeemer of Israel".

Similarly the tenth benediction uses phrases borrowed from Isa. 11:12; 27:13; 43:5; 45:20; 60:9; Jer. 51:27; and Deut. 30:4, in order to bless God who "gathers our exiles". The fourteenth refers to God the "Builder of Jerusalem" using phrases from Zech. 8:3; Ps. 147:2, etc. The fifteenth refers to God who causes the Davidic Messiah to rise, using phrases borrowed from the Prophets' writings (namely Jer. 23:5; 33:15; Isa. 53:2; Zech. 3:8) and the Psalms.

This rapid glance is enough to point out that in the liturgy itself we find a twofold use of Scripture.

a) A number of key texts were recited, thus explicitly used: the Ten Commandments, the three texts of the *Shema* and the Priestly Blessings. These texts were actually representing the whole of Torah in a summary form. Recited again and again they structured not only the worship service but also the life of the worshipping community. We could say here that Torah, recited word for word, was here a *locus* of revelation.

b) The rest of the liturgy composed of prayers and benedictions, served a similar function. Yet significantly, in these texts the emphasis was not at all on Scripture itself. In an anthological use of Scripture, the biblical texts were used for their language, which served to express the faith of the community. The attention of the worshipper was not at all focused on Scripture but on the very act of worshipping, which took preeminence over Scripture itself. It is as though a *locus* of revelation were discovered in the worship itself, Or in other words, it is as if the Presence of God were no longer found in Scripture but in prayer,[139] in the worshipping community which embodied Scripture.

This twofold use of Scripture in the Synagogue points to two *loci* of revelation (on the one hand Scripture in itself, on the other hand the worshipping community in itself) which were kept in balance, and which thus qualified each other.[140]

The above is valid mainly for the Temple worship, for in the Synagogue a third use of Scripture was also incorporated into the service: the reading from Scripture and its explanation in homilies and targumizations. As we saw, in the latter case, the interpretation of Scripture as actualization suggested a third locus of revelation: the cultural situations which were part of the concrete life of the Jewish community.[141] Thus we could say that, in the Synagogue

---

[139] This is underscored when one notes with Idelsohn, *op. cit.*, 25, that the fixed formulae of the liturgy were only the framework for improvised meditations and prayers.

[140] This balance was somehow upset in the Dead Sea Community, as we shall see when studying the use of Scripture in the *Manual of Discipline*.

[141] This "interpretation of Scripture in tension with the cultural changes" will be shown more clearly in our study of the use of Scripture in the Schools (ch. V).

service, the Presence of God was apprehended at once in Scripture, in the worshipping community and in that community's cultural situations, the three *loci* of revelation balancing each other. Yet the third locus of revelation played a very secondary role in the Synagogue. By contrast its role was quite important in the hermeneutic practiced in the Schools.

CHAPTER V

THE USE OF SCRIPTURE IN THE SCHOOLS: WRITTEN AND ORAL TOROTH

What we said about the use of Scripture in the Synagogue as witnessed by the reading cycle (Sedarim and haftaroth), homily and Targum, is valid for the haggadic use of Scripture as found in the Tannaitic Midrashim (*Mekilta*, *Sifra* and *Sifre*). The same exegetical methods are used with the same attitude toward, and understanding of, Scripture. This is apparent not only in the fact that the very haggadic *middoth* attributed to R. Eliezer were already used in the Targum, but also in the fact that often the haggadic targumic interpretations of specific texts were identical to those found in the Tannaitic Midrashim.[1] As already mentioned these similarities can be explained by a common *Sitz im Leben*: the Synagogue.

A development on the haggadic use of the Bible in the Tannaitic Midrashim would, therefore, be repetitious. There, as in the Targum, we would find the "circle" which we mentioned in order to express the relationship of Scripture and Tradition. We shall spell out more precisely its significance, but only after examining another aspect of this Tradition, the Oral Torah, i.e., the halakic tradition. For indeed haggadic and halakic traditions cannot be separated in

---

[1] Cf. for instance, Le Déaut, *La Nuit Pascale*, 132, n. 2, where the author points out the great similarity of the Palestinian Targum with the Mekilta.

this discussion of the relation between Scripture and Tradition. Both were modes by means of which the same men expressed their faith: this explains the fact that we find the halakah in the Synagogue, *Sitz im Leben par excellence* of the haggadah,[2] and the haggadah in the school, *Sitz im Leben par excellence* of the halakah. Furthermore, it is even possible that in their origins they were not distinguished.[3]

As is well known the use of Scripture in the School must be qualified as *halakic*: it aimed at interpreting the biblical laws and prescriptions in such a way that they might be carried out by the Jewish community in all aspects of its daily life. In order to apprehend the halakic hermeneutical process we need assess the relationship between the halakah and Scripture. For this purpose we shall examine a) what is implied in the phrase "Oral Torah" as designation of the halakah: our concern will be to point out the principles (or axioms) which governed the belief that, as interpretation and supplement of Scripture, the Oral Torah had an authority comparable to that of the Written Torah; b) the Oral Torah as living Tradition. A study of the criteria which were used to establish the halakah will point out more specifically the halakic hermeneutical process. We hope to show that revelation (i.e., the divine Will) was discovered in the contemporary culture as well as in Scripture.

ORAL TORAH, HALAKAH AND JURISPRUDENCE

Through our whole discussion of the relationship between halakah and Scripture we shall have to bear in mind the fact that one of the proper renderings for the term "halakah"[4] is

---

[2] Cf. the Yelammedenu homilies.

[3] Cf. W. Baker, "The origin of the word Haggada", *Jewish Quarterly Review* IV, 1892, 406-29.

[4] As is well known, "halakah" is derived from הלך, to walk, and means therefore custom, law. Cf. for instance, Joseph Jacobs, "Halakah", *J.E.*, vol. VI, 163.

jurisprudence. For indeed, although the Jewish community was at one time a theocracy in which the High priest, the "vicar of God", so to speak, had the supreme authority over the entire community on temporal as well as spiritual matters,[5] it became a nomocracy during the Maccabean period. During that period the Sanhedrin (*Beth Din*) was established[6] as a supreme court. Thereupon the supreme authority in temporal as well as religious matters was no longer expressed in the law and decrees of the High Priest, but only in the Law (i.e., Torah) which the Sanhedrin was supposed to enforce as the communal way of life (halakah). Israel became a Torah-centered nation. Yet in this nomocratic situation Torah had to involve more than the mere Written Torah: it needed to include also what has been finally called the Oral Torah.

Let us sketch what the Rabbis designated by the phrase תורה שבעל פה, which we translate by "Oral Torah".[7] In one sentence we could characterize the Oral Torah as being the result of the "adjustment of Torah to life".[8] This adjustment was absolutely necessary not only because of the changing conditions of life through the centuries but also because the community wanted to consider Torah as a Code regulating its civil as well as religious life. For indeed, many ritual and

---

[5] For a description of the High Priest toward the end of this theocratic period, cf. ben Sirach, ch. 50. That the High Priest had authority on temporal as well as spiritual matters is already implied in Ezra 7:25-26, where Ezra--the Scribe but also the son of Aaron the chief Priest (7:5)--received from the Persian King the authority to punish those who would not follow "the Law of thy God, and the law of the King".

[6] Cf. S. B. Hoening, *The Great Sanhedrin. A Study of the Origin, Development, Composition and Functions of the Bet Din Ha-gadol during the second Jewish Commonwealth*, Philadelphia, 1953, Hasmonean, High Priest and ethnarch (who died 135 B.C.). Yet the *Beth Din* existed before that time.

[7] As usual we shall point out only those characteristics of the Oral Torah which are needed for our discussion of the use of Scripture. For complete presentations of the Oral Law see Lauterbach, "Oral Law", *J.E.*, vol. IX, 423ff.; Bonsirven, *Le Judaïsme Palestinien*, vol. I, 263ff.; Moore, *Judaism*, vol. I, 251ff.

[8] To use the title of S. Zuckrow's book: *Adjustment of Law to Life in Rabbinic Literature*, Boston, 1928.

civil laws are very sketchy in the Pentateuch; they would have been impossible to carry out without a priestly tradition of ritual details or without a juridical tradition of specific legislations.[9] Thus there is no doubt that such an Oral Torah (called first "Tradition", קבלה or מצוה זקנים) was used very early in order to *supplement* the Written Torah and to *interpret* it for specific situations.

ORIGINS OF THE ORAL TORAH

Our last sentence summarizes the whole problem of the relation between the Oral Torah and the Written. Is the Oral Torah made out of customs and traditional laws which had their origin in cultures foreign to Scripture? In other words, was the Oral Torah originally independent from Scripture? Or on the contrary was the Oral Torah the result of an interpretation of Scripture? We shall be obliged to recognize that the Oral Torah at the beginning of the Christian era was made out of both independent elements and results of midrashic interpretations. And yet it was called Torah.

If we could specify at least the original form of the teaching of the Oral Torah, we could hope to have a less ambiguous situation. Yet the limited number of evidences allow for nothing more than speculation. Thus has arisen the debate between two eminent Jewish scholars: J. Z. Lauterbach and S. Zeitlin. They agree that the halakah was taught in two forms: the mishnaic and the midrashic. When taught in the mishnaic form the Oral Torah was presented without Scriptural proof texts thus as teachings not directly connected with the Written Torah. On the contrary in the midrashic form the halakah is presented as an interpretation and exposition of the Written Torah. But the scholars disagree on the question

---

[9] For examples, cf. Moore, *op. cit.*, 251-54, and S. Zeitlin, "The Halaka: Introduction to Tannaitic Jurisprudence", *J.Q.R.* 39, 1948-49, 4ff. Zeitlin gives specific examples of laws mentioned in the Prophets and Hagiographa but not in the Pentateuch.

of which form is the older. J. Z. Lauterbach, in an essay entitled "Midrash and Mishnah"[10] maintained that "of these two forms of teaching the halakah, the Midrash is the older and the Mishnah the later".[11] On the contrary Solomon Zeitlin, in his essay "The Halaka: Introduction to Tannaitic Jurisprudence",[12] attempted to refute this theory[13] by pointing out that Lauterbach and his followers "ignored the fact that the Jews of that period were a living nation, the creators of the laws".[14] Such a debate is impossible to summarize here. It would necessitate our bringing out too many minute details about the exegesis of texts covering the whole period from the biblical books of Nehemiah (ch. 8 and 10:30) and Ezra (7:10)[15] to a text by Sherira Gaon.[16] Furthermore we could conclude only that there is a greater degree of probability in favor of Zeitlin's thesis on the original form of the teaching of the Oral Law.

By-passing the question of origins and turning back to that Judaism which formed the background of the New Testament, we find the two scholars agreeing. During that period the Oral Torah was taught under the two forms. Thus Lauterbach[17] points out that it is "not to be doubted" that Jose b. Joezer (who died about 165 B.C.) taught halakoth which were

---

[10] First published in *J.Q.R.*, 1915-16. This article has been reprinted in J. Z. Lauterbach, *Rabbinic Essays*, Cincinnati, 1951, 163-256.

[11] *Op. cit.*, 164.

[12] *J.Q.R.* 39, 1948-49, 1-40.

[13] In this he has been followed by David Daube, "Rabbinic Methods of Interpretation and Hellenistic Rhetoric", *H.U.C.A.* 22, 1949, 239-64, cf. especially 244f.

[14] Zeitlin, *op. cit.*, 17. Yet it is to be noted that Zeitlin did not refute all the points made by Lauterbach and that actually his argument was only against one of several conclusions Lauterbach reached. The others were apparently acceptable to Zeitlin.

[15] Lauterbach, *op. cit.*, 164; Zeitlin, *op. cit.*, 8.

[16] Lauterbach, *op. cit.*, 166; Zeitlin, *op. cit.*, 15.

[17] Lauterbach, *op. cit.*, 185 and 213ff.; cf. also 195ff.

independent from Scripture.[18] This and other evidences help him to conclude that independent halakoth were taught since the reorganization of the Sanhedrin (*circa* 190 B.C.), because already during the preceding period the people followed new laws and customs which were not based on the teaching of the early Sopherim.[19] On the other hand Zeitlin points out that at least in the time of Hillel, and possibly earlier, "the Pharisees had developed an array of Laws which they held were based not only on tradition but also on the Pentateuch and which were derived by hermeneutic rules".[20] He states further that "the method of Midrash used in interpreting the biblical verses in order to establish halakoth came into vogue very early".[21] By "very early" Zeitlin means since the "canonization" of the Pentateuch in the period of the Restoration after the exile.

Lauterbach and Zeitlin agree therefore that there were two sources for the Oral Torah: customs and traditions on the one hand, and on the other hand interpretations of Scripture. On the one hand, then, the Oral Torah was made out of customs and laws which emerged in the *living* Jewish community independently from Scripture and which were legitimated afterward by means of Scriptural proof texts;[22] in this case the cultural elements (customs) were primary and Scripture was

---

[18] According to *Eduy.* 8:4.

[19] Lauterbach, *op. cit.*, 206ff.

[20] Zeitlin, *op. cit.*, 10.

[21] Zeitlin, "Midrash: A Historical Study", *J.Q.R.* 44, 1953, 30.

[22] The reason for this legitimation is different according to the theory held. For Lauterbach (*op. cit.*, 230ff.) it was in order to justify the authority of the Tradition by the only authority: Scripture. For Zeitlin (*op. cit.*, 10) and Daube (*op. cit.*, 244ff.) it was seen as a way of countering the Sadducees (who recognized only the authority of the Written Torah) by taking "a leaf out of the other party's book". On the contrary, this confrontation between Pharisees and Sadducees is considered by Lauterbach (*op. cit.*, 232ff.) to be at th e origin of the Mishnah form. The Pharisees suppressed any Scriptural proof texts, for indeed, because of the artificiality of the exegesis involved, they could have been easily refuted by the Sadducees.

secondary. On the other hand the Oral Torah was made out of the results of midrashic interpretations: in this case Scripture was primary. The followers of the two theories agree also that before the beginning of the Christian era the Oral Torah was considered as having been revealed. It was therefore possible to speak of two Toroth (שתי תורות)[23] in order to express the similar authority of the two sources of religious teaching. As Lauterbach notes[24] such a belief "made it of little consequence whether a halakah was taught in the Midrash form, as derived from the Written Law, or in the Mishnah form, as a traditional Law".[25] Consequently, we can suggest that revelation was found in two *loci*: culture and Scripture. This is in conflict with the explicit doctrine of Scripture which affirms that Torah is the complete and final revelation. We need therefore to assess the conviction on which was based the belief in a similar authority of the Oral Torah with the Written Torah.

THE AUTHORITY OF THE ORAL TORAH: THE CONTROVERSY BETWEEN THE SADDUCEES AND THE PHARISEES

The controversy between the Pharisees and the Sadducees reveals this conviction. The Pharisees' belief in a comparable authority of the two Toroth was at the heart of their dispute with the Sadducees who denied any authority to the Oral Torah. This is to say that this controversy reflected the conflict of two hermeneutics. We cannot but follow Lauterbach's study of this controversy, as expressed in

---

[23] This phrase has been ascribed first to Hillel: cf. *Shab*. 31a, and Lauterbach, "Oral Law", *J.E.*, vol. IX, 423ff.

[24] "Midrash and Mishnah", 231.

[25] Let us note that generally speaking the Written Torah is more authoritative than the Oral Torah. Yet the authority of the latter is such that in a few instances the halakah superseded Torah. See the examples given by Zeitlin, "The Halakah . . .," 12.

three essays: "The Sadducees and Pharisees", "A Significant controversy between the Sadducees and the Pharisees", "The Pharisees and their Teachings".[26] These essays are highly praised by scholars as various as R. Travers Herford[27] and G. Vermès.[28]

As we read in Josephus:

> "The Pharisees had passed on to the people certain regulations handed down by former generations and not recorded in the Law of Moses, for which reason they are rejected by the Saducean group who hold that only those regulations should be considered valid which were written down (in Scripture), and that those which had been handed down by former generations need not be observed".[29]

Therefore one of the points[30] on which the Pharisees and Sadducees were opposed was that the latter did not accept the authority of the Oral Torah, and this because the Written Torah was for them the sole Torah. Lauterbach pointed out that the reason for this (as well as for the whole dispute) is to be found in two irreconcilable conceptions of the authority of the Torah.

---

[26] 1913, 1927, and 1929, reprinted in *Rabbinical Essays*, Cincinnati, 1951, 23-159. We shall refer to these essays by indicating the page numbers of this edition.

[27] He based his book, *The Pharisees*, London, 1924, on the first essay, which he qualified as "the master-word on the subject". For our topic cf. especially 53-87.

[28] "Notes sur la Formation de la Tradition Juive", *Cahiers Sioniens*, 1953, 320-42. Cf. especially 321-30. On this topic cf. also *inter alias*: K. Kohler, "Pharisees", *J.E.*, vol. IX; "Sadducees", *J.E.*, vol. X; L. Finkelstein, *The Pharisees: The Sociological Background of their Faith*, 2 vol., Philadelphia, 1946; A. Finkel, *The Pharisees and the Teacher of Nazareth*, Leiden, 1964, especially 11-127, and I. Abrahams, *Studies in Pharisaism and the Gospels*, 2 vol., Cambridge, vol. I, 1917; vol. II, 1924, and especially vol. I, 1-17, 129-35, and vol. II, 4-14, 29-32 and 120-28.

[29] *Ant.* XIII, 10,6: R. Marcus' translation, *Josephus*, Loeb Classical Library, London, 1961, vol. VII, 375ff.; cf. also *Ant.* XVIII, 1-3.

[30] For other points of disagreement between Pharisees and Sadducees according to Josephus see: *Bell. Jud.* II, 8, 14.

In spite of Josephus[31] we recognize that the Sadducees were the older party and the Pharisees the innovators who brought in a new understanding of Torah. Before the appearance of the Pharisees and from the time of Ezra, the authority of Torah was absolute. Lauterbach discovers the nature of this authority in Neh. 10:1, 29-30, which he interprets as follows: ". . . in order to insure allegiance to the Torah and obedience to its laws it was deemed necessary for the people to enter a covenant and pledge allegiance by oath".[32] This oath was regarded as being eternally binding; it imposed a curse upon its transgressors.[33] The authority of Torah was not, therefore, inherent in Torah, but was a consequence of the pledge which Israel took by curse and oath "to walk in God's Law which was given by Moses the servant of God, and to observe and do all the commandments of the Lord our Lord, and his judgments and his statutes".[34] Thus Torah was understood at the time of Ezra (and was still understood in the same way by the Sadducees)[35] as the laws imposed by God upon Israel, which Israel accepted in order to secure for itself the favor of God. The Israelites of all time must carry them out in order to avoid the curse stipulated in the oath taken by the forefathers. No interpretation, no adaptation, was therefore necessary: to observe the laws according to the letter was sufficient. It was enough that not a single law of the Torah be violated or neglected. On the other hand any other law (not written in Scripture) was not binding since it was not included in the pledge of the forefathers. This does not mean that the Sadducees did not

---

[31] Cf. *Bell. Jud.* II, 8, 2, and *Ant.* XVIII, 1-3.

[32] Lauterbach, *op. cit.*, 113.

[33] Cf. Deut. 29:9-30:20; Dan. 9:11ff., *passim*.

[34] Neh. 10:29.

[35] That this role of the oath and curse was still stressed in the time of the Sadducees is confirmed by the Dead Sea Scrolls. The Dead Sea community, which is also of priestly origin, attached a great importance to them. Cf. G. Vermès, "La Formation de la Tradition Juive", *op. cit.*, 324.

follow traditional customs and laws:[36] they themselves, as priestly leaders of the community, were the possessors and transmitters of the old traditions. Furthermore they issued decrees and supplementary laws which alone could allow the Jewish community to function. If we may indulge in an anachronism, we could say that for the Sadducees there was a distinction between a secular and a religious life. The religious realm was strictly limited to the letter of the Torah, and therefore it allowed beside it a secular realm which could accommodate itself to any new situation and to any culture (Persian, Hellenistic or Roman), so long as it did not conflict with the letter of the Torah.

It is precisely on this point that Lauterbach sees the essential difference which opposed Sadducees and Pharisees. For the Pharisees *Torah was co-extensive with life*: "the Torah comprised all and expressed all".[37] Furthermore it appears that in their interpretation of Scripture, they did not believe that authority was bestowed upon Torah from without (by an oath or the covenant): it was inherent in Torah itself, i.e., in its divine origin. Torah is not imposed by a "dictatorial" God. It is a *gift* for the benefit of man in order that he may live a good life, and thus come nearer to God. As Lauterbach says boldly, "the Pharisees did not become the slaves of the Law; they were its masters".[38]

To illustrate this attitude let us take the example of their interpretation of the commandments about the Sabbath. It can be summarized by a quotation from the *Mekilta*, "The Sabbath is given to you and you are not given to the Sabbath".[39] The Sabbath is given to man that he may delight in its rest, this according to the prophetic teaching *viz.* Isa. 58:13-14, "If you call the Sabbath a delight . . . then you shall take delight in the Lord". Thus instead of limiting themselves to the letter of the commandments concerning the Sabbath (e.g., Exod. 16:29; 35:3), they interpreted it

---

[36] Cf. Zeitlin, "The Halakah", *op. cit.*, 10.

[37] Lauterbach, *op. cit.*, 112.

[38] *Ibid.*, 131.

[39] Lauterbach ed., vol. III, 196.

according to the prophetic teaching which allowed them to remove any consideration of the Sabbath as a Tabu day.

This twofold conviction that Torah was a *gift* and that it was *co-extensive with life*, appears as the convictional foundation on which the Sages built their whole interpretation of the Law. Indeed for them the Torah (Pentateuch) was the comprehensive revelation. Yet, as we saw in the preceding example, it needed to be interpreted in the light of the prophetic teaching, that is דברי קבלה, the words of Tradition. These were not new laws in opposition to Torah.[40] As "words of Tradition", however, they explain the Torah, which must therefore be interpreted in terms of them. They were consequently included in the term Torah (together with the Hagiographa).

In order that Torah might be really co-extensive with life, it had to include even more, *viz.* traditional customs and laws which were followed and carried out by the people. These were adopted either in order to fill up the gaps of the biblical code or in order to adapt it to new cultural situations. In other words Torah had to include what has been finally called the Oral Torah, which came to be considered as being derived from the Written Torah by what we could call a projection of their own understanding of Torah on the past. The Pharisees believed in good faith that these laws were regulations enacted by former priestly leaders on the authority that they had as *interpreters* of Torah. Because of their different understanding of the nature of Torah, the Pharisees could not imagine that these priestly leaders had acted on their own authority, independently of Torah.

For the Pharisees, then, there could be no more conflict between the Oral Torah and the Written than between the Pentateuch and the rest of the Bible. The midrashic interpretation of Scripture could not but coincide with the halakoth. Scripture had to be interpreted in terms of the Oral Torah. And the discovery of proof texts for the

---

[40] Cf. *Sanh.* 90a; *Hor.* 4b; *Meg.* 14a, and already *Sifra* on Lev. 27:34 (cf. Bonsirven, *Textes*, 49 and 267).

halakoth[41] was nothing but the re-discovery of the interpretations which gave birth to them. Those for which no proof texts could be found were simply considered as having been handed down orally from Moses,[42] that is, as having been revealed in the same way as the Written Torah.

Such was certainly the rationale behind the belief in the two Toroth during the Tannaitic period. We need to emphasize that what became the bulk of the Oral Torah was believed to have divine authority before it was tallied with Scripture. Such a belief (possibly never shared by the ruling class) was of a popular character and was common in Hellenistic culture,[43] for which the unwritten law was a gift of the gods. It seems therefore that it was this popular belief which those lay teachers assumed who were the originators of the Pharisaic movement.[44] It is nevertheless clear that the Pharisees did not blindly accept as authoritative all the traditions.[45] Just as later they made a distinction between *halakoth* and *gezeroth*.[46]

Speaking from our modern perspective, we could say that they recognized divine authority in what was the result of a cultural process which included changes in the people's way of life, as well as influences of foreign cultures. We have already hinted at this attitude in speaking of the haggadic traditons, but let us emphasize that here it is even more

---

[41] That this was done retroactively is clear in the many instances where several proof texts are given for the same halakah. Cf. an extreme example in *Pes.* 84a, where eight different proof texts are given by different Tannaim for the same halakah.

[42] Cf. *Aboth* 1:1.

[43] As pointed out by Zeitlin, "The Halaka . . .", *op. cit.*, 8-11, and by Daube, "Rabbinic Methods . . .", *op. cit.*, 242ff., and *passim*.

[44] On this cf. the presentation of the origins of the Pharisees by L. Finkelstein. Cf. also S. H. Blank, "The Dissident Laity in Early Judaism", *H.U.C.A.* XIX, 1945-46, 1-42.

[45] Cf. Lauterbach, *op. cit.*, 130ff.

[46] Cf. below.

clearly apparent: these traditional laws and customs were proclaimed to be nothing less than Torah.[47]

THE ORAL TORAH AS LIVING TRADITION: CULTURAL CHANGES AND SCRIPTURE

What was the precise relationship between culture and Scipture at the time of the origin of the Pharisaic movement? We cannot say. We do not know what criteria were used to select the traditional customs and laws which were to be considered as authoritative.[48] Happily for the period just preceding the Christian era we know the main criteria which were used for this same purpose: the seven *middoth* of Hillel together with the distinctions made between *halakah, gezerah, takkanah,* and *minhag,* and the concept of the "fence around the Torah".

In that period the Sages were not only concerned to show the unity of those halakoth already accepted as authoritative along with the Written Torah, but also to adapt the Oral Torah to the ever changing culture in which they lived. For indeed,

---

[47] It is to be noted that this conclusion contradicts openly the *explicit* teaching of the Tannaim. For instance in the *Sifra* on Lev. 18:4, the biblical text, "Ye shall keep my ordinances to walk therein" is interpreted as follows:
> "That is, you are to make them the main purpose of your life, and not a subsidiary thing: all thy business is with them alone, and other matters (or better: other words [commandments] of the world) must not be mixed with them. Do not say 'Now that I have learnt the wisdom of Israel, I will go and learn the wisdom of the nations of the world' for the Torah says 'to walk in them'. . . ."

(This is followed by the proof text Prov. 5:17, which was read: "Let them be thine only ones, and let no strange things be with thee" instead of ". . . not strangers be with thee"). Montefiore and Loewe's translation, parentheses mine. Yet such Tannaitic statements imply what Lauterbach called the "naive belief" that the Oral Torah was an integral part of Torah.

[48] Lauterbach's remark "in the final analysis it was reason that determined the selection" is at once too vague an answer and even perhaps misleading. The eminent Jewish scholar is here following Josephus too closely, forgetting the apologetic character of the latter's writings.

in spite of the authority recognized in it, the Oral Torah was *not "closed"*. It remained a living tradition which was constantly expanded, adapted, adjusted, actualized and this in three different ways:

a) By means of the incorporation of new, independent halakoth: the *gezeroth* or decrees.

b) By means of new midrashic interpretations of the Written Torah. This permitted the promulgation of new halakoth either in order to adjust the Torah to the actual situation of the people (namely by means of *takkanoth*) or in order to make a "fence around the Torah".

c) By means of interpretation of authoritative halakoth: this was a kind of midrash on the Oral Torah.[49] We shall not dwell on this latter aspect since it took place mainly after the codification of the Oral Torah in the Mishnah. Let us note simply that this is inherent to any jurisprudence: the laws have to be applied to any special case even if this latter is not explicitly taken into account in the laws.

1) *The Gezeroth*

This adaptation to new cultural situations is particularly clear in the *gezeroth*.[50] A *gezerah*[51] is a decree which is issued on the sole authority of the Sanhedrin (or of its leader, the *Nasi*) independently from Scripture. This practice was justified on the basis of Deut. 27:11 in which the Israelites are required to walk not only according to the Law of Moses but also according to the ordinances of the

---

[49] This is designated in the Talmud as "midrash Torah" or "midrash Halakah" according to S. Zeitlin, *op. cit.*, 21; Lauterbach says that these phrases designate the Oral Torah "as an interpretation and exposition of Torah", *op. cit.*, 163. But both agree on the existence of this kind of expansion of the Oral Torah.

[50] Cf. J. H. Greenstone, "Gezerah", *J.E.*, vol. V, 648ff., and Zeitlin, "The Halakah", *op. cit.*, 21ff.

[51] From the root נזר, to cut, to decide.

priests, levites and *judges*; likewise on the basis of Deut. 32:7, "ask your father, and he will show you your elders, and they will tell you".[52] Yet its use was limited because it was in open contradiction to Deut. 4:2: "You shall not add to the word which I command you nor take from it", which implied that Torah itself was the complete revelation. Consequently a *gezerah* was authoritative only as long as the particular situation that it was supposed to meet lasted. When the reason for it disappeared the *gezerah* became void.[53]

During the Second Commonwealth many such laws were decreed. Thus, for instance, Jose b. Joezer and Jose b. Johanan decreed the levitical uncleanliness of the lands of the pagans. To understand why, we have to remember that they issued this *gezerah* during the Maccabean war. According to Zeitlin[54] the purpose of its promulgation was to prevent the Jews from migrating to foreign countries. It was also directed against Onias' Temple in Egypt. When this situation disappeared it became void; it had to be decreed again by Shammai and Hillel when another situation demanded it.[55]

Thus in the case of the *gezerah* we feel the strong reluctance to introduce laws independently from Scripture. The case has to be exceptional as well as limited in time. In other words, the Sages accepted the dynamic impulse of cultural changes only in so far as they could do so in terms of Torah; they behaved thus, as mentioned earlier, not because they were th e slaves of Torah, rather, to put it bluntly, because they sought to retain Torah as their sole system of reference.

---

[52] Cf. *Shab.* 23a; and also *Ab.R.N.* 25b.

[53] It became void after a decision of the sanhedrin: *Eduy* 1:5.

[54] Zeitlin, *op. cit.*, 21ff.

[55] Cf. *Y. Shab.* 1, quoted by Zeitlin, *ibid.*, for further examples see Greenstone, *op. cit.*, *passim*.

2) *The Takkanoth*

This tendency is apparent furthermore in the *takkanoth*,[56] whose purpose was precisely to harmonize Torah and life. Contrary to the *gezerah*, the *takkanah* must always find support in Scripture even if it actually amended a pentateuchal law. A *takkanah* is indeed deduced from a biblical prescription. Yet it makes a radical interpretation of the biblical law in terms of new circumstances; it may be regarded as a new prescription.

Takkanoth were ascribed not only to Ezra and the Men of the Great Synagogue but also to Moses himself, Joshua, David, Solomon, the Prophets.[57] Yet as Zeitlin showed for those ascribed to Ezra and Solomon, takkanoth were certainly introduced only during the early Tannaitic period. The takkanah which is the most famous, because also the most daring in contradicting the pentateuchal prescription, is the takkanah known as the *Prosbul* of Hillel. It is described in the Mishnah as follows:[58]

> "Seeing that the law which prescribed the release of all debts every seventh year[59] brought about the harmful consequence that people refused to loan to one another and thus violated what was written in the Law, namely, that a money loan should not be withheld because of the approach of the Sabbatical year(60) Hillel instituted the Prosbul".

The Prosbul is a declaration made in court (πρὸς βουλῇ) mentioning that the loan may be collected *whenever the loaner*

---

[56] Cf. S. Ochser, "Takkanah", *J.E.*, vol. XI, 669-76, which offers a large (if not comprehensive) list of *Takkanoth*; Zeitlin, *op. cit.*, 23ff.; and "Takkanoth Ezra", *J.Q.R.* VIII; Lauterbach, *op. cit.*, 287ff.; J. Neusner, "Studies on the Taqqanot of Yavned", *Harvard Theological Review* 63, 1970, 183-98.

[57] Cf. S. Ochser, *op. cit.*, 670, where the author gives a list of them.

[58] *Sheb.* 9.3, trans. J. H. Greenstone in "Prosbul", *J.E.*, vol. X, 219.

[59] Deut. 15:1-3.

[60] Cf. Deut. 15:9-11.

desires it.[61] Such declaration was to the effect that the law requiring the release of debts upon the entrance of the sabbatical year shall not apply to such a loan. Thus Hillel introduced this modification of the pentateuchal law because of the needs created by the economic life of the Jews in his time.

In the same way the takkanah of *Erub*[62] amended the law about the Sabbath "Remain every man of you in his place, let no man go out of his place on the seventh day".[63] First the words "his place" were taken to mean "his city"; then it was added that a man could walk four cubits (beyond the city limits) and even later on, two thousands cubits. This was done by successive emendations of the law. It was emended further by instituting the legal fiction of the *erub*: the place where a person deposited certain food (the *erub*) on the eve of the Sabbath was interpreted as belonging to his house.[64] As a last example let us take a takkanah dealing with one of the laws about marriage. Simon b. Shetah (first century A.D.) emended the law about the *mohar* (the sum of money the groom had to pay the father of the bride).[65] Instead of paying the *mohar* the groom had to write a *ketuba* in which he pledged all his property up to the amount of the dowry as security for his wife in case of his death or divorce.[66] By such a takkanah the woman possessed rights of her own (instead of being considered as a property of her father), and she was protected economically.

These examples are sufficient to show that by means of the takkanoth all kinds of pentateuchal laws (ritual as well

---

[61] Cf. *Sheb*. 9.4.

[62] This takkanah was ascribed to Solomon: cf. *Sheb*. 14b.

[63] Exod. 16:29.

[64] Cf. *Erub* (most of the tractacte and mainly) 2:6ff.; cf. also what we said above about the delight of the Sabbath.

[65] This was a halakah deduced from Exod. 22:16.

[66] Cf. *Ket*. 8 end.

as economical and civil laws) were emended in order to adapt Torah to new cultural situations. We could add that by so doing the Sages were not merely following cultural changes. It is rather as if, scrutinizing the signs of cultural changes, they looked for what was valuable in them. In traditional terms we could say that they looked for what was in the "spirit" of Torah, or in other words for what could be considered of divine origin and could therefore be incorporated into Torah. By so doing, then, they did not simply comply to the demands of cultural changes. On the contrary they transformed into actual cultural changes what were only "signs". Let us take again the example of the takkanah of *ketuba*. There was in that time a movement in favor of the rights of woman, as well as in favor of the rights of any human being. This was a fact of the dominant Hellenistic culture. By this takkanah the "sign" was actualized: women actually received their rights.

Let us stress that the Sages were not simply complying with the culture of their time: they scrutinized it in order to see what was valuable enough to be interpreted in terms of Torah and therefore to be incorporated to it. One of the criteria which the Sages used is apparent when we look at the customs and traditional laws which they refused to incorporate into the Oral Torah, *viz.* the *minhagin* (usages).[67] The *minhagin* were often very authoritative,[68] yet they were not recognized as part of the Oral Torah, because they were only the customs or laws of a particular locality (Palestine, Babylonia, Jerusalem . . .), or only the customs of a certain part of the population (certain families, very pious people, scholars or common people). A *minhag* did not become part of the Oral Torah because the latter must apply to every Jew everywhere. In the same way that God is One,[69] Torah must be universal.

---

[67] Cf. J. H. Greenstone, "Custom", *J.E.*, vol. IV, 395-98.

[68] According to the Amoraim they were authoritative enough to nullify a halakah: cf. Y. *B. M.* 7:1.

[69] Cf. the *Shema*.

3) *The Takkanoth and the Sanctification of the Name*

In all this we should indeed never lose sight of the belief in the divine origin of Torah. Nor should we forget the relationship, in the belief of the Sages, between the carrying out of the laws of Torah and God. This relationship was expressed in one of the key dogmas of Tannaitic Judaism: the sanctification of the Name.

The Israelites have been elected (saved from Egypt) in order that they may sanctify the Name.[70] It is with each element of his life that the Israelite must sanctify God.[71] What is it to sanctify the Name? It is to celebrate it. It is to recognize its Presence and action in order to bless God.[72] But also, and this is essential for the Sages, to sanctify the Name is to provoke in others the urge to bless God. Thus to carry out the commandments faithfully is to sanctify the Name; other people, seeing that you follow the commandments will be reminded of the Name and will bless It.[73] For this reason the Jew must be especially careful, when dealing with pagans, to be not only just but good, in order that they may bless the Name instead of profaning It.[74] The supreme sanctification of the Name is martyrdom.[75] Inversely the supreme sin is the profanation of the Name.[76] Any transgression of any commandment is a profanation of the

---

[70] *Sifra* on Lev. 23:33. This text as well as those referred to in the following footnotes are all given in translation by Bonsirven in *Textes, ad loc.*

[71] Cf. *Ber.* 4:1.

[72] Cf. *Sifre* on Deut. 23:5.

[73] *Mek.* on Exod. 15:2, Lauterbach ed., vol. II, 23ff.

[74] Cf. the tradition about Simeon b. Shetah in Y. *Bab. M.* (II,5) 8c, quoted by Montefiore and Loewe, *Rabbinic Anthology*, 393-94.

[75] *Sifra* on Lev. 22:32.

[76] Cf. e.g., *Sifra* on Lev. 22:32; *Sifra* on Deut. 33:3.

Name[77] and actually diminishes the Sanctity of God,[78] as the Sages put it boldly. Yet it is at once stated that the divine sanctity is not diminished in itself, but in the world, among men who, because of these transgressions, would not be placed in the Presence of God and consequently would not bless his Name. The fulfillment of the commandments for their own sake is not alone important. Their fulfillment in order that other people may bless God and recognize his Presence in the world[79] is as important if not more.

As can be seen by the references we gave from Tannaitic sources,[80] this belief in the sanctification of the Name is part of the context in which we have to understand the *takkanoth*. Torah was emended, in the face of new cultural situations in order to promote the sanctification of the Name, either positively or negatively. The sanctification of the Name was positively promoted in the case of the *takkanah* of *ketuba*: the woman who has her own rights and security at the death of her husband or in divorce, will be in a better situation to bless God. This is true also of all the takkanoth which emended the laws about the Sabbath in order to make out of this day a delight, a day during which God could be blessed.[81] The sanctification of the Name was also promoted negatively, i.e., in order to prevent its profanation. In this category we can put all the takkanoth

---

[77] *Sifre* on Deut. 32:18; cf. also *Sifre* on Deut. 27:1 and on Deut. 23:10.

[78] *Sifre* on Deut. 32:18.

[79] That this is so can be seen in different sayings of the Sages, which specify that if one cannot avoid transgressing a commandment he must do it in secret (*Kid.* 40a; *Tanh. B. Hukkat* 61a, cf. Montefiore and Loewe, *op. cit.*, 305ff.). Even worshipping an idol to save one's life is allowed if it is done in secret (according to R. Ishmael: *Sifra* on Lev. 18:4).

[80] For latter developments, namely philosophical developments of this belief see H. Slonimsky, "The Philosophy Implicit in the Midrash", *H.U.C.A.*, 1956, specially 258-68.

[81] The same kind of comments could be made about many other *takkanoth* as for instance the *takkanah* ascribed to Simeon b. Shetah on the compulsory attendance at School: *Ket.* 8 (end) and *Shab.* 14b.

which made the pentateuchal laws more lenient, going so far as to abrogate them purely and simply when these laws were too often transgressed. After the emendation there were no more transgressions of the law, that is to say, no more profanation of the Name.[82]

4) *Making a fence around Torah*

Over against this lenient way of interpreting Torah, we find the principle of multiplying the *halakoth*, *takkanoth* and *gezeroth* in order to make "a fence (סייג) around the Torah".[83] Instead of making the laws easier to carry out, the Sages made them more difficult. Thus according to the halakah, fowl and cheese must not be eaten at the same time. Yet if they are placed on the same table (which was not forbidden) one might be tempted to eat both. Therefore the school of Hillel introduced the preventive measure (a fence around the Torah) that they should not be placed on the same table.[84] We could multiply the examples, for indeed as R. Akiba said, "the Tradition is a fence around the Torah".[85] Yet this example is sufficient to show that this principle had a purpose similar to that of the *takkanoth*: to prevent as far as possible the profanation of the Name. This time the emphasis was on the Jew's sanctification of the Name by his being "holy" as God is

---

[82] A striking example of this is the *takkanah* about the abolition of the ritual governing trials of adulterers (the bitter water) because adulterers multiplied (*Sotah* 47a). In this way the adulterers were no longer exposed publicly: they would be punished, indeed, by God himself, but their profanation of the Name would be as limited as possible.

[83] Cf. *Aboth* 1:1; 3:13; *Sifra* 86b (Weiss ed.); *Ber.* 4b. This phrase is found very rarely in the Tannaitic literature, but the principle involved shaped many Tannaitic halakoth: cf. Zeitlin, "Halakah", *op. cit.*, 27.

[84] Cf. *Hul.* 104b: it is to be noted that the school of Shammai did not agree with this teaching.

[85] *Aboth* 3:13. R. Akiba uses here the term "masoreth" in its original meaning to designate the Oral Torah. Cf. Blackman's note *ad loc.*, and D. Daube, "Rabbinic Methods", *op. cit.*, 242, n. 10.

"holy".[86] We should note that in the concept of holiness the connotation of "separation" was stressed.[87] In the "fence", therefore, we have the "separation" of Israel as the holy people of God which sanctifies God by this very separation, rather than the sanctification of the Name by provoking the celebration of God—whether through good deeds or through making the Law a delight.

Nevertheless it was *together* that the *takkanoth* and the prescriptions making a "fence around the Torah" contributed to the expansion of the Oral Torah; the attitude of the two were not contradictory. If the first (the takkanoth) emphasized the importance of the culture, the second (the fence) emphasized the importance of Torah as the necessary system of reference, without which Israel would no longer be Israel. She would lose her identity. It is worthwhile here to emphasize the wisdom of the Pharisees, and after them of the Tannaim, in keeping these two poles more or less in balance. For if either were suppressed the very purpose of the election of Israel (the sanctification of the Name) would be lost. Either Israel would become one of the nations by conforming to their culture (which was prevented by the requirement that the takkanoth be related to Scripture) or Israel would build such a high fence around herself that she would no longer be able to communicate with the nations of which she should be the "priesthood".[88] Pharisaism and Rabbinic Judaism had the tendency to succumb to this second temptation.[89] Yet generally speaking we can say that these two poles have been more or less kept in balance. We find witness to this in the criticisms which sectarian Judaism addressed to the Pharisees.

---

[86] Cf. *Sifra* on Lev. 20:26 (Weiss ed., 93d; Bonsirven, *Textes*, 45).

[87] Cf. *Mek.* on Exod. 19:6; Lauterbach ed., vol. II, 205, and also *Sifra* on Lev. 28:4 (Weiss ed., 86a; Bonsirven, *Textes*, 42).

[88] Exod. 19:5-6; cf. the warning against building to high a fence in *Ab. R. N.* 1, 2a: a fence should not be higher than the object which it is to guard.

[89] See the description of the Pharisees in the New Testament. On the value of this description see the well-balanced article by G. Vermès, "La formation de la tradition juive", *op. cit.*, especially 330-42.

The latter were considered as being too open to the culture of their time. The continual controversy which had opposed liberal and conservative schools since the creation of the sanhedrin[90] contributed to this balance.

5) *The Hermeneutical Rules (middoth) of Hillel*

Another important aspect of the relationship between halakah and Torah, *viz.* the hermeneutical rules (*middoth*) generally ascribed to Hillel,[91] will allow us to illustrate further the preceding remarks.

As mentioned earlier the distinction between halakic and haggadic interpretations is artificial. In both we find the same basic principles which we stressed when dealing with the Targum and which are valid for the haggadic Midrash.[92] Yet there is one difference which is important for our discussion. The halakic interpretation was much more limited by the Tradition than the haggadic. The latter, as we saw, was indeed limited by the Tradition's general influence on their whole way of thinking; but its authority was not brought to bear explicitly on every point.[93] In the case of the halakic

---

[90] That is, from the "first pair", Jose b. Joezer (conservative) and Jose b. Johanan (liberal), down to the well-know opposition between the Schools of Hillel and Shammai. Cf. Zeitlin, "The Halaka", *op. cit.*, 31ff.

[91] Yet certainly Hillel was not their author: the text of the *Tosephta* which mentions them implies merely that Hillel used these *middoth* in his controversy with the Bene Bathyra: *Tos. Sanh.* 7 (end). On these rules see H. L. Strack, *Introduction to the Talmud and Midrash*, Philadelphia, 1931, 94 and 284-85 (notes). On the relationship of these rules with Hellenism, see S. Lieberman, *Hellenism in Jewish Palestine*, New York, 1950, 46-82; and D. Daube, "Rabbinic Methods", *op. cit.*, 251-60.

[92] Cf. J. Bonsirven, *Exégèse Rabbinique et Exégèse Paulinienne*, Paris, 1939, 14, who agrees on this with G. Aicher, *Das Alte Testament in der Mischna*, Freiburg, 1906, 152.

[93] As we noted above, the haggadic interpretation was strictly limited by the Tradition at a later date.

interpretation, from very early, the Oral Torah was recognized as authoritative in such a way that exegesis could not contradict the existing halakah.[94] This is apparent in the controversy which opposed Hillel to the Bene Bathyra.[95] The controversy concerned the slaughtering of the Paschal Lamb on the Sabbath. Was it permitted or not? In other words does the Passover override the Sabbath or not? The Bene Bathyra did not know. Hillel proved that the Passover overrides the Sabbath by means of three hermeneutical rules: a) by *heqqesh* (assimilation of two laws because of analogy of subjects): the Passover sacrifice can be assimilated to the *Tamid* (perpetual sacrifice) since both are sacrifices of the community. Therefore since the *Tamid* does override the Sabbath, the Passover sacrifice does it also. b) by *Qal wahômer* (*a minori ad majus*, i.e., reasoning by *a fortiori*). The omission of the sacrifice of the *Tamid* is *not* punished by *kareth* (excommunication), and it overrides the Sabbath. A *fortiori* the Passover sacrifice, whose omission *is* punished by *kareth*, must override the Sabbath. c) by *Gezerah Shawah* (analogy of words in two laws). "In its appointed time" is stated about the *Tamid* as well as about the Passover sacrifice.[96]

Yet the Bene Bathyra did not accept Hillel's ruling, on the following grounds: a) one cannot assimilate the two kinds of sacrifice, because for the *Tamid* the quantity is fixed and not for the Passover sacrifice. b) one cannot argue *a fortiori* in this case, because the *Tamid* is "a holy of holies" and the Passover sacrifice is of inferior holiness. c) finally they could not accept his argument by analogy

---

[94] Yet as we shall see it is too hasty a generalization to say that the exegesis could not do anything else than justify an existing halakah. Thus Bonsirven, *op. cit.*, 13: "cette exégèse n'invente pas mais seulement justifie, une loi qui tire toute sa valeur de la tradition. . . . C'est un principe reçu qu'un raisonnement ne peut fonder une loi si elle n'a déjà autorité". **cf.** also 4**5**-51.

[95] Cf. Y. *Pes.* 6, 1, 33a. Cf. also *Pes.* 66a, which gives a shorter version.

[96] במועדו: about the Tamid in Num. 28:2; about the Passover sacrifice in Num. 9:2.

(*Gezerah Shawah*), because one cannot present a conclusion by means of such a rule if this conclusion is not supported by the Tradition.

Hillel proposed other arguments using other hermeneutical rules. They refuted these also. But when he finally said that he had received the tradition that the Passover sacrifice may be performed on a Sabbath from his teachers Abtalion and Shemaiah, the Bene Bathyra accepted it and appointed Hillel Nasi over the sanhedrin.

To this the Babylonian Talmud adds that the Bene Bathyra did not know if it was allowed to carry the knife for the slaughter on the Sabbath. Hillel answered: "I have heard this law (i.e., I have received a tradition aboutthis law) but have forgotten it. But leave it to Israel: if they are not prophets, yet they are the children of prophets".[97] The day of the Passover (which was on a Sabbath) the Jews who brought lambs for the sacrifice stuck the knife in their wool. Seeing this Hillel remembered the halakah and said: "Thus have I received the tradition from the mouth(s) of Shemaiah and Abtalion".[98]

This example is representative, in spite of its late redaction. In the time of Hillel there were hesitations about the respective authority of halakic tradition (independent from Scripture) and of halakic rules resulting from midrashic interpretation.

As we have seen,[99] for a long time many halakoth existed and were decreed independently from Scripture. On the other hand, for a long time also new halakoth were deduced from Scripture, and this, at first, by a "simple" exegesis which was presented as the plain meaning of the text. We can find traces of these very ancient interpretations in the Tannaitic

---

[97] *Pes.* 66a, Epstein's translation. Parentheses mine.

[98] *Ibid.*

[99] Cf. our comments above 91ff. on the debate between Zeitlin and Lauterbach and on the *Gezeroth*.

midrashim,[100] which, in the same way as the *takkanoth*, do not hesitate to contradict the text. Thus in the *Mekilta* "an eye for an eye" (Exod. 21:24, the Talion law) is understood to refer to a monetary compensation, as if this were the plain meaning of the text! But such "simple" interpretations were not satisfactory anymore in the time of Hillel. Thus, as in the example just mentioned, the Sages used stricter hermeneutical rules in their attempt to justify the conclusions of ancient midrashic interpretations as well as the halakoth which originated independently from Scripture. All the deductions by analogy were strictly limited to this role. Thus, as is clear in the controversy between Hillel and the Bene Bathyra, the rule *Gezerah Shawah*[101] was limited by existing halakoth (this was, *a fortiori*, the case with the rule of *heqqesh*, analogy by subjects, which is not even mentioned among the *middoth* of Hillel although it was used by him).

The rules of logical deduction (דין) were used more freely: thus the דין par excellence viz. Qal Wahomer. Its limitation was not Tradition but Scripture:[102] the result of any logical conclusions could not outrun its Scriptural premises.

Without going into a detailed study of these rules,[103]

---

[100] They are often introduced by אלא . . . אין "nothing else than", cf. for instances in *Mekilta*: Lauterbach ed., vol. I, 27 (line 68); 67 (line 95); 207 (line 35); 213 (line 116); vol. III, 24 (line 78); 45 (lines 56 and 58); *passim*. Cf. also the examples given by Lieberman, *op. cit.*, 51, and Bonsirven, *Egéseses*, 42ff.

[101] The second of the seven *middoth* of Hillel. It is to be noted that this rule (like most of the other rules by analogy, with the exception of the sixth rule of Hillel, which is significantly omitted by Ishmael) refers not to an analogy of content but to an identity of words. Cf. what we said about the tallying of haftaroth and sedarim, above.

[102] According to the principle of דיו: "it is enough for him". See for instance the *Mekilta* on Exod. 21:2 (Lauterbach ed., vol. III, 5) where this limitation is expressed: "It is enough for that which is derived by inference to be like that from which it is derived".

[103] For this cf. Adolf Schwarz, *Die hermeneutische in der talmudischen Litteratur*, Vienna, 1897; *Der hermeneutische Syllogismus in der talmudischen Litteratur*, Vienna, 1901; *Die*

it is relevant here to note the conclusions of Lieberman and Daube on their relationship with Hellenistic rhetoric.[104] As these scholars have shown, we cannot ignore an important influence of Hellenism on the hermeneutical rules.[105] If the Sages could no longer be satisfied with the "simple" exegesis, it was because of changes in the Jewish community's very way of thinking, which was imperceptibly molded by Hellenism. The Jews could not but think in the logical categories of Greek rhetoric. And indeed, as Daube has shown, each of the seven hermeneutical rules finds its equivalent in Hellenistic rhetoric; indeed, so does the very distinction between Written Torah and Oral Torah![106] Yet as Daube notes, "Just as the Romans succeeded in latinizing the rhetorical notions they used, so the 'classical' Tannaitic Rabbis succeeded in hebraizing (them)".[107] This they did by their use of the phrase תורה שבעל פי, literally "Torah *by mouth*" to designate the Oral Torah. It means indeed "by heart", "from memory". But in this the Sages were alluding to Scriptural texts like Num. 9:23 which, translated literally, can be rendered: "According to the mouth of the Lord they rested, and according to the mouth of the Lord they journeyed, they kept the charge of the Lord according to the mouth of the Lord in the hand of Moses"; Josh. 1:8: "This book of the Torah shall no depart out of thy mouth, but thou shalt meditate therein day and night . . ."; and Ps. 119:72f.: "The Torah of thy mouth is

---

hermeneutische Induktion in der talmudischen Litteratur, Vienna, 1909; *Die hermeneutische Antinomie in der talmudischen Litteratur*, Vienna, 1913. For brief presentation of this topic see Bonsirven, *Exégèses*, 77-144, and J. Z. Lauterbach, "Talmud Hermeneutic", *J.E.*, vol. XII, 30-33.

[104] Cf. Lieberman, *op. cit.*, 47-82, and D. Daube, "Rabbinic Methods", *op. cit.*, 251-60.

[105] This they defended against the then conventioned view that these rules were completely of Jewish origin.

[106] Reminiscent of the pair νόμοι ἔγγραφοι and νόμοι ἄγραφοι or *ius scriptum* and *ius non scriptum*, Daube, *op. cit.*, 248.

[107] *Ibid.*, 258.

better unto me than thousands of gold and silver. . . ."[108] Thus in their hermeneutic the Sages used Hellenistic categories. The rhetorical rules have been hebraized to become the *middoth*. This last sentence implies all the complexity of the relationship between classical Judaism and Hellenism. We cannot become involved in this discussion: it would carry us too far from our topic, for indeed we would have to attempt to evaluate the nature of Palestinian Hellenism. Suffice it here to note, in view of our preceding chapters, that such Hellenistic influence on the *middoth* and other hermeneutical methods largely shaped the categorical presuppositions of the hermeneutic, but not nearly so effective in that hermeneutic's results. Thus the various haggadic and halakic developments which we have mentioned would hardly have satisfied the typically Hellenistic demands for univocity and non-contradiction. Why is it so? Because, as we stressed in our introduction, hermeneutical rules derive from the exegesis of the text. Such exegesis expresses a contemporary, "culture-bound" understanding of the nature of the text. In the case of an early Jew this meant to look at Scripture from the complex Judeo-Hellenistic culture. We can therefore assume that a complex exegesis was implied. As a Jew involved in a Jewish community and its synagogal services, one apprehended the nature of Scripture as witness to the election of the Chosen People and as Torah. As a man influenced by Hellenism, the Jew apprehended the nature of Scripture let us say with the devices of Hellenistic rhetoric (if we may risk this generalization without discussing it).

Such a situation could have led to two distinct hermeneutics: the scholars' and the worshippers'. Yet clearly this was not the case, as we pointed out earlier; halakah and haggadah belonged together. Furthermore the synagogal understanding of Scripture was the explicit doctrine of Scripture. Thus if Hellenistic categories were to be used, in Daube's words, they had to be hebraized. In other words they had to fit into the hermeneutic process of classical Judaism.

---

[108] Daube's translation, *ibid*. He refers also to Josh. 22:9; Exod. 17:1; 38:21; Num. 3:51; Ezra 1:1; II Chr. 36:22.

Thus indeed the hermeneutical rules were influenced by Hellenism. Yet these Hellenistic elements have been submitted to a "coherent deformation".[109] The Hellenistic categories were no longer rhetorical rules, they were *middoth*. The discourse which prolonged the discourse of Scripture could *not* be a philosophy by means of which the Jews would have to express their identity as the Chosen People of God. Rather, it was haggadah and halakah. In haggadah, according to their Jewish exegesis, the Jews prolonged the Scriptural discourse about the election and vocation of Israel in a new discourse, in which they understood themselves as being this very Chosen People. Similarly in the halakah they prolonged the Scriptural discourse on how to carry out that very vocation in their contemporary cultural setting. Our next chapter will develop these conclusions.

---

[109] This is a phrase that Malraux used about the poetic language. It is quoted by Merleau-Ponty in *Signs*, Evanston, 1964, 91.

CHAPTER VI

CLASSICAL JUDAISM AND SCRIPTURE

As a way of crystallizing what we have learned through our exploration of the different ways in which classical Judaism used Scripture, we shall try to describe what R. Bloch has called the "midrashic genre".[1]

We have first to specify what is the relationship of Tradition and Torah in the midrashic genre. R. Bloch[2] expressed this by saying that the midrash is an *"actualization* of Scripture". That cannot be contested; the midrash is often a way to make Scripture relevant for the actual life of the Jewish people. The Tradition is the result of such actualization, which allows Scripture to be incarnated in the community.[3] We saw many examples of this. Yet the phrase

---

[1] It is clear that here this phrase does not designate a "literary genre", but the *attitude* toward Scripture which is found indeed in the midrashim, but also in the homilies, targumim, and halakic teachings. We say this in order to avoid the ambiguity in R. Bloch's writings which Wright points out. Cf. A. G. Wright, "The Literary Genre Midrash", *C.B.Q.* 28, 1966, 105-38 and 417-57, especially 106ff. As R. Le Déaut notes in his excellent review of this study ("A propos d'une définition du Midrash", *Biblica* 50, 1969, 395-413), it is not legitimate to reduce the significance of the term *midrash* to that of a literary genre. It has a broader sense, mainly in the period we are considering. Therefore we cannot use Wright's definition of the term, which is a projection upon the past of the latter literary genre. We use the term to express an attitude toward Scripture.

[2] "Midrash", *S.D.B.*, vol. V, col. 1253ff.

[3] Cf. A. Lacocque, *op. cit.*, 16.

"actualization of Scripture" has the connotation that the interpretation was always a movement starting from Scripture in order to meet a concrete situation. Actually that was a tradition brought about by cultural changes and recognized as authoritative apart from Scripture. The midrashic interpretation was in this case a *legitimation* of this tradition rather than an actualization of Scripture. In order to show what is implied in this distinction between "actualization of Scripture" and "legitimation by means of Scripture" we need to investigate the original meaning of the word "midrash".

THE MIDRASH AS THE "INQUIRING OF GOD"

Let us first note, following S. Zeitlin,[4] that the word "midrash" is derived from the verb דרש, "to inquire". In the Hebrew Bible it has often the connotation of inquiring *of God*, either for a solution (when one was in difficulty) or for a knowledge of the future (in order to know the outcome of such or such situation).[5] This inquiring of God was generally done through the intermediary of the seers and prophets.[6] With the book of Ezra, that is, in the time when the prophets disappeared from the life of Israel, the Torah took their place as the intermediary for this "inquiring of God": "Ezra had set his heart to inquire (of) the Torah of the Lord".[7] Thus Torah came to assume the role of intermediary between God and Israel. "Inquiring of God" became synonymous with "inquiring of Torah". This could actually help to explain, as Zeitlin pointed out,[8] why prophecy ceased precisely at the

---

[4] "Midrash: A Historical Study", *J.Q.R.* 44, 1953, 21-36.

[5] See the examples given by Zeitlin, *op. cit.*, 21ff.

[6] Cf. I Sam. 9:6-10; 28:6-7; I Kings 14:1-4; 22:5-7; II Kings 1:2-16; 3:11; cf. also II Chr. *passim*.

[7] Ezra 7:10, transl. mine. It is to be noted that this inquiring of God is also mentioned in the book of Ezra in a worship setting: cf. Exra 4:2 and 6:21.

[8] *Op. cit.*, 26ff.

time when the Pentateuch was canonized. The role of the prophets had been taken over by the Sages, who were inquiring of the Torah (of God) and teaching Israel.[9] They were those who, from then on, gave solutions to the questions which concrete life was raising for the Jewish people of their time. According to the Rabbinic literature they did this by interpreting Torah precisely as the prophets did. We should not forget that the books of the prophets were understood in classical Judaism as nothing but commentaries on Torah. Yet the Sages in their midrashic activity did not perform the whole of the prophetic function. For indeed the prophets had also the power to foretell the future by interpreting the meaning of history. They had this because they were inspired by the "Holy Spirit", *Ruah Hakodesh*, which in classical Judaism refers exclusively to the Spirit of prophecy.[10] The disappearance of the prophets meant also the departure of the Holy Spirit, which was felt as a loss due to the sins of Israel.

When considering classical Judaism from our perspective, and no longer in its own terms, we can view this loss in terms of the Sages utter inability[11] to interpret the history of their own time. They did not discover in history new acts of the living God, as the prophets had.[12] Yet it is correct to

---

[9] Cf. Ezra 7:10, the end of the verse.

[10] Cf. H. Parzen, "The *Ruah Hakodesh* in Tannaitic literature", *J.Q.R.*, 1929, 51-76, and L. Blau, "Holy Spirit", *J.E.*, vol. VI, 447-50.

[11] There are a few exceptions. Thus the Sages have interpreted historical events like the Fall of Jerusalem (in A.D. 70). Yet the emphasis is not on this event as a new act of God in history but on the new cultural situations it brought about, as the work of Yohanan b. Zakkai at Yabneh shows. This point will be clarified when we deal with sectarian Judaism.

[12] The *Bath Qol* cannot be said to have assumed this function. It was merely a kind of divination by means of Scripture. For instance one understood what he should do, or what would be the future, from a verse of Scripture which he overheard children saying when passing by a school. Cf. Lieberman, *op. cit.*, 194-99, and mainly L. Blau, "Bath Qol", *J.E.*, vol. II, 588-92, who notes that it cannot be identified with prophecy.

claim with Lauterbach that classical Judaism is heir to the prophets.[13] Like the prophets, the Sages "inquired of God" not in Torah by itself (as did the Sadducees) but in Torah *and* in the concrete situation of the life of the Jewish people, an attitude which gave rise to the doctrine of the Oral Torah. That is, although the Sages did not interpret the whole of their contemporary history, they did interpret part of it. Which part?

We need here to use the distinction between two levels of history which we mentioned in our introduction. On the first level we place the events which orient decisively the history of a man, a family, a community or a nation, that is, the *salient* features of history. We call this "the salient history". On the second level we place the cultural changes, i.e., the continuous changes in the concrete situations of life, in the laws, the current ideas, the ways of thinking, and the folklore. We call this second level the "history of cultural changes".

Unlike the prophets who took the "salient history" seriously into account, classical Judaism focused its attention *almost* exclusively on the history of the cultural changes.

Such a statement may seem at first to be objectionable. There are indeed in the Rabbinic literature exceptions to this principle. One of them is the midrashic interpretation of Deut. 26:5. It reads in the Midrash: "An Aramean sought to destroy my father" (the Aramean is here identified with Laban), instead of reading: "A wandering Aramean was my father". As L. Finkelstein,[14] J. L. Seeligmann,[15] and L. H. Silberman[16] showed, such an interpretation is understandable only when one recognizes the identification of the Aramean Laban with Antiochus Epiphanes. As long as one makes no

---

[13] "The Ethics of the Halakah", in *Rabbinic Essays*, 272.

[14] "The Oldest Midrash", *Harvard Theological Review* 31, 1938, 291-317.

[15] *The Septuagint Version of Isaiah*, Leiden, 1948, 85-86.

[16] "Unriddling the Riddle", *R.Q.* 3, 1961, 324-25, who quotes the former.

distinction between different kinds of "contemporization" one can agree with Seeligmann and Silberman that this is not an isolated instance. But when we distinguish between "contemporization by reference to the salient history" versus "contemporization by reference to the history of cultural changes" we must admit that the former is exceptional in Rabbinic literature and may even be looked on as the remnant of an Apocalyptic interpretation which has been incorporated into the Rabbinic literature.[17] Thus in spite of this and other exceptions we can maintain that classical Judaism focused its attention almost exclusively on the history of cultural changes. It is as if the Sages had discovered an ultimate significance in the "history of cultural changes" or more precisely in the traditions which evolved from that history. Such traditions could therefore be considered as having come "from the mouth of God" (i.e., as Oral Torah). In other words they could be considered the results of the revelatory activity of God not in the "salient history" but in the "history of cultural changes".

Yet as we have seen, not all the traditions and customs were recognized as authoritative. Besides the *takkanoth* were the *minhagin*. Why was one accepted and the other rejected? We saw that the criterion used here was the "sanctification of the Name", that is to say, the vocation of the Chosen People. Traditions and customs were recognized as "from the mouth of God" if they could be apprehended as *signs showing how to be the Chosen People in the new situation*. These signs were therefore "instructions", "teaching", a "guide for life": in one word, Torah. This Torah was to be followed as a consequence of the election. In this respect it was mainly an ethical teaching.

But how was this election revealed to the Jewish community? No new sign of the election was discovered in history. Now that prophecy had ceased and the Holy Spirit had departed from Israel, the "salient history" of their time was silent, as if the living God were acting now only in the

---

[17] This will serve to remind us that classical Judaism and Apocalyptic Judaism were not strictly separated from each other.

"history of cultural changes". The election of Israel was now apprehended only by means of Scripture. Or more precisely this election was discovered only in the acts of God in the "salient history" *of the past* as recorded in Scripture. The only remaining sign of this election was Scripture.

THE TWO FUNCTIONS OF SCRIPTURE IN CLASSICAL JUDAISM

Scripture appears therefore as having two functions:

A) *It gave the Jewish community its identity as the Chosen People with the vocation of sanctifying the Name*. In this, Scripture was self-sufficient. It contained the complete and only revelation of Israel's election: the "past sacred History" was the only sacred History. Here Scripture can be considered "closed". The only witness to the election of Israel, it had to be, necessarily, the system of reference by means of which the Jewish community could *discover its identity*. A closed system of signs, Scripture was interpreted by Scripture. An integrated system of reference, Scripture could be telescoped.

In all this classical Judaism constantly based its interpretation on the *words* of Scripture, and especially on rare words or phrases. As we have seen this was almost always done to tally one text with another. Such a use of Scripture points again to the image of a closed system of signs which refers back and forth to each other *ad infinitum*. Also implied here is the notion of Hebrew (Biblical Hebrew) as a holy language,[18] together with the concern to preserve an accurate holy text. The latter concern emerged out of the conviction that Scripture had inexaustible possibilities.[19] Yet such a conviction did not lead to wild metaphysical speculations: indeed each word of the holy text was meaningful and had to be interpreted, but not by itself. It

---

[18] On this topic cf. A. Lacocque's article in C.T.S. *Register*, 1968.

[19] Cf. Gerhardsson, *op. cit.*, 41.

had to be interpreted with the system of signs of Scripture.[20] To interpret Scripture by Scripture amounted to a better understanding of the events recorded therein. This sort of interpretation always referred, implicitly if not explicitly, to the election and vocation; it was the *uncovering* of the revealed identity of the worshipping community.

The Synagogue was the *Sitz im Leben par excellence* for such an understanding of Scripture. The reading of Scripture, the homily, the Targum, the liturgy itself, contributed each in its own way to the community's consciousness of itself as the Chosen People. Thus each contributed to the *embodying* of this revealed identity. This was reenforced by the constant choice of happy endings for the *haftaroth*: these betokened the promise that Israel's election would be fully manifested in the Messianic age. Yet this revelation of the election was addressed to a concrete people. Hence Scripture had to be made understandable. Homily and Targum worked together to ensure that nothing in Scripture be left without meaning. In these haggadic developments, rewritings and translations, we have found already an actualization of Scripture which met this need. Yet it was a quite moderate actualization since it remained within the boundaries of the worshipping community. Such was the first function of Scripture, that we can term a *liturgical* function since it belonged to the worshipping community, and we find it primarily exemplified in the haggadah.

B) In its second function, Scripture served as a set of criteria which would enable the community to discover how to fulfill this vocation in the concrete situations of life. This characterized, above all, the halakah. Scripture provided instructions and laws: Torah. Here also Scripture

---

[20] By contrast the allegorists used the words not in order to refer to another text but in order to discover in them a hidden (generally spiritual) meaning. This was the attitude not only of Philo but also of Palestinian allegorists known as the *Dorshe Reshumot* whose teachings were rejected. Cf. Lauterbach, "The Ancient Jewish Allegorists in Talmud and Midrash", *J.Q.R.* N.S. I, 1910-11, 291ff. and 503ff. They were rejected on the ground that Torah was conveyed "in the language of man" as R. Ishmael expressed it (*Y. Yeb.*, 8, 8d and *Y. Ned.*, 1, 36c).

was interpreted by Scripture. Commandments were interpreted by means of other Scriptural passages, and these interpretations were limited by Scripture. Yet here the actualization of Scripture was much more important. Scripture was interpreted in terms of the cultural situations in which these "instructions" were to be carried out. Thus Torah, by these midrashic interpretations, participated in the concrete life of the Jewish people. It participated therefore in the dynamism of the "history of cultural changes". It was not, as for the Sadducees, a static and sclerosed Torah but an ever living God,[21] who demands that his will be carried out in the history of cultural changes. On the other hand as we suggested earlier, the will of God was also apprehended directly in customs and traditions, and then legitimated by means of Scripture.

This halakic use of Scripture implies therefore that the "inquiring of God" was done either by scrutinizing Scripture in the light of the new cultural situation or by scrutinizing Tradition in the light of Scripture.[22] We emphasize these two opposite processes in order to make clear that revelation appears between the two poles: Scripture and Tradition. Actually for the Sages, as well as for the Jewish community, these two processes were not distinguished from one another. Legitimating a halakah by means of a Scriptural proof text was not considered to be something different from deriving it directly from Scripture. In both cases the halakah demanded by the new situation was considered to be *inherent* in Scripture. This was the consequence of the fact that they

---

[21] Cf. A. Lacocque, "Tradition dans le Bas Judaïsme", *R.H.Ph.R.*, 1960, 3-16, who writes: "Ce sera l'oeuvre unique de la Tradition d'empêcher la sclérose, de faire que l'Ecriture ne soit pas statique, mais dynamique. Grâce à la Tradition, la Bible participera à la réalité vivante dont elle témoigne, elle participera à la vie, au dépassement de tout cadre, de toute analyse, de toute fixation, de tout statisme", p. 6.

[22] See again the very explicit example we gave: Hillel did not know if it was allowed or not to carry the knife for the slaughter of the Paschal lamb on the Sabbath. He rules according to the way the Jews were doing it traditionaly (*Pes.* 66a). In other words he recognized the custom as authoritative: the Jews are sons of the prophets!

could not look at the cultural changes of their time in any other way than through Scripture from which they received their identity as the Chosen People of God. Likewise they could not look at Torah in total withdrawal from the broader cultural situations of their time. They were not indeed an "a-temporal", spiritual Israel, but a concrete, worldly Israel, involving itself in the cultural changes of its age in order to perform its function as Chosen People: to sanctify the Name of God.

In order to show more clearly this twofold hermeneutic of Scripture in classical Judaism, let us oppose it to that of the Sadducees.

EXEGESIS, HERMENEUTIC AND THE SADDUCEES

For the Sadducees Scripture was to be understood in the framework of the oaths and curses of a juridical covenant. The Sacred History contained in Scripture was for them, on the one hand, a witness to the sins and punishment of Israel, and on the other hand, to the faithfulness to the covenant and the blessing of Israel. Bluntly put, Scripture was for them the revelation of how to be blessed and not cursed by God. Such were the results of the Sadducees' implicit exegesis. Let us note that such an exegesis was not illegitimate. It was an understanding of Scripture in terms of Deut. 27 and 28 and many other passages of the same type, including I and II Chronicles. To place oneself in the perspective of Scripture meant in this case to follow strictly the letter of the commandments in order to avoid the curses. As a consequence Scripture concerned only a part of their life: their religious life and not their secular life. In brief, for the Sadducees Scripture was absolutely closed; it contained the complete and final revelation, to which nothing could be added. We could say that for them there was actually no real hermeneutic. For indeed it was not a question of extending the vectors of the Biblical Text up to themselves in their concrete life situation. It was not a question of prolonging the discourse of the Biblical Text in a new discourse. On the contrary, the Sadducees went themselves "into the Text", they made the discourse of the Text their own. For the Sadducees it was as if revelation were wholly *contained in* Scripture.

EXEGESIS, HERMENEUTIC AND THE PHARISEES

For the Pharisees Scripture was also to be understood in the framework of the covenant. But their concept of covenant was quite different:[23] it was mainly considered in terms of the election. The Sacred History contained in Scripture was the revelation of Israel as the Chosen People, whose vocation was to sanctify the Name. Such a vocation could only be conceived as co-extensive with life. The biblical Laws were understood in this context as ways to carry out this vocation. This appears to have been the characteristic result of the Pharisees' exegesis. To place oneself in the perspective of Scripture meant, on the one hand, to discover oneself as a member of the Chosen People. Here the *loci* of revelation were Scripture itself and the worshipping community. On the other hand, it meant to be in a constant quest for the way in which one might hope to fulfill this vocation in new situations, that is to fulfill the concrete will of God. Here the *loci* of revelation were Scripture and the history of cultural changes. For the Pharisees, then, and for classical Judaism as a whole, it was as if revelation, far from being contained in Scripture, occurred in the tension among Scripture, the worshipping community, and the history of cultural changes. Such are the main characteristics of the hermeneutical structure which governed the use of Scripture in classical Judaism.

Therein Torah was a closed system of reference in the following sense: no new signs of Israel's election were to be

---

[23]Cf. Annie Jaubert, *La Notion d'Alliance dans le Judaïsme*, Paris, 1963, 289-92. Yet she is much too negative toward what she sees as a reduction of the notion of Covenant in classical Judaism.

found in the "salient history" of the early Jews' time. Therefore the *uncovering* of their revealed identity as Chosen People had to take place in an interpretation of Scripture by Scripture. The *embodying* of this revealed identity, i.e., the process which enabled the Jewish community to become consciously the Chosen People, could not but take place in the Scriptural system of reference provided by the Scripturally structured liturgy. Through this *embodying* of the revealed identity the worshipping community itself became locus of revelation (as we noted when discussing the liturgical texts and the Targum).

Beyond this "biblical world" of the liturgy, the early Jewish community had to carry out its vocation in the secular world. Here Torah was open in the following sense: in the cultural changes of their times they could perceive signs pointing to the ways in which they and their community could *live* as the Chosen People. These ways were seen as belonging to an open, growing Torah. This opening, which gave rise to the Oral Torah, had necessarily an ethical orientation. The fact that the only new signs of "the hand of God" in history were of this sort led necessarily to a moralistic attitude, i.e., to a reduction of the whole Jewish religion to certain practices, a regulated mode of life; halakah became the characteristic of classical Judaism. And indeed, as Zeitlin notes, "the word that has connotation of religion is *dat*, law". This was the case from very early Tannaitic times.[24] Therefore the election was simply assumed: it was enough to be the children of Abraham[25] and to carry out the commandments of Torah, understood as co-extensive with life, to be indeed the Chosen People.

---

[24]"Halakah", *op. cit.*, 38.

[25]Cf. Mat. 3:9.

PART II

THE USE OF SCRIPTURE IN SECTARIAN JUDAISM

CHAPTER VII

THE PROBLEM OF THE SOURCES

The phrase "sectarian Judaism", when opposed to the "classical Judaism" of the Pharisees applies to the Sadducees, the Samaritans, the Apocalyptists and the (Dead Sea) Covenanters.[1] Concerning the Sadducees and their use of Scripture we have actually very few witnesses: we employed them as far as we could in the preceding part, when comparing the Sadducees with the Pharisees. On the Samaritans, we have

---

[1] The list could be longer. Yet any other sectarian group can be included legitimately in one of these four categories. For instance the *Zadokite Document*, in spite of the fact that it is witness to a group certainly different from the Dead Sea community, can be considered together with the literature of the latter because of clear affinities. We designate these groups by the generic name: "Covenanters" rather than others such as, for instance, the name "Essenes". Although this latter designation seems plausible to us in view of the evidences brought out by Dupont-Sommer, *Les Ecrits Esseniens decouverts pres de la Mer Morte*, Paris, 1959, G. Vermes, *Les Manuscrits du Desert de Juda*, Paris, 1953, and many other scholars, we prefer to avoid it since we cannot indulge ourselves in this discussion. A lengthy argument would be required in order to refute the hypothesis that the Covenanters were Zealots. The best case for this hypothesis was made by G. R. Driver in his important work, *The Judean Scrolls*, Oxford, 1965. Let us say simply that in view of the archeological evidences (if for no other reasons) it is difficult to doubt that the Covenanters existed already before the beginning of the Christian era: the organization of the Dead Sea Community seems to antedate the emergence of the Zealot movement.

indeed access to an important literature. Yet its later date[2] allows only conjectures for our special topic.

We are therefore left with two sectarian groups: the "Apocalyptists" and the "Covenanters". The distinction between them is legitimate, especially because of the different degrees in which they were separated from classical Judaism. Yet it is often difficult to distinguish them radically: the Covenanters can be said to be Apocalyptists (although with specific characteristics of their own), and indeed at the level of the sources it is not always easy to discern what is specifically the Covenanters', since they made use of several Apocalyptic books.

THE SOURCES

The question dating the sources is much less complex than for classical Judaism. We have access to a number of

---

[2] This would not be the case if the so-called *Assumption of Moses* could be ascribed to the Samaritans, as has recently been proposed by K. Haacker, "Assumptio Mosis - eine samaritanische Schrift?", *T.Z.* 25, 1969, 385-405. Yet in our estimation his argument is not conclusive. The fact that this book is exclusively concerned with Moses does not make it necessarily a Samaritan work: Moses was a very important figure for early Judaism. The strong antipathy against the Maccabees and the Hasmoneans which is expressed in this book could have come from sectarian Jews just as well as from the Samaritans. Furthermore the parallels which the author discovered between, on the one hand, the *Assumption of Moses*, and on the other hand, the *Memar Marqah* and the Samaritan *Chronicles* are not unique. John Bowman in his "The Exegesis of the Pentateuch among the Samaritans and the Rabbis", *Oud testamentische Studien*, P. A. H. De Boer ed., Leiden, 1950, pointed out many such parallels with the Rabbinic literature: this does not give the latter a Samaritan origin! Furthermore Haacker's stronger argument, i.e., that there is no reference to the Prophetic writings and to the Hagiographa is not valid. As we shall show it below (ch. VIII,V,D) these parts of Scripture were used in the *Assumption of Moses*. Thus we shall assume for this book a sectarian (and *not* Samaritan) origin. On the Samaritans and their literature see: Moses Gaster, *The Samaritans. Their History, Doctrines and Literature*, Schweich Lecture 1923, London, 1925; *Samaritan Oral Law and Ancient Tradition*, vol. I, London, 1932; John MacDonald, *Memar Marqah. The Teaching of Marqah*, 2 vols., Berlin, 1963; and *The Theology of the Samaritans*, Philadelphia, 1964. (The latter work includes extensive bibliography on Samaritan studies).

writings which clearly emerged out of these two groups and which can be dated in the period with which we are concerned.

Thus we can list the following Apocalyptic books in an approximate chronological order:[3]

a) I Enoch (from 163 B.C. onward).[4]
b) The Book of Jubilees (*circa* 153-105 B.C.).[5]
c) The Sibylline Oracles Book III (from *circa* 150 B.C. onward to the first century A.D.).[6]
d) The Testaments of the Twelve Patriarchs (latter part of the second century B.C., yet with Christian interpolations).[7]
e) The Psalms of Solomon (between 70 and 30 B.C.).[8]

---

[3] We are following the dating given by contemporary scholars who took into account the discovery of the Dead Sea Scrolls rather than the classical dates given by R. H. Charles in his basic work: *The Apocrypha and Pseudepigrapha of the Old Testament*, Oxford, 1913.

[4] This is a composite work which can be dated as follows according to M. Rist, "Enoch", *I.D.B.*, vol. II, 103ff.:
Introduction 1-5 (*circa* 150-100 B.C.).
Book I: Angels and Universe 6-36 (*circa* 100 B.C.).
Book II: Similitudes 37-71 (*circa* 100-80 B.C.) in spite of Milik, *Dix ans de decouverte dans le Desert de Juda*, Paris, 1957, 31, and Dupont-Sommer, *Les Ecrits Esseniens decouverts pres de la Mer Morte*, Paris, 1959, 312: the argument *a silentio* (no fragments of this part of Enoch have been found among the Dead Sea Scrolls) by J. T. Milik is not adequate.
Book III: Heavenly Luminaries 72-82 (150-100 B.C.).
Book IV: Dream visions 83-90 (163-130 B.C.).
Book V: Admonitions ot Righteousness 91-105 (100-80 B.C. with the exception of the so-called "Apocalypse of Weeks" therein 93:1-10; 91:12-17, to be dated *circa* 163 B.C.).
Conclusions 106-108 (100-80 B.C.).

[5] Cf. S. Tedesche, "Book of Jubilees", *I.D.B.*, vol. II, 1002ff.

[6] Cf. D. S. Russell, *The Method and Message of Jewish Apocalyptic*, Philadelphia, 1964, 54ff.

[7] Cf. M. Smith, "Testaments of the Twelve Patriarchs", *I.D.B.*, vol. IV, 575ff., and Russell, *op. cit.*, 55ff.

[8] Cf. P. Winter, "Psalms of Solomon", *I.D.B.*, vol. III, 958ff. On their "sectarian" (rather than Pharisaic) origin cf. J. O'Dell, "The religious background of the Psalms of Solomon", *R.Q.* III, 1961, 241-58.

f) The Assumption of Moses (A.D. 6-30).[9]
g) The life of Adam and Eve (or The Apocalypse of Moses), (shortly before A.D. 70).[10]

The rest of the Jewish Apocalyptic literature (*viz*. the Apocalypse of Abraham, The Testament of Abraham, II Enoch, the rest of the Sibylline Oracles, II Esdras, also called IV Ezra, II Baruch and III Baruch) are of later date and need not be considered in our study. We will have sufficient evidence from the texts falling within our period.[11]

At least three of the Apocalyptic works were in the possession of the Dead Sea Covenanters. Thus, fragments of at least nine manuscripts of the *Book of Jubilees* (in its Hebrew original) were found among the remnants of their library. In the same way, fragments were discovered from at least eleven manuscripts (in its Aramaic original) of the *Book of Enoch*, fragments corresponding to four of the five parts of this composite work.[12] To these should be added fragments of the Testaments of Levi (in Aramaic) and of Naphtali (in Hebrew): thus at least these two parts of the *Testament of the Twelve Patriarchs* were in the possession of the Covenanters.

The fact that these books were found among the Dead Sea Scrolls does not mean that we should ascribe the authorships of these books to the Covenanters: it points out simply the close affinity of this group with the Apocalyptists. Among the Dead Sea Scrolls were also found works which had their origin in this or similar communities and which were altogether unknown before 1947.

We shall list the most important of these writings (with their abbreviations) according to their different uses of Scripture. Four categories will suffice: A. Texts written

---

[9] Cf. M. Rist, "Assumption of Moses", *I.D.B.*, vol. III, 450ff.

[10] Cf. B. J. Bamberger, "Books of Adam", *I.D.B.*, vol. I, 44ff.

[11] We are not excluding the possibility that they contain traditions which are the results of earlier interpretations of Scripture.

for the needs of the community. These, we shall see, make constant use of Scripture, although most of the time implicitly. B. The commentaries that is, the so-called *Pesharim*, to which we shall add a few other exegetical works. C. The more specifically Apocalyptic books. D. What we could call the "re-writings" of Scripture.

A. Texts written for the needs of the community.
- Manual of Discipline: 1 QS[13] and its two annexes:
- The Rule of the Congregation: 1 QSa
- The Scroll of Benedictions: 1 QSb
- The Thanksgiving Hymns: 1 QH

To which we may add:
- The Prayer for the Feast of Weeks: 1 Q 34 and 34bis
- and The Zadokite Documents: CD

B. Commentaries.
- The Pesher on Habakkuk: 1 Qp Hab.
- The Pesher on Isaiah: 4 Qp Isa.
- The Pesher on Micah: 1 Qp Mic. (1 Q 14)
- The Pesher on Nahum: 4 Qp Nah.
- The Pesher on Hosea: 4 Qp Hos.
- The Pesher on Psalm 37: 4 Qp Ps. 37
- The Pesher on Zephaniah: 1 Qp Zeph. (1 Q 15)

To which we may add:
- The Florilegium: 4 Q Florilegium
- The testimonia: 4 Q Test.
- The Patriarchal Blessings: 4 Q Patriarchal Blessings

C. Apocalyptic Books.
- The War of the Sons of Lights with the Sons of Darkness: 1 QM
- The Prayer of Nabodinus: 4 Q Prayer of Nabodinus
- The Book of Mysteries: 1 Q Myst. (1 Q 27)

D. Re-writings of Scripture.
- The Genesis Apocryphon (which is actually a Targum): 1 Q Gen. Apoc.

---

[12] Cf. Dupont-Sommer, *op. cit.*, 307-18.

[13] The number at the beginning of the abbreviation designates the cave in which the manuscript was found.

- The Sayings of Moses: QDM (1 Q 22). This is a re-writing of Deuteronomy.[14]

Such are our sources. As far as their dates are concerned, they present less difficulties than the sources of our first part, and their volume is relatively smaller, although still quite sufficient. Therefore, as earlier, we shall limit ourselves to a number of representative examples which will allow us to point out the main characteristics of the sectarian uses of Scripture.

We shall deal successively with the Apocalyptic books as a whole and then with the Dead Sea Scrolls. Yet before that we need make a few remarks about the eschatological dimension which can be found to a greater or lesser extent in each of these.

ESCHATOLOGY AND APOCALYPTICISM

In order to avoid any confusion let us define briefly the way in which we shall use the terms eschatology and apocalypticism.[15] "Eschatology" is derived from τὸ ἔσχατον or τὰ ἔσχατα: it refers therefore to doctrines about "the last things", i.e., either to the fate of the individual after death or in a collective sense to the fate of the whole world "at the end of time" (e.g., destruction of the world, general resurrection, judgment and establishment of the Kingdom of God . . .). Such is the traditional meaning of the word, that we shall use rather than its modern use by Bultmann and his followers, who stress the existential decision involved in the eschatological attitude.[16]

---

[14] This list does not pretend to be exhaustive. Together with numerous fragments we have left aside scrolls which are not relevant to our research, for instance the Copper Scroll.

[15] The following are proposed as working definitions. We do not pretend to deal with all the aspects of Eschatology and Apocalypticism, in a few lines. On this topic, besides the works quoted below, see the bibliography given by D. S. Russell, *op. cit.*

[16] Cf. e.g., Bultmann, *Jesus and the Word*, New York, 1934, *passim*, and especially his introduction.

"Apocalypticism" is derived from ἀποκάλυψις: revelation. In the Apocalyptic literature "the last things" are *revealed*. This is expressed either directly in descriptions of the world's end or indirectly by reference to "mysteries" concerning the origin of the world, and its history. These eschatological transcendental "mysteries" allowed the Apocalyptists to deduce what would be the nature of the end time and why it would be such. Apocalyptism is therefore characterized by a specific set of eschatological doctrines both explicit and implicit. Yet the term is frequently used to denote the characteristic features of Apocalyptic literature, *viz*. the colorful symbolism which is used in often detailed descriptions of the end time. It includes, for instance, the description of the huge catastrophes which will herald the divine judgment, and a developed angelology. In this latter "literary" sense the term "Apocalypticism" often carries a negative connotation in which emphasis is given to its fanciful character.[17]

Unless otherwise specified we shall use the term "Apocalypticism" in order to refer to the sectarian Judaism which is presented in the Apocalyptic literature. Thus the phrase "Apocalyptic use of Scripture" will mean the use of Scripture found in this literature. When we speak of the "Apocalyptic" character of such or such a passage in another body of literature we shall refer to its similarities, either in literary genre or otherwise, with the Apocalyptic books. Our use of this terminology is therefore purely pragmatic and does not intend to imply what is the fundamental character of Apocalypticism.

According to these conventions only a number of the Covenanters' writings can be said to be Apocalyptic, although their literature as a whole, as well as the Apocalyptic literature, can be qualified as eschatological. What they have in common (and what distinguishes them from the literature of classical Judaism) is a view of history. This appears clearly in the Apocalyptic books: the "revelation"

---

[17]Cf. *inter alios*, J.B. Frey, "Apocalyptique", *S.D.B.* I, 1928, col. 350f.

contained therein concerns past history, "present" situations (i.e., present to the writer) and future events in which God is said to be acting (directly or indirectly by means of angels). For indeed history is understood as led by God toward a predetermined *telos*: the establishement of the divine Kingdom.[18] In the same way that God acted in "past" history, he is acting "now", in the present of the writers, in the "salient" history (rather than in the history of cultural changes). The events of their time were meaningful. They were heading toward the supreme goal of history, even if in mysterious ways which required a "revelation" to understand them. The Apocalyptists and the Covenanters were therefore aware of God's activity in their "present" salient history: they believed the "eschaton" was imminent. They lived in the last days (in the last generation): the events which they foretold were coming in the near future. How near a future? It varied according to the writers. But for all of them their "present" history belonged to the last stages of history's course.[19]

Thus the eschatology which we find in these Jewish sectarian writings was not a mere doctrine, as in classical Judaism: it was also a consciousness which appeared during the desperate period of the Maccabeans' war. This eschatological consciousness commanded their uses of Scripture in many ways and it was reflected in them.

---

[18] But the phrase "Kingdom of God" is used in an eschatological sense, to our knowledge, only in the *Sibylline Oracles*, book III, 767, and *Assumption of Moses* 10:1. For the use of this phrase in Apocalyptic Judaism and in the Dead Sea Scrolls, see the remarks by O. Betz in *What do we know about Jesus?*, London, 1968, 33ff.

[19] For a more precise exposition of this concept of history see below.

CHAPTER VIII

THE USE OF SCRIPTURE IN APOCALYPTIC LITERATURE

LIMITATIONS FOR OUR STUDY

We mentioned that the Apocalyptic literature allows for relatively precise dating. These texts offer in this regard fewer difficulties than the sources we used for the study of classical Judaism. Yet they present other problems which limit research into their use of Scripture.

First, with the exception of a few fragments, they are known to us only in various translations (ranging from Ethiopian to Greek and Latin), and even sometimes in translations of translations. This fact alone limits our study. Reading the homilies, the Targum and the Midrash in their original language, we saw how subtle were the hints which allowed us to understand the mechanisms of their interpretations of Scripture. A translation (not to speak of multiple translations) at best will cover up these hints and at worst dismiss them, especially when the relationship with Scripture is no longer the concern of the translator. Thus it will be quite difficult to grasp the precise relationship between these texts and the biblical text which they either imply o r interpret in "haggadic-like" developments. Because of this we shall not be able to show as precisely as before the logic inherent in their use of Scripture. Yet after what we have learned of classical Judaism, we are not ready to consider these writings the product of the mere fancy of the Apocalyptists. This hypothesis would be considerably weaker in our view than the conjecture that they used Scripture according to a logic similar to that used by classical Judaism, however different their purposes. For indeed the term "sectarian" should not mislead us. Although not the official teaching of the Synagogue,[1] Apocalyptic Judaism was not strictly separated from it. Apocalyptic-minded people were participating in the Synagogal and Temple worship: this is witnessed in the uprising provoked by the Zealots (Apocalyptists *par excellence*) to prevent the defilement of the Temple.[2] Actually the Apocalyptists did not consider themselves separate from Judaism. They saw themselves rather as the truly faithful part of the Jewish community, as Jews who, because of their extreme piety, were adding not only much stricter halakoth but also special beliefs to the teachings of the Synagogue.[3] This implied indeed a new attitude toward Scripture, yet there is no reason to think that they abandoned such basic exegetical principles as the interpretation of

---

[1] It is quite possible that the Apocalyptic teaching was present in the Synagogue itself: its relative absence in the texts of classical Judaism may be due to its systematic suppression after the failure of the Apocalyptic movement in the disaster of A.D. 70. As we noted earlier the origin of the *Psalms of Solomon* is open to discussion. For indeed besides clear Apocalyptic teaching one can see in it Pharisaic elements. These Psalms can be considered evidence of the overlapping of classical and Apocalyptic Judaism: cf. O'Dell, *op. cit.*, 256-57.

[2] Cf. Josephus, *Ant.* XV, 8, 1-4.

[3] We could say that each of the Apocalyptic groups was an *ecclesiola in ecclesia*. In our view they should be considered similar to the *habhuroth* (the "companies") which are mentioned in the Rabbinic literature. The latter, in spite of an organization which allowed them to be very rigorous in their observance of the Law, were not cut off from the Synagogue, so that we may compare them more readily to the Apocalyptists than to the Covenanters, who were strictly separated. The latter comparison has been made by S. Liebermann, "The Discipline in the so-called Dead Sea Manual of Discipline", *J.B.L.*, 1952, 199-206, and more extensively by G. Vermes, *Les Manuscrits du Desert de Juda*, Paris, 1953, 53-57.

Scripture by Scripture, and the tallying of different texts by verbal similarities. Nevertheless as mentioned, this is very difficult to establish.

A second limitation (which may explain the relative vagueness of the preceding comments) is due to the fact that we have very little information about the *Sitz im Leben* of this literature. Although it is clear that its emergence was connected with the Maccabean war and the Zealot movement, we have no precise information about the life of these Apocalyptic groups, nor about how these texts were used. Practically all we can say concerning the *Sitz im Leben* of these texts is that they were used in a community, or rather several little groups, which were characterized by the eschatological consciousness we described earlier.

To say that the Apocalyptic books may have been read by these groups in some kind of worship setting like the Scripture-reading in the Synagogue, as Hartmann has proposed,[4] is mere conjecture. At any rate besides the broad statement that these books had their origin in a *milieu* characterized by an eschatological consciousness, it is clear that we cannot assume the same *Sitz im Leben* for all of them; we cannot do so, if for no other reason, because of doctrinal differences which often do not allow any systematization,[5] and because of the various dates of these books. The impossibility of grasping precisely the *Sitz im Leben* of these texts is a second important limitation for our research.

A third limitation is due to the fact that this literature does not express any explicit doctrine of Scripture which could give us a starting point.[6]

---

[4] Cf. Lars. Hartmann, *Prophecy Interpreted. The Formation of some Jewish Apocalyptic Texts and of the Eschatological Discours of Mark. 13 Par.*, Lund-Sweden, 1966. 52.

[5] e.g. the angelologies cannot be systematized because of irreconciliable differences. D. S. Russell, *The Method and Message of Jewish Apocalyptic*, Philadelphia, 1964, 240f.

[6] The only exception is the repeated mention of the "tables of the Law" and the "heavenly Tables" (see below), if we can consider these mentions an explicit doctrine of Scripture.

These three limitations are quite a handicap. Happily they do not exist for the Dead Sea Scrolls, which are, as we mentioned, of a similar nature. Looking forward to a more detailed study of the use of Scripture in the Dead Sea Scrolls, we shall deal with the use of Scripture in the Apocalyptic literature in a synthetic way. Such an approach is legitimate in that our purpose, as said above, is the discovery of the axioms which govern the use of Scripture in this body of literature.

We shall certainly take into account the different literary genres: "re-writing" of Scripture (as in the *Book of Jubilees*); testament-form and pseudonymous-form (as in the *Testaments of the Twelve Patriarchs*, the *Book of Enoch* . . .); the hymnic form (as in the *Psalms of Solomon*); the visionary genre (found in most of the Apocalyptic writings).[7] As far as is possible in view of the limitations mentioned above, we shall point out their significance for an understanding of the axioms which govern the use of Scripture by the Apocalyptists. Yet we shall have to leave open the interpretation of several genres. We cannot, therefore, structure our presentation exclusively on the genres.

Taking advantage of our study of classical Judaism, we shall first investigate the Apocalyptic literature with two questions in mind:

1) Is there in the Apocalyptic literature something similar to the relationship we observed in classical Judaism between Written Torah and Oral Torah?

2) What is the relationship between "history" and Scripture in Apocalyptic Judaism?

These two questions will allow us to enter into the Apocalyptic literature and to indicate how Scripture is used in some of its literary genres. We shall point out a) the broad biblical patterns which are used to structure the

---

[7] We list here only the main Apocalyptic literary genres. These literary genres are often found combined in the same Apocalyptic book, although each of these books may be characterized as predominantly belonging to one or the other.

Apocalyptic writings; b) the significance of pseudonymity for our topic; c) the "anthological" and "structural" style of the visionary passages.

In conclusion we shall attempt to deal with the topic: visions, inspiration, and Scripture.

I

TRADITION, ORAL TORAH, AND APOCALYPTICISM

We shall begin our study by using the *Book of Jubilees* as fully as possible, for it has the advantage of being explicitly connected with specific Scriptural passages. We shall assume that the main axioms underlying the use of Scripture in this book are valid for the other Apocalyptic books, although there they are less readily discernible.

SIMILARITIES WITH THE TARGUMIC USE OF SCRIPTURE

The *Book of Jubilees*[8] can be called a haggadic commentary,[9] in spite of the fact that it also contains many halakic developments. Here as in the Targum one purpose of this "re-writing" of Scripture (in this case Genesis and Exodus) is clearly didactic if not homiletic. It expands the text in order to uncover moral teachings[10] and in order to

---

[8] For translation see "The Book of Jubilees" in R. H. Charles (ed.), *Apocrypha and Pseudepigrapha*, Cambridge, Mass., 1913, vol. II, 1-82. We shall quote from this translation.

[9] "Ein haggadischer Commentar zum biblischen Texte", E. Schürer, *Geschichte Des Jüdischen Volkes im Zeitalter Jesu Christi*, Leipzig, 1898, vol. III. 274.

[10] This is also one of the characteristics of the *Testaments of the Twelve Patriarchs*. We are not dealing extensively with this book because of the great similarity of its content with the *Book of Jubilees*. Furthermore the study of this text is complicated by the delicate problem of the Christian interpolations. On this see Charles, *The Greek Versions of the Twelve Patriarchs*, Oxford, 1908 (and especially his important introduction); M. De Jonge, *The Testaments of the Twelve Patriarchs*, Assen, Netherlands, 1953 (who ascribes to this book a Christian origin!), and his more balanced article, "Christian Influence in the Testaments of the Twelve Patriarchs", *Nov. Test.* 4, 1960, 222ff.; and M. Philonenko, *Les interpolations chrétiennes des Testaments des Douze Patriarches et les manuscrits de Qoumrân*, Cah. Rev. Hist. Phil. Rel. 35, Paris, 1960.

explain those difficulties which the biblical text presented for the author and his group.

For instance, in order to avoid any hint of Jacob's being a liar, the author made him answer only "I am thy son" instead of "I am Esau thy first born".[11] In the same way, commenting on Gen. 27:3, "and he (Isaac) discerned him not", the author adds "because it was a dispensation from heaven to remove his power of perception":[12] this was no longer a deception of Isaac by Jacob but by God. Thus Jacob could be a moral type for the readers of the *Book of Jubilees*. This is true also of the other Patriarchs, who were depicted like him as carrying out all the commandments before their promulgation at Sinai. Let us take only one example of this latter characteristic: the laws of purification after the birth of a child, Lev. 12:2-5, are carried out even for the creation (birth!) of Adam and Eve. They are brought into the Garden of Eden (a holy place like the Temple) only after the period of purification required by the Levitical laws, the origin of which is explained by this, their first application.[13]

This point toward a first difference[14] with the Targum: the rigor with which the commandments were interpreted. Thus not only was the Levitical law prohibiting fornication by a priest's daughter (Lev. 21:9) now applied to any daughter of Israel, but also her marriage with a heathen was considered to be fornication. To give one's daughter in marriage to a heathen was considered giving her "to Moloch" (Lev. 20:2).

---

[11] Cp. Jub. 26:13 and Gen. 27:18.

[12] Jub. 26:18, cp. also 26:19 with Gen. 27:24.

[13] Cf. Jub. 3:8-14.

[14] The pre-eminence given to Jacob is also sometimes found in Tannaitic literature: God chose Israel when he chose Jacob, cf. *Sifra* on Deut. 32:9, Pisqa 312. Cf. also E. Mihaly, *op. cit.*

Consequently such a man should be stoned to death and his daughter "burnt with fire".[15]

We should have to multiply these examples of "haggadic" and halakic developments if our purpose were to compare the *teachings* found in classical Judaism with those in the *Book of Jubilees*.[16] Yet in our case this could not give us any new insights on the use of Scripture which we called "re-writing". Let us note simply that despite the fact that we are often faced with quite divergent interpretations, especially in halakic matters,[17] we find here a similar attitude toward the biblical text, together with similar exegetical techniques (especially the interpretation of Scripture by Scripture).[18] The Apocalyptic re-writings of Scripture were didactic, i.e., they aimed at making possible the embodying of Scripture by believers. As we saw, this was also one of the characteristics of the interpretation of Scripture in the Synagogal liturgigal setting. This suggests that the Apocalyptic re-writings have a "liturgical *function*" (yet this phrase does not imply a formal liturgical setting), although

---

[15]Cf. Jub. 30:7-17: "If there is any man who wishes in Israel to give his daughter or his sister to any man who is of the seed of the Gentiles he shall surely die, and they shall stone him with stone . . . and they shall burn the woman with fire" (7). The sin of the man is further explained: "he has given of his seed to Moloch" (10). In the same way, as mentioned also in this text, adultery will be strictly punished by the death of both adulterers.

[16]On this see L. Finkelstein, "The Book of Jubilees and the Rabbinic Halakah", *Harvard Theological Review* XVI, 1922, 39-61, and the remarks of S. Zeitlin in "The Book of Jubilees, its Character and its Significance", *J.Q.R.* XXX, 1939, 1-31.

[17]Yet, let us emphasize that in haggadic matters the *Book of Jubilees* reflects often similar traditions to those found later on in classical Judaism. On this see G. Vermès, *Scripture and Tradition*, 81, 84ff., 97f., 116, 119, 183ff., 197, 209, 215.

[18]Here the tallying of different biblical texts by means of verbal similarities is less clear, either because we have the *Book of Jubilees* only in an Ethiopic translation of the Greek translation of the Hebrew original (and I should add that since the Ethiopic language is unknown to me, I had to read an English translation!) or, and this is probable, because the tallying was done more often by means of *themes* than in classical Judaism.

the divergence in specific interpretations emphasizes that other factors have to be taken into account: these factors, alone, will help us to understand the rigor of halakic interpretations.

Before doing so let us stress that under the influence of the traditions and beliefs of the community for which he wrote,[19] the author of the *Book of Jubilees* emphasized certain of the characteristics of the targumic interpretations of Scripture: especially giving dates to biblical events and telescoping the sacred history.

We found in the Targum a tendency to give a date to the different biblical events in order that they might fit the religious calendar of the Synagogue. Here this practice has become one of the major preoccupations of the author, to such an extent that the complete calendar which he used can be rebuilt from the elements we find in the *Book of Jubilees*.[20] Without going into any discussion of the particularities of this solar calendar (as opposed to the lunar calendar used in classical Judaism), we need to emphasize two of its characteristics: a) As A. Jaubert and J. Morgenstern showed, traces of this calendar can be found in the biblical text itself. It was not therefore merely read into Scripture. b) Further and characteristically for the *Book of Jubilees*, this religious calendar was expanded to the whole of history, which was divided into jubilees. Just as the basic unit of the

---

[19] Dupont-Sommer has suggested (*op. cit.*, 307ff.) that it was the Qumran Community or at least an early form of this sect. Cf. also Michel Testuz, *Les idées religieuses du Livre des Jubilés*, Geneve, Paris, 1960, which brings forth several pieces of evidence in favor of this thesis.

[20] On this see A. Jaubert, "Le calendrier des Jubilés et de la secte de Qumran; ses origines bibliques", *V.T.* III, 1953, 250-64; "Le calendrier des Jubilés et les jours liturgiques de la semaine", *V.T.* VII, 1957, 35-61; and *La date de la Cène*, Paris, 1957, especially the first part entitled, "Un calendrier juif ancien"; J. Morgenstern, "The Calendar of the Book of Jubilees, its Origin and its Character", *V.T.* V, 1955, 34-76; E. Wiesenberg, "The Jubilee of Jubilees", *R.Q.* 3, 1961, 3-40; and the comprehensive study by J. van Goudoever, *Biblical Calendars*, Leiden, 1961, *passim*. A similar calendar is to be found in the *Testaments of the Twelve Patriarchs* and in *I Enoch*, as is pointed out by these scholars. See, for instance, for the former, A. Jaubert, *La date de la Cène*, 56ff. and *passim*. For the latter, 19 and *passim*.

calendar was the week of seven days,[21] so the years were computed by "weeks of years", by jubilees (seven "weeks of years", i.e., 49 years),[22] and by "jubilee of jubilees"[23] (i.e., 49 times 49 years). The "jubilee of jubilees" was especially holy; it was the opening of a new era. Thus it had been on such a "jubilee of jubilees" that the Torah was given to Moses on Mt Sinai,[24] and Israel was to spend this holy jubilee "learning the commandments of the Lord".[25] Furthermore Moses was said to have received the revelation of "all the divisions of the days in the law and in the testimony", and of "the weeks and the jubilees unto eternity, until I descend and dwell with them throughout eternity".[26] When will the Lord come to dwell with his people? This is not specified, yet it can be understood that it will be in the following "jubilee of jubilees", since the jubilees after the reception of Torah were described as follows:

> "And the jubilees shall pass by, until Israel is cleansed from all guilt and fornication, and uncleanness and pollution, and sin and error, and dwells with confidence in all the land and there shall be no Satan or any evil one, and the land shall be clean from that time for evermore".(27)

---

[21] The year had exactly fifty two weeks, i.e., 364 days as it is explicitly stated in Jub. 6:30 and 38.

[22] And not 50 years as in the Pentateuch where these concepts are used: cf. e.g., Lev. 25. The "years of jubilee" of the Pentateuch was, therefore, for the author of the *Book of Jubilees* not the end of the period but already the first year of the next one.

[23] Cf. Jub. 2:30.

[24] Jub. 50:4.

[25] *Ibid.*

[26] Jub. 1:26, cf. also 1:29.

[27] Jub. 50:5.

THE "TABLES OF THE LAW AND OF TESTIMONY" AND THE "HEAVENLY TABLES"

The interpretation of Scripture in terms of this "Jubilee Calendar" appears to find its roots in the author's belief about the "Heavenly Tables". This belief was based on mentions in the Book of Exodus (24:12; 31:18; 34:1) of the two Tables which were given to Moses. These two Tables of the Law are called Tables of the testimony (העדח) in Exod. 31:18. It is to be noted first that in the *Book of Jubilees* these Tables appear to have been interpreted as containing not only the Law but also the secrets of the whole history of the world. How the author (or this community) reached this conclusion cannot be pointed out with certainty. We can conjecture that in Exod. 31:18 the word עדח (reminder, testimony) could have been interpreted in terms of the word עד, which is from the same root (עוד) and has the double connotation of "witness", עד (thus referring to the past) and of "everlasting time", עד (thus referring also to the future). It is possible that עדח was understood with a similar double connotation, i.e., as testimony not only of the past but also of the future.[28] At any rates it is clear in the *Book of Jubilees* as well as in *I Enoch* and the *Testaments of the Twelve Patriarchs* that "the tables of the testimony" were interpreted as being "heavenly Tables" containing the secrets of world history.[29] That it was so can be seen, for instance, in the very introductory chapter of the *Book of Jubilees* where, after the quoting of Exod. 24:12 and 18, we read: "and God taught him (Moses) the earlier and the later history of the divisions of all the days of the law and of the testimony".[30] Then Moses is said to

---

[28] Besides its meaning of "witness" עד was frequently used with the "everlasting time" connotation. It is to be noted that in the Dead Sea Scrolls עד was used almost exclusively in this latter sense: cf. K. G. Kuhn, *Konkordanz zu den Qumrantexte*, Göttingen, 1960, 155f.

[29] Cf. *I Enoch* 81:2; 93:2; 106:19; 107:1; 108:7, *passim*. *Test. of Asher* 2:10; 7:5; *Test. of Levi* 5:4.

[30] Jub. 1:4.

have received the revelation of the history of Israel from its beginning up to the time of the writer.[31] Furthermore it is mentioned that the rest of the history of the world was also revealed to Moses.[32] The author specified even that these revelations were copied down from the "Heavenly Tables" by Moses, who wrote under the dictation of the "Angel of the Presence". These revelations could therefore be more or less identified with the "Heavenly Tables".[33] Thus according to the *Book of Jubilees* the revelation to Moses on Sinai had a twofold aspect: it was on the one hand the Law *and* on the other hand the secrets of history from its beginning to its end. Thus Scripture, here primarily the Pentateuch, Moses' writings, must be read not only in order to learn the commandments, moral teachings and ritual laws which must be carried out to satisfy the demands of God, but also in order to learn the mysteries of history. We should emphasize here that it was not merely the mysteries of past history, but also those of present and future history which were thus revealed.

WRITTEN AND ORAL TOROTH
VERSUS OPEN AND SECRET REVELATIONS

It appears also that the two tables "of the law and testimony" were not coextensive with the "Heavenly Tables".

---

[31] It is to be noted that Jub. 1:7-25 and 28 are possibly an interpolation which would refer, according to M. Testuz (*op. cit.*, 39ff.) to events after the redaction of the *Book of Jubilees* (*circa* 110 B.C.), *viz.* up to the middle of the first century B.C. This interpolation removed, the meaning of the text remains the same: the history of Israel is simply presented in a shorter form.

[32] Jub. 1:26-27 and 29.

[33] We cannot say that they were completly identified with them, as will be explained below. Let us note the parallelism between this conception of Scripture as "Heavenly Tables" and what we said about the concept of the "pre-existing Torah" in classical Judaism. Yet they did not have the same content. The "pre-existing Torah" did not include the secrets of history (at least as far as this concept was understood during the period we are considering; later on this concept became more complex: cf. *Ber. Rab.* 1:1). It was nothing but the Torah which was revealed to Moses; it was either written down or transmitted orally and *openly*, cf. above.

The latter were actually seven.[34] Nevertheless they were totally revealed to Moses and also to Jacob[35] and the other Patriarchs.[36]

Can we conclude that we have here a distinction similar to the one which we found in classical Judaism? In one sense this is indeed the case. Just as besides the Written Torah there was the Oral Torah which was received by Moses on Mt Sinai, so for the author of the *Book of Jubilees* besides the Written Scripture (containing the laws and the revelation of the secrets of history) was another revelation which was also given to Moses.[37] Yet we find here not a distinction between written and oral revelations, but rather one between the common revelation (open to anybody) and the secret revelation which was to be found in "secret books" like the *Book of Jubilees*[38] and which was reserved for specific circles of people (*viz.* circles of especially pious people). Like the common revelation (Scripture), these "secret books" contained the twofold revelation of laws and secrets of history. Thus the *Book of Jubilees* introduced not only new elements about the secrets of history, but also new laws: for instance there is mentioned the otherwise unknown law about covering one's nakedness.[39]

---

[34] Jub. 32:21-22.

[35] *Ibid.*

[36] Thus at least implicitly, Jub. ch. 20, 21, and 22 present Abraham just before his death as having knowledge of the future of Israel.

[37] This very parallelism between Oral Torah and secret revelation can be found in IV Ezra 14. Cf. the interpretation of this passage by D. S. Russell, *op. cit.*, 85ff.

[38] Let us not forget that the *Book of Jubilees* was presented as consisting of these revelations given to Moses. Cf. Jub. ch. 1 and also ch. 2:1 and 50:13. Several other books containing these secret revelations are also referred to as having been written by Enoch (Jub. 4:17; 21:10), Noah (10:13; 21:10), and Jacob (32:26; 45:16). The just mentioned "Book of Enoch" was certainly not the book which we have, yet possibly a first version of it.

[39] Jub. 3:30-32.

One may be tempted to point out the similarities between these "secret revelations" and the Oral Torah. And indeed they are worth emphasizing if one does not forget to point out also the radical differences.

Thus just as Scripture was to be read in terms of the Oral Torah which had an authority comparable to Scripture, so for the Apocalyptists, Scripture was to be read in terms of these secret revelations, whose authority, again, was comparable to that of Scripture.

The fact that the Oral Torah and the secret revelations of the Apocalyptists had a comparable relationship to Scripture explains why, in spite of their different contents, they can find expression in a similar literary genre. As noted earlier, the *Book of Jubilees* can be compared on this ground with the Midrash and the Targum. Like the Sages the author does not appear to have thought that he was expressing anything more than what was implicit in Scripture. By definition the Oral Torah could not contradict Scripture, nor could the secret revelations. The author of the *Book of Jubilees* did not fear therefore to refer his reader to the first "Law".[40]

APOCALYPTICISM AND THE "HISTORY OF CULTURAL CHANGES"

We can compare further the ways in which the Sages and the Apocalyptists used Oral Torah and secret revelations respectively for the interpretation of Scripture by asking: what was the role of cultural changes in the Apocalyptic literature?

---

[40] Jub. 6:22. Cf. on this point Charles, *op. cit.*, vol. II, (introduction to the *Book of Jubilees*), 1 and 7. There is no need to argue with Spiro (*op. cit., passim*) that such a re-writing was possible because the text of Scripture was not accessible to the common people, who could not therefore compare the re-writing with the biblical original. Moreover such an argument has no bearing on sects like the Qumran Covenanters where the accessibility of Scripture is well attested. As mentioned, it is probable that the *Book of Jubilees* found its origin in a similar circle.

From our stand point the *Book of Jubilees* appears to result from a reading of Scripture through spectacles colored by a tradition which was much influenced by cultural elements. Yet we should add right away: *unconsciously* influenced. For indeed such a statement is going against one of the most important characteristics of the *Book of Jubilees*: its radical rejection of any ideas, customs, practices which could have originated in the heathen culture which surrounded the author and his community. What good can come from heathen people when one knows that they are subjected to the demons and their chief Mastema (i.e., Beliar or Satan).[41] They are nothing but corruption and wickedness. All their sciences are nothing but errors, ignorance and abominations.[42] Thus the author of the *Book of Jubilees* exhorted his readers to despise the other nations and their culture:

> "Separate thyself from the nations, and eat not with them; and do not according to their works, and become not their associate; for their works are unclean, and all their ways are pollution and abomination and uncleanness".(43)

This strict separation from the Gentiles included also a separation from those Israelites who followed their ways by following the calendar of the Gentiles.[44] They were assimilated to the Gentiles for they excluded themselves from the Covenant.[45] Who were these unfaithful Israelites? They can be safely identified not only with those who abandoned the Jewish faith but also with the Pharisees, who not only followed the lunar calendar but were also open to the Hellenistic culture. Thus, far from finding an ultimate meaning in the "history of cultural changes" the Apocalyptists

---

[41] Jub. 10:1, 9-10.

[42] Thus the astrology: cf. Jub. 8:3 and 15:31.

[43] Jub. 22:16.

[44] Cf. Jub. 6:32-38, and especially 35, where are condemned those who "walk according to the feasts of the Gentiles after their error and ignorance".

[45] Killing them is not murder, as can be seen in Jub. 38:2, where the pious and righteous Jacob is said to have killed his brother Esau after his exclusion from the Covenant. Cf. M. Testuz, *op. cit.*, 104-05.

looked at it as meaningless and even as the very manifestation of Evil (symbolized by Mastema).

The very reaction against their contemporary culture led the Apocalyptists to give an absolute authority to a different culture, which influenced Judaism before the Hellenistic period and which they identified with the biblical teaching. Here I allude to the influence that the Persian culture had on Judaism before the Hellenization of the Middle East (thus before 323 B.C.). For indeed it is striking to find in the Apocalyptic literature not only a considerable expansion of the angelology and demonology,[46] but also such dualistic doctrines as the doctrine of the two ways (i.e., the two opposite moral ways in which men live depending on who leads them, the evil spirits or God)[47] and the expectation of an Apocalyptic war during which the forces of evil will be completly destroyed (Jub. 24:29-30). Confronted with these and other facts one cannot but ask if such developments do not reveal the influence of Persian religion, namely Mazdeism. Russell demonstrates that such a Persian influence "can hardly be denied".[48]

Yet in the eyes of the author of the *Book of Jubilees* all these doctrines were not of foreign origin, they were part of the culture of the faithful Israel.[49] Thus despite his aversion for alien influences he interpreted Scripture in

---

[46] It would require a long list to point out all the amplifications of Scripture along this line: cf. for some examples M. Testuz, *op. cit.*, 75-92. This emphasis on angelology and demonology will be seen to have been even greater in other Apocalyptic writings namely *I Enoch* and the *Testaments of the Twelve Patriarchs*.

[47] This doctrine will be much more explicit in the Dead Sea Scrolls, cf. 1 QS 3:13-4:26.

[48] D. S. Russell, *op. cit.*, 19. Cf. also 185, 228f., 239, 258ff., 266, 270f., 281, 347f., for the influence of the Persian religion on specific Apocalyptic teachings.

[49] This might have been due to the fact that Persian ideas were expressed in Aramaic, which was the language of Israel, as opposed to the foreign, heathen Greek. We can conjecture that by reaction against Hellenism all cultural influence which were carried by the Aramaic language were more readily received as part of the Jewish heritage.

terms of these cultural elements and the latter in terms of Scripture.[50] In this he was following what had been done before him by the author of the book of *Daniel*.

When we compare classical Judaism with the *Book of Jubilees* as far as their respective attitudes toward cultural changes, it appears that the reactionary and exclusivist attitude of the author of the *Book of Jubilees* against the Hellenistic culture led him, so to speak, to canonize a former culture. By contrast let us remember the carefully balanced attitude of classical Judaism which affirmed Israel's particularity as a Chosen People in terms of the new cultural situations.

The opposing attitudes toward cultural changes found their roots once again in the different understandings which classical Judaism and Apocalypticism had of the Oral Torah and of the secret revelations respectively. The Oral Torah was not considered a new revelation: the whole, complete and final revelation of the election was contained in the Written Torah. The Oral Torah was only the unfolding of this final revelation in new cultural situations. By contrast, for the Apocalyptists, the "secret revelations" were new revelations, that is revelations not contained in Scripture. Scripture was only one part of the total revelation: only two of the seven Heavenly Tables![51] This is to say that for the Apocalyptists these new revelations were in no sense linked with cultural changes. They were "heavenly secrets" opposed by nature to the "evil" cultural changes. These secrets further revealed the weakness of this "evil generation".

---

[50] e.g., the dualism was strongly attenuated by emphasizing that angels and demons were created by God (Jub. 2:2). They were therefore submitted to God who *allowed* the demons to act after the time of the Flood in order to lead astray the wicked men (Jub. 10:8ff.).

[51] Jub. 32:21-22.

The author of the *Book of Jubilees*, therefore re-wrote Scripture not only in order to uncover the revelation present in it, but also to point out the full meaning of Scripture in the light of the "heavenly secrets". We shall see that this full meaning of Scripture was uncovered by means of typology.[52]

---

[52] It should be noted here that the typological interpretation of Scripture did not comprise the whole process by means of which the secret revelations were uncovered. We shall see that this process included, for the Apocalyptists, visionary experiences: we find indirect references to these in the *Book of Jubilees* in the description of the revelations to the Patriarchs.

II

SCRIPTURE AND HISTORY IN APOCALYPTIC
LITERATURE: TYPOLOGY

If the author of the *Book of Jubilees*, as well as the Apocalyptists in general, rejected any possibility of discovering a positive meaning in the history of cultural changes, he was open to the discovery of a meaning in the "salient " history,[53] even in his contemporary "salient history", which he interpreted with the help of Scripture.

Such an interpretation of contemporary history was clearly not the first preoccupation of our author (since we find it explicitly only in Jub. 23:11-26), yet by his re-writing of Scripture, he was laying down the foundations which allow such an interpretation.

A "COSMOLOGIZATION" OF THE BIBLICAL CONCEPT OF SACRED HISTORY

We already mentioned the interpretation of the two tables "of the law and of testimony" as copied from the "Heavenly Tables". Here we need to emphasize that these Heavenly Tables contained besides additional laws the record of the whole history of the world. They included therefore not only the record of past history,[54] but also that of future history until the establishment of the world to come.[55]

This doctrine implies that the whole course of history

---

[53] Henceforth in our comments on Apocalyptic Judaism, "history" will designate "salient history" unless otherwise stipulated.

[54] And therefore it included the record of the good and evil deeds of each man. This record would be used at the final Judgment. Cf. Jub. 30:21-22.

[55] Cf. Jub. 1:29.

was pre-determined. Thus, certain people could not but be sinners and rejects, and others could not but be faithful and therefore elected.[56] Yet man was nevertheless held responsible for his actions, and would be punished or rewarded accordingly. Thus despite the determinism we just noted man's freedom was affirmed. The following statement in the *Book of Jubilees* illustrates this point: "The judgment of all is ordained and written on the heavenly tablets in righteousness . . . even (the judgment of) all who depart from the path which is ordained for them to walk in" (Jub. 5:13). In this course of history, fixed once and for all, God took into account the wickedness of man. Their sins, corruptions, evil deeds, including their persecutions of the righteous, were parts of God's plan. In this perspective sacred history was viewed as including both these events which could be called "acts of God" and any other events as well. Sacred history was conceived as being coextensive with the whole of history. Any event had a part in it, even the evil deeds of the heathen.[57] What we have here is a "cosmologization" of the notion of sacred history. Even God could not provoke a "surprise" in history, as the biblical God could.[58] This is not to say that we have here a cyclical view of history: there was a *telos*, an end. Yet as we pointed out with regard to the calendar of the *Book of Jubilees*, there were analogies between the different periods of history.

The preceding remarks help us to understand that in the *Book of Jubilees* as well as in other Apocalyptic books the Creation, the Flood, and the events of the Exodus-Sinai were considered as *types* of the eschatological events which either were happening in the Apocalyptists' time or would happen in the near future. Similarly the Patriarchs were presented not only as moral types, but also as the types of the faithful

---

[56] Cf. Jub. 10:5ff.

[57] As D. S. Russell notes, this "deterministic" re-interpretation of the biblical concept of sacred history reflects the influence of Persian culture. *Op. cit.*, 19.

[58] Indeed He gained in power and majesty but He lost His "freedom".

Israel of the end time (they were considered as *prophets* who received the revelation of future history by being allowed to read the heavenly tables).

We need to specify here what we mean by "type" and "typology".[59] Typology is actually a peculiar way of looking at history. In such a perspective the *types* can be persons, institutions or events described by Scripture which are regarded as models or better as prefigurations of persons, institutions or events contemporary with the Apocalyptists, or belonging to the future history.

Let us take as an example the re-writing of the Flood story in the *Book of Jubilees* (ch. 5): this text provides examples of the typological interpretation of a biblical event (the Flood), a person (Noah), and an institution (the feast of the renewal of the Covenant).

The author first followed the text of Genesis (6:1-5) expressing the causes of the corruption of men: "the angels saw that they (the daughters of men) were beautiful to look upon and they took themselves wives of all whom they chose and they bare unto them sons and they were giants. And lawlessness increased on earth. . . ." (Jub. 5:1-2) The biblical text did not elaborate on this lawlessness, except to specify that it was *all* flesh which was corrupted (Gen. 6:12). The *Book of Jubilees* emphasized that also, then continued its presentation. God saw this corruption and decided to destroy mankind except for Noah, who was found to be righteous. Then, strangely enough, the destruction took place not by means of the Flood but by means of a *war*. First, if I interpret this difficult passage correctly, the sons of the angels, i.e., the giants, were slain by the angels themselves (Jub. 5:7). The text continues:

---

[59] On the question of typology see L. Goppelt, *Typos. Die typologische Deutung des Alten Testaments im Neuen*, Gütersloh, 1939; J. Coppens, *Les Harmonies des deux Testaments*, Tournai-Paris, 1949, especially 60-61, and 123; J. Danielou, *Sacramentum futuri*, Paris, 1950. In *Essays on Old Testament Hermeneutics* (ed. by Claus Westermann, Richmond, 1963) see the essays by G. von Rad, "Typological Interpretation of the Old Testament", 17-39, and W. Eichrodt, "Is Typological Exegesis an Appropriate Method?", 224-45. Cf. also C. Downing, "Typology and the Literary Christ Figure", *J.A.A.R.*, 1968, 13-20.

> "He (God) sent his sword into their[60] midst that each
> should slay his neighbour, and they began to slay each
> other till they all fell by the sword and were destroyed
> from the earth. . . . And He *destroyed* all from their
> places, and there *was* not left one of them whom He
> judged not according to all their wickedness. And
> He *made* for all His works a new and righteous nature,
> so that they should not sin in their whole nature for
> ever, but should be all righteous each in his kind
> always. . . ." (Jub. 5:9ff., my italics).

The author went forth from here to the topic of the final judgment. Then the author came back to the biblical text and described, this time, the destruction of the corrupt world by means of the Flood.

This interpretation is quite significant. The original Flood story has been identified typologically with the period preceding the establishment of the divine kingdom at the end of history--that is, with the eschatological punishment and judgment of the wicked. This typological identification was not new; its germ can be found already in Isaiah ch. 24 (where the prophet describes the judgment of God, pointing out that nobody can escape, "for the windows from heaven are open", v. 18) and in other Scriptural passages. Among these is Dan. 9:26, in which war and flood are closely associated in the same way as in our text: "The people of the prince that shall come shall destroy the city and the sanctuary; and the end thereof shall be with a flood (שטף)".[61] In the *Book of Jubilees* (ch. 5) this very identification was made in such a way that one wonders of which "flood" the author is speaking! In the earlier quotation we italicized the verbs "destroyed", "was", "made", all of them in the past tense, indicating the

---

[60]"Their" may designate either the men or the giants! According to the context this war may refer to a war of the giants among themselves. Yet the details of the description seem to refer to men. In this twofold character, the text refers to both wars: the war of the giants and the eschatological war.

[61]Cf. also Isa. 28:14-18 (with the idea of the overflowing wrath of God); Isa. 54:8-9; Ezek. 14:14. On the typology of the Flood see J. Danielou, *Sacramentum futuri. Etudes sur les origines de la typologie biblique*, Paris, 1950, 55-94, and J. P. Lewis, *A Study of the Interpretation of Noah and the Flood in Jewish and Christian Literature*, Leiden, 1968, 7-9 and 10-41.

first flood, but one is tempted with Charles[62] to emend the text in order to introduce the future tense, thus pointing to the eschatological "flood".

What were these wars to which the text refers? In the light of Jub. ch. 1 and 23 and of other Apocalyptic texts, we can safely assume that these were the wars contemporary[63] with our author, which he interpreted as the beginning of the destruction of wickedness on the earth--the beginning of the eschatological war. Reading into the biblical text the interpretation which he had made of his history, he introduced this into the Flood story, which was in his view a prefiguration of the eschatological destruction of the world. Thus again we find an interplay between the biblical text and an element of the life of the author (this time an element of the salient history). Yet it is impossible to distinguish whether he interpreted his history in terms of Scripture or rather Scripture in terms of his history. For him they were not separable: one is the promise, the other is the fulfillment.

Similarly Noah appeared as the type of those who would be saved from the "eschatological flood". He was therefore the moral type to be imitated. Yet he was also the type of the eschatological Israel with which God would renew the Covenant; the eschatological Israel would be a "new Noah".

Still in the same text we have an example of an institution which was presented as a type: the institution of the "feast of oaths"[64] (Jub. 6:17-22). This was the feast of the revewal of the eternal Covenant. This feast had been

---

[62] Cf. *op. cit.*, note on Jub. 5:11-12.

[63] Or belonging to the recent past, the Maccabean wars for example. For the identification of these events, see Charles *ad loc.*

[64] Or feast of weeks. שבועות has the twofold meaning of "weeks" (used by early Rabbinic Judaism: thus "feast of weeks") and "oaths". This latter meaning may be the original one in the *Book of Jubilees*, which does not allude to the seven *weeks* after Passover which gave their name to the feast in early Rabbinic Judaism. On this see M. Testuz, *op. cit.*, 147ff.

celebrated already in Heaven since the Creation.[65] Yet it had been forgotten again and again and reestablished after each historical renewal of the Covenant (Jub. 6:19), *viz.* with Abraham (Jub. 14:18), Jacob (Jub. 25:15-23 and especially 32:18ff.) and Moses (Jub. 1:5ff.; 6:11, *passim*). Its celebration by Noah (as well as its celebration by Abraham, Jacob and Moses) was therefore the type of the reestablishment of the "feast of oaths" in the end time, i.e., in the time of the supreme renewal of the Covenant (Jub. 1:29, *passim*). Thus, as we mentioned earlier about the calendar, these successive renewals of the Covenant, and especially that which took place at Sinai, were presented as the prefigurations of the eschatological renewal.

A LITURGICAL VIEW OF HISTORY

Comparing this typological interpretation of Scripture with our observations about the use of Scripture in the Targum, and especially with the "telescoping" of biblical history, we cannot but be struck by the similarities. In Apocalyptic Judaism we have the same telescoping of history, but this time it involves systematically the contemporary history of the Apocalyptists.[66] We noted that in classical

---

[65] Jub. 6:18.

[66] Yet this does not mean that the Sages and the Apocalyptists lacked a *chronological* sense of history. The elaborate calendar of the *Book of Jubilees* should be a reminder of this. And this is also true of biblical thought, as J. Barr reminded those scholars who, in order to stress the qualitative notion of time, had the tendency, following O. Cullmann (*Christ and Time*, Engl. trans., London, 1951), to deny a chronological understanding of time. Cf. J. Barr, *Biblical Words for Time*, London, 1962, 96, 130f., 144, 153, *passim*, and also *The Semantics of Biblical Language*, Oxford, 1961, 78ff., where he shows that there is no evidence in the Hebrew verbal system for an idea of contemporaneity. Thus we should avoid speaking too easily of a "sense of contemporaneity" characterizing the Hebrew and Jewish way of thinking about time, according to which two events with similar contents (or, to use Boman's phrase, similar "psychological contents") were considered identical regardless of their place in the course of history. Cf. Thorleif Boman, *Das hebraïsche Denken im Vergleich mit dem Griechischen*, Göttingen, 1959, 118-26.

Judaism this telescoping of history was done mainly for a liturgical purpose in the Synagogal setting. In Apocalypticism this liturgical view of history seems to have been used much more extensively: the liturgical calendar became the only valid calendar. It even became the cosmic calendar. This was so not only because such a calendar was written down on the Heavenly Tables (Jub. 50:13, *passim*), but also because it was observed by God himself (Jub. 2:18) and the angels (Jub. 2:17-21).[67] It is as if the emphasis on the liturgical calendar had led the Apocalyptists to consider their whole life almost exclusively in this broad liturgical setting, that is, *in a situation where the essential was the encounter with God*. In such a perspective we could say that the contemporary history of the Apocalyptists was forced into the framework of the liturgical calendar determined by biblical events.[68] The encounters with God in contemporary history were therefore presented by means of biblical historical sequences;[69] one might even say that they were forced into this pattern. Contemporary events were molded in order to fit the biblical models. In this way they lost their specificity but received a meaning. On the other hand, the biblical types were enriched by the new events in which they were embodied: instead of a vague type, each became a concrete reality with the complexity and precision of a multitude of details.

Thus when compared with the telescoping of history in classical Judaism, there is only one essential difference: the synthetic sacred history of the Apocalyptic texts also included the history contemporary to the Apocalyptists. And yet, even this fact is not totally new. For indeed, as we pointed out, the classical Judaism synthetic sacred history included, in addition to the biblical sacred history, the

---

[67] Cf. also *I Enoch* ch. 72-82.

[68] As we saw, it was not only a yearly calendar but also a division of the whole course of history into periods (jubilees).

[69] Cf. Barr, *Biblical Words for Time*, 144, where he follows W. Eichrodt, "Heilserfahrung und Zeitverständnis im Alten Testament", *T.Z.* XII, 1956, 103-25.

events of the eschatological time. This was so also for the Apocalyptists. The difference is found, of course, in the fact that for classical Judaism the eschatological time was considered as totally belonging to the future, and that, by contrast, for Apocalyptic Judaism the eschatological time was already present (this was the "last generation"). Because of this eschatological consciousness[70] the typological interpretation of Scripture systematically involved the contemporary history of the Apocalyptists.

As a consequence the sacred history was no longer closed (until the ever-future eschatological time); in the same way that God Acted in the biblical history, he Acts in the present of the Apocalyptists. These are revelatory Acts of God, i.e., Acts in which God reveals anew what was revealed in the biblical sacred history *viz.* the election and vocation of His people. For classical Judaism, this revelation of the identity of the Chosen People was totally expressed in the Bible. The Jewish community received this identity in its worship which was structured by Scripture. Scripture was the necessary system of reference by means of which the community could discover its identity as Chosen People. The liturgy, whose function was precisely to allow the community to discover and then to embody this revealed identity was therefore structured by Scripture and the biblical sacred history.

For Apocalyptic Judaism it could not be so; God was also revealing this identity of the Chosen People in new Acts in the contemporary history. The Synagogal liturgy could not but burst open; the "true" liturgy needed to be structured by the whole revelation of the election and vocation of God's People. It had therefore to include these new Acts of God and consequently to be structured by the whole sacred history, including the "*present* sacred history". The liturgical calendar could not be contained in the closed fence of the

---

[70]Cf. W. Eichrodt, "Is Typological Exegesis an Appropriate Method?" in *Essays on Old Testament Hermeneutics*, ed. by C. Westermann, English trans., Richmond, 1963, 234: "It (typology) is extremely closely connected with the eschatological hope and must be explained from the same fundamental forces as the latter".

past sacred history. Since the sacred history was co-extensive with history itself the liturgical calendar had to be the "Jubilee calendar" which we described above. Each new historical event (new event of the *salient history*) became a sacrament which in one way or another was revelation as the past biblical events were. And the different events of "past sacred history" found in Scripture were thought to prefigure these new historical events which were also eschatological events. This is confirmed by the fact that again and again in the Apocalyptic literature in general, and in the *Book of Jubilees* in particular, we find broad biblical patterns applied to the description of the "end time".[71]

---

[71] A possible origin for such typology will be pointed out below when we deal with the Dead Sea Scrolls.

III

THE USE OF BROAD BIBLICAL PATTERNS
TO STRUCTURE APOCALYPTIC WRITINGS

Up to this point we have focused investigation on the characteristics of the Apocalyptic use of Scripture which we could discover in the *Book of Jubilees*. The relationship of this book with Scripture is clear: it is a re-writing of Scripture. Now we have to widen our investigation to include the Apocalyptic literature as a whole. In most cases, far from being clear from the outset, the relationship of these texts with Scripture has to be demonstrated before we can proceed to elucidate the axioms which governed such a use of Scripture. For this reason we shall conduct our investigation in such a way as to let appear the different levels at which Scripture was used in these texts. We shall deal first with the more general uses of Scripture a) as *broad biblical patterns* and b) as the basis for *Pseudonymity* (section IV). Then we shall deal with the uses of Scripture within this general framework: we shall call them the *anthological* and the *structural* styles (section V).

The use of *broad biblical patterns* emphasizes again the "liturgical" character of typology: in the same way that the liturgy was structured by what was considered in classical Judaism as being key biblical texts (the Ten Commandments, the three texts of the *Shema* and the Preestly Blessings), in the same way the Apocalyptic texts were structured by what was considered in Apocalyptic Judaism as being key biblical texts (although these were only alluded to rather than recited).

Such broad biblical patterns were so commonly used that they became stereotyped, so that today they are often looked at as mere characteristics of the Apocalyptic way of thinking. This is the case with the following pattern, which structures many Apocalyptic texts.

A. There are evil times (all kinds of corruptions).
B. God intervenes (by himself or by means of the Messiah).
C. There is judgment and punishment of sinners.
D. The righteous are saved from this punishment and rejoice.

This very common pattern (sometimes in more elaborated forms) is again and again applied to the end time.[72] We should note first that it is not specific to the Bible. It can be found in Babylonian as well as in Persian mythologies: the primeval evil times (i.e., "chaotic" times) are overcome by a destruction of the chaotic powers (the sinners), and then a cosmic order is established, in which the "righteous" can live in peace and rejoice.[73] Yet the Apocalyptists discovered this pattern first of all in Scripture. They saw it for instance in the story of Noah and the Flood and also in the Exodus tradition (Exodus 1-15). In that the Apocalyptists were not innovators. As Daube has shown, the Exodus pattern was already used in Scripture itself as a framework for many biblical laws and stories.[74] Furthermore the Apocalyptists found this pattern already applied (more or less extensively)

---

[72] Hartman, *Prophecy Interpreted*, Lund, 1966, 55ff., finds it in more than twenty texts, among which are Jub. 23:11-31; *I Enoch* 10:16-11:2; 80:2-8; 91:6-11; 99:1-16; 100:1-9; 102:1-11; 103:1-15; 104:1-105:2; *Test. Lev.* 4:1-4; 4:1-16:5; *Test. Jud.* 21:6-22:3; *Test. Zeb.* 9:5-9, to which we may add *Ps. Sol.* 17. Furthermore such a pattern is found in larger units as the very structure of whole Apocalyptic books. Cf. for instance E. M. Laperrousaz, "Le Testament de Moise (Generalement appele 'Assomption de Moise')", *Semitica* 19, 1970, 1-134, cf. especially 82ff. where the author points out this structure.

[73] The establishement of the cosmic order was understood as taking place *either* in a primeval time (thus identified with the Creation), as for the Babylonians, or at the end of history, as for Zoroastrianism (and also for many Apocalyptic writings). Cf. on this for the Babylonian mythodologies: James B. Pritchard, *Ancient Near Eastern Texts relating to the Old Testament*, third ed., Princeton, 1969; for Persian mythologies: M. J. Dresde, "Mythology of Ancient Iran", in *Mythologies of the Ancient World*, ed. by S. N. Kramer, New York, 1961, 331ff. and his bibliography.

[74] Cf. D. Daube, *The Exodus Pattern in the Bible*, London, 1963.

to the future judgment of God, for instance in Dan. 7:23-27; Ezek. 38-39; Isa. 59:1-21; Ps. 68:2-4.[75]

The use of such broad biblical patterns by the Apocalyptists in general and the author of the *Book of Jubilees* in particular[76] cannot be considered as a specific use of Scripture. Yet it is to be noted that it corresponds more or less to the "unfulfilled prophecies" found in Scripture about the Day of the Lord (Amos 5:18), and especially to these prophecies which point to the judgment and punishment of the whole world (Zeph. 1:2, 3, 18; 3:8; Isa. 34; Jer. 25:15ff.; Hag. 2:32; Joel 1 and 2), to the eschatological war (Ezek. 38-39; Zech. 6:1-8, *passim*), and throughout the above, to the Messianic age and the golden age. Thus the Apocalyptic literature as a whole can be understood as a re-interpretation of these "unfulfilled prophecies" with the aim of pointing, with the help of typology, to the beginning of their fulfillment in the time of the Apocalyptists.

Before taking a specific example of the use of a broad biblical pattern we should note that these patterns were always used in combination with other uses of Scripture. The patterns did indeed allow the Apocalyptists to understand the general course of history. But in order to interpret the details of their contemporary history they used, in addition, a great number of Scriptural passages. The broad biblical patterns provided only the general framework. Within each we find other uses of Scripture. They can be considered as belonging to two major categories, a) the structural use of Scripture and b) the anthological use of Scripture. We shall deal with them at length later on (ch. VIII, section V). Yet we need to note some of their characteristics here, in order to understand what we shall bring forth when taking an example of the use of a broad biblical pattern.

By the structural use of Scripture (or *structural style*) we refer to the structuring of Apocalyptic texts by one or

---

[75]Cf. Hartman, *op. cit.*, 57-60.

[76]In Jub. 23:11-31: Evil times, 23:11-21; God intervenes, 23:22-23; judgment and punishment of the sinners, 23:22-26; the righteous rejoice, 23:27-31.

several biblical passages. In this case it appears that Scripture itself is the primary locus of revelation. The anthological use of Scripture (or *anthological style*) is akin to the use of Scripture which we pointed out in the liturgical texts of classical Judaism. Here also Scripture is used as a mere *language*. The Apocalyptists' teaching is expressed by means of numerous biblical phrases, to such an extent that it is possible to consider many of these Apocalyptic texts a kind of anthology of biblical phrases. For this reason, following Andre Robert, we name this use of Scripture "anthological style".[77] We noted when examining the liturgical texts of classical Judaism that such a use of Scripture was not focused on Scripture in itself: therein the locus of revelation was the worshipping community rather than Scripture. Similarly, here this "anthological style" is not focused on Scripture itself. Once again Scripture is only a language. And indeed in any given part of the broad framework, the Apocalyptic teaching, cloaked in this anthological style, is structured by events of the contemporary history of the author. The biblical texts and phrases were brought together in a theme which these events suggested. The primary locus of revelation appears to be, therefore, these events rather than Scripture.

This being said, we can present one example[78] of the use of a broad biblical pattern and show how within it Scripture is further used. We shall take as an example the seventeenth of the *Psalms of Solomon*.[79] An examination of this text will show not only how a broad biblical pattern was used but also

---

[77] Cf. A Robert, "Genres Litteraires", *DBS* V, col. 411ff. cf. also for concrete examples of this style given by A. Robert his articles: "Les attaches litteraires bibliques de Prov. I-IX", *R.B.* 43, 1934, 47ff., 172ff., 374ff.; 44, 1935, 344ff., 502ff.; "Le sens du mot 'Loi' dans le Ps. CIX", *R.B.* 46, 1937, 182-206; "Le Ps. CIX et les Sapientiaux", *R.B.* 48, 1939, 5-20; "Le Yahwisme de Prov. X,1-XXII,16; XXV-XXIX" in *Memorial Lagrange*, Paris, 1940, 163-82; "Le genre litteraire du Cantique des Cantiques", *R.B.* 52, 1944, 192-213.

[78] For other examples see Hartman, *op. cit.*, 55ff. We do not need here to repeat them.

[79] On the Apocalyptic origin of the *Psalms of Solomon* see O'Dell, "The Religious Background of the Psalms of Solomon", *RQ* 3, 1961, 241-58.

how in it the contemporary salient history was interpreted in terms of Scripture, and Scripture in terms of this history.

After a brief introduction (1-4) on the kingship of God[80] we find the biblical pattern mentioned above with the addition of the Messiah theme.

    A. The evil times are described at length (6-22).
    B. God's intervention is then promised (23): the Messiah, Son of David will be God's agent.
    C. The heathen and sinners are punished (24-27).
    D. The rule of the Messiah is presented: Israel rejoices and is at peace (28-51).

This pattern possibly follows Exod. 1-15. The Messiah's role is interpreted in terms of Moses' participation in the Exodus events (cf. also Isa. 8:1-9:7 and Jer. 30-31).

It is the first part (6-22) which interests us here.[81] In it we find the following sub-structure:

1) Sinners rose up and took over the throne of David (6-8a). This refers, as is generally recognized, to the Hasmoneans and more specifically to Aristobulus I and the later Hasmoneans.
2) They and their family were punished by "a man alien to our race". The people suffered as well (9-14). This refers certainly to Pompey and his intervention in Palestine.
3) The idolatry of the Foreigner in Jerusalem is described, as well as the idolatry of the people of Israel[82] (15-17).
4) The pious fled into the wilderness (18-20a).
5) The punishment of God came forth because of the sins of the people (20b-22).

---

[80]It was possibly built on Exod. 15. In Ps. Sol. 17:1a we have indeed a direct allusion to Exod. 15:18; in Ps. Sol. 17:1b, a possible allusion to Exod. 15:1 (the glory is mentioned in both although not with the same predicament); Ps. Sol. 17:3a may refer to Exod. 15:2a; Ps. Sol. 17:3b to Exod. 15:13b and possibly 6a; Ps. Sol. 17:4 again alludes directly to Exod. 15:18.

[81]For the following analysis we are indebted to G. B. Gray, "The Psalms of Solomon", in *Apocrypha and Pseudepigrapha*, vol. II, 625-52 (we shall quote from his translation unless otherwise stated) and J. Viteau, *Les Psaumes de Salomon. Introduction, texte grec et traduction*, Paris, 1911.

[82]We shall see below the problems raised by this passage.

Here then we have four[83] historical events which are presented in their chronological order and which form the framework of this passage. Each of these events was interpreted by means of biblical passages. It will be enough to show this for verses 6-12.[84]

> 6 - "But for our sins, sinners rose up against us.
> They assailed us and thrust us out. What Thou hast
> not promised to them, they took away with violence".

This biblical theme has been in common use since the exile: the Gentiles (sinners) are sent against Israel because of her sins (see for instance Jer. 6:19ff. and also Jer. 5 and Isa. 5:18ff.). As sinners, the Hasmoneans are identified with these Gentiles. The author may have had in mind also Deut. 28:63-65, where the sinner Israel is depicted as being expelled from and dispossessed of the land, although it is the promised land. This idea is implied at the end of our verse: Gray translates it "they took away (*from us*) with violence". Thus here we have the use of biblical themes in quite general terms.

> 7- "And they did not glorify Thy honourable Name
> (τὸ ὄνομά σου τὸ ἔντιμον). They gloriously
> established a monarchy in exchange for their
> elevation (ἀντι ὕψοθς αὐτῶν)".[85]

τὸ ὄνομά τὸ ἔντιμον is actually the LXX translation of the phrase השם הנכבד found in Deut. 28:58. In the latter text Israel's punishment (we noted that its description is akin to Ps. Sol. 17:6) results from the fact that the people did not glorify the "glorious and fearful Name" of God. The corollary follows: they glorified themselves.

> 8 - "They laid waste the throne of David in tumultuous
> arrogance. But Thou, O God, didst cast them down, and
> remove their seed from the earth -9- in that there rose
> up against them a man that was alien to our race".

Common biblical phraseology about the punishment of the sinners is here used to represent a series of historical events. "They laid waste the throne of David . . ." refers

---

[83] The fifth one may be, as we shall see, projected upon history because of biblical interpretations.

[84] It is to be noted here that the verses 8-11 are in the future tense. This will be understandable after studying the phenomenon of Pseudonymity. Here we follow Gray and use the past tense throughout.

[85] My translation.

possibly to the deposing of Hyrcanus.[86] That they were "cast down", refers to Pompey's intervention in Palestine ("the man alien to our race"). And that their seed was removed from the earth refers to the destruction of Aristobulus' family.

> 10 - "According to their sins didst Thou recompense them, O God: so that it befell them according to their deeds -11- God showed them no pity: he sought out their seed and let not one of them to go free. -12- Faithful is the Lord in all his judgments which He doeth upon the earth".

Here again we have the use of biblical phraseology and of biblical themes (the same image of merciless hunting is found in I Sam. 23:22f. which describes Saul searching for David).

This example will suffice to show how loosely Scripture is used here. We could even say that it is not properly speaking a use of Scripture: the anthological style is relatively weak. It is mainly an interpretation of contemporary history by a man whose way of thinking has been shaped in his meditation on or hearing of Scripture. Thus although he set contemporary history within a broad biblical pattern, his Psalm is mainly structured by the historical events of his time.

Thus here two poles are kept in tension: on the one hand we have Scripture, represented by the broad biblical pattern and the weak anthological style, and on the other had we have the events of the author's time. The Psalm is the product of this "revelatory" tension: it presents the ultimate meaning which the author discovered in his contemporary history. Yet the process itself is not described. We shall see that this process is often expressed in terms of visionary experiences.

---

[86] Thus J. Viteau, *ad loc*.

IV

SCRIPTURE AND PSEUDONYMITY

Another broad use of Scripture in the Apocalyptic literature is the "Testament form", which is one of the expressions of the phenomenon of Pseudonymity. An understanding of the "Testament form" and of Pseudonymity will help us to specify the nature of the Apocalyptic typology.

As mentioned earlier, the biblical heroes were presented as having read in the "Heavenly Tables" what would be the course of all history. Consequently they were considered prophets; the Apocalyptists were, accordingly, presenting their secret prophecies. In this way the whole of past history, as well as the actual future, could be presented in the form of prophecy. The fact that most of these prophecies (i.e., those referring to past events) had indeed been fulfilled, gave strength to the actual predictions which were put in the mouths of these biblical heroes.

This Pseudonymity is one of the most obvious characteristics of the Apocalyptic literature. The very title of these books expresses it: *Book of Enoch*, *The Testaments of the Twelve Patriarchs*, and later the *Apocalypse of Abraham*, the *Book of Ezra* (IV Ezra), and so on. The *Book of Jubilees* itself was actually presented as a "Testament of Moses",[87] although it refers primarily to the revelation given to Moses of the history preceding his time. This Testament literary form itself indicates the Apocalyptists' attitude toward Scripture.

Let us note first that pseudonymity is to be found already in Scripture. For example in Gen. 49, the Blessing of Jacob, which was written in the period of the early monarchy,[88] the history of the twelve tribes was put as a

---

[87] This title was indeed used for the book: cf. Charles, *op. cit.*, 2.

[88] Cf. R. de Vaux, *La Genèse*, Paris, 1962, *ad loc*, note c

prophecy into the mouth of the Patriarch. We find the same phenomenon in the Blessing of Moses (Deut. 33). Furthermore the book of Deuteronomy as a whole reflects the same form, since it gives laws of the period of the kingship (and even post-exilic laws) in the name of Moses. Many psalms are ascribed to David in the same fashion, and the wisdom literature (Proverbs and Ecclesiastes) to Solomon. So in using the pseudonymous form the Apocalyptists were not innovators.

What is the significance of this adoption of pseudonymity by the Apocalyptists? In one of the most acute parts of his book,[89] Russell points it out quite well. First he refuses to consider the phenomenon of pseudonymity as one which claims or implies "deception on the part of the writers". Neither the desire to avoid persecution[90] (which could be avoided by an anonymous text), nor the supposed Jewish love and respect for "antiquarianism"[91] nor again the desire to accredit these writings as inspired after the end of prophecy[92] are sufficient to explain the general use of pseudonymity. The two latter solutions charge the Apocalyptic writers with plain fraud.[93] As Russell notes, such fraud would be irreconcilable with the very character of these writings. To reduce the pseudonymity to a mere literary convention, as H. H. Rowley does,[94] stops short of the goal. It is a literary convention, indeed, yet if it is only that the authority of these texts would rest upon their author. This may be satisfactory for a modern mind, but it was not necessarily so for the Jewish mind of that time.

---

[89] Russell, *op. cit.*, 127-39.

[90] Cf. J. B. Frey, *DBS*, vol. I, 1928, cols. 334ff.

[91] Cf. C. C. McCown, "Hebrew and Egyptian Apocalyptic Literature", *Harvard Theological Review* 18, 1925, 357-411.

[92] Cf. Charles, *op. cit.*, VIIIf. and *Eschatology*, second ed., 1913, 198ff.

[93] It attributes also an amazing credulity to its readers.

[94] *The Relevance of Apocalyptic*, London, 1947, 37ff.

Thus Russell proposes to try to understand this phenomenon by taking into account the specific Jewish "psychology", namely "the idea of corporate personality, the peculiar time-consciousness of the Hebrew and the significance of the proper name in Hebrew thought".[95] For when reading the Apocalyptic books it appears quite clearly that, even for the writers, these are genuine revelations which rest upon the authority of the biblical heroes to which they are ascribed. This can be explained with the help of H. Wheeler Robinson's idea of corporate personality. Since there was "an identity of the individual and the group to which he belongs",[96] and since this identity was extended to the past and future members of the group, the Apocalyptists could have felt so indebted to the tradition of a specific Apocalyptic group that "they could rightly regard themselves not as original writers at all, but simply as inheritors and interpreters of what, under divine inspiration, they had already received".[97] Thus "as spokesmen of the tradition, they were, in fact spokesmen of the seer himself and could justifiably assume his name".[98] This view is strengthened when we take into consideration the way in which the proper name is used in Hebrew thought. The name is not, as for us, a mere appellation: it expresses the man's personality, his very self.[99] To interpret revelations which were believed to have been first expressed by a biblical personage was to express "*him*". It was therefore legitimate to speak in his name.

Furthermore, as we shall see below, the Apocalyptic teachings reflect actual ecstatic experiences. The writers believed that they had received these revelations (which they

---

[95] Russell, *op. cit.*, 132. Yet these concepts have to be used with caution, as we noted earlier referring to the work of J. Barr.

[96] H. Wheeler Robinson, *Inspiration and Revelation in the Old Testament*, Oxford, 1946, 70.

[97] Russell, *op. cit.*, 133.

[98] Russell, *op. cit.* 134.

[99] Cf. J. Pedersen, *Israel: Its Life and Culture*, I-II, Engl. ed., Copenhagen, 1926, 254-59.

considered as being the very revelations previously disclosed to a biblical personage) under divine inspiration. In this way their experiences could be regarded by them as similar to those of the biblical heroes (envisioned as prophets or seers). In a telescoping of history characteristic of the Jewish consciousness of that time, they could assimilate these two experiences as one and the same. Contemporary with the seers' vision, the Apocalyptist could actually say that his own vision was the seer's, all the more so if the historical situation behind this vision was similar to that of the biblical heroes.

We can even say that the Apocalyptists saw in the biblical heroes, "types" of themselves, prefigurations of themselves either as individual seers or, in a corporate way, as the righteous community of those who had received the revelation of the secrets of the end time.

In such a perspective it is possible to understand why Noah was one of the names so often used in Apocalyptic writings. The righteous man in a time of corruption before the destruction of all evil, he was an obvious "type" with which the righteous community in an evil time preceding the eschatological judgment could identify itself. In the same way they could identify themselves with Enoch. According to the Apocalyptists' beliefs Enoch had testified against the sinners (and against the watchers, cf. Jub. 4:17-22).[100] Furthermore he had received the complete revelation of the secrets of history. Similarly Moses and Ezra were ideal types since they both had renewed the Covenant, which would be renewed at the end time, i.e., in the Apocalyptists' time. Such identifications and the resulting pseudonymity were, as noted above, further facilitated by the fact that the Apocalyptists had themselves visionary experiences which were similar, according to their beliefs, to those of the biblical heroes. This cannot be doubted after a careful reading of the numerous visionary passages, which we shall examine now.

---

[100] This is an interpretation of Gen. 5:22 and 24 where it is twice mentioned (of him alone before Noah) that "he walked with God". He was therefore the only righteous man in this wicked generation and testified to them of their sins.

V

THE VISIONARY TEXTS: ANTHOLOGICAL AND STRUCTURAL USES OF SCRIPTURE

Our purpose in studying the visions[101] found in the Apocalyptic texts is once again to see how Scripture was used therein. Since the visionary texts as pseudonymous are to be understood in the context of the general typological interpretation of Scripture, we could expect that in them the use of Scripture would be limited to such typological interpretations and to the use of broad biblical patterns. This is the case when the vision was merely a literary form; then the author was consciously creating an Apocalyptic work, using Scripture according to the (conscious) Apocalyptic doctrine. We shall present an example of the vision used as a mere literary form. In order to appreciate its character, we need to emphasize that in many Apocalyptic texts the visions were not mere literary forms; they reflected the actual experiences of the writers.

VISION AS LITERARY FORM AND AS ECSTATIC EXPERIENCE

As a literary form the visions are pseudonymous. The Apocalyptic writers presented visions as having been experienced by biblical heroes. We need to know if the vision is a mere literary device, or if on the contrary it reflects the actual experience of the Apocalyptic writers. It is clear that no definite answer can be given. Russell[102] discusses the question in detail. Suffice it here to give his

---

[101] We use the word in a broad sense, that is, not only in the sense of visual revelations but also of auditions, dreams, trances, translations. . . .

[102] Russell, *op. cit.*, 158-77.

conclusions. He argues first that it is quite unlikely that the Apocalyptists would present the inspired message in a form which would fail to reflect, in their eyes, an actual mode of inspiration. Studying the different modes of inspiration presented in these texts, Russell emphasizes the concrete details used to describe these experiences and especially the different methods by means of which trance states were induced (*viz*. fasting, Dan. 9:3, IV Ezra 5:20 and 6:31; eating special foods, Dan. 1:12, Martyrdom of Isaiah 2:11, IV Ezra 9:23-25; drinking special drinks, IV Ezra 14:38-42). This investigation led him to the following conclusions, which he qualifies as "a matter for inference", but "for strong inference":[103] "In not a few cases, the claim to psychical experience on the part of the ancient seer may well indicate similar experiences on the part of the Apocalyptic writer himself who thereby believes that he is writing under divine inspiration",[104] and this in a manner similar to that of the Prophets.

Thus, we can assume that the Apocalyptists believed themselves to have been divinely inspired, either in a personal psychical experience which they presented as that of the biblical heroes, or in the very process of writing down their teaching in the conventional literary framework.[105] In such a case we can expect to find a use of Scripture beyond that which is prescribed by the Apocalyptic doctrine.

THE NATURE OF APOCALYPTIC INSPIRATION

This leads us to the difficult question of the nature of inspiration and of its role in the Apocalyptic use of Scripture. On the one hand the Apocalyptists wrote messages which they thought were received by divine inspiration. On

---

[103] Russell, *op. cit.*, 159.

[104] Russell, *op. cit.*, 172.

[105] Just as the Prophets were inspired, although they used the conventional form of Hebrew poetry.

the other hand, it is clear that they made use of material learned earlier either in a conscious intellectual effort or unconsciously, as if it had been infused in them through their culture. This means we must consider this inspiration as one of the many aspects of *creative imagination*. Without going into the different theories about the latter,[106] let us note simply that the creative imagination brings together elements which belong to different levels of consciousness. The associations which arise from different ideas, traditions, or previously learned material indeed follow a "logic", that is, are governed by a basic structure. Nevertheless this "logic" is not necessarily the logic of the conscious intellectual level. We can expect that they used Scripture in this way. Thus, in these visionary texts we can hope to apprehend directly the very hermeneutical structure which governed unconsciously the Apocalyptists' use of Scripture.

In these Apocalyptic visions we are indeed confronted with a very special use of Scripture. The latter did not appear as explicit quotations or interpretations. Yet these visionary writings are, so to speak, permeated by Scripture. This was precisely what made them *Jewish* inspired texts. The material which the creative imagination used either in a psychical experience or in the very process of writing came to a very large extent from Scripture. We should add: from Scripture as read in the writer's milieu, that is, in the Jewish Palestinian milieu of that time. Thus some of the associations which allowed them to tally various biblical texts with it, imposed themselves on the Apocalyptists because of the way the texts were used in the Synagogal readings, or in other circumstances which lie for the most part, beyond any possible investigation. Thus it is not surprising to find a continuity, as G. Vermes has shown, between the traditional biblical interpretations in classical Judaism and in Apocalyptic literature.[107] In addition, as already noted, we

---

[106] On this see for instance Arthur Koestler, *The Act of Creation*, New York, 1964, especially 101ff., and the bibliography therein.

[107] G. Vermes, *Scripture and Tradition*, 9-10 and *passim*.

need not be surprised to find the same kinds of associations (namely verbal associations). Let us stress again that such associations were made at different levels of consciousness, and even unconsciously.

ANTHOLOGICAL AND STRUCTURAL STYLES

An inspired and faithful Jew, the Apocalyptist was nourished by Scripture. He was impregnated by Scripture, he meditated it day and night (Deut. 6:7). His inspired message appears therefore as a "mosaic" of biblical phrases and allusions. As said, we call the amalgamation of biblical phrases to express a new inspired message, an *anthological* use of Scripture.[108] We distinguish this from the *structural* style. In the latter case specific biblical texts are used as framework of an Apocalyptic passage.

The anthological style, either in a dense form or in a weak one, can be found in practically any Apocalyptic text. Nevertheless, because we have these texts only in translations, we are often unable to decide which of several texts has been used. We are limited to conjectures. Furthermore many biblical phrases which were used in the original are certainly hidden or missing in the translation. The anthological style can easily be seen by consulting the different translations which refer in their footnotes to biblical passages where similar ideas or images can be found.

---

[108] Following A. Robert. For bibliography cf. above note 77. It is to be noted that A. Robert does not make the distinction between "anthological Style" and "structural style". Such a distinction is necessary for reasons which will be clear in our study of the Dead Sea Scrolls. Let us state already that as we will show, the structural style expresses not only the content of the revelation, but also the process of "uncovering" it with the help of Scripture. The anthological style either expresses the result of this "uncovering" (the biblical phrases being what remains of the former use of Scripture) or as we saw earlier, it points to something else than Scripture itself as primary locus of revelation.

Therefore we shall not take any example of mere anthological style.[109]

The structural style is less frequent, yet it is more difficult to detect, just as the haftarah, as structure of the homily, is difficult to graps even in the original language. The haftarah as well as the biblical passages which structure the visionary texts are only the "thread" which links together the thoughts which are themselves expressed, in an anthological style, by means of biblical phrases borrowed from other texts. We can be sure that such a thread has been in many instances hidden in the process of translation to which the Pseudepigrapha have been submitted. Therefore, despite the fact that we can only point to a limited number of examples of structural style which we can actually indicate we may assume that it was used fairly frequently and especially in those passages which at first appear fanciful.

We shall illustrate this structural use of Scripture in four examples. These are chosen so as to contribute to our understanding of the relationship between visionary revelation and Scripture. We shall study successively the following passages: *Sibylline Oracles* III:8-91, *I Enoch* 90:13-19; *I Enoch* 1:3-9, *Assumption of Moses* 10:1-10.[110] In the analysis of these texts the frequent use of typology should be noted.

A. *Sibylline Oracles III:8-91*

This Oracle is presented as a divinely inspired message. It describes a psychical experience which may be, beyond the literary convention, the description of an actual experience of the Apocalyptist:[111] his heart is "fluttering", his soul "lashed with a spur from within" (Or. Sib. 3:4-5). He is thus compelled to announce the message.

---

[109] We shall cite several examples of this style in the Dead Sea Scrolls, examples which will be useful for other purposes.

[110] For other examples, see Hartman, *op. cit.*

[111] So, Russell, *op. cit.*, 160.

There are three pericopes in this message, 3:8-45; 3:46-61; 3:62-91. While the second presents a simple anthological style (it is structured by contemporary historical events) the first and the third present a structural style.

Or. Sib. 3:8-45

This first pericope is structured by a prophetic text: Isa. 40:18ff. Other biblical texts are tallied with this main text (the thread) by means of either thematic or verbal associations. The Sibyl addresses men "that bear the form that God did mould in his image"[112] asking them why they err and walk not in the straight path and forget the Creator (9-10: a common biblical theme about the sinful Israel).

The following lines (11ff.), describing how incomparable is God over against the idols, are strongly reminiscent of Isa. 40:18ff.[113] Thus "No mason's hand did make him, nor does some model formed from gold or ivory by the varied skill of man represent him" (13-14). Compare Isa. 40:19-20. "He, himself Eternal, hath revealed himself as One who is and was before, yea, and shall be hereafter" (15-16). This interprets Isa. 40:21. The latter refers to the revelation of God as the one who *is* from the beginning. The idea that God is eternal, is found in Isa. 40:28: "Have you not heard. The Lord is the everlasting God, the Creator . . .".

This use of Isa. 40 allows the association of other biblical texts about the way in which God reveals himself. He cannot be seen by mortal eyes (17: alluding to texts like Exod. 33:20, Judg. 13:22, etc.). Even traditional doctrines are brought in: his Name cannot even be heard (18-19). Thus God reveals himself in his Creation (20-23), which is the very topic of Isa. 40:22-26. The Sibyl emphasizes furthermore that God created everything by his word (20). Compare Isa. 40:26,

---

[112] Here, as well as below, we quote Lanchester's translation: "The Sibylline Oracles", in *Apocrypha and Pseudepigrapha*, Charles ed., vol. II, 368-406. It is clear that we are also much indebted to his notes.

[113] The same interrogative style is used.

"he calls them all by names by the greatness of his might". This idea is explicitly expressed in Ps. 33:6-7, which may have been used also, since the elements of the creation are presented in Or. Sib. 3:20 in the very same order as in the Psalm.

Then follows an acrostic on the name of Adam: "Yea it is God himself who fashioned four-lettered Adam . . ., who completes in his name morn and dusk, antarctic and arctic" (24-26). The four letters of Adam are understood as representing the initials of East, West, South and North, i.e., the four "ends of the earth". At first it seems that we are far from Isa. 40. Yet a more careful examination of the biblical texts shows that God is presented in Isa. 40:28 as "the Creator of the ends of the earth". This acrostic may be understood as a development on this phrase.

The mention of Adam seems to have brought into the author's mind the description of the creation in Gen. 1 and 2. So there follows a further brief description of the creation in a vocabulary reminiscent of these texts (27-28).

Then the text comes back to the denunciation of idolatry (29ff.) with, at times, a vocabulary reminiscent of the Prophets'. The Sibyl says to the idolatrous men: "Ye weary the God who ever is . . .," which can be compared with "you have wearied me with your iniquities" of Isa. 43:24. This association may have been provoked by the mention of the weariness of God in Isa. 40:28, although there it is in the negative; God does not weary. Therefore this tallying of the two biblical texts would have been by verbal association (by means of the root יגע). The supposition that Isa. 43:24 is used here is reinforced by the fact that its setting is in the Temple. So Or. Sib. 3:32 speaks of "Godless temples". We gain reinforcement too from the fact that in 34f. the ideas of judgment and God as "Eternal Savior" are presented. In Isa. 43:26 we also find the idea of Judgment, and in Isa. 43:25 God is presented as a Savior "that blots out your transgressions . . . and will not remember your sins".

Then the denunciation of idolatry continues (36-45):

idolatry is associated with immorality and injustice, as often in the Prophets' writings.[114]

We leave aside Or. Sib. 3:46-61, which interprets historical events of the seer's time with the mention of "the holy prince", i.e., the Messiah. I could not find in it any reference to specific biblical texts, although biblical phrases are used. This passage presents therefore an *anthological style* and not a *structural one*.

Or. Sib. 3:62-91

In a similar fashion, this pericope is structured by Deut. 13. It describes the coming and destruction of Beliar.[115] The text at first glance does not seem to use any biblical texts. Yet checking the few biblical texts which mention the name of Belial,[116] we find Deut. 13:14. There the "sons of Belial" are presented as having led astray the men in idolatry. Comparing the whole chapter, we could not but be struck by the similarities.

Our pericope is introduced by these words "I will tell out in particular all those cities in which men are to suffer woe" (61-62): Deut. 13:15-16 proclaims that the cities led astray by "the sons of Belial" will be put to anathema. We have thus a first hint.

Then the coming of Beliar is described as performing signs and wonders: "Beliar shall come in later time[117] and shall raise the mountain heights and raise (or still) the sea, shall make the great fiery sun and the bright moon stand still, and he shall raise up the dead and shall perform many signs for men" (63-67).[118] Certainly we have here a

---

[114] There is possibly a closer association with Amos ch. 3 and 4.

[115] This passage may be a later (first century A.D.) interpolation; we will nevertheless deal with it, but briefly.

[116] The biblical form of Beliar.

[117] Here we find again the Prophetic pseudonymous style.

[118] We follow here some of Hartman's interpretations of the text: cf. *op. cit.*, 73.

description of the coming of Beliar in the very terms of the biblical theophanies such as Exod. 15:8, Ps. 65:6-7, Isa. 38:8, Hab. 3:10f.[119] Yet, as Hartman did not see, the main purpose of the author is to describe Beliar as a false prophet. In this he follows Deut. 13:2: "If a prophet arises among you . . . and gives you a sign or a wonder, and the sign or the wonder come to pass, and if he says, 'Let us go after other gods'". The last part of this verse is also interpreted: "he deceives mortals" (68, cf. also 69f.).

The vengeance of God against Beliar is then described as a fire which burns up Beliar and his followers (71-74), which is precisely how the idolatrous will be destroyed according to Deut. 13:16. In the following passage the author interpreted, in the light of his preceding comments on the coming and destruction of Beliar, elements of the history of his time. For this purpose he used other biblical texts as well.[120]

Thus in each of these two pericopes it appears that we have a structural style: the message of the Apocalyptists is built on a main biblical text (Isa. 40:18ff. for the first and Deut. 13 for the second). This is complemented by the use of other biblical texts which are tallied with the main text by means of either thematic or verbal associations. Yet each of these texts are used only implicitly. The result is therefore comparable to a midrash without any biblical quotations. This suggest that it has been created in a different way than a midrash (in which the tallying and the interpretation are done generally at a relatively high level of consciousness). Let us remember that the Apocalyptist believed that he delivered an *inspired* message.

B. *I Enoch 90:13-19*

This vision brings at once to mind Ezek. 34, which is indeed the text which structures it, as Hartman has shown.[121]

---

[119] As Hartman suggested: *ibid*.

[120] Like Isa. 34:4 and Ps. 102:26 in Or. Sib. 3:82: (God) "shall roll up the heaven as a book is rolled".

[121] Hartman, *op. cit.*, 82-87.

Without going into the details of the analysis which can be found in Hartman's work, let us summarize his conclusions. The vision reads:[122]

> 13 - "And I saw till the shepherds and eagles and those vultures and kites came and they cried to the ravens that they should break the horn of that ram, and they battled and fought with it, and it battled with them and cried that its help might come.
> 14 - "And I saw till that man who wrote down the names of the shepherds and carried up into the presence of the Lord of the sheep and he helped it and showed it everything: he had come down for the help of that ram.
> 15 - "And I saw till the Lord of the sheep came unto them in wrath and all who saw him fled and they all fell into (his) shadow from before his face.
> 16 - "All the eagles and vultures and ravens and kites were gathered together and there came with them all the sheep of the field, yea, they all came together, and helped each other to break that horn of the ram.
> 17 - "And I saw that man, who wrote the book according to the command of the Lord, till he opened that book concerning the destruction which those twelve last shepherds had wrought and showed that they had destroyed much more than their predecessors, before the Lord of the sheep.
> 18 - "And I saw till the Lord of the sheep came unto them and took in his hand the staff of his wrath and smote the earth and the earth clave asunder and all the beasts and all the birds of the heaven fell from among those sheep and were swallowed up in the earth and it covered them.
> 19 - "And I saw till a great sword was given to the sheep, and the sheep proceeded against all the beasts of the field to slay them, and all the beasts and the birds of the heaven fled before their face".

This pericope, as well as the passages before and after it, makes fundamental use of a metaphor from Ezek. 34. The latter expresses the reproof of the bad shepherds who neglected the sheep (Israel). Thus saith the Lord, "my sheep have become a prey, and . . . food for all the wild beasts" (34:8). God punished the shepherds (10) and becomes himself the shepherd of his flock (12) before setting up David as a shepherd over them (23ff.).

---

[122] Charles' translation. We shall give this in the order of the text and not in the amended order proposed by Charles, *op. cit.*, vol. II, 258.

The interpretation of how the bad shepherds neglected the sheep (Ezek. 34:2-7) has been given in the preceding passages of I Enoch. With our text begins the interpretation of Ezek. 34:8, which is viewed in terms of Dan. 8, where the flock, Israel, is described as a ram. Dan. 12:1 (and its context) is also interpreted: Michael ("that man who wrote down the names of the shepherds", I Enoch 90:14) intervenes in favor of Israel.[123] This introduces the idea of the angel's help to Israel. By means of verbal association (the mention of time of trouble עת צרה) Dan. 12:1 is tallied to Isa. 33:2f. The latter text seems to have been used although there it is Yahweh who intervenes and not an angel. The successive uses of Dan. 12:1 and Isa. 33:2f. bring about the following succession of ideas, which at first seems illogical.[124] First there is the mention of the *angel*'s help (14) and then the fleeing of Israel's enemies before *God* (15). The latter is a detail found in Isa. 33:2f.

In I Enoch 90:16 the text returns to the heathen assault. This has been amended by Charles as being a *doublet*. Yet it is not necessarily so. The Apocalyptist knows that the destruction of the heathen must be complete from texts like Ezek. 38f. or Zech. 12:1-9. This assumption seems confirmed by some similarities between I Enoch 90:16 and Ezek. 38:7ff., and Zech. 12:2f. These texts seem to have been associated, somehow, with Dan. 7:9ff.: the books are opened and the beasts are destroyed (I Enoch 90:17-18). Yet with 90:18 we come back to Ezek. 34 and to the metaphor of God as a shepherd with his staff. This allows a new association with "the staff of his wrath" (Isa. 10:5), striking the earth (Isa. 11:4), which brings the image of the earth splitting as a result and the association with Num. 16:30ff., where Korah and his followers are swallowed up by the earth.

In the following passage we find again an apparently illogical mention: the sheep are given a sword and slay the beasts. Were not the beasts destroyed?[125] Hartman finds

---

[123] Cf. also Dan. 10:13ff.

[124] Charles proposes there an emendation.

[125] Again Charles amends the text here.

the explanation in the use of Ps. 63:10f. where we read: "Those that seek my soul, to destroy it, shall go into the lower parts of the earth. They shall fall by the sword". The text of I Enoch follows here the order given in the Psalm.

Thus here again we find indeed a basic text used throughout (the "thread") in association with others which complement it. Here also we have been able to point out a verbal tallying. Yet we should not forget that since our text is a translation, others might be due to a similar tallying with terms used by the Apocalyptist himself, although we cannot detect these connections any longer.

C. I Enoch 1:1-9

We chose this last illustration of the structured style because it presents a more complex structure. It is built on three basic texts: Deut. 33:1ff., Hab. 3:3ff., and Mic. 1:2ff.[126]

The introduction of the Book of Enoch begins as follows: "The words of the blessing of Enoch wherewith he blessed the elect and righteous" (1:1). This uses obviously Deut. 33:1: "This is the blessing, with which Moses the man of God blessed the children of Israel". The phrase "man of God" is furthermore interpreted in I Enoch 1:2, "Enoch a righteous man, whose eyes were opened by God, saw the vision of the Holy One in heaven. . . ." Thus in I Enoch 1:1-3a, Deut. 33:1 is interpreted in eschatological terms, with the help of biblical texts or phraseology.[128]

---

[126] Hartman dealt with this text (*op. cit.*, 112-18) yet we cannot agree with his interpretation. He did not see the basic biblical passages underlying this chapter, mainly because he focused his attention too much on the oracle 1:3-9 by itself. Hartman points out only what we call an anthological style.

[128] Like Isa. 45:4, 65:9, 15:22; Jer. 16:19; Obad. 14; Nah. 1:7; Hab. 3:16; Zeph. 1:15; Ps. 18:28; Isa. 10:20; Ezek. 14:14; Num. 23:7, 24:3-4; Dan. 8:15ff., 10:12ff.; Ps. 78:4ff., as pointed out by Hartman, *op. cit.*, 113.

For the rest of the chapter the Apocalyptist went on using the following verses of Deut. 33, where we find first a theophany. Deut. 33:2 reads:

> "The Lord came from Sinai, and rose up from Seir unto them, he shone forth from Mount Paran and he came with ten thousands of saints: from his right hand went a fiery law for them".

Then follows a description of God's love for his people: "Yea, he loved the people: all his saints are in your hand" (Deut. 33:3a).

Likewise there is in the oracle (I Enoch 1:3-9) a description of the eschatological theophany (3-7) where God is described as coming forth. It is even mentioned that "he will appear with his hosts" (1:4), (cf. Deut. 33:2: "with ten thousands of saints"). We find also the mention of "flame" (6), (cp. "the fiery law"). Then the bliss of his people (1:8) is described, which is the interpretation of Deut. 33:3. There follows almost explicit quotation of Deut. 33:2 in 1:9: "He cometh with ten thousands of saints",[129] which is interpreted in terms of the eschatological judgment.

Thus at the foundation of this whole chapter we find Deut. 33:1-3a, which as usual was interpreted in a n eschatological perspective with the help of other biblical texts.

The tallying of these texts seems to have begun with the mention of Mount Paran in Deut. 33:2, which is also mentioned in Hab. 3:3. Thus the designation of God as the Holy One (Hab. 3:3) is introduced in our text. The use of קדוש may well have provoked the tallying of the other text used here, Mic. 1:2-3.[130] Here we have the interesting phenomenon which we noted in classical Judaism: the sentences are separated in a different way from that used in the Massoretic text. Mic. 1:2b-3a reads:

אדני מהיכל קדשו

---

[129] Or "holy ones" as Charles translates correctly, since the "saints" were understood as being angels.

[130] This tallying is re-inforced by the mention of mountains in both texts.

(Adonai from his Temple of holiness); then a new sentence begins:

כי-הנה יי יצא ממקומו

("For behold Yahweh comes forth from his place"). The author apparently had in mind the following sentence

קדשו כי-הנה יי יצא ממקומו[131]

which gives us almost exactly the text of I Enoch 1:3b, "The Holy (great) one will come forth from his dwelling". In the following part of our text we shall find indeed a combination of the three texts, Deut. 33:1ff., Hab. 3:3ff., and Mic. 1:2-4.

I Enoch 1:4, "And the eternal God will tread upon the earth (cp. Mic. 1:3b), on Mount Sinai (cp. Deut. 33:2a) and appear with his hosts (cp. Deut. 33:2b) and appear in the strength of his might from the heaven (cp. Hab. 3:3-4)".

5, "And all shall be smiten with fear (cp. Hab. 3:6) and the warchers shall quake, and great fear and trembling shall seize them unto the ends of the earth".[132]

6, "And the high mountains shall be shaken (cp. Hab. 3:10) and the high hills shall be made low (cp. Hab. 3:6) and shall melt like wax before the flame" (Mic. 1:4 and Deut. 33:2b, where אש is also found).

7, "And the earth shall be rent in sunder" (cp. Hab. 3:9). These images are further interpreted in terms of the eschatological judgment (using biblical phraseology). Possibly they interpret in this way the "fiery law" of Deut. 33:2.

Then we find the interpretation of Deut. 33:3: "he loved the people, all his saints are in your hand. . ." and

---

[131] כיהנה יי is certainly understood as an explanation of קדשו in this strange construction.

[132] This may be an interpretation of Hab. 3:6, where the "nations", possibly interpreted as the watchers (since the latter reign over the nations), are said to jump or to quake as well as the rest of the earth (יתר is interpreted as coming from the root חרר, to jump, to startle: on this cf. Dhorme, *Bible*, *ad loc*).

this in terms of the Aaronite blessing of Num. 6:24-26.[133] It is interesting to note here that the Aaronite blessing is interpreted as being fulfilled, since the Apocalyptists described the eschatological bliss:

8, "But with the righteous he will make peace (Num. 6:26b) and will protect the elect (Num. 6:24b) and mercy shall be upon them (Num. 6:25b). And they shall all belong to God (cp. Deut. 33:3b) and they shall be prosperous and they shall all be blessed (Num. 6:24a) and light shall appear unto them" (Num. 6:25a).

Here the mention of light (in the verbal form in Num. 6:25) links back to Deut. 33:3, where God is described as "shining" forth from Mount Paran.[134] We are not surprised therefore to find in the next sentence (I Enoch 1:9) the following part of Deut. 33:2:

9a, "And behold, he cometh with ten thousands of saints". Again as in I Enoch 1:5 and 7, the end of Deut. 33:2 is interpreted in terms of judgment using biblical phraseology.

9b, "to execute judgment upon all, and to destroy (all) the ungodly: and to convict all flesh of all the works that they have ungodly committed. . . ."

Thus again the unity of this chapter is discovered in the implicit use of three basic texts: Deut. 33:1ff., Hab. 3:3ff., and Mic. 1:2ff.

It is apparent in these three examples that the visionary texts (inspired texts) are structured either by events of the Apocalyptist's contemporary history (Or. Sib. 3:46-61 and 75-91) or by a few basic biblical passages. The primary locus of revelation is either the contemporary salient

---

[133]The passage is certainly tallied with Deut. 33:1, by virtue of the fact that it is another blessing and that the root of the latter word is found, as we can expect, in both texts. Hartman saw the influence of Num. 6:24-26 without being able to explain this association, since he disregarded Deut. 33.

[134]This is so in spite of the fact that the vocabulary is not the same, but there is no longer any need for tallying. The two texts are already associated in the mind of the Apocalyptist.

history or Scripture. We emphasize this second possibility for it implies that despite the Apocalyptic doctrine of Scripture (as expressed in the belief about the Heavenly Tables) sometimes, these visions are primarily interpretations of Scripture, albeit quite possibly unconscious interpretations. Thus besides the general use of Scripture in typology (which is emphasizing the contemporary salient history as locus of revelation) we find that the Apocalyptic hermeneutic was concurrently emphasizing Scripture as the locus of revelation.

How generalized was this structural use of Scripture among the Apocalyptists is difficult to assess for two reasons:

a) First, as we noted earlier, the very fact that we have access only to translations (and often to translations of translations) of the Pseudepigrapha is a very serious handicap. If we had in front of us the original of the many texts which present a mere anthological style in their translation, it is quite possible that we could discover in them a Scriptural "thread" as we did above in three examples, and as Hartman did elsewhere.[135]

b) Second, the very fact that these visions were incorporated in literary works had the possible effect of removing them from the actual psychical experience, that is, from the setting of the Apocalyptic hermeneutic which interests us here. The vision became a literary genre; in such a case it is structured logically by a succession of ideas. It does not present any longer the Apocalyptic visionary hermeneutic. A brief discussion of *Assumption of Moses* 10:1-10 shall suffice to illustrate this. For a more detailed interpretation, see Hartman's analysis.[136]

---

[135]Cf. Hartman, *op. cit.*, 118ff. He found them in I Enoch 46:1-8 (an important text about the Son of Man) and IV Ezra 6:13-28. His other example taken from Ass. Mos. 10:1-10 is not an example of structural style. We shall discuss it below.

[136]Hartman, *op. cit.*, 126-32.

D. *Assumption of Moses 10:1-10*

We want to make only three general remarks about this text.

First, it is quite clear that this text made abundant use of biblical texts from the Prophets and the Hagiographa: we emphasize this in order to dismiss the claim that the *Assumption of Moses* could be of Samaritan origin.[137]

Second, as Hartman rightly shows, the structure of this text is not to be found in a continuous association of biblical texts (in the form of a chain). Here, by contrast, we have a coherent construction going logically from one idea to another. The different biblical texts are brought together not by means of verbal tallying, as in the preceding examples, but by direct connection with the author's ideas. The use of Scripture appears fundamentally different compared with what we found up to now. In the preceding examples of structural style it appeared that the author's own conception had been introduced into a biblical structure and molded into it and by it. By contrast here the biblical elements appear to have been brought into the author's doctrine almost as proof texts. This points out to a different mode of composition. The author used here the literary conventions of the Apocalyptic style, rather than transcribing what was revealed to him under some kind of inspiration. We have here an intellectual work, rather than one which could be considered the product of a creative imagination.[138]

Third, at several places the author is using Scripture not according to the Hebrew text but according to its targumic

---

[137] See above, our comments on K. Haacker's article: "Assumptio Mosis - eine samaritanische Schrift?", *Theol. Zeit.* 25, 1969, 385-405. For a much more balanced hypothesis about the origin of this book see E. M. Laperrousaz, *op. cit.*, 88-99.

[138] For this distinction see again Koestler, *op. cit.*, 85ff.

rendering.[139] Thus we can conclude with Hartman that "the author has made use of a text recited in public worship in an interpretative translation"[140] or expounded in a Midrashic form.

In order to substantiate these remarks we shall give here Charles' translation including in it the references to the main biblical passages which, according to Hartman, are used (leaving aside those which present merely a similar theme or phraseology).

As. Mos. 10:1,

"And then His Kingdom shall appear (Isa. 40:9, Targum) throughout all his creation (cp. Isa. 40:5) and then Satan shall be no more and sorrow shall depart with him (Isa. 35:10).(141)

2, "Then the hands of the angel shall be filled (Dan. 12:1) who has been appointed chief and he shall go forth to avenge them of their enemies (cp. Isa. 35:4).

3, "For the Heavenly One will arise from His royal throne (a common biblical phrase) and he will go forth from his holy habitation (cp. Isa. 26:21, Mic. 1:3) with indignation and wrath on account of his sons.

4, "And the earth shall tremble: to its confines shall it be shaken: and the high mountains shall be made low (Isa. 2:12ff., 40:4; Hab. 3:6, etc.) and the hills shall be shaken and fall

5, "the sun shall not give his light and he shall be turned into darkness, the horns of the moon shall be broken and it shall be turned wholly into blood (Joel 3:4) and the circle of the stars shall be disturbed(142)

6, "And the sea shall retire into the abyss and the fountains of waters shall fail and the rivers shall dry up (cp. Nah. 1:4)

7, "For the Most High will arise, the Eternal God alone, and He will appear to punish the Gentiles and will destroy all their idols (cp. Mic. 1:7)

---

[139] As Hartman showed, it is indeed the Assumption of Moses which made use of the Targum and not the Targum which has been influenced by the Assumption of Moses, cf. Hartman, *op. cit.*, 127f.

[140] Hartman, *op. cit.*, 132.

[141] Isa. 40:9 and Isa. 35:10 may be verbally tallied in their targumic renderings.

[142] My translation: I followed the latin text for this verse rather than Charles' emendations; in this verse allusions to several biblical texts can be found: *viz.* Isa. 13:10; Joel 2:10, 3:4, 4:15; Zech. 14:6.

8, "Then thou, O Israel, shalt be happy and thou shalt mount upon the necks (cp. Deut. 33:29, Targum) and wings of the eagle (cp. Isa. 40:31, Targum). And they shall be ended.
9, "And God will exalt thee and will cause thee to approach (cp. Ps. 37:34) to the heaven of the stars
10, "And thou shalt look from on high and shalt see thy enemies in Gehenna(143) and thou shalt recognize them and rejoice and thou shalt give thanks and confess thy Creator (cp. Ps. 37:34 and also 91:8, 92:12, 118:7; Isa. 66:14, 24).

After such an example we are disappointed. We have the feeling of being confronted with a second hand message. Under the same disguise of biblical phraseology and traditional Apocalyptic symbols and style, we find no inspiration, no creation. We have the feeling that this is a mere repetition of the message of other Apocalyptists who themselves were inspired. It is significant to note that the *Assumption of Moses* was not a text of the first generation of Apocalyptic books; it is generally accepted that it was written at the beginning of the first century.

---

[143] According to Charles' emendation of the text rather than "on the earth".

VI

VISIONS, INSPIRATION AND SCRIPTURE

We just implied distinction between "inspired Apocalyptic messages" and "repetitions" of these messages. By that we do not deny the value of the latter; not everybody can or must be a prophet. There is room for both prophets and disciples who propagate their message, which becomes tradition in this way. The prophets *uncover* the new revelation, their disciples are concerned with the embodying of this revelation by the faithful community. Such literary works as the *Assumption of Moses* had precisely this latter function, although the disciples may deceive a community by presenting themselves as prophets. By saying this we are proposing to see in these Apocalyptic messages which are structured on biblical texts the results of a psychical experience of one kind or another.[144] This demands explanation, for indeed the opposite conclusion could appear as valid as ours.

First let us emphasize that for the Jewish Apocalyptic circles the concept of inspiration involved a use of Scripture, as cannot be doubted after our survey. We saw, studying Or. Sib. 3, that the Apocalyptists were conscious of the problem of false prophecy: Beliar was the model of the false prophets. This is to say that the psychical experience was not in itself a proof that such an inspiration was coming from Yahweh, the One God: Beliar also performed signs and wonders! The validity of this inspiration was guaranteed rather by its relationship with Scripture. Yet it is clear now that this did not mean that the inspired message was to be a mere repetition of Scripture. As noted already we can describe this inspiration as the work of the creative imagination of a man permeated with Scripture.

---

[144] As we showed by our last example there are nevertheless exceptions.

For the understanding of this process it would be useful to have a detailed knowledge of the way of life of these Apocalyptic circles: in this the Dead Sea Scrolls will be most helpful. Yet a cautious reference to modern Apocalyptic circles may throw some light on the question. I would like, if I may, to refer to the Pentecostal circles that I have had the chance to observe.

After studying Jewish Apocalypticism one is not lost in such circles. Although strongly colored by the Christian perspective, their symbolism is characteristically Apocalyptic. It is borrowed from the Book of Daniel, from the Apocalyptic passages of the New Testament and especially from the Book of Revelation. Furthermore we find there a similar eschatological consciousness. As is well known, in the doctrine of these circles a great place is given to the Holy Spirit as the source of the inspiration active in the community, and consequently to what Paul calls the gifts of the Spirit,[145] namely glossolalia and prophecy. If we leave aside the glossolalia, the inspiration described in the Apocalyptic books is quite similar to the psychical phenomena[146] which I was able to witness.

In these circles one can find besides the regular worship service and its preaching, intensive biblical studies in special meetings and in private. The truly faithful Pentecostalist meditates Scripture day and night, to such an extent that one cannot talk with him without being struck by his "biblical slang". These circles also have prayer meetings: this is the setting for the psychical phenomena. There I had the opportunity to witness men and women, in a trance-like attitude, rising and prophesying. If often these prophecies were purely fantastic if not incoherent, others were actually striking in their use of Scripture. I remember

---

[145] Cf. I Cor. 12 and 14.

[146] The nearly complete absence of any mention of the Holy Spirit in the Apocalyptic books is only a question of vocabulary. As Russell has shown, "the belief is strongly expressed in the accessibility of man's nature to invasive force sent forth from God as means of inspiration", *op. cit.*, 160; cf. also 158-73.

one man, quite-well educated, prophesying on the theme of the role of his community in the contemporary historical situation, which he described in symbols that he was "seeing". It was quite clear that it was not an intellectual game: he was "possessed by the spirit", literally in trance. As always his discourse was in biblical phraseology, yet I could not but be struck by several references to the crossing of the Jordan river. Listening more carefully it became clear that despite the multitude of other biblical texts or phrases used (especially from the New Testament) the whole of his prophecy was structured by Joshua ch. 4, although often apparently we were very far from it.

The community was quite impressed by this prophecy, and significantly in other meetings I found it mentioned in a sermon, and by other "prophets". Yet on these occasions the connection with Joshua ch. 4 was no longer to be found. The symbols alone were kept in the well- elaborated sermon.[147]

This, indeed, does not prove anything about the inspiration of the visionary passages in the Apocalyptic books. Yet it provides me with a strong reason to doubt that these passages, so well-structured on biblical texts, are necessarily the product of a conscious intellectual effort. The forms of inspiration may vary: as we noted above, for the Apocalyptists they included not only visions and trances but dreams (during the night or awake), auditions, and also literary inspiration. Yet even in the latter case, the structuring of the Apocalyptic message is not necessarily the outcome of a conscious intellectual effort.

This structuring of the Apocalyptic messages on specific biblical passages can be pointed out only in a limited number of Apocalyptic pericopes. Yet, as mentioned earlier, it is certain that many other instances have been covered up by the

---

[147] Let us note also that in such communities the Spirit must submitted to Scripture. I had a chance to make a tape recording of a beautiful example of this, in a Pentecostal Church in Chicago. The congregation, almost as a whole, was in trance. The minister could not control it any longer. After many unsuccessful attempts to bring some order in the congregation, he finally said, "Now, open your Bible . . ." and the disorder stopped immediately.

translations. Many of the numerous passages in which we find an anthological style could be the vestiges of a structural style after translation.

CONCLUSION

Let us now crystallize the results of our investigation by listing the axioms which appear to have presided over the use of Scripture in the Apocalyptic literature.

The first axiom, strikingly different from those we found governing the use of Scripture in classical Judaism, is that Scripture by itself is not the complete revelation. In classical Judaism the Torah, given *openly* to Israel through Moses,[148] was the complete and final revelation of the election: "Nothing is left from it in heaven".[149] For the Apocalyptists , indeed, Scripture was given openly, but it was not the complete revelation: part of it was left in heaven (the "Heavenly Tables") and this was now revealed at the end of time to the Apocalyptists. The "Heavenly Tables" had been revealed indeed to the Patriarchs and Moses, but this revelation remained sealed until the last generation, i.e., the Apocalyptists' generation.

Thus for them there was a new revelation (ἀποκάλυψις). This was not understood so much either as the revelation of God himself or as the revelation of God's will, but rather as the revelation of the meaning of history (the salient history). It was therefore a revelation of how God governs history, acts in history, despite the power of evil.

Thus instead of using Scripture in tension with cultural situations (the "history of cultural changes"), in which classical Judaism discovered demands for the reinterpretation of Torah, the Apocalyptists were using Scripture in tension with their contemporary history (salient history), in which they discovered signs of the end of time.

In this context we were led by our investigation to distinguish between two kinds of Scriptural use. Scripture was used, on the one hand, in the process of uncovering the

---

[148] *Mek.* on Exod. 19:2 and on 20:20, cf. Lauterbach ed., vol. II, 234.

[149] *Deut. Rab.* 30:11-14.

"secret revelations" (namely in the visionary passages)[150] and on the other hand, in the process of drawing the consequences which these "secret revelations" had for the life of the Apocalyptic groups (namely in halakic passages, moral teachings and the re-writing of Scripture).

In the passages which express the uncovering of secret revelations, we noted that the Apocalyptic teaching was structured by both Scripture and contemporary history: they can be looked on as being in sequence. Scripture expressed the *past* of this pre-determined sacred history, which unfolded itself in the new events of their time. Yet the metaphor of unfolding eliminates the necessity of inspiration, and thus of new or secret revelations, which we find constantly implied in the Apocalyptic literature. A better metaphor would be that of two poles in tension: revelation appears *in* this tension between Scripture and the contemporary history. This tension could then represent the eschatological consciousness, with its expectation of (tension toward) the End. The typology was used as the means to relate these two poles: this process took place in the experience of inspiration which, so to speak, allowed the spark of revelation to flash between the two poles.

This metaphor may help to show why these texts are structured by both Scripture and contemporary history, although according to the passages one or the other predominates. On the one hand biblical passages structure more directly the new revelation (structural style), and the contemporary history is then molded into this structure; in this first case the text still manifests the uncovering of the new revelation. On the other hand, contemporary history structures the new revelation. Scripture furnishes only the vocabulary to express it (anthological style). Yet in this second case, Scripture still furnishes a general framework (which we called the broad biblical pattern). As noted above, this type of use of Scripture manifests the embodying process of these new revelations (their function is comparable to that of the liturgy in the Synagogue).

---

[150] Yet not necessarily all of them.

On the basis of these new (secret) revelations, Scripture is further used in order to draw out implications for the life of the Apocalyptic group. Here the exegetical techniques are similar to those found in classical Judaism (although some of them are amplified because of the demands of the new revelation). The commandments are no longer reinterpreted in terms of new cultural situations (as was the case in classical Judaism), but in terms of the new revelation, that is, of the new acts of God in history. It is noteworthy here that this reinterpretation of the commandments results from belief in the new acts of God in history. We have here, therefore, the same Covenant pattern which one can observe in Exodus 19 and 20, where the commandments are given as the consequence of the election (represented by the event of the Exodus) and of the vocation of the people expressed therein.[151]

In the Apocalyptic passages using Scripture in this way, we find then a kind of halakic interpretation, as well as the use of biblical characters as moral (or anti-moral) types. This new revelation implies also a new reading of Scripture, which is expressed in the re-writing that we found in the *Book of Jubilees*, but which can be brought out also in several other Apocalyptic books (although less extensively). Among the latter are the *Testaments of the Twelve Patriarchs* and *I Enoch*, which contains passages of a *Book of Noah*.[152]

All these uses of Scripture were nevertheless influenced by cultural elements which had their origin outside the Jewish people (this is particularly noticeable in the extra- biblical symbolism). This happened against the Apocalyptists' very intention: they denied indeed any value to cultural changes. We have noted that this attitude led the Apocalyptists to "canonize" a former culture.

---

[151] By that we are denying the existence of the other understanding of the Covenant which we emphasized when speaking of classical Judaism. On these two understandings see A. Jaubert, *La Notion d'Alliance*, especially 27-66.

[152] I Enoch ch. 106.

Several of these conclusions, which we have been able to draw despite the limitations we noted earlier, will be refined and confirmed in our upcoming investigation of the use of Scripture in the Dead Sea Scrolls.

CHAPTER IX

THE USE OF SCRIPTURE IN
THE DEAD SEA SCROLLS

With the Dead Sea Scrolls[1] we find ourselves in a quite different position than when studying the use of Scripture in the Apocalyptic books. Here not only do we have the original Hebrew (or Aramaic) texts, but also we can reach the *Sitz im Leben* of this use of Scripture: in these documents the life of the community is partially described. Furthermore we find statements which can be looked on as expressing explicitly the sect's doctrine of Scripture. So before examining the different ways in which Scripture has been used, according to the different literary genres of the main scrolls, we shall

---

[1] For this part of our research we generally used the Hebrew text of the Dead Sea Scrolls as edited by E. Lohse in *Die Texte aus Qumran Hebräisch und Deutsch*, München, 1964, rather than A. M. Habermann, *Megikloth Midbar Yehuda. The Scrolls from the Judean Desert*, Jerusalem, 1959. I constantly compared these texts with the multi-volume standard texts edited 1) by D. Barthelemy, J. T. Milik, and J. M. Allegro, *Discoveries in the Judaean Desert*, Oxford, 1955-1968; 2) by M. Burrows, J. C. Trever, and W. H. Brownlee, *The Dead Sea Scrolls of St. Mark's Monastery*, vol. I and II, New Haven, 1950 and 1951; and 3) by E. L. Sukenik, *The Dead Sea Scrolls of the Hebrew University*, Jerusalem, 1954, in order to check the completions or reconstructions of the accidental lacunae in the manuscripts. Passages quoted are from different translations. I chose them according to their closeness to my own interpretation (see the footnotes). When no reference is made to English translations, although I may have used them, I introduced into the text my own interpretations and translations. I cannot therefore claim the authority of another scholar to justify the latter. For the *Zadokite Documents* I used mainly Chaim Rabin's *The Zadokite Documents*, second revised ed. Oxford, 1958.

sketch briefly the main characteristics of the community (in so far as they are useful for our study) and point out the main texts which express its doctrine of Scripture.

I

THE ESCHATOLOGICAL COMMUNITY
AND SCRIPTURE

The community existed for a relatively long period and underwent a number of changes. This could explain why the description of the community varies in detail from one scroll to the other. Yet beyond this diversity there are major characteristics which can be found in each of these documents. For our purpose it is enough to present in a synthetic way a general picture of the community. We can therefore include in our description characteristics mentioned in the *Zadokite Documents*, although this text refers certainly to another community than that established at Kirbet Qumran. In other words, in spite of our synthetic approach, it should not be forgotten that the Dead Sea Scrolls refer not only to the Dead Sea community but also to other communities representing other branches of the same movement. For indeed we conceive the Covenanters' movement as being similar to that of the *haburot* of the Talmudic literature.[2]

---

[2]On this see P. Wernberg-Møller, "The Nature of the *Yahad* according to the *Manual of Discipline* and related documents" in *The Annual of Leeds University Oriental Society*, vol VI, Leiden, 1969, 56-81. The other possibility would be to interpret these passages as referring to the historical development of the sect. In our view these two interpretations must be taken into account in order to understand the nature of the community. At any rate an attempt to point out the different stages of the organization of the community would be quite conjectural, at least for the time being. It would demand a relative chronology of the origin of the different Qumran texts. Such a chronology is very difficult to establish because of the composite character of the main texts describing the community, namely the *Manual of Discipline* (1 QS) and the *Zadokite Documents* (CD): cf. A. Jaubert, *La Notion d'Alliance dans le Judaïsme aux abords de l'Ere Chrétienne*, Paris, 1963, 117f. To my knowledge the only serious attempts to deal with this problem are those by A. M. Denis, "Evolution des Structures dans la Secte de Qumran", in *Aux Origines de l'Eglise*, Recherches Bibliques VII, Louvain, 1965, (cf. also his *Les Thèmes de connaissance dans le Document de Damas*, Louvain, 1967), and by J. Murphy O'Connor, "La Genèse littéraire de la Règle de la communauté", Revue Biblique 76, 1969, 528-49. Cf. also the excellent article by

Our chief sources of information about the organization of the community are the *Manual of Discipline, The Hodayot* and secondarily the *Zadokite Documents*.

This community was an eschatological one. Without going into the discussion of all its eschatological characteristics, we need at least mention how the sectarians referred to themselves. Their community (יחד: union) was the "covenant" (ברית). Thus to enter the community meant nothing less than to enter the covenant.[3] The Zadokite Documents specify further that it was the "New Covenant".[4] For indeed they considered themselves the Remnant of Israel (in terms of Isa. 65). They were the true and faithful Israel for whom the Covenant had been renewed,[5] although the final, messianic renewal of the Covenant was still in the future.[6]

We cannot indulge ourselves in an exposition of the concept of covenant in the Dead Sea Scrolls. This would carry us too far from our topic and could not but repeat the excellent and complementary studies by A. Jaubert[7] and Otto Betz.[8] Let us simply state that the community of the Covenant

---

D. Winton Thomas, "The Dead Sea Scrolls: what may we believe?" in *The Annual of Leeds University Oriental Society*, vol VI, 1969, 7-20. He points out "the many uncertainties which surround the study of the scrolls", especially as far as their dates and the identification of the different historical allusions therein are concerned.

[3] Cf. e.g., 1 QS 1:16, 18, 20; 5:7-9.

[4] Cf. CD 6:19; 8:21 and 20:12. The phrase is also possibly used in 1 Qp Hab. 2:4, which presents, unhappily, a lacuna.

[5] 1 QSb 3:26; 5:21; 1 Q 34bis 3, II 6.

[6] 1 QSb 5:20-23; 4 Q Patriarchal Blessings 3-4, cf. also 1 QS 4:25.

[7] *La Notion d'Alliance dans le Judaïsme aux abords de l'Ere Chrétienne*, Paris, 1963, 116-249.

[8] "The eschatological interpretation of the Sinai tradition in Qumran and in the New Testament", *R.Q.* 6, 1967, 89-108, cf. also his "Le ministère cultuel dans la secte de Qumran et dans le christianisme primitif", in *La Secte de Qumran et les Origines du Christianisme*, Louvain, 1959, 163-202.

understood itself in terms of the Sinai-tradition (Deut. 33:2-5 and Exod. 19). Waiting for the final renewal of the Covenant, they made the holy status which was required of the people in front of Mount Sinai (cf. 1 QSa 1:26) into their permanent (because eschatological) way of life. This attitude was associated further with the ritual purity of the priests in the Temple: they considered their community the substitute for the defiled Temple of Jerusalem.[9]

We just mentioned that the Covenanters expected the eschatological fulfillment. Here we should qualify this statement: the eschatological fulfillment concerned primarily the "men of iniquity" who would be judged at that time. As far as the Covenanters themselves were concerned, this eschatological fulfillment was already beginning in their community. They were living in the eschatological era. They were in communion with the angels.[10] Thus the eschatological reality was already present in the community. The latter was the place between heaven and earth, between future and present, where the eschaton was already realized, yet still future. Such are the conclusions of the study by H. W. Kuhn on the eschatology of the Hodayot.[11]

These brief remarks should be sufficient to let appear the eschatological setting that the Dead Sea community provided for the Covenanters' use of Scripture. Following the demands of our topic we shall mention other aspects of the life of the community. Let us simply emphasize a significant difference between the concrete settings for the use of Scripture by the Covenanters and by classical Judaism. There were *two Sitze im Leben* for the interpretation of Scripture in classical Judaism: the Synagogue and the School. For the Covenanters' interpetation of Scripture there was only *one Sitz im Leben*: the community. This formal difference

---

[9] Cf. on this B. Gärtner, *The Temple and the Community in Qumran and the New Testament*, Cambridge, 1965, especially 4-46, and the bibliography therein.

[10] Cf. e.g., 1 QH 3:2; 1 QS 11:7-8.

[11] *Enderwartung und gegenwärtiges Heil, Untersuchungen zu den Gemeindeliedern von Qumran*, Göttingen, 1966. Cf. namely ch. 10 and 11.

symbolizes already a major difference which separates the
hermeneutical structure of classical Judaism from that of the
Covenanters (and also of the Apocalyptists): the former is
twofold, the latter is integrated around a single center.

THE BASIS FOR THEIR SECTARIANISM: SCRIPTURE

This eschatological community was a *sect*. The
Covenanters were quite aware that the basis for their
sectarianism was their interpretation of Scripture. The
following passage of the Manual of Discipline expresses it:[12]

> "Everyone who enters into the council of the
> community shall enter into the Covenant of
> God in the presence of all the volunteers
> and he shall obligate himself by a binding
> oath to return to the Law of Moses according
> to everything which he prescribed, with all
> his heart and all his soul, following the
> priests, the keepers of the Covenant and
> seekers(13) of his will, and to the multitude
> of the men of their covenant they who
> volunteer together for this truth and to walk
> in his will. And he shall undertake by the
> Covenant to separate himself from all men of
> iniquity that walk in the ways of wickedness.
> For they are not reckoned in His Covenant,
> for they have not sought (בקשו) nor searched
> (דרשהו) (14) in His Laws (בחוקיהו) to know
> the hidden things (הנסתרות) in which they
> have erred, incurring guilt, and the manifest
> things (הנגלות) they have done high-handedly".(15)

This text is quite representative. It shows clearly
what was the reason for the separation from the rest of
Judaism: a different attitude toward Scripture. The "men of
iniquity" were those who had not "sought nor searched in his

---

[12] Let us note its "covenant" setting.

[13] דורשי

[14] ודרשו: cf. E. Lohse, *Die Texts ans Qumran, Hebräisch und Deutsch*, München, 1964, 18, note c.

[15] 1 QS 5:7-12.

Laws". בקש and דרש[16] were both used with the meaning "to consult", "to inquire of" God (Exod. 33:7) or His word (Amos 8:12). This consultation of the precepts of God was to be done "in order to know the hidden things". The Covenanters were not therefore merely rejecting people who neglected the study of Scripture, but those who were not practicing the same approach toward interpreting Scripture as theirs.

The Covenanters' doctrine of Scripture is therefore expressed a) in the characteristics of their approach toward interpreting Scripture (it was to be an inspired interpretation), as well as b) in the statements which describe what they expected to discover in Scripture (the "hidden things" and "mysteries").

THE TEACHER OF RIGHTEOUSNESS, INSPIRED INTERPRETER OF SCRIPTURE

Scripture (the Book) was to be studied by the whole of the community ("the Many") for one third of every night (1 QS 6:7). Thus it is not surprising that the *Zadokite Documents* refer to the community as a "House of the Torah" (בית התורה).[17] The study of Torah was therefore the enterprise of the community as a whole. Yet there were men who were specially appointed for this task. In each place where there were ten members of the sect there was to be a man studying Torah day and night (1 QS 6:6, this according to Josh. 1:8 and Ps. 1:2). He was a *Doresh ha-Torah*, an Interpreter of Torah, a title which was used not only for these men and the Teacher of Righteousness,[18] but also for the *Doresh ha-Torah* par

---

[16] Cf. above.

[17] This phrase, which occurs twice (CD 20:10 and 13), is to be compared with the similar phrase בית האמת "House of truth" (1 QS 5:6, cf. also 1 QS 8:9).

[18] Cf. CD 6:7 which I interpret as referring to the Teacher of Righteousness, following N. Wieder, *The Judean Scroll and Karaism*, London, 1962, 9, note 4.

excellence, namely the Priestly Messiah who would rise with the Davidic Messiah (4 Q Florilegium 1:11[19] and CD 7:18).

The Teacher of Righteousness himself was primarily an interpreter of Scripture.[20] His function was described not only as that of an interpreter of Torah but also (and mainly) as an interpreter of the Prophets. Thus we read in the *Pesher on Habakkuk*:[21]

> "God told Habakkuk to write down the things that were to come upon the last generation, but the end of the epoch he did not make known to him. And as for the words 'he that readeth it, may do so swiftly' this refers to the Teacher of Righteousness to whom God made known all the secrets of the words of His servants the Prophets".

The function of this priestly[22] Teacher was "to explain all the words of His servants the Prophets through whom he foretold what was to come upon his people" (1 Qp Hab. 2:8-10).

Thus the Teacher of Righteousness was the *inspired* interpreter of the Prophets' writings. This is not to say that the Teacher of Righteousness knew more than the Prophets, as the beginning of the text quoted above (1 Qp Hab. 7:1-2)

---

[19] Where II Sam. 7:11-12 is interpreted as follows: "He is 'the shoot of David' who will rise with the Interpreter of the Law. . . ." (דורש התורה).

[20] Here let us note that, following *inter alios* G. W. Buchanan, "The Priestly Teacher of Righteousness", *R.Q.* 6, 1969, 553-58, we consider this title as referring to a position or function rather than to a specific individual. We agree nevertheless that the first who fulfilled this function was without any doubt considered as the Teacher of Righteousness :*par excellence* and had a considerable role in the organization of the community. Several Qumran texts can be attributed to him, namely some of the *Hodayot*: cf. M. Mansoor, *The Thanksgiving Hymns*, Grand Rapids, Mich., 1961, 45ff., and the bibliography therein. Yet we should note that, taking into account the *Zadokite Documents* (1:1ff.), the phrase Teacher of Righteousness does not seem to refer to the founder of the sect (cf. A. S. Van Woude, "Le Maître de Justice et les deux Messies", in *La Secte de Qumran et les Origines du Christianisme*, Louvain, 1959, 127f.).

[21] 1 Qp Hab. 7:1-5 interpreting Hab. 2:2. N. Wieder's translation.

[22] Cf. 4 Qp Ps. 37; 3:15.

has sometimes been interpreted.[23] Yet he was inspired [24] in the sense that he had the gift of "explaining" these records, especially the mysteries, the secrets contained in them. These mysteries, as we shall see below, concerned the last generation (1 Qp Hab. 1:7), hence the eschatological period (although not the end of it). We find the inspiration of the Teacher of Righteousness expressed in the *Hodayot* in the repeated mention that the author received the gift of the Holy Spirit. The author is generally identified with the Teacher of Righteousness: "But I, Thy Servant, know, by the Spirit which Thou hast given me . . ." (1 QH 13:18-19). "And me, Thy servant, Thou hast favoured with the Spirit of knowledge . . ." (1 QH 14:25).[25] He is therefore the one of whom it can be said, "Thou hast laid it in his heart to open the fountain of knowledge unto all who understand" (1 QH 2:18).

We should note here that although the Teacher of Righteousness is described as inspired by the Holy Spirit,[26]

---

[23] Thus Millar Burrows, *The Dead Sea Scrolls*, New York, 1956, "The Habakkuk commentary, it will be remembered, says that the teacher of righteousness was given insight surpassing that of the Prophets themselves", 284 (although he does not mention his source we think the author interprets here 1 Qp Hab. 7:1-2). Cf. also, along the same line: J. T. Milik, *Ten Years of Discovery in the Wilderness of Judea*, 113f. G. Vermès, *Discoveries in the Judean Desert*, 128. We follow Dupont-Sommer, *Les Ecrits Esséniens découverts près de la Mer Morte*, Paris, 1959, *ad loc.*, who interprets this same text as follows: "*Nul* ne connaît ni le jour ni l'heure" (italics mine); and N. Wieder, *op. cit.*, 86f., "The whole intention of the author of the *Habakkuk Commentary* in observing that God did not reveal to Habakkuk when the 'end of the epoch' would occur . . . was to explain why the *moreh sedeq* was ignorant of that crucial date".

[24] This may have been explicitly stated in the corrupted text of 1 Qp Hab. 2:8; cf. also: B. J. Roberts, "The Dead Sea Scrolls and the Old Testament Scriptures", *B.J.R.L.* 36, 1953, 75-96 and especially 83f.

[25] Cf. also 1 QH 7:6-7; 12:12; 17:26, *passim*.

[26] Cf. the relevant passages in O. Betz, *Der Paraklet: Fürsprecher im häretischen Spätjudentum, im Johannes. Evangelium und in den neugefundenen gnostichen Schriften*, Leiden, 1963, *passim*, and *Offenbarung*, 110ff., and *passim*. For a sketch of this doctrine see F. F. Bruce, "Holy Spirit in the Qumran Text", in *Annual of Leeds University Oriental Society*, Leiden, 1969, 49-55.

there is no explicit reference to any kind of visionary experiences (psychical experiences) comparable to the Apocalyptists'. Here Scripture had a much more central role in the uncovering of the "hidden things" and of the "mysteries". Revelation occurred in an *inspired search of Scripture*.

Thus the Teacher of Righteousness was the inspired interpreter of the Prophets. In spite of the stress put on his interpretation of the Prophets, he was also the interpreter and expounder of the Law, i.e., a *Doresh ha-Torah*. For the community, to follow the Law of Moses meant indeed to carry out "every commandment of the Law of Moses in accordance with all that has been revealed of it to the sons of Zadok" (1 QS 6:6-7), that is also to the priestly Teacher of Righteousness. We shall return to this "halakic" exegesis of the sect. Let us note simply, as we did for the Apocalyptic literature, that it was a very rigorous interpretation. This explains why the opponents of the sect were called the "seekers of smooth things", that is the *dorshe halaqot* (דורשי החלקות), which is certainly to be understood as a term of derision for the *dorshe halakot* (דורשי הלכות).[27]

"HIDDEN THINGS", "MYSTERIES", AND SCRIPTURE

According to the text quoted above (1 QS 5:7-12) the purpose for searching Scripture was "to know the hidden things" (הנסתרות). What were these "hidden things?" Also, what were the "mysteries" or "secrets" that we found mentioned in the *Pesher* on Habakkuk (1 Qp Hab. 7:5 and also 7:8, 14, *passim*)?[28] What was this "knowledge" (which one is tempted to

---

[27] 4 Qp Nahum 2 and 3; on this cf. S. B. Hoenig, "Dorshe Halakot in the Pesher Nahum scrolls", *J.B.L.* 83, 1964, 119-38.

[28] Cf. Kuhn's concordance under רז and סוד for the numerous instances where these concepts can be found through most of the Dead Sea Scrolls.

call with Dupont-Sommer a "gnosis"[29]) which was imparted to the Teacher of Righteousness and his followers in their interpretation of Scripture?[30]

Did all these terms refer to an esoteric teaching? This has been maintained by some authors.[31] Yet one hesitates. It is true that several passages stress that the peculiar teaching of the sect must be jealously guarded and not revealed to anyone outside the community.[32] Yet the *Hodayot* described the "men of iniquity" as those who refused the instruction of the Teacher of Righteousness.[33] This implies that the teaching had been exposed to them. The Teacher of Righteousness seems to have preached his doctrine openly. As A. M. Denis pointed out for the *Zadokite Documents*, this discrepancy may be due to the composite character of the Dead Sea Scrolls. They reflect different stages in the evolution of the community, which was first open and which later on[34] fell back upon itself with a strong esoteric tendency.[35] It seems therefore (and this will be substantiated below) that these secret teachings were "secret" because they were hidden until that time (until the last generation). What we have seen about the Apocalyptists' understanding of their own "secret revelation" is valid here also. According to the Covenanters' and the Apocalyptists' belief, certain

---

[29] Dupont-Sommer, *op. cit.*, 372. Against such a qualification see G. R. Driver, *The Judaean Scrolls*, Oxford, 1965, 562-70.

[30] Cf. 1 QS 7:17-18, *passim*.

[31] Cf. e.g., Dupont-Sommer, *op. cit.*, 58, who does not hesitate to speak of the strictly esoteric character of the sect: ". . . le caractère strictement ésotérique de la secte essénienne. Or ce même caractère est également des plus accentués dans la secte de Qumran". Cf. also J. Licht, *The Thanksgiving Scroll*, 49.

[32] Cf. 1 QS 4:6; 5:15-16; 9:16-19; 10:24-25.

[33] Cf. e.g., 1 QH 4:7ff.; 15:18ff.

[34] Persecutions certainly played an important role in this evolution of the sect.

[35] Cf. A. M. Denis, *Les Thèmes de Connaissance . . .*, 208-12.

revelations were known to the Patriarchs, Moses, and the Prophets (the last mainly according to the Covenanters). Yet these revelations were hidden, kept secret until the "appointed time" for their unveiling.

We need now to see more specifically what was meant by the terms "hidden things", "mysteries" and "knowledge". Let us examine first the use of the general term: "knowledge" (דעה).[36] It is very striking that דעה refers to a knowledge of which God is the object only in 1 QH 12:11 and 1 QSb 5:25. The latter is clearly a quotation of Isa. 11:2; thus we have only one instance.[37] We can therefore conclude negatively that this knowledge was not a mystic knowledge which would have as its consequence a "communion" with the Divinity.

This knowledge[38] appears much more often as belonging to God, who was called the "God of knowledges".[39] This phrase had two distinct connotations. On the one hand, as "God of knowledges" God was the One with whom the sinner was confronted.[40] In other words the notion of knowledge was connected in this case with the question of the observance of the divine commandments. On the other hand, in other passages, as in 1 QS 3:15, God was called the "God of knowledges" because as the Creator he knew, before even creating them, "all the works which creatures would accomplish during all ages for ever" (1 QH 1:7-8).[41] It was also he who had fixed the heavenly calendar.[42] We find therefore the same

---

[36] We dismiss those passages which refer to common human knowledge such as CD 10:10; 1 QS 1:11-12; 2:26-3:2. . . .

[37] 1 QH 12:11 is itself possibly reminiscent of Hos. 13:5.

[38] On this see Kuhn, *op. cit.*, ch. 8-9, on the theme of knowledge in the *Hodayot*, and Denis, *Les Thèmes de Connaissance, passim*, on the *Zadokite Documents*.

[39] אל הדעות

[40] 1 QH 1:26-27. The phrase "God of knowledges" is used here in the same sense as in I Sam. 2:3.

[41] Cf. also CD 2:8, *passim*, 1 QH 13:11; 15:14-15, *passim*.

[42] 1 QH 12:10-13.

deterministic concept of history as the one we pointed out in
the *Book of Jubilees*. Since God was in this sense the "source
of knowledge (מקור דעה)",[43] it is not surprising to see that
this knowledge referred to the mysteries of history and
especially to the mysteries of the eschatological time (the
last generation).

This twofold conception of the "God of knowledges"
reflects the distinction between the objects of this
knowledge, *viz.* the "hidden things" and the "mysteries", that
the Covenanters expected to discover by means of their
interpretation of Scripture. We shall now discuss these two
concepts.

A. *The "Hidden Things"*

The "hidden things" (הנסתרות), according to the context
of 1 QS 5:7-12, clearly referred to specific teachings
discovered in the commandments. Interestingly enough these
were opposed to the "manifest things" (הנגלות) which the "men
of iniquity" knew and interpreted correctly, yet transgressed
"high-handedly". Thus it appears that this peculiar
interpretation of the commandments was not one which applied
to every commandment. In other words this was not an
interpretation which would attempt to discover an esoteric
teaching in each biblical precept. On the contrary such an
interpretation concerned only the precepts which, because of
their vague wordings, could be interpreted in different ways
(and which therefore were one of the causes of the division in
Palestinian Judaism).

In the *Zadokite Documents* we find a list of these
"hidden things":

---

[43] Cf. 1 QS 10:11-12 and 1 QH 12:29.

> "But with them that held fast to the commandments
> of God who were left over of them, God established
> His covenant with Israel for ever, by revealing to
> them hidden things (הנסתרות) concerning which all
> Israel had gone astray: his holy sabbaths and his
> glorious appointed times, his righteous testimonies
> and his true ways and the requirements of his
> desire which man shall do and live thereby"
> (CD 3:12-16).(44)

Thus for the author of the *Zadokite Documents* sabbaths and festivals were typical examples of these "hidden" commandments which needed a peculiar interpretation. Why the Sabbath? Because, as is well known, the Scriptural basis for the *halakoth* concerning its observance is actually very vague.[45] The sect's observance of this commandment was very rigorous, as can be seen in the *Zadokite Documents* (10:14-11:18).[46] The same can be said about the festivals. Yet in the latter case we should note also the sect's preoccupation with holding the festivals at the proper time, that is, according to the sect's calendar, which was itself a "hidden thing"[47] that could be discovered in Scripture[48] by means of a through "search". The "men of iniquity" could be condemned therefore because they did not practice such a study of Scripture.[49] Thus this search of Scripture did not have in

---

[44] For a similar list with reference to the "true laws" see 1 QS 1:11-15. Here we cannot follow Denis' interpretation of נסתורות (cf. *op. cit.*, 25ff.). For indeed this author identifies them too easily with the mysteries (or secrets): he did not give enough weight to the parallel passage in 1 QS.

[45] As was also recognized by the Rabbis: cf. Hag. 1:8.

[46] We shall not go into the discussion about the sect's possible practice of reckoning the Sabbath from sunrise instead of from sunset. In favor of this theory see S. Talmon, "The Calendar Reckoning of the Sect from the Judaean Desert", *Scripta Hierosolymitana* IV, 187ff. Against it see N. Wieder, *op. cit.*, 54f.

[47] Cf. e.g., 1 QS 10:1.

[48] As A. Jaubert has shown. On this cf. the bibliography we gave about the calendar of the *Book of Jubilees*.

[49] Cf. 1 QS 5:7-12.

itself an esoteric character; such a search was open to everybody.⁵⁰ The outcome was nevertheless apprehended as a revelation.⁵¹ It was an "uncovering" which, as we have seen, was the result of a gift of God. It was an inspired interpretation of Scripture.⁵²

These "hidden things" were designated also by the more general phrase "his true ways", i.e., the Lord's true ways. This phrase occurs quite often under one form or another⁵³ in order to designate the peculiar conception which the sect had of Judaism.⁵⁴ This designation had its origin in the community's interpretation of Isa. 40:3: "Prepare the way of the Lord, make straight in the desert a highway for our God". The Covenanters applied this text to themselves. Its interpretation is given in the *Manual of Discipline*:

> "This is the study of the Torah (מדרש התורה) (which) he commanded through Moses, in order to act according to all that has been revealed from time to time and according to that which the prophets have uncovered by his holy spirit" (1 QS 8:15-16).(55)

---

⁵⁰Cf. N. Wieder, *op. cit.*, 54ff.

⁵¹Cf. CD 3:14.

⁵²We find here as in the *Book of Jubilees* both determinism *viz.* the gift of the revelation of "hidden things", and on the other hand the responsibility of man, *viz.* his condemnation for not discovering these "hidden things" in Torah. On this complex relationship of "determinism" and "grace" in the Dead Sea Scrolls cf. e.g., A. Jaubert, *La Notion d'Alliance*, 131-43.

⁵³Cf. e.g., 1 QS 3:10; 3:20; 4:2, *passim*.

⁵⁴Cf. e.g., CD 20:18, דרך יי. The Covenanters were "those who chose the way" (1 QS 9:17f.). Their opponents were "those who deviated from the way" (CD 1:13; 2:6).

⁵⁵Cf. the excellent interpretation of this passage by O. Betz (*Offenbarung*, 155ff.). He notes th e differences in meaning which the passage of Isa. 40:3 had for the prophet himself, for the Qumranites, and for the writers of the Gospels. Here the "way" to be built was this very interpretation of Torah, this *halakah*, which was "built" in the wilderness by means of the study of Torah. For the Gospels the wilderness was only the place where the injunction to build a way for the Lord was cried out. For the Prophet it was the actual road along which the people would walk when coming back from exile. Thus in the Dead Sea Scrolls and in

Thus the preparation of the "way of the Lord" was first of all the study of Torah, which resulted in an "uncovering" of the Law. In other words it resulted in a special *halakah* which the community had to follow. We need emphasize here with N. Wieder[56] that the Covenanters conceived such a revelation as progressive.[57] There was a specific revelation for each stage of the sacred History in its course toward the *eschaton*. This is implied in the already mentioned distinction between the "hidden" and "manifest" things.[58] This same concept of progressive revelation is also certainly implied in 1 QS 1:8-9, in which the Covenanters were called to "walk before him (God) perfectly according to all that has been revealed at the times set for making them known".[59] As the context implies, this sentence refers to the interpretations of the commandments given by God "through Moses and the Prophets" (1:3), which were revealed at certain divinely "appointed times". Thus these interpretations amounted to the revelation of the right way of life for that "appointed time", the last generation's time. They expressed this further by speaking of the search into Torah as "the

---

the Gospels we have an actualization of the biblical text as it was applied to two historical situations. It was understood as a prophecy of these two historical events by the respective communities.

[56] *Op. cit.*, 67ff.

[57] "From time to time", עת בעת. Cf. 1 QS 8:15 and 9:13. Cf. also 1 QS 9:12 and CD 12:21.

[58] 1 QS 5:7-12.

[59] Leaney's translation: A. R. C. Leaney, *The Rule of Qumran and its Meaning*, Philadelphia, 1966. The phrase למועדי תעודרתם has been interpreted quite differently by Dupont-Sommer, *op. cit.*, *ad loc.*, and G. Vermès, *The Dead Sea Scrolls in English*, Baltimore, 1962. They interpret it as follows: ". . . in accordance with all that has been revealed concerning *their appointed times*" (Vermès), or "their regular feasts" (Dupont-Sommer). This interpretation has rightly been rejected by P. Guilbert, *Les Textes de Qumran traduits et annotés*, vol. I, Paris, 1961, 22; P. Wernberg-Møller, *The Manual of Discipline*, Leiden, 1967, *ad loc.*; and O. Betz, *Offenbarung*, 45, because of his understanding of the preposition ל. O. Betz supports the interpretation "at the times set for making them known" by pointing to the parallel texts: 1 QM 14:13 and 1 QH frgt. 5:11.

digging of the well".[60] In this interpretation of Num. 21:18 we find the same conception of a progressive uncovering of Torah. What had been revealed until now to the community involved in the "search of Torah" was a revelation for the "epoch of wickedness" in which they lived. Yet the final "uncovering" of the Law would take place only in the time "when shall arise he who teaches righteousness in the end of days".[61] It is nevertheless clear that for the community the "uncovering" of Scripture was already almost complete. The interpretation given by the community was the final rule which should be strictly followed.[62] Any other interpretation was a "snare of Satan".[63]

It is hardly necessary to point out that this study of Torah was to be implemented in a practice of the Law.[64] Here, as in the Hebrew Bible, "knowledge" was always a "practical" knowledge. We should not forget that this study of Scripture was undertaken in the framework of the Covenant. We can say therefore that the purpose of this "search" and practice of Torah was to live up to the election as the holy and faithful people of the last generation.[65]

---

[60] Cf. CD 3:16. In this text the image was used in order to explain "the uncovering of hidden things" and especially "of his true ways", cf. also CD 6:3-11. For an interpretation of the use of Num. 21:18 and Isa. 54:16 in this passage, cf. J. A. Fitzmyer, "The Use of Explicit Old Testament Quotations in Qumran Literature and in the New Testament", *N.T.S.* 7, 1960-61, 320f.

[61] CD 6:11.

[62] Cf. 1 QS 5:8-9.

[63] Cf. CD 4:15-17, on this see G. Vermès, "The Qumran Interpretation of Scripture", in *The Annual of Leeds University Oriental Society*, Leiden, 1969, 84-97, especially 86-89.

[64] Cf. e.g., 1 QS 5:20ff.; 6:18.

[65] On this cf. G. R. Driver, *The Judaean Scrolls. The Problem and a Solution*, Oxford, 1965, 564ff.

B. *The "Mysteries"*

The term "mystery" (רז) referred precisely to the discovery of this election. The election was understood to be the meaning of the salient history at large: i.e., the history as involving not only the life of the community, but also all of human history and even the whole creation. It was indeed to this second kind of revelation that the term "mystery" (רז) most often referred.[66] The phrase "mysteries of God" is particularly meaningful.[67] In each of its occurrences (1 QS 3:23; 1 Qp Hab. 7:8; 1 QM 3:9, 16:11 and 16) it referred to the mysterious ways in which God acted in history in order to realize His purpose, especially by the suppression of all evil and iniquity. Thus רז referred to the divine plan to bring about the messianic age. As noted already in connection with the Teacher of Righteousness as interpreter of the Prophets, these mysteries of God's government of history were revealed to the Prophets and could be discovered by a "study" of their oracles. The knowledge of this mysterious plan of God enabled the Covenanters to interpret present history; they were living in the eschatological time ("the last generation") about which the Prophets had written. These mysteries referred mainly to the extirpation of wickedness, that is, so to speak, to the "negative" acts of God in history. Nevertheless the contexts of these passages show that the establishment of the community of the New Covenant was itself a mystery. This appears clearly in the *pesharim*, as we shall see below. It is also to be found in the first part of the *Zadokite Documents* in which the Covenanters were exhorted to "consider the works of God"[68]

---

[66] We leave aside the term "secret" סוד, which is less typical. Let us note that the term "mystery" (רז) was also sued in order to refer to the "hidden things" of the Law, as for instance in 1 QS 9:18. Yet our distinction between הנסתרות and רז is justified by the specific connotation of the latter in most of its occurrences.

[67] On this cf. E. Vogt, "'Mysteria' in Textibus Qumran", *Biblica* 37, 1956, 247-57.

[68] CD 1:1-2.

which involved not only the punishment of the wicked but also the establishment of the community.[69]

This is to be understood as the same deterministic view of history which we found in the *Book of Jubilees*.[70] In the same way this divine plan included also the government of the universe (cf. e.g., 1 QH 1:11, 13, 21). We do not need therefore to elaborate further on this.

To conclude this discussion, let us emphasize that the distinction which we have discovered between the "hidden things" and the "mysteries" as two different contents of the Covenanters' revelation, is similar to what we discovered in the Apocalyptic literature. To unveil the "mysteries" of contemporary history was to uncover a new election of the faithful community (i.e., to unveil the new acts of God which brought about the new Covenant). As we may already anticipate, such an uncovering was the result of the confrontation between Scripture and contemporary salient history, just as in the Apocalyptic literature. The uncovering of the "hidden things" was apparently the outcome of a subsequent use of Scripture, interpreting the way of Torah for a community which had earlier discovered the "mysteries" of its identity as Chosen People of the end time. Thus the search of Scripture which brought about the uncovering of the "hidden things" was made in terms of a previous understanding of the revealed nature of the community.

---

[69] Cf. A. M. Denis, *Les Thèmes de Connaissance*, 11-82. The author presents therein a study of CD 1:1-4:6 focused on this topic.

[70] On this see for instance G. R. Driver, *op. cit.*, 550-62, although I do not agree with his conclusions that such a view could not have been held in the first or second century B.C.

THE EXPLICIT QUOTATIONS
OF SCRIPTURE

Let us add a few general remarks about the explicit quotations of Scripture in the Dead Sea Scrolls.[71] We are referring here to the passages in which the sectarians made appeal to Scripture consciously and deliberately. These remarks will deal specifically with the introductory formulae of the forty-four explicit quotations.[72] They are significant because of the doctrine of Scripture they express.

In eight of them the verb כתב (to write) is used (1 QS 5:15; 8:14; CD 11:18, 20; 7:19; 9:5; 5:1 and also 4 Q Florilegium 1:2, 12, 15, 16). This implies that the sectarians considered the Old Testament to be their normative *Scripture*, in the same way that it was the normative Scripture for the rest of Judaism (and the New Testament). Yet the verbs meaning to say (הגיד; דבר; אמר) are used even more frequently in these formulae (twenty-two times). This points to an understanding of the Old Testament similar to the one found in classical Judaism, that is to say to a conception of the Old Testament as a dynamic, living reality, a word addressed to the concretness of the life of the hearers and not merely an eternal and atemporal truth. In some passages the formulae clearly refer to the Old Testament as the Word of God.[73] Yet in a few instances the formulae refer also sometimes to the human author[74] emphasizing his instrumentality.

---

[71] Cf. on this J. A. Fitzmyer, "The Use of Explicit Old Testament Quotations", *N.T.S.* 7, 1960-61, 296-333; we do not take into consideration here the use of Scripture in the *Pesharim* and the *Testimonia* (we shall deal with them later on).

[72] We shall follow here J. A. Fitzmyer, 299ff. to whom we are indebted for the following remarks. For the list of the forty-four explicit quotations see this work.

[73] Cf. namely CD 6:13; 8:9; 9:7 (and possibly 3:7) and 1 QM 11:5-6, *op. cit.*, 302.

[74] Cf. CD 6:7-8; 8:14; 19:26-27; 5:8; 1 QM 10:1.

One is struck by the lack of "fulfillment or realization formulae" so frequently found in the New Testament.[75] We should have expected them, since on the one hand they are found in the Old Testament itself (I Kings 2:17, II Chr. 36:21), and on the other hand, as we noted above, the Covenanters believed that the prophecies of the Prophets were realized in their time. This should remind us that the faith of the Covenanters was still primarily forward looking toward the *eschaton*,[76] in spite of the embryo of realized eschatology which we suggested.

We shall deal with the specific role which these explicit quotations played when we study the use of Scripture in the different scrolls. Here let us note simply that whenever their original meaning could not be directly applied to the life of the Covenanters, they were "modernized" and even transformed by different devices[77] in order to accommodate the new situation.[78] Furthermore it appears that the Covenanters did not see the need to create new quotation formulae. They tacitly agreed with classical Judaism : the Hebrew Bible is Scripture, Word of God, that is, locus of revelation. Yet, as we shall see, the Covenanters' understanding of Scripture as locus of revelation was quite different from that of classical Judaism. This is to say that the extent of this agreement was limited to two basic convictions: a) that the biblical text has an ultimate meaning for the believer and consequently that everything is meaningful in Scripture; and b) that as Word of God who is One, Scripture is One.

---

[75] Three formulae of this kind can, indeed, be found (CD 7:10-11; 19:7 and 1:13) yet they refer to either future or past events, cf. Fitzmyer, *op. cit.*, 303f.

[76] On the other hand the New Testament is "characterized by a backward glance, seeing the culmination of all that preceded in the advent of Christ", *ibid*. Although such a statement should be qualified.

[77] Among these devices were that of giving the words another meaning than the one they had in the biblical text, the omission of words, and the atomization of the biblical text.

[78] Cf. Fitzmyer, *op. cit.*, 305-30.

As we saw when discussing the interpretation of Scripture in the Targum, these convictions were what demanded the use of the *middoth* for haggadic interpretation (which atomized the biblical text and interpreted Scripture by Scripture in order to discover its meaning for the believer). We should not be surprised to find that these very *middoth* were used by the Covenanters for their interpretation of Scripture (as we shall see when discussing the *Pesharim*). This is to say that the *middoth* symbolize, at once, elements of the Apocalyptic hermeneutical structure of classical Judaism and that of the Covenanters (and Apocalyptists). Or better, they symbolize what these two hermeneutical structures have in common: the conviction that the Hebrew Bible is locus of revelation. This suggests that the difference between these two hermeneutical structures is to be found in the other loci of revelation that they set in tension with Scripture. This implies that we cannot expect to distinguish these two hermeneutics at the levels of the methods of interpretation (the *middoth*).

This concludes our general remarks about what appears as the Covenanters' explicit doctrine of Scripture. Let us turn now to the study of the way in which the Covenanters actually implemented this doctrine in their writings. In this way we may hope to further our understanding of the Covenanters' hermeneutic.

For this purpose we shall examine how Scripture was used in the various Dead Sea Scrolls. For the most part, such a study has already been done by scholars who have focused their attention on one or the other kind of use of Scripture, often in a specific Qumran text.[79] For the pursuit of our

---

[79] Cf. for instances W. H. Brownlee, "Biblical Interpretation among the Sectaries of the Dead Sea Scrolls", *Bibl. Archael.* 14, 1951, 54-76; B. Gärtner, "The Habakkuk Commentary and the Gospel of Matthew", *Stud. Theol.* 8, 1954, 1-24; P. Wernberg-Møller, "Some Reflexions on the Biblical Material in the Manual of Discipline", *Stud. Theol.* 9, 1955, 40-66; J. Carmignac, "Les citations de l'Ancien Testament dans 'la guerre des Fils de Lumière contre les Fils de Ténèbre'", *Rev. Bibl.* 63, 1956, 234-60 and 375-90; and "Les citations de l'Ancien Testament et spécialement des Poèmes du Serviteur, dans les Hymnes de Qumrân", *R.Q.* 2, 1059-60, 357-94; J. A. Fitzmyer, "The Use of Explicit Old Testament Quotations in

investigation we are greatly indebted to these scholars' works. We hope nevertheless to be able to contribute something to the on-going discussion by setting it in the broader perspective of our investigation. We shall attempt therefore to present a "panoramic" view of the different uses of Scripture by the Covenanters.[80] Such a panoramic view alone can allow us to graps the axioms which governed their hermeneutic as a whole.

We shall examine successively the uses of Scripture in the *Genesis Apocryphon*, the *Zadokite Documents*, the *Hodayot*, the *Manual of Discipline*, the *War Scroll*, various shorter texts, and the *Pesharim*.

Qumran Literature and in the New Testament", *N.T. Studies* 7, 1960-61, 297-333; F. F. Bruce, *Biblical Exegesis in the Qumran Texts*, London, 1959; O. Betz, *Offenbarung und Schriftforschung in der Qumransekte*, Tübingen, 1960; J. Amusin, *The Qumran Commentaries and their Significance for the History of the Qumran Community*, Moscow, 1967; E. Slomovic, "Toward an Understanding of the Exegesis in the Dead Sea Scrolls", *R.Q.* 7, 1969. 3-15; G. Vermès, "The Qumran Interpretation of Scripture in its Historical Setting", *Annual of Leeds University Oriental Society*, Leiden, 1969, 84-97, and S. Lowy, "Some Aspects of Normative and Sectarian Interpretation of the Scriptures", *ibid.*, 98-163. To these should be added the different works on the *pesharim*. Among them see especially: K. Elliger, *Studien zum Habakuk-Kommentar vom Toten Meer*, Tubingen, 1953; M. Delcor, *Essai sur le Midrash d'Habacuc*, Paris, 1951; W. H. Brownlee, *The Text of Habakkuk in the Ancient Commentary from Qumran*, J.B.L. Monograph series, vol. XI, Philadelphia 1959; Ch. Rabin, "Notes on the Habakkuk Scroll and the Damasan Document", *V.T.* 5, 1955, 168-77; L. Silberman, "Unriddling the Riddle", *R.Q.* 3, 1961, 224-64; A. Finkel, "The Pesher of Dreams and Scriptures", *R.Q.* 4, 1963, 357-70. Cf. also the notes below.

[80] Such a panoramic view is missing in most of the studies mentioned above. They are focused on one specific use of Scripture. Such a panoramic view is nevertheless to be found in O. Betz, *Offenbarung*, and a number of short articles, including G. Vermès, "The Qumran Interpretation of Scripture in its Historical Setting", in *Annual of Leeds University Oriental Society*, Leiden, 1969.

II

THE RE-WRITINGS OF SCRIPTURE: GENESIS APOCRYPHON, BOOK OF JUBILEES AND SAYING OF MOSES

As the title of this work, *Genesis Apocryphon* (1 Q Gen. Apoc.) suggests, it is a re-writing of Scripture. This literary genre can be found also in other Dead Sea Scrolls and fragments: according to a preliminary report, fragments of a *Targum of Job* have been discovered in cave 11,[81] as well as fragments of an Aramaic version of Leviticus 16:12-15, 18-21.[82] Furthermore, as we shall see, certain parts of other scrolls can be considered re-writings of Scripture, although of a quite different type than that found in the *Genesis Apocryphon*.

The *Genesis Apocryphon*,[83] an Aramaic text, presents characteristics reminiscent of the *Book of Jubilees* and the *Book of Noah* (I Enoch ch. 106). What can be deciphered of this often badly damaged scroll (with the exception of col. XIX-XXII) indicates that it was a re-writing of Genesis ch. 5[84] to 15. Written in the first person,[85] it has therefore a pseudepigraphic character. Yet unlike the *Book of Jubilees*,

---

[81] Cf. J. van der Ploeg, "Un Targum du livre de Job: Nouvelle Découverte dans le désert de Juda", *Bible et Vie Chrétienne* 58, 1964, 79-87.

[82] Cf. J. T. Milik, *Ten Years of Discoveries in the Wilderness of Judaea*, Naperville, 1959, 31.

[83] Here we are indebted mainly to N. Avigad and Y. Yadin, *A Genesis Apocryphon. A Scroll from the Wilderness of Judaea*, Jerusalem, 1956; J. A. Fitzmyer, *The Genesis Apocryphon of Qumran Cave I. A Commentary*, Tome, 1966; and also to M. R. Lehmann, "I Q Genesis Apocryphon in the Light of Targumim and Midrashim", *R.Q.* 1, 249-63, and G. Vermés, *Scripture and Tradition*, 96-126.

[84] Yet it is quite possible that the re-writing began even earlier. The beginning of the scroll is lost. As it stands now, col. I-V deal with the birth of Noah (Gen. 5:28-29).

[85] With the exception of col. XXI:23-XXII:34.

which was presented as the *revelations* made to Moses, it presents the *memoirs* of the Patriarchs. By this very fact it is much more akin to the Targum than to the Apocalyptic re-writing. The Patriarchs were *not* conceived by the author as prophets proclaiming in a more or less cryptic way what would happen in later generations and especially in the eschatological time. They were simply presented as revealing details of their lifes which are not contained in Scripture. In this way the *Genesis Apocryphon* solves some difficulties of the biblical text. For instance 1 Q Gen. Apoc. 21:32-33 reads: "The King of Sodom was defeated and fled and the King of Gomorrah fell into the pits". This conflicts with the text of Genesis 14:10 which states that both kings fell into the pits. The change is brought about in order to solve the difficulty of this biblical text. Gen. 14:17 mentions indeed that the king of Sodom came out to meet Abram. How, then, could he have fallen into the pit? Jubilees 13:22 solves the problem in the same way. The Midrashim do it by mentioning a rescue of the king of Sodom (cf. *Gen. Rab.* 42:7). Later we find a harmonizing of the Genesis text with Num. 13:22 in 1 Q Gen. Apoc. 20:14: the years of Abram's wanderings are harmonized with what is said in Numbers about the building of Zoan. In the same way the author makes use of Ezek. 42:16-19 in col. 21:8ff. and of Ps. 76:2 in col. 22:13 in order to explain details of the text of Genesis.[86]

Actually the *Genesis Apocryphon* mainly presents haggadic traditions, often very loosely connected with the text. Such is the long haggadic development (approximately col. I-V) on the birth of Noah (which presents striking similarities with the fragment of the *Book of Noah* contained in I Enoch ch. 106): this is a development of the very short passage of Gen. 5:28-29.

Besides these Midrashic interpretations of the Massoretic Text, we find also literal translations. The latter are often interwoven in the Midrashic developments and seem to have been used as a leading thread. (There are

---

[86] On this cf. Avigad and Yadin, *op. cit.*, 24ff. and 36.

nevertheless a few exceptions where the biblical sequence is not respected).[87] There are also longer passages of quasi-literal translation (namely in the last section of the scroll, 21:23-22:26).

Thus the use of Scripture which we find in the *Genesis Apocryphon* is akin to the Targumim (with the alternation of Midrashic developments and literal translations) and to the Midrashim, rather than to Apocalyptic re-writings like the *Book of Jubilees* and the *Book of Noah*. A comparison of their respective haggadic developments[88] shows often that all these books witness to the same traditions, although the *Genesis Apocryphon* contains a few haggadic developments which cannot be found elsewhere.[89]

Apart from the fact that it was found together with texts whose origin in the Qumran community cannot be doubted, there is no evidence that the *Genesis Apocryphon* originated in the sect.[90] Yet its belonging to the Covenanters' library indicates that such a use of Scripture was not meaningless for them. This conclusion is reinforced by the discovery of the fragments of a Targum of Job which hopefully will be soon published.

This is not to say that the Covenanters did not themselves practice a re-writing of Scripture. We may assume that theirs was an Apocalyptic re-writing. As we noted earlier, it is actually quite possible that the *Book of Jubilees* itself originated among the Covenanters. Furthermore

---

[87]Cf. 20:33-34 and 21:9. On this see M. R. Lehmann, *op. cit.*, 252.

[88]For a comparison of 1 Q Gen. Apoc. with Targumim and Midrashim see Lehmann, *op. cit.*, 252-63, and Fitzmyer, *op. cit.*, 26-34. For a comparison with the books of Jubilees and of Noah, see mainly Avidag and Yadin, *op. cit.*, 16-37.

[89]Cf. for instance col. 19 which explains the story of Sarah and Pharaoh by means of a dream in which Abram saw two trees, a cedar and a palm-tree: the cedar is saved by the palm-tree. This is interpreted to mean that there will be an attempt to kill Abram, but he will be saved by Sarah. See also the numerous haggadic details found in col. 20. Cf. Avidag and Yadin, *op. cit.*, 25-26.

[90]Thus Fitzmyer, *op. cit.*, 12.

fragments of similar Apocalyptic re-writings have been found among the Dead Sea Scrolls. Among these are the fragments called "sayings of Moses" (1 QDM).[91] Although they are badly damaged these fragments seem to belong to an Apocalyptic re-writing. Was it a re-writing of the whole Book of Deuteronomy, similar to that of the Book of Genesis in the *Book of Jubilees*?[92] Perhaps. Yet it should be noted that these fragments could as well be described as fragments of a "Testament of Moses" (thus like the *Testaments of the Twelve Patriarchs*). The fragmentary nature of this text does not allow a firm conclusion, although the second hypothesis seems more probable: the passages of Deuteronomy which are used therein do not follow the sequence of this biblical book. Since we have dealt at length with the re-writing in the Apocalyptic literature, we do not need to elaborate on the use of Scripture in the "sayings of Moses". It is characterized by the usual prophetic style (namely col. I, 1-10) and a dense anthological style in the interpretation which it gives for the basic texts from Deut. 31:28-29; 27:9-10; 6:11; 8:14; 9:1; 30:20, used in this order.

Several other shorter fragments could fit into this category of Apocalyptic re-writings: among them *4 Q Patriarchal Blessings*.[94]

---

[91] Cf. J. T. Milik in *Discoveries in the Judaean Desert. I. Qumran Cave I*, ed. by D. Barthélemy and J. T. Milik, Oxford, 1955, 91-97 and plates XVIII-XIX.

[92] Thus Dupont-Sommer, *op. cit.*, 310, and J. Carmignac, *Les Textes de Qumran*, vol. II, 247f.

[94] Cf. J. M. Allegro, "Further Messianic References in Qumran Literature", *J.B.L.* 75, 1956, 174-76.

III

THE USE OF SCRIPTURE IN
THE ZADOKITE DOCUMENTS

In the *Zadokite Documents* we find a much more diversified use of Scripture. Following O. J. R. Schwarz[95] we can divide it into three main categories, corresponding to the three literary genres found in these texts: A. The *narrative texts* (they deal with the history of the community and with the ways of God in favor of the righteous and against the wicked): CD 1:1-13a; 2:2a-13; 2:14-3:20; 4:4-12. B. The *exegetical texts* (they actualize Scripture): e.g., CD 1:13b-2:1; 3:20-4:2; 4:12-14; 5:13-6:4.[96] C. The *juridical texts* (halakic interpretations): e.g., CD 4:19-5:13 and 20:1-34.[96]

A. The Use of Scripture in the Narrative Texts

In the narrative texts we find a use of Scripture which is akin to re-writing. These are re-writings of the history of Israel. Such is CD 2:14-3:20, [97] which we shall take as example.

The introduction to this passage gives the purpose of this re-writing, or better of this re-reading, of the sacred history:

---

[95] O. J. R. Schwarz, *Der erste Teil der Damaskusschrift und das Alte Testament*, Lichtland/Diest, 1965.

[96] For other instances see below.

[97] Our quotations generally (yet not consistantly) follow C. Rabin's translation, *The Zadokite Documents*, second edition Oxford, 1958. We are also indebted to his notes.

> "And now, children, hearken unto me, that I may
> uncover your eyes to see and to consider the
> works of God to choose that in which He delights
> and to reject what he hates,(98) to walk uprightly
> in all his ways and not to seek after thoughts of
> guilty inclinations and eyes of whoredom"
> (CD 2:14-16).(99)

In this admonition it appears that the purpose of this re-writing of Israel's history was twofold. On the one hand, it was done in order to penetrate, to scrutinize[100] "the works of God", in the past sacred history. On the other hand this knowledge had a practical purpose: it was to be used in order to discern the righteous way to be followed by the Covenanters and also possibly, if we adopt Rabin's interpretation, in order to distinguish the righteous from the wicked among men.

The re-telling of the sacred history began with the fall of the Angels (Gen. 6:1-14): the angels and their sons (the giants) were given as the type of the wicked who walk "in the stubbornness of their hearts" (CD 2:17-18). Their punishment was stressed at once: "All flesh that were on the dry land they died" (CD 2:20). This sentence, which is reminiscent of Gen. 7:22, was interpreted by means of Obadiah 16: "they shall be as though they had not been"[101] because they have done their own will instead of keeping the commandments of their Maker (CD 2:21).

Then, after a brief mention of the punishment of the sons of Noah and their families,[102] our text presents Abraham and with him Isaac and Jacob as types of the righteous. Abraham was indeed "keeping the commandments of God and not choosing the desire of his own spirit" (CD 3:2-3). The

---

[98] This translation seems to me better, because of the parallelism, than the one proposed by C. Rabin, "to choose him in whom He delights and to reject him whom he hates".

[99] Let us note incidentally the use of Num. 15:39 in the last part of this passage (2:16). This is a first example of anthological style in these documents.

[100] בִּין: for the meaning of this term in the *Zadokite Documents*, cf. A. M. Denis, *op. cit.*, 11-16.

[101] This refers, in the text of the Prophet, to the destruction of the heathen.

[102] Alluding possibly to the Tower of Babel.

Patriarchs were furthermore presented as "the friends of God"[103] "and his covenanters for eternity" (CD 3:4). They were therefore the types of the member of the community of the "new Covenant".

After the Patriarchs, the sons of Jacob, (the people of Israel) through all their history in Egypt, in the wilderness, during the period of the kingship, and up to the time of the establishment of the community, were presented as walking "in the stubbornness of their hearts". Thus the sons of Jacob were all along types of the wicked, and because of that they "were given over to the sword" (CD 3:4-12).

Such a re-telling of the history of Israel does not fail to remind us of the confessions of sins which one may find in Dan. 9:4-19; Ezra 9:6-15 and Neh. 9 (as a whole but especially 32-37). Just as in their confession of sins Daniel, Ezra, and the Levites presented themselves as sinners within the general framework of the sinful history of Israel, so as to ask for forgiveness, in the same way the author of the *Zadokite Documents* confessed: "They were defiling themselves with impiety of man and ways of impurity, and they said: Because it is ours! And God in his marvellous mysteries forgave their iniquity" (CD 3:17-18).[104]

When reading this passage of the *Zadokite Documents* together with the biblical passages just mentioned, one cannot but wonder if the latter were in the mind of the author. We could not find any phrase reminiscent of them in CD 2:14-3:20; yet in the preceding passages, which deal also with the history of the sect, especially in their introduction, we read: "when He remembered the Covenant of the forefathers,[105] He caused a remnant to remain of Israel and gave them not up to be consumed" (CD 1:4-5). As C. Rabin notes, the latter

---

[103] This according to Isa. 41:8.

[104] The same idea is found again in CD 4:9-10, in the conclusion of another re-telling of the history of Israel.

[105] Quasi-quotation from Lev. 26:45: for an interpretation of its use here and in CD 6:2, by comparison with the Targum, cf. Le Déaut, "Une citation de Lévitique 26:45 dans le Document de Damas 1:4; 6:2", *R.Q.* 6, 1967, 289-92.

part of this passage is strongly reminiscent of Ezra 9:14, in which the same vocabulary was used, although in the interrogative-negative form. The following verse (Ezra 9:15) presents the same idea in the affirmative form, and all against the background of God's judgment just as in the *Zadokite Documents*.

Such light evidence cannot be a proof that the author built up his text on the pattern of Ezra 9. It is striking nevertheless that it was by reference to this text (rather than texts like Isa. 10:20-23) that he introduced the idea of the "remnant" and so cast the history of the sect into the framework of Israel's general history. As can be expected, the sect's history was presented not only in this broad biblical context, but also with the help of a great number of prophetic texts.[106]

In this passage (CD 2:14-3:20) as well as in CD 1:1-13a; 2:2a-13 and 4:4-12, we find an interpretation of Scripture which had the purpose of showing the place of the community in the framework of the sacred history—exactly at the end of the sacred history (at the consummation of time: CD 4:10). Whether or not this re-telling of the sacred history was done by following the framework of the biblical confessions of sin, at any rate it is clear that we have here a conception of history quite similar to that which we found in the Apocalyptic literature. It is characterized by the same determinism. This is expressed in CD 2:2ff. and especially 2:9-10:

> "And He knows the years of life and the number, together with the exact date of the times of all the events of the ages, and the things to come, all that comes to pass in the seasons of all the everlasting years".(107)

---

[106] See on this the notes given by C. Rabin on these passages of the *Zadokite Documents*. Cf. also O. Schwarz, *op. cit.*, 77-82.

[107] Dupont-Sommer's translation. Cf. *The Essene Writings from Qumran*, translated by G. Vermès, Cleveland-New York, 1962, *ad loc.*

We also find a similar twofold typology. On the one hand the events of the past sacred history were considered as the *types of the contemporary events* in which the faithful community and the wicked were involved at the end of time. On the other hand (and consequently) the biblical characters were seen as *moral types* of the righteous or of the wicked.

Here as in the Apocalyptic re-writing of Scripture, we have the feeling that we witness a use of Scripture which was subsequent to a former one. It was assumed that the community was the community of the "new Covenant". This revealed identity was a fact for the author. The process by means of which it was discovered (with the help of Scripture, as we shall see) was not described. Thus in this re-telling of the sacred history, Scripture was used in tension with the revealed identity of the community. This use of Scripture was, as we shall see when studying the *Hodayot*, akin to a liturgical use (which likewise assumes the revealed identity of the worshipping community).[108]

B. THE USE OF SCRIPTURE IN THE EXEGETICAL TEXTS

This leads us to the second kind of use of Scripture which is found in what O. Schzarz called the "exegetical texts". Actually these passages have been artificially singled out. Some of them are parts of the narrative texts we just mentioned. At any rate they are parts of a wider context in which an anthological use of Scripture can be found. Most of the time they explain a given historical situation by means of a biblical passage.

Thus in CD 1:11-12 the historical situation was first described: (God) "raised for them a teacher of righteousness to lead them in the way of his heart and to make known to the last generation that which He would do to the last generation,

---

[108] For this use of Scripture in an actual liturgical setting, see below the section on the use of Scripture in the angelic liturgy and other "liturgical texts".

the congregation of the faithless". What was this "last generation", this "congregation of faithless"? This was explained by means of Hosea 4:16, "There are those that backslide from the way; that is the time about which it was written: 'Like a backsliding heifer thus did Israel slide back'" (CD 1:13). Having explained this, the author went on to the next element of his narrative.

Similarly the following biblical texts were used to interpret historical situations which were first described: Ezek. 44:15 (in CD 3:20-4:2); Isa. 24:17 (in CD 4:12-14); Num. 21:18 (in CD 6:3-4);[109] Mal. 1:10 (in CD 6:13-14); Num. 30:17 (in CD 7:8-9); Isa. 7:17 (in CD 7:9-14); Deut. 32:33 (in CD 8:9-10); Deut. 9:5 (in CD 8:14-18); Zech. 13:7 (in CD 19:5-9); Hosea 5:10 (in CD 19:15-16).[110] Each of these texts was introduced by a formula like: "As He (God) spoke by the hand of the prophet Isaiah son of Amoz saying. . ." (CD 4:14), or "As for that which Moses said to Israel. . ." (CD 8:14), or again "As God said. . ." (CD 6:13).

This is to say that these biblical passages were introduced as proof texts in order to strengthen the claim that the Covenanters were indeed the "new Covenant" and consequently that those Jews who did not belong to the community were a congregation of faithless. We are not witnessing here the process of uncovering of these "mysteries". Rather we have an apologetic argumentation which was based on the results of the pesher interpretation and which referred to it; the biblical texts quoted were quite possibly the very texts which presided over the uncovering of this revealed identity in a pesher interpretation.

This observation is reinforced by the fact that in a few instances the author interpreted for his readers some biblical

---

[109] This interpretation of Num. 21:18 is actually of an allegorical type, so far as the interpretation of the "well" (as the Torah) is concerned. Such an allegorical interpretation is very scarce. In the Dead Sea Scrolls we can say that it is at the embryonic stage: cf. O. Betz, *Offenbarung*, 176-81, who points out the few other examples of this use of Scripture. See below our comments on *the angelic liturgy*.

[110] *Passim*. Cf. O. Schwarz, *op. cit.*, 90ff.

passages in a pesher-like manner. Instead of having first the description of a situation and then its explanation by means of a biblical text, we find the reverse order. The text is given first, and its meaning is found in the contemporary situation. This is the very use of Scripture characteristic of the *Pesharim*, which we shall deal with later[111]

It is to be noted that this pesher-like use of Scripture in the *Zadokite Documents* always follows up a proof text. It is as if, after a quotation, the author could not help but look further in the biblical text. A preceding interpretation had proved that this text was a prophecy concerning his time, since it explained a contemporary event. He could therefore expect to find in it other insights for the understanding of his situation.

A good example of this is CD 3:19-4:5. The author first described the situation. God pardoned the sins of the Covenanters "and he built them a sure house in Israel, the like of which has not stood from ancient times even until now. They that hold fast to it are destined for eternal life and all glory of man is theirs" (CD 3:19-20). This described the community as seen by the Covenanters. Then Ezek. 44:15 was quoted in order to show that this community was indeed the eschatological sacerdotal community, the spiritual temple of God, which had been promised by God:

> "As God swore to them by the hand of
> the prophet Ezekiel saying: 'The priests
> and the levites and the sons of Zadok,(112)
> who kept the charge of my sanctuary when
> the children of Israel strayed from me,
> they shall approach me to minister unto me,
> and they shall stand before me to offer me
> fat and blood'" (Ezek. 44:15; CD 3:21-4:2).

---

[111] The technical term "pesher" is to be found only once in the *Zadokite Documents*, CD 4:14.

[112] The Massoretic Text reads: והכהנים הלוים בני צדוק (the priest-levites sons of Zadok) and not הכהנים והלוים ובני צדוק. This small alteration of the text was made to prepare for the coming interpretation. This was a common practice in the case of the *pesharim*, as we shall see below.

Then the author looked for further insights in the text. He did this in the *pesher* style: "The priests are they that turned (from the impiety) of Israel[113] who went out from the land of Judah; and (the levites are) they that joined themselves[114] with them; and the sons of Zadok are the elect of Israel the men called by name[115] who shall arise in the end of days" (CD 4:2-4). Thus the details of the "prophecy" which had not yet been applied to the situation were used in order further to understand the present reality of the eschatological-sacerdotal community.[116]

We shall soon deal with the *pesher* use of Scripture at length. Yet let us note that in the *pesharim* this technique of interpretation was applied to a complete prophetic book and not, as here, merely to brief independent passages.

Leaving aside for the moment the *pesher*-like passages, let us compare the use of Scripture in these exegetical texts with the one we found in the narrative texts. We should emphasize first that with the exegetical texts we are closer to the process by means of which the community discovered its revealed identity. Yet here again the identity of the community seems to have been assumed. The biblical texts were brought forward as "proof" texts in order to back up the author's claim that he was a member of the eschatological faithful community. This remark may give us a clue for the understanding of the *Zadokite Documents*: this use of Scripture seems indeed to reflect an *apologetic* character. The author appears to have wanted, among other things, to set forth the revealed identity of the community in such a way as to convince his readers. Were these, prospective members of

---

[113] Based on Isa. 59:20.

[114] Based on Gen. 29:34 and Num. 18:2, 4.

[115] Based on Num. 16:2.

[116] In this process other biblical texts were also included. For other examples of this *pesher* use of Scripture see CD 4:14-19; 6:4-11; 7:14-21; 8:10-12; 19:9-13 and 22-24. For a commentary on them see O. Schwarz, *op. cit.*, 112-15. It is to be noted again that CD 7:14ff. can be considered as an embryo of allegorical interpretation. See below our comments on *the angelic liturgy*.

the community? The elect of Israel at the end of days?[117] Or new members? We cannot say.

It is nevertheless quite possible that these Scriptural passages were the very ones which were formerly used in order to discover this identity. Such an assumption is strengthened by the *pesher*-like passages. In the latter new elements of the community's identity were discovered in the Scriptural texts which were no longer interpreted in terms of the community's revealed identity but this time in terms of its actual historical situation. As we have suggested the latter process involved other biblical passages, which were alluded to in the anthological style. In the latter case Scripture appears to have revealed the community's identity, when it was placed in tension with the historical events which took place during the community's forming. For the example we took (CD 4:2-5), the key event was the going out into the wilderness of a group of priests with their followers. The author discovered the prophecy for this in Ezek. 44:15. He could therefore interpret the text further and conclude that the elect of Israel would join the Covenanters at the end of days. Thus here, instead of having Scripture in tension with the community's revealed identity, we have Scripture in tension with the community's historical situation. We should emphasize that such an interpretation of Scripture also involved an interpretation of Scripture by Scripture. We find traces of this in the anthological style.

This *pesher*-like interpretation looks almost "accidental". For indeed the *Zadokite Documents* are chiefly characterized by what we could call an *apologetic use of Scripture*. This allows us to explain at once the re-telling of the sacred history and the "proof-text" method. The apologetic use of Scripture was indeed subsequent to a previous use of Scripture which we can identify with the "pesher". This is to say that the apologetic use of Scripture here cannot be identified with other such uses elsewhere (e.g., in Philo's writings).

---

[117] Cf. Cd 4:2-5.

C. THE USE OF SCRIPTURE IN THE JURIDIC TEXTS

We find here a halakic exegesis. As in classical Judaism, we find, here both halakic interpretations which do not mention the biblical laws they were interpreting (cf. CD 19:33-20:1; 20:1-8, 8-13, 13-17, 17-22, 22-24, 24-25, 25-27, 27-34)--as in the Mishnah--and others which quote the biblical text (cf. CD 4:19-5:13 on Gen. 1:27; CD 6:11-7:6 on Mal. 1:10; CD 7:6-9 on Num. 30:17; CD 8:2-9 on Deut. 32:33).[118]

This halakic interpretation was, as mentioned, similar to that of classical Judaism. But let us note that, generally speaking, it involved a more rigorous interpretation of the laws. Thus the marriage of a man with his niece, which was allowed in classical Judaism, was forbidden here (CD 5:8-11) on the ground of Lev. 18:13, which explicitly prohibits only the marriage between an aunt and her nephew. In the same way polygamy was strictly forbidden (CD 4:20-5:2).[119]

We need not elaborate further on this kind of use of Scripture. Let us simply add that this rigor appears to result from the fact that the halakic interpretation was done *in terms of the revealed identity of the eschatological community*. This has to be contrasted with the halakic interpretation of classical Judaism, which was done in terms of cultural situations.

---

[118] *Passim*, cf. O. Schwarz, *op. cit.*, 136-60.

[119] Cf. G. Vermès, "The Qumran Interpretation of Scripture", 88-89. The same rigorous interpretation is found in *4 Q Ordinances*: cf. J. M. Allegro, "An Unpublished Fragment of Essene Halakkah (4 Q Ordinances)" in *Journal of Semitic Studies*, 1961, 71-73. Cf. also below our remarks on the *Manual of Discipline*.

IV

THE USE OF SCRIPTURE IN
THE HODAYOT (1 QH)

The *"liturgical"* character of these hymns[120] has long been recognized, although the actual meaning of this qualification must be discussed. Were these hymns used by the worshipping community of Qumran in the same way as the individual hymns of thanksgiving in the canonical Psalms? Despite the close resemblance between the former and the latter,[121] there is an important difference. In the canonical Psalms there are specific allusions to a cultic setting.[122] Such allusions, if not totally absent, are indeed limited in the Hodayot to a few passages[123] which allude to musical instruments.

This raises the question of the *Sitz im Leben* of the Hodayot. Two main theses have been proposed. One, represented chiefly by H. Bardtke,[124] claims that the Hodayot did *not* have a worship setting: their purpose was first of all didactic. To support his thesis Bardtke emphasizes the desintegration of the Psalm style in the Hodayot.[125] He argues that the prayer style was abandoned in favor of a kind of intellectual reflection (as in 1 QH 11:11-14; 13:17-18, etc.). The Hodayot are catechistic in style. Bardtke

---

[120] For the sake of this discussion we shall include in the *Hodayot* 1 QS 10:8b-11:22. In this we follow Th. Gaster, *The Dead Sea Scriptures*, New York, 1964, 126ff.

[121] Cf. on this G. Morawe, *Aufban und Abgreuzung der Loblieder von Qumran*, Berlin, 1961.

[122] This has been shown by H. Gunkel and J. Begrich in *Einleitung in die Psalmen*, Göttingen, 1933, vol. I, 265ff., as Dupont-Sommer reminds us, *op. cit.*, 199.

[123] 1 QH 1:28-29; 11:22ff.

[124] In his article "Considérations sur les Cantiques de Qumran", *R.B.*, 1956, 220-33.

[125] Cf. Bardtke, *op. cit.*, 223-26.

concludes therefore that the Hodayot were composed for the edification of the individuals in the community. They were recited by the individual as a kind of spiritual exercise. Thus Bardtke is not denying the prayer-like nature of the Hodayot. He emphasizes it. Yet he argues at the same time that their didactic content makes recitation in an assembly quite improbable.

As Dupont-Sommer notes,[126] Bardtke has certainly exaggerated the didactic character of these hymns and neglected their lyric character. Furthermore, as S. Holm-Nielsen notes,[127] once the actual proportion of the didactic material is recognized, it remains to determine the purpose for which these hymns were written. Granted that they may have been used in the individual manner described by Bardtke, this does not explain their prayer-like nature, which would not have been necessary of a didactic purpose.

Holm-Nielsen proposes[128] that these hymns were written for liturgical use. He supports this thesis by pointing out, on the one hand, the different allusions to worship services in the other scrolls. He finds allusions to the practice of morning and evening prayers by the community (1 QS 10:10) and to the reciting of a grace at table during the communal meal (1 QS 10:15 and 6:5). He also finds allusions to worship services in the several references to the assembly of the "Many" (e.g., 1 QS 6:8ff.). This assembly may have had a cultic form. As Holm-Nielsen suggests, the assembly of the "Many" can possibly be identified with the "Holy" assembly mentioned in 1 QS 2:1ff. On the other hand he notes that if it is clear that the songs of praise, "the offering of the lips", replaced the sacrifice (1 QS 10:6-8), it should be emphasized that this spiritualization of the sacrifice did not eliminate the worship setting. Although the faith of the

---

[126] Dupont-Sommer, *Le livre des hymnes découvert près de la Mer Morte*, Semitica VII, Paris, 1957, 16.

[127] Holm-Nielsen, *Hodayot Psalms from Qumran*, Aarhus, 1960, 338ff.

[128] Holm-Nielsen, *op. cit.*, 345ff.

individual was stressed, its communal expression is also quite apparent, if only in the passages just mentioned.

We should add to Holm-Nielsen's argument in favor of a worship setting for the *Hodayot* the remarks of Bo Reicke.[129] Although one cannot identify the Qumranites and the Therapeutai,[130] Philo's description of the latter can be useful for drawing analogies to Qumranites' ways of worship. Particularly meaningful, is the "banquet" of the Therapeutai in *De vita contemplativa* (# 65ff.). Omitting the description of the Scriptural interpretation which was presented to the community by the "President", let us quote Philo's reports on how the hymns were sung at the end of the meal.

> "Then the President rises and sings a hymn composed as an address to God, either a new one of his own composition or an old one by poets of an earlier day who have left behind them hymns in many measures and melodies, hexameters and iambics, lyrics suitable for processions or in libations and at the altars, or for the chorus whilst standing or dancing, with careful metrical arrangements to fit the various evolutions. (131)
> After him all the others take their turn as they are arranged and in the proper order while all the rest listen in complete silence except when they have to chant the closing lines or refrains, for this they all lift up their voices, men and women alike".(132)

The procedures at the Qumranites' sacred meals may have been similar. Many features of the Hodayot could be readily explained in such a setting, especially their personal character (expressed so often by the "I") and their didactic

---

[129] "Remarques sur l'Histoire de la Forme (Formgeschichte) des textes de Qumran" in *Les Manuscrits de la Mer Morte*, Colloque de Strasbourg, 1955.

[130] G. Vermès in his article "Essenes-Therapeutai-Qumran" in *Durham University Journal*, 1960, 97ff., shows their close relationship, although he may go too far: Philo himself was cautious enough to distinguish the Essenes from the Therapeutai! Cf. *De vita contemplativa*, # 1f.

[131] These "old" hymns may refer to the canonical Psalms which were described in a similar way (i.e., with allusions to Greek metres) by Josephus, *Ant*. 7:12, 3. Cf. F. H. Colson, *Philo*, vol. IX, Cambridge, Mass., 1941, 524.

[132] *De vita contemplativa*, # 80, F. H. Colson's translation, *op. cit.*, *ad loc*.

content. Let us not forget that the "President" was *teaching* (interpreting Scripture) in the preceding part of the sacred meal.

With Dupont-Sommer, Holm-Nielsen, and Bo Reicke one can argue therefore that even the "individual hymns" were liturgical in the specific sense of the term. The near absence of cultic references could mean simply that they were used in different liturgical settings of the community's life, rather than a definite one.[133]

Other hymns appear to have had a more definite *Sitz im Leben*. As Holm-Nielsen pointed out there is a close relationship between a) the description of "ritual for the entry in the Covenant" (1 QS 1:16-2:19, cf. also 5:7ff.) and b) 1 QH 14:8-22; 14:23-28; 16:1-7; 16:8-20; 17:9-15; 17:17-25. The same motives, themes, and even phrases are found in the "ritual" and in these hymns. Holm-Nielsen therefore concluded that these psalms or portions of psalms "are part of a liturgy which belonged to this occasion".[134]

In the same line G. Morawe[135] and after him H. W. Kuhn[136] distinguish between two kinds of Hodayot: 1) *Individual Thanksgiving Hymns*. These are characterized by two constant themes: on the one hand, a confession of personal needs and weakness and on the other, the reference to a medium of revelation. Yet as we saw above their personal character does not exclude a liturgical setting. 2) *The Hymns of the Community* which do not contain these two elements or, if they do, express them in terms of the community.[137] In addition to the passages pointed out by Holm-Nielsen and listed above (1 QH 14:8-22, etc.) these include 1 QH 3:19-36; 7:26-33 and 11:3-14. Kuhn sees their *Sitz im Leben* either in the ritual

---

[133] Yet this is not excluding a parallel "private" use of the *Hodayot* as Holm-Nielsen, *op. cit.*, 346ff., emphasizes also.

[134] Holm-Nielsen, *op. cit.*, 344f.

[135] *op. cit.*

[136] *Enderwartung und gegenwartiges Heil*, Göttingen, 1966.

[137] Cf. e.g., 1 QH 3:19-36.

for entry into the community or in the ceremony for the renewal of the Covenant: these need not necessarily be distinguished from each other.

Although Holm-Nielsen does not make this distinction, he shows that the passages which we called, following Kuhn, the "Hymns of the community" have a more specific liturgical character than the other Hodayot.[138]

On the basis of the research of these scholars we can assume, therefore, a liturgical setting for the Hodayot as a whole: a definite setting for most of the hymns of the community and an undefinite setting for the Individual Thanksgiving Hymns. Let us examine now the use of Scripture in these Hodayot. We shall use the distinctions made by Morawe and Kuhn, although as we shall see, our study will demand a more complete classification of the Hodayot.

A. THE USE OF SCRIPTURE IN THE HYMNS OF THE COMMUNITY

In this group we can place: 1 QH 3:19-36; 7:26-33; 11:3-14; 14:8-22; 14:23-28; 16:1-7; 16:8-20; 17:9-15; 17:17-25.

If one wishes to limit his study to the specific uses of Scripture, these hymns or part of hymns could be left aside; the only use of Scripture we find in them is the use of Scriptural phraseology.[139] This is significant in itself, nor is it surprising after our remarks on the use of Scripture in the liturgical texts of classical Judaism.

The Scriptural phrases used in these passages have been pointed out by S. Holm-Nielsen,[140] J. Carmignac,[141] and M.

---

[138] Cf. Holm-Nielsen, *op. cit.*, 75; 141; 188; 223-24; 344f.

[139] Among the very few exceptions, we may note the combination of Isa. 19:8 and Ezek. 12:13 (or 17:20) in 1 QH 3:26.

[140] *op. cit., ad loc.*

[141] *Les Textes de Qumran*, vol. I, Paris, 1961, 127ff.

Delcor.[142] We need not repeat here the results of their comprehensive studies. They are generally in agreement about the origin of the different biblical phrases found in these hymns.[143] Yet a close study of the anthological style of these hymns reveals that the density of biblical phrases varies with the theme. Certain beliefs of the Covenanters were expressed in a relatively dense anthological style (as in 1 QH 3:19-36), others in a weak anthological style (as in 1 QH 11:3-14). An examination of these two hymns will allow us to be more specific.

1 QH 3:19-36 presents a relatively dense use of biblical phrases.[144]

> 19a: "I thank thee, O Lord, (a) for Thou hast released my sould from the grave, (b)"

The first part of line 19 is clearly made of two biblical phrases. The first (a) is a very common one, although it is generally found with Yahweh as a designation for God. Yet it is found with אדרני (Adonai) in Ps. 57:10. The second (b) is also a stereotyped phrase belonging to the biblical thanksgiving Psalms; it is found in Pss. 30:4; 31:6; 49:16; Isa. 38:17; Job 33:28. Although the wording appears to be closer to Pss. 30:4 and 49:16, this should not necessarily be looked at as a specific use of one of these Psalms.

> 19b-20a: "And from the abyss of sheol (a) Thou hast raised me up (b) to an eternal height"

(a) The words שאול (sheol) and אבדון (abyss) are never combined in the Old Testament. Yet they occur in parallel phrases in Job 26:6 and are juxtaposed in Prov. 15:11, as

---

[142] *Les Hymnes de Qumran*, Paris, 1962, *ad loc.*

[143] J. Carmignac and M. Delcor add nevertheless their own insights to the basic work of Holm-Nielsen. Let us note also the tendency of J. Carmignac to speak of these biblical phrases in terms of "quotations" (e.g., *op. cit.*, 132): as will be clear in the following example, this term does not fit the use of Scripture which we find in these texts.

[144] We use here Holm-Nielsen's translation. We introduce in it letters which will help us to designate the parts of the passages cited. It is clear that we are greatly indebted for our remarks on this passage to the works of the three scholars just mentioned.

Holm-Nielsen notes. Thus we may have here an echoing of these two texts. (b) In Ps. 30:4 we find a similar phrase: "Thou hast brought up my soul from sheol". Thus (a) and (b) could be a combination of Ps. 30:4 and Prov. 15:11. The next phrase ("to an eternal height") has no parallel in the Old Testament.

> 20b-21a: "So that I can wander in the plain without limit (a) and so that I know that there is hope for (b) him whom Thou hast formed out of dust (c) unto an eternal fellowship (d)".

(a) Excluding the mention of the plain (במישור), one can see here with Carmignac a combination of Ps. 119:45 with either Ps. 26:12 or Mal. 2:6. (b) The phrase יש-מקוהל is found in Esd. 10:2. (c) This phrase is reminiscent of Gen. 2:7 in vocabularly as well as in symbolism. (d) This phrase belongs to the specific terminology of the sect and refers to the community of Qumran.[145] If this interpretation is accepted we have, here and in the following lines, allusions to the ritual for the entry into the community. This allows us to see this ritual as the *Sitz im Leben* of our hymns.

> 21b-22a: "And the perverted spirit Thou hast cleansed from the great transgression (a) to stand in the assembly with the host of the saints, and to come into communion with the congregation of the sons of heaven (b)".

(a) The latter part of this phrase is reminiscent of Ps. 19:14. The first part of it, although using a biblical vocabulary, has no parallel in the Old Testment. (b) The rest of the passage does not contain any biblical phrase. Yet it is clear that the vocabulary as well as the symbolism are biblical.

> 22b-23: "And for man Thou hast cast an eternal lot with the spirits of insights (a), to praise Thy name (b) in the assembly [of rejoicings] (c), and to proclaim Thy wonders (d) before all Thy creatures".

---

[145] With Kuhn, Holm-Nielsen, Carmignac, against Dupont-Sommer, Delcor, M. Mansoor. The latter scholars see in this phrase a reference to the heavenly community. Yet if one takes into account 1 QS 2:23 and 25, this interpretation is difficult in spite of the following sentence of our text.

For (a) there is no direct biblical parallel. (b) is a biblical phrase frequently used in the Scrolls. (c) shows the possible influence of Isa. 52:8; Ps. 98:8 or Job 38:7. (d) is a frequent phrase in the Psalms (cf. Pss. 9:2; 26:7; 25:2).

The first part of this hymn is quite typical of the use of Scripture in the rest of it (1 QH 3:24-36). It is merely anthological. This is not only true of this hymn but also of each of the "hymns of the community", in which this use of Scripture is even less important. As mentioned earlier, the hymn presents the denser use of biblical phrases. The other extreme is 1 QH 11:3-14, which uses specific biblical phrases in only two instances (11:6 and 12). In the rest of it only biblical symbols and ideas are used. It is obvious in either case that Scripture is not the center of attention. Scripture is used as a mere language. One can expect such a phenomenon in a community in which Scripture is studied day and night.

The use of Scripture which we qualified as anthological is characteristic of liturgical texts. The anthological style appears therefore as second to that other use of Scripture, the study or search which gave rise to the *Pesharim*. The uncovering, the act of revelation, had already taken place. The worshipping community was now the depository of this revelation, or better it was now the *locus* of this revelation. In the Hodayot "Nothing is said directly about how, where and when the revelation of God came. . ." concludes Holm-Nielsen.[146] These Thanksgiving Hymns expressed only the "what" of this revelation which the community possessed. Beyond the dynamism of the uncovering they are the means by which the community became an incarnation of this revelation. Repeated again and again in liturgical hymns, the revelation permeated the community.[147]

---

[146] *op. cit.*, 286.

[147] This function of the liturgy can be said to be didactic. H. Bardtke's insight was not therefore without foundation, although his argument is not well enough balanced. Yet the qualification of "didactic" has to be understood here in a broad sense: the teaching was that of the community as a whole and not of a specific teacher.

The anthological use of Scripture which we find in these hymns signifies the importance of Scripture's role in the manner of this revelation. This hymn which presents a relatively dense use of biblical phrases refers to what was specific to the Covenanters' revealed identity: to their specific election and vocation. In symbolic terms it alludes to *how* this community had become the depository of the revelation. The biblical phrases reflect the search of Scripture which enabled the community to uncover these revelations. Yet other revelations which were embodied by means of other hymns do not appear as having been as closely related to Scripture.

A perfect example of this is the hymn in 1 QH 11:3-14. There are only two biblical phrases used in it, although the vocabulary and the symbols are reminiscent of the Old Testament: Scripture fades into the background. What is the topic of this hymn? It praises God for His revelation. God has given the Psalmist "insight" into his "wonderful deeds" (4, cf. also 8) revealing his "mercy", his "greatness" (5), his "Glory", "the abundance of (his) goodness) (6, cf. also 9). He has "made known unto them the counsel of (His) truth" (9) and "into the mysteries of (His) wonders (He) has given them insight" (10, cf. also 12 and 14). The result of this revelation was that its recipients were introduced into the eternal congregation (with eternal hosts and spirits) in which they sang praises unto God (13 and 14).

Thus this hymn was clearly focused on the *"what"* of revelation. It expressed the revelation in a "dogmatic" way. Such a hymn made a very weak use of Scripture. When by contrast the focus shifted toward *"how"* this comunity has become the depository of the revelation (as in 1 QH 3:19-36), the density of biblical phrases increased considerably even if, as in the hymn just mentioned, this did not yet express the actual process of the uncovering of the "mysteries" and of the "hidden things". The individual thanksgiving hymns present clearer examples of this phenomenon.

B. THE INDIVIDUAL THANKSGIVING HYMNS

In the hymns presenting features which seem to indicate a liturgical setting, we found that the use of Scripture was merely anthological, more or less dense according to the topic of the hymn. Among the rests of the Hodayot we find a number of hymns presenting the same kind of use of Scripture. If we limit ourselves to the well-preserved passages[148] and if we make a distinction between "weak anthological style" (as in 1 QH 11:3-14) and "anthological style" (as in 1 QH 3:19-36) we can list them as follows:

1. *Weak anthological style*: 1 QH 1:1(?)-39; 9:37-10:12; 11:29-12:36;[149] 13:1-21; 18:1-33. We add here 1 QS 10 and 11.

2. *Anthological style*: 1 QH 2:7(?)-19; 2:20-30; 7:6-25; 15:1-26.

A third group of hymns presents a stronger use of Scripture: a structural style.

3. *Structural style*: 1 QH 3:3(?)-18; 5:5-19; 5:20-7:5 and 8:4-9:36.

As is clear, these distinctions have no absolute character. The first and second categories have the same anthological style. Yet the grouping is helpful in that it allows a comparison of the relative importance of the use of Scripture according to the topics.

---

[148] It is impossible to evaluate the use of Scripture with any certainty as soon as the text becomes fragmentary.

[149] We take into account only 1 QH 12:2-12, the rest of it being badly damaged. 1 QH 10:14-11:2 and 11:15-28 may fall into this category too. But their fragmentary nature does not allow us any certainty.

1. Weak Anthological Style

1 QH 11:29-12:36:[150] in the well-preserved part of this text the use of biblical phrases is remarkably weak. In what could be an introduction to the whole passage, the Psalmist expressed his dependency on God's compassion, mercy, and cleansing, which make praise possible (11:29-34(?)). In so doing he used only two biblical phrases besides the stereotypes (like "Praised be Thou, O God"). In col. 12:4-11a we found only one instance: it is the use of the phrase "the God of knowledge" which is found in at least three other places in the scroll. This passage is not at all cast in a hymnic style. It is rather a liturgical instruction (very similar to 1 QS 10) about the proper times for worship: it alludes to the revealed sacred calendar of the community. Later in the text (12:11b-24a) the hymn alludes to the "what" of the revelation (as in 1 QH 11:3-14),[151] then to the organization of the community as recipient of this revelation. The last part of the hymn emphasizes that man could not have any "knowledge" (wisdom), if not for the fact of God's revelation (12:24b-36).

Although it is quite clearly a hymn (the hymnic motives are dominant in this passage,[152] and one can even point out strophes[153]), let us emphasize the text's instructional character and the focus on the community. The text makes a remarkably weak use of Scripture.

---

[150] We consider this passage as a whole, although it is quite possible that we have here two hymns, as J. Carmignac suggests (*op. cit., ad loc.*). There can be no certainty about how to distinguish between the different hymns of this passage: there are large lacunae.

[151] This is as far as we can interpret the badly damaged text.

[152] As Holm-Nielsen showed, *op. cit.*, 208f.

[153] With J. Carmignac, *op. cit.*, 262-67, although it is difficult to say anything about the rhythmic construction because of the damaged condition of the text.

1 QH 13:1-21: in spite of the fragmentary condition of most of this text, it appears that Scriptural phrases are a little more frequent in it. Yet it is still a very weak anthological style. The topic of this hymn is similar to that of 1 QH 11:3-14: God brings man to an understanding of his mysteries and his glory in his works, despite the poverty of the earthly and sinful man.

In *I QH 18:1-33*, we find again the same theme. Although other biblical phrases were certainly used, the condition of the text allows only two relatively sure idnetifications (besides the stereotypes): Isa. 61:1-2 furnished the terminology for 18:14-15 and Ezek. 11:19, or 36:26, supplied the phrase "heart of stone" which if found in 18:26.

1 QS 10 and 11 present the same weak anthological style. The hymnic character of the passage need not be proved. Nor do we need go into the discussion of its unity. Let us note simply that we follow here the scholars who emphasize its unity (among them A. Dupont-Sommer, A. R. C. Leaney, and Th. Gaster).[154] As far as we are concerned this passage is characterized throughout by a weak anthological use of Scripture,[155] which suits well its clearly didactic nature. Besides the instruction about when God should be worshipped (10:1-17), (which includes the instruction about the sacred calendar, 10:1-8a, similar to 1 QH 12:4-11a), we find ethical resolutions (10:17b-11:2a) and dogmatic affirmations about the revelation, the glory of God and the poverty of earthly man (11:2b-15a and 15b-22). Thus the whole passage which can be entitled, following Th. Gaster, "Hymn of the Initiants", can be said to be a liturgical instruction.

To these texts we can add 1 QH 1:1(?)-39. Although it is denser, its use of Scripture is less important than in the

---

[154] P. Guilbert sees in this passage a succession of four hymns (10:1-8a; 10:8b-11:2a; 11:2b-15a; 11:15b-22). By so doing he stresses the different themes of this passage. Yet several themes may be found in the same hymn.

[155] For biblical phrases used see P. Guilbert, *op. cit.*, 66-80. The only relatively long phrases are to be found in 11:10 in which Isa. 9:1 and Jer. 10:23 are used.

next series. Biblical phrases are used only in five lines:[156] from Isa. 29:24 in line 21; from I Sam. 2:3 in line 26; possibly from Hos. 14:3 in line 28; from Isa. 26:3 in line 35; and from Ps. 119:111 in line 36. This passage expresses themes quite frequent in those Old Testament Psalms in which God is praised as the Creator. Thus for instance lines 9-14 give praise to God as the Creator of the universe in a way similar to that of Pss. 104:2-7 and 135:6-7. Yet in spite of similar images and style we cannot establish a direct dependency of our text upon them. In like manner the following parts (on God's creation of man and man's weakness as contrasted with the might of God, and the final exhortation to praise God) indeed make use of biblical themes. Yet again no direct dependency on specific Psalms can be pointed out. Let us stress that this hymn with weak anthological style is dogmatic in content.

Our survey of these passages and their use of Scripture allows us therefore to reach conclusions similar to those we reached about the "Hymns of the community". Although because of their content we cannot attribute a definite liturgical setting to these hymns,[157] they are nevertheless liturgical texts. We saw also that they present a weak use of Scripture which can be readily understood when we take note of their purpose: expressing praise about the "what" of the revelation, these hymns push Scripture into the background.

---

[156] To which may be added line 6 in which a biblical phrase could have been used according to the reconstruction of the text (it would have come from either one of the following: Exod. 34:6; Joel 2:13; Jonah 4:2; Pss. 86:15; 103:8; 145:8).

[157] 1 QS 10 and 11 is an exception. From the position of this passage at the conclusion of the *Manual of Discipline* we may assume with Th. Gaster that its setting is the ritual of entry into the community. Cf. Th. Gaster, *op. cit.*, 124-25.

2. Anthological Style

1 QH 2:7(?)-19: The use of Scripture is quite important in this last part of a hymn,[158] indeed so important that Holm-Nielsen wrote: "in fact, everything in the psalm can be explained from Old Testament models".[159] The passage makes a very comprehensive use of biblical phrases in a quite *pure* anthological style. The biblical phrases are used out of context, and no single biblical text (or combination of biblical texts) structures the hymn as far as we can see.[160]

In this hymn the "I" clearly has a personal nature.[161] Neither purely a psalm of thanksgiving nor a psalm of complaint, it rightly been called "a psalm of confidence".[162] The author (with whom the community as a whole could eventually identify itself) describes his situation as that of the faithful depository of "truth and insight" (2:10) and as "banner unto the chosen of righteousness" (2:13). On the other hand, the author describes himself as a "snare for the sinners" (2:8) and as an object of scorn for the ungodly

---

[158] With Dupont-Sommer, Th. Gaster, Holm-Nielsen, taking into account the thematic change, we assume that the beginning of this hymn was in the lacuna at the head of the column. Here we do not follow J. Carmignac, who understands our texts as the continuation of that of the first column because of the similar length of the strophes he discovers in these passages. We do not need here to take a position in this debate: we use the first classification because it is convenient. The use of Scripture is different in this passage and in 1 QH 1. But, as we shall see, this cannot be used against Carmignac's argument: different uses of Scripture can be found in the same hymn.

[159] *op. cit.*, 39.

[160] Nevertheless we cannot be absolutly certain of this: a decisive clue may have been lost in the lacuna. There is not enough evidence, in our opinion, to say that the phrase from Isa. 8:14 about "the snare" which the author became for the sinners (2:8), structures the rest of the hymn as J. Carmignac suggests. This *theme*, however, is quite important indeed.

[161] This allows several scholars following Dupont-Sommer to attribute it to the Teacher of Righteousness.

[162] Holm-Nielsen, *op. cit.*, 39.

(e.g., 2:10-11). This is to say that the biblical phrases found in this hymn are used in order to describe the condition of the faithful author, that of the sinners, and their tense relationship. Although there is no clear reference to them, one has the distinct feeling that the text is constantly alluding to specific situations and events. We can assume that these had been previously interpreted by means of the biblical texts, here represented only by the biblical phrases. This assumption is justified by the existence of the *Pesharim* (which interpret biblical texts in terms of present events) as well as by the examples we took in the *Zadokite Documents*: there the events were interpreted by means of biblical texts.

If we can consider this assumption to be correct, then we have in this text what resulted when biblical texts were used to interpret situations in the author's life. Now there is no reason to deny a liturgical use to this hymn when such use is accepted for the Old Testament's thanksgiving Psalms and Psalms of complaint. Thus, once more, in a liturgical text we find the author's convictions expressed by means of biblical phrases, which are the remnant of the process by which the author acquired these convictions. Yet here the focus is no longer on this process and therefore no longer on Scripture. The focus is on these very convictions, or better on the "I", the author, who becomes the embodiment of the revelation. Here the term "revelation" is to be understood not, as before, as a "dogmatic revelation", but as a "dynamic" revelation in line with the sacred history. In this light the author appears both among the Covenanters and among the sinners, as the manifestation of God's action.

A detailed study of 1 QH 2:20-30 and 7:6-25 would be repetitious: let us note simply that what we said for 1 QH 2:7-19 applies to these two hymns, which are also characterized by a dense anthological style. (1 QH 2:20-30 can even be characterized as a mosaic of biblical phrases). Both these hymns are focused in the clearly personal "I".[163]

---

[163] A detailed study which points out the biblical phrases used (although not the significance of their use) can be found in works by Holm-Nielsen, J. Carmignac and M. Delcor.

1 QH 15:9-26: This passage presents a very substantial use of biblical phrases (although not quite as substantial as in the three preceding texts). Yet despite its anthological style it needs to be studied by itself.

In this fragment of a hymn, we can speak properly of an anthological style only for 1 QH 15:17b-20, the rest presents what we have called a weak anthological style (15:12-17a, 21-26).[164]

In 15:17b-20 we find three almost verbatim quotations from Jer. 12:3 in 15:17, from Isa. 65:2 in 15:18 and from Deut. 28:46 in 15:20.[165] To those we can add other phrases, possibly borrowed from Ps. 107:18 in 15:18; from Jer. 32:23 in 15:18b-19a; a common phrase from Ezekiel "to execute great judgment upon them before the eyes of"[166] in 15:19b-20; a combination of Hab. 2:14 with Deut. 9:29, Jer. 32:7 or Neh. 1:10 in 15:20b. This passage (15:17b-20) deals with the ungodly. It first describes their rejection of God's Covenant and commandments, then it announces their punishment and its purpose.

By contrast, if we look at the use of Scripture in 15:14b-17a (a passage of about the same length) we find only what may *possibly* be two uses of biblical phrases: from both Isa. 63:15 and Gen. 42:21 in line 15:16, with no quasi-quotation. What is the theme of this part? Since it is introduced by "and I, I know" (ואני ידעתי) and proceeds to express, in dogmatic terms, the relationship between the righteous creature and his creator, it can readily be called "dogmatic".

Here we may have a clue which will help us further to understand why in certain hymns we have a weak, and in others a dense, anthological style. First 15:17b-20 deals with a favorite theme found in the *Pesharim*: the sinners, their

---

[164] We leave aside the beginning of the hymn; it is fragmentary.

[165] Yet in this last passage the use of the biblical text is less direct.

[166] לעשות בם שפטים גדולים לעיני, cf. e.g., Ezek. 16:41; cf. also Exod. 6:6; 12:12 and Num. 33:4.

ways, and their punishment. This theme is, so to speak, the
negative side of the "dynamic" revelation which we saw in 1 QH
2:7(?)-19. We know from the number of examples found in the
Dead Sea Scrolls that this theme was the major preoccupation
of the Covenanters when searching Scripture. Thus the
discrepancy in the density of biblical phrases may simply
reflect the varying importance of the use of Scripture in
playing upon these themes. This seems to be confirmed by the
Hodayot we have studied so far. When the theme involved an
interpretation of events concerning the community and the
Psalmist or their negative counterparts, the sinners, we found
an important use of biblical phrases (as in 2:7(?)-19, 20-30;
7:6-25; 15:17b-20, as well as in 3:19-36 which deals with the
situation of the community). But when the theme becomes
dogmatic, the anthological style gets weaker (as in 15:14-17a,
but also 11:3-14; 11:29-12:36; 13:1-21 and 18:1-33, as well as
in 1 QS 10 and 11).

These observations confirm the general impression one
has when reading the Dead Sea Scrolls: although a dogmatic
search of Scripture is not absent, it is less important than
the dynamic "sacred historical" search of Scripture. But in
both cases we have liturgical texts: the use of Scripture
stays in the background. The worshipping community or the
Psalmist are now either the embodiment of the dynamic
revelation or the depository of the dogmatic revelation, and
Scripture is reduced to the role of a language.

3. *The Structural Use of Scripture
in the Hodayot*

In our remarks on 1 QH 15:17b-20 we did not emphasize
the fact that we found in it at least two quasi-quotations
(from Jer. 12:3 and Isa. 65:2). Here Scripture tends to
become more than a mere language. It is as if it were not
sufficient to present the results of a search of Scripture,
i.e., as if the author needed to strengthen his point by

alluding to "how" it was "uncovered". This leads us to another use of Scripture, which can be found in the *Hodayot* and which cannot be properly qualified as anthological: we have called it the structural use of Scripture. Such a use of Scripture can be found more or less extensively in the following hymns: 1 QH 3:3(?)-18; 5:5-19; 5:20-7:5 and 8:4-9:36.

As we shall show by a number of examples, each of these hymns is at least partly structured on one or several biblical passages. The hymn exposits this (these) passage(s) with the help of other biblical passages or phrases which are tallied to it (or them). Here Scripture is at the center of the hymn. The process of "uncovering" revelation is still present, although the focus is already on its result.

Let us note from the outset that each of these texts deals with the situation of the righteous author (possibly representing the community as a whole) as opposed to his enemies, the sinners. They are not concerned therefore with dogmatic themes.

1 QH 3:3(?)-18: The central symbol of this hymn is quite clearly that of the "distress of a woman giving birth". This is expressed in line 7 with vocabulary borrowed from Jer. 4:31 and Jer. 13:21. This theme is combined with that of the distress of the sailors at sea (which was possibly already mentioned in line 6, if the restitution of the lacuna by םי is correct). The second theme echoes, above all, Ps. 107:23-30.

The first theme is expressed in a combination of terms from Jer. 4:31 and Jer. 13:21. We should note here that the image of the woman giving birth is used in Jer. 4:31 to speak of the "daughter of Zion" threatened by her enemies. Taken out of context the verse can be understood as referring to the suffering of the righteous daughter of Zion. In Jer. 13:21 by contrast, the distress of the woman appears quite clearly as the punishment of her wickedness. The author of our hymn used this twofold image typologically. He saw in the woman "daughter of Zion", a type of himself (and the righteous community). In the woman suffering because of her wickedness he saw the type of his enemies.[167] This twofold interpretation is made by means of other biblical passages, which are tallied to the former in a fashion similar to that of Midrash.

Thus in lines 7-12 in order to express the typological identification of the author (or community) with the woman giving birth we find the use of biblical phrases from the following passages (in their Old Testament sequence): I Sam. 4:19; Isa. 9:5, 13:8, 26:17, 37:3, 66:7; Jer. 22:23, 49:24; Dan. 10:16, 9:11, 13:13; Mic. 2:10; Ps. 18:6 and Job 39:3. They are tallied quite often by key words. Such tallyings allow a very subtle combination of meanings. Most of the key words of our text received in this way an ambiguous meaning from their multifold context. Because of this, it is practically impossible to have a proper translation of our text.[168] Let us note that most of the passages are used only here in the *Hodayot*[169] This confirms our assumption of a conscious use of the biblical phrases in this passage.

---

[167]This is a typological interpretation (and not an allegorical one) since it interprets the image as referring to historical situations of actual people. As mentioned earlier we understand the allegorical interpretation as one which discovers in the biblical text a purely spiritual meaning.

[168]For a detailed description of the interweaving of these texts see the remarkable analysis of Holm-Nielsen, *op. cit.*, 56-64. Cf. also that of J. Carmignac, *op. cit., ad loc.* For the interpretation of the meaning of this text, beside the translations see: J. V. Chamberlain, "Another Qumran Thanksgiving Psalm", in *Journal of Near Eastern Studies*, 1955, 32-41, and "Further Elucidation of a Messianic Thanksgiving Psalm from Qumran", same periodical, 1955, 181-82; A. Dupont-Sommer, "La mère du Messie et la mère de l'Aspic dans un hymne de Qoumrân", in *Revue de l'Histoire des Religions*, 1955, 174-88; L. H. Silberman, "Language and Structure in the Hodayot (1 QH 3)", *J.B.L.*, 1956, 96-106; M. Delcor, "Un psaume messianique de Qumrân", in *Mélanges Bibliques rédigés en l'honneur de André Robert*, Paris, 1957, 334-40; O. Betz, "Die Geburt der Gemeinde durch den Lehrer", *N.T.S.*, 1957, 314-26, and "Das Volk seiner Kraft: zur Auslegung der Qumran-hodajah III, 1-18", *N.T.S.*, 1958, 67-75; G. Hinson, "Hodayot III, 6-18: in what sense messianic?" in *R.Q.*, t. II, 183-204.

[169]This can be seen if we compare this list with the complete list of biblical passages used in the *Hodayot*. The latter is given by Holm-Nielsen, *op. cit.*, 354-59.

In the same way the woman is identified typologically with the wicked, as one who is pregnant with wickedness (if we interpret אפעה, serpent, figuratively, cf. Isa. 30:6, 59:5 and Job 20:16). The phrase may have been borrowed from Isa. 59:6, which mentions the hatching of the serpent. This image is combined further with a phrase from II Sam. 22:6a, tallied to the preceding by the mention of Belial (Satan, serpent) in II Sam. 22:5. In this very verse occurs the mention of "the waves of death" (משבר משברי-מות, a phrase which is used also in connection with birth in Isa. 37:3 and Hos. 13:13); this mention allowed the author to pass to the image of the sea and the distress of the man on the sea (Ps. 107:23ff.). Several other biblical phrases are tallied to the latter image in the same fashion, composing lines 14-16. Among them Job 38:16 ("the springs of the waters" נבוכי מים) in line 15b, allows Job 38:17 to influence lines 17-18 in which the image of the pregnant woman is again used.[170]

Although we cannot take time to mention all the biblical phrases used in this text and how they relate to each other,[171] this is enough to show that the hymn is completely structured on a limited number of biblical passages, which are themselves interpreted by means of other biblical passages.

The same is true of 1 QH 5:5-19, which is structured on Dan. 6:17-24 (used in lines, 7, 9, 11, 13-14, 19). This basic biblical passage is combined and interpreted by means of many other biblical passages in a manner similar to that which we found in 1 QH 3:6-18. This time the typology identifies the author with Daniel and his enemies with the lions.[172]

Likewise in 1 QH 5:20-7:5, the passage which portrays the misery of the author is apparently built on Ps. 107:10-18, which is tallied with several other passages. For instance in

---

[170] Job 38:17 seems to be combined with Ps. 107:18 and Jonah 2:7. Yet no certain conclusion can be drawn because the text is damaged.

[171] For this cf. the studies mentioned above.

[172] The tallying here is a little more difficult to follow because of the passage from Aramaic to Hebrew. For details see Holm-Nielsen and J. Carmignac, *ad loc*. Yet let us note that Ps. 107:27 is used here again in line 18.

5:37-38, Ps. 107:16 is tallied with Jonah 2:6-7. This combination occurs again in 6:27-28. References to the Book of Jonah are found also in 6:22-23 and later at the end of our passage in 7:5.

In 1 QH 8:4-9:36, although a large part of this passage presents simply an anthological style, the first part, 8:4-26, appears to be structured on Ps. 80:9-15. In this way the situation of the author (and of the community) is expressed in terms of a plantation or a garden, although Ps. 80 refers only to the vine. Yet as usual the image of Ps. 80 is combined with several other biblical passages: from the outset with Isa. 44:3, 49:10, 41:18, possibly 58:11, and 60:13, and Gen. 2-3. (The first use of a phrase from Ps. 80 appears only in line 7).

A Threefold Locus of Revelation: Scripture, the Community, the Salient History

This examination of the use of Scripture in the *Hodayot* sharpens the observations we made when dealing with the quasi-explicit doctrine of Scripture in the Dead Sea Scrolls and when dealing with the *Zadokite Documents*. First it appears that the Covenanters used Scripture primarily in order to understand their "identity" as a community, this over against the "identity" of the wicked. As we say they apprehended this "identity" in the context of the historical situations in which they lived. Witnesses to this are: a) the dense anthological style found when the topic of the hymn is this "identity"; b) the structural style, which reflects the process which allowed the inspired author to discover elements of this revealed identity.

A corollary of the first remark is that the Covenanters made a very weak use of Scripture in acquiring their dogmatic theological beliefs. Witness to this is the weak anthological style of the dogmatic passages. The implication is that on these matters the Covenanters relied on common haggadic traditions. This is confirmed by the fact that we find such traditional haggadic material as the *Genesis Apocryphon* among the Dead Sea Scrolls. Thus we can assume that the Covenanters did not deny the value of classical haggadic interpretations and the doctrinal revelation which these expressed. As far as the Covenanters were concerned these haggadic beliefs were so much manifest that they did not any longer require an extensive search of Scripture; the weak anthological style in which they were expressed in the hymns is witness to this.

Yet for the Covenanters such haggadic interpretations did not provide a sufficient interpretation of the non-halakic biblical passages. It was essential to discover in these passages the dynamic revelation of the living God acting in the salient history of their time; they did this by means of typology and *pesher* interpretation.

A third concluding remark is demanded by the *liturgical* character of these texts. This character seems to be the reason for the limited role of Scripture in the *Hodayot*: Scripture is used in most instances as a mere language.[173] Studying the *Zadokite Documents* we noted that the revelation of the community's identity was assumed.[174] Consequently both the re-telling of the sacred history and the "halakic" interpretations were done in terms of this revealed identity. The "re-telling" of the sacred history was either a way of reminding the community of its revealed identity or a way of teaching the latter to prospective members. It was the ground for any subsequent use of Scripture and for the halakic interpretations. The *Hodayot*, as *liturgical* texts, had a similar function. Yet now this function was directed exclusively toward the community. The communal recitation of these hymns (as well as the individual meditation on them), was the reaffirmation of the community's revealed identity as an eschatological community. The worshipping community thus became the locus of revelation, its embodiment. If this

---

[173] With the exception of the hymn which present a structural style.

[174] With the exception of the *pesher*-like passages.

revelation had been doctrinal in nature (the revelation of an eternal truth), they could have limited themselves from that time on to the liturgical-anthological use of Scripture. Yet because this revelation was dynamic in addition to the liturgical use, they had to search further in Scripture, as is attested by the several references to the Covenanters' constant study of Scripture. This direct use of Scripture may well have taken place in the same sort of "worship service" which Philo pointed out for the Therapeutai.[175]

---

[175]*De vita contemplativa*, # 65ff.

V

THE USE OF SCRIPTURE IN THE
MANUAL OF DISCIPLINE (1 QS)

In the *Manual of Discipline* we find various uses of Scripture which we have met already in other scrolls. For indeed the use of Scripture in this scroll presents at once similarities to what we found in the *Zadokite Documents* and in the *Hodayot*. Yet it is identical neither to one nor the other: actually this twofold kinship points to a specific use of Scripture.

EXPLICIT SCRIPTURAL QUOTATIONS

Although less often than in the *Zadokite Documents*, we find explicit quotations in three passages: 1 QS 5:14, 17 and 8:14.[176] The limited number of occurrences shows that this use of Scripture is not at all characteristic of the *Manual of Discipline*, which can be said consequently to be much less apologetic.

In the first two passages (1 QS 5:14, 17) the biblical texts (respectively Exod. 23:7 and Isa. 2:22) are introduced to justify the injunctions to the new Covenanters to be separated from every "perverse man who walks in the way of wickedness" (5:10-11). Here we have a use of Scripture which can be assimilated to the halakic Midrash. The text quoted is the biblical passage which is interpreted in the preceding *halakah*.[177] In 1 QS 8:14 we find a use of Isa. 40:3 which is

---

[176] They are introduced by the formulae כאשר כתוב (1 QS 5:17 and 8:14) and כיא כן כתוב (1 QS 5:15).

[177] As often in the Midrash we are surprised by the choice of the Scriptural text. As Leaney pointed out (*op. cit.*, 174), the same teaching could have been found more readily for instance in Lev. 18:3, 24, 30; 20:23 . . . than in Exod. 23:7, although the context of the latter which deals with the Covenant, may have motivated the choice.

more akin to the use found in the *Zadokite Documents*. A historical situation is first presented: the settlement of the community in the wilderness (1 QS 8:12-13). Then the Prophetic text is introduced as the key which allows us to understand this historical situation (1 QS 8:14). Then occurs a further interpretation of the situation in terms of the text in a *pesher*-like manner: the preparation of the way is the study of Torah. We have noted the importance of this text: it is a description by the sectarians themselves of their use of Scripture.

HALAKIC INTERPRETATIONS

Besides the use of Scripture in explicit quotations, we also find halakic interpretations in the *Manual of Discipline*. These are gathered together in 1 QS 5:1-7:25. In the fragments of the *Manual* found in Cave 4, which seem to give an older version of this passage,[178] this part of the text is introduced, significantly, by the phrase מדרש למשכיל על אנשי החורה. This can be translated as follows: "Interpretation for the instructor concerning the men of the Law"; it is an authoritative halakic interpretation of Scripture which the "instructor" should teach and implement in the community. Yet except for the few passages where the Scriptural text is either explicitly quoted (1 QS 5:17 quoting Isa. 2:22) or "quasi-quoted" (e.g., 1 QS 5:4 which uses Jer. 11:8), the relationship between the *halakah* and Scripture is not obvious at all.[179] We saw that this was also the case for the halakah of classical Judaism. This is not to say that Scripture was not important in itself; the contrary is repeatedly emphasized in these very passages (e.g., 5:8, 21; 6:6, 22). Just as the Oral Torah did not abolish the Written but complemented and

---

[178]Cf. Milik's review of P. Wernberg-Møller's book (*The Manual of Discipline*, Leiden, 1957) in *R.B.* 67, 1960, 410ff.

[179]Most of P. Guilbert's notes refer only to biblical phraseologies. Cf. *op. cit., ad loc.*

interpreted it, the Qumranite halakah complemented and interpreted the Law of Moses, which was to be carefully studied and followed.

Yet an examination of the use of Scripture in terms of classical Judaism's distinction between Oral and Written Toroth may be misleading, because this does not take into account the specific nature of the community. For indeed there is a fundamental difference. When classical halakah took some freedom from Scripture (either by interpretating it freely or by promulgating new laws without direct Scriptural connections), it was as if the Sages considered that the action of God was manifested in cultural changes. In other words, it was as if the locus of revelation were, for them, the tension between Scripture and the cultural changes which affected the whole society. By contrast the Qumranite *halakah* is narrowly focused on the life of the community as such. It is as if the locus of revelation, for the Covenanters, were the tension between their community and Scripture.[180] In this the *Manual of Discipline* is like the *Zadokite Documents*.

ANTHOLOGICAL USE OF SCRIPTURE

Let us now consider the rest of the scroll. Although explicit uses of Scripture are rare, Scripture is implicitly used to such an extent that it could be said to be a mosaic of biblical texts.[181] Such a statement must be qualified. If some passages are indeed a dense mosaic of biblical passages, there are others presenting a weaker anthological style. We do not need to elaborate on this. Let us note simply that

---

[180] Indeed one could explain the different connotations of the halakah by the different concrete situations of the community. For instance the passage 5:1-6:23 could have been written before the "foundation" of the "monastery" of Qumran, that is, at a time when the Covenanters were still in contact with the other Israelites. On this see Leaney, *op. cit.*, 174.

[181] This appears clearly when the biblical phrases are printed in a different type, as for instance in Guilbert's translation.

various densities of anthological style are to be found in the different sections of the scroll, although no definite pattern emerges. Thus in the doctrinal section dealing with the doctrine of the two spirits (1 QS 3:13-4:26), we find passages with a weak anthological style (1 QS 3:13-4:1 and 4:23b-26) and others with a denser one (4:2-23a). The same is true of the passages which we could call hortatory, expressed in the form of a rule, (1 QS 2:24-3:12; 5:1-6:9; 8:16-9:11),[182] and again of the passages dealing more specifically with the organization of the community (as in the rule for the "assembly of the Many", 1 QS 6:8-23, and also in 1 QS 8:1-16, which deals with the establishment of the community in the wilderness, but without reference to any specific events).

THE STRUCTURAL USE OF SCRIPTURE

One section clearly presents a structural use of Scripture:[183] 1 QS 1:16-2:18. It describes the "rite for the entry into the Covenant".

We cannot discuss the actual setting of this rite at length. It has generally been identified with the Feast of the Weeks, i.e., the feast of the Renewal of the Covenant.[184] Among the various biblical texts which could have served as a structure for this liturgy, it appears that Deut. 27-30 was chosen. The characteristic phrase "עבר בברית" of the opening sentence of our passage (1 QS 1:16, cf. also 1:18) is indeed borrowed from Deut. 29:11. As in Deut. 27-28 the people (here

---

[182] Thus for instance, as P. Guilbert pointed out, 1 QS 5:20-25 describes the hierarchic order of the members of the community (established according to the Covenanters' "understanding" and works with regard to the Law). It uses phrases from II Chr. 15:12; Exod. 18:16; Prov. 12:8; Deut. 8:18, 6:17; Ps. 45:5; Mic. 6:8.

[183] Although such a use of Scripture may be present elsewhere in the scroll, we were not able to detect any other instance in which this structural style could be assumed with a reasonable degree of certainty.

[184] Thus e.g., Guilbert, Leaney, Dupont-Sommer.

the Covenanters) will be blessed and cursed.[185] As in Deut. 27:14ff. the curses are proclaimed by the Levites and the people respond "Amen".[186] Furthermore the second set of curses (1 QS 2:11-18) follows very closely Deut. 29:17-19.[187]

Yet this text, which served as framework for the rite, stays in the background. It is combined with other biblical passages used as quasi-quotations (namely Lev. 16:21, Ps. 106:6 and Num. 6:24-26), which are themselves introduced and interpreted by means of biblical phrases. Let us now follow part of the text to point out more specifically this use of Scripture.[188] In parentheses we note the origin of the main biblical phrases.

> 1:18ff.: "And when they pass into the Covenant (Deut. 29:11) the priests and the Levites shall bless the God of Salvation (Isa. 12:2) and all the works of his faithfulness (Ps. 33:4) and all who pass into the Covenant (Deut. 29:11) shall say after them 'Amen, Amen'".
> 21f.: "And the priests recount the righteous deeds of God (Ps. 40:40) in the works of his power and proclaim all the favour of mercy towards Israel".

According to this introduction, after a general blessing of God the past sacred history was recited. In this the Covenanters followed biblical models like Deut. 26:5-10; Pss. 78, 105, 106; Neh. 9:6ff.

> 22bff.: "And the Levites recount the iniquities of the sons of Israel and all their guilty rebellions and their sins (Lev. 16:21) under the dominion of Belial".

Here we have the parallel ritual, in which the transgressions of the people were recited. This served as an introduction to the confession of sins just as in Pss. 78, 105, 106 and Neh. 9:6ff.

---

[185] It is in that order in Deut. 27:12-13, as in our text, although the specific curses precede the benedictions in the following passage of Deuteronomy.

[186] But in 1 QS the response is a double "Amen" following Num. 5:22 and Neh. 8:6.

[187] As O. Betz showed, *Offenbarung*, 170ff.

[188] We shall generally follow the translation given by Dupont-Sommer and Vermès, although often we shall introduce our own interpretations. For the biblical references we are much indebted to P. Guilbert.

> 24ff.: "And all who pass into the Covenant
> (Deut. 19:11) confess (Lev. 16:21) after them,
> saying: 'we have been sinful, [we have rebelled],
> we [have sinned] we have been wicked (I Kings 8:47;
> Dan. 9:5; Ps. 106:6) we and our fathers (Ps. 106:6)
> before us, by going [against the Covenant of] truth
> and righteousness [and God has passed] His judgment
> upon us and upon our fathers. But he has bestowed
> upon us mercies of his favour (Isa. 63:7) for ever
> and ever'" (Ps. 103:17).

Here we have the classical formula of confession with, in addition, brief remarks pointing out the contrast between the action of God and that of Israel, as in Ps. 106 for instance. In the parallel passage in CD 20:28-30, where the formula of confession is also used, the second part of the text is more developed: it alludes more directly to features of the life of the sect. The different use of the formula of confession is readily understandable when we remember the "historical" and "apologetic" character of the *Zadokite Documents*, as opposed to the "liturgical" character of the *Manual of Discipline*.

> 2:1bff.: "And the priests bless all the men of
> the lot of God who walk perfectly in all his
> ways (Gen. 17:1; Pss. 15:2, 101:2) and say. . ."

The idea of the people as the "lot" of God can be found in Deut. 32:9 and Eccl. 17:17. Yet it is not the same term which is used here. The term גורל is used, interestingly enough, in Lev. 16:8 about the two goats: one is for Yahweh, the other for "Azazel". As mentioned above, the formula by means of which the sins are put on the scapegoat (Lev. 16:21) has just been used (1:23). Thus it is quite possible that by the phrase "lot of God" they identified themselves with the goat designated for Yahweh, and that by the phrase "lot of Belial" (2:5) they identified the wicked men with the scapegoat.

Then follows the blessing which is an expansion of Num. 6:24-26, benedictions by Aaron and his sons. It is said, naturally, by the priests. This passage has been commented upon many times. We need not repeat these comments here.[189] It is enough to say that these benedictions are complemented by specific references to the sect's doctrine of "knowledge".

---

[189] Cf. for instance the excellent commentary in Betz, *Offenbarung*, 166ff.

The curses (2:4b-9) represent the negative side of the blessings. The same text (Num. 6:24-26) is therefore used as a framework, complemented by means of biblical phraseology.

The last part of the ritual is, as mentioned, built upon Deut. 29:17-19 in a similar fashion.

THE MANUAL OF DISCIPLINE: A QUASI-LITURGICAL TEXT

Our brief examination of this passage will suffice to show the liturgical character of the text and the use of Scripture in it. What is remarkable, when we compare it with the *Zadokite Documents*, for instance, is that this passage says nothing specific about the historical situation of the community. There are only vague hints concerning the enemies of the community even in the curses which could have so readily been used to attack them specifically.

This is true of the scroll in general: the historical situation of the community is, at most, barely hinted at. This is not surprising in itself: it simply reflects the character of this scroll as a rule of the community. Yet this is worth emphasizing for our purposes; it has implications for our understanding of the use of Scripture therein. Coming back to the metaphor we used previously, we could say that here Scripture is used neither in tension with historical situations, nor in tension with the identity of the community as discovered in this historical setting, but in tension with *the community as living Temple* ("sanctuary in Aaron" and "House of truth in Israel").[190] Indeed we should not forget that the consciousness of the community was structured by what we could call (by an analogy with the main feature of Apocalyptic literature) a broad biblical pattern: namely a combination of Temple symbolism and of Sinaitic Covenant symbolism.

---

[190] Cf. 1 QS 5:6.

As we have pointed out already, this general biblical pattern is the one which structures the self-consciousness of the sect. We have to take it seriously into account in the study of this scroll. For indeed the general purpose of the writers[191] is clear. It is to give a "rule" which will structure the life of the community. Thus the authors do not intend either to make a commentary upon such or such biblical passages, or to point out the identity of the community in its historical setting, but primarily to organize the life of the community as the true and faithful Israel of the eschatological time. Their use of Scripture is therefore commanded by this purpose.

As in the *Zadokite Documents*, what we called the revealed identity of the community is assumed. Yet here, with few exceptions, there are no longer any "proof texts", no longer apologetic aims or historical settings. The authors write for the community itself, to give a rule to its members.

Our scroll is more akin to the liturgical texts than to the *Zadokite Documents*. This is indicated by the important role which the Temple symbolism has for the consciousness of the community. In addition to what we said about the use of Scripture in the *Hodayot* as liturgical texts, we should bear in mind here our brief comments on the uses of Scripture in the Temple and Synagogal liturgies.

The *Manual of Discipline*, as the rule which sets the structure of the "Sanctuary in Aaron" and the "house of truth in Israel" (1 QS 5:6), can be legitimately considered a "quasi-liturgical" document.[192] Now we were able to conclude from our examination of the use of Scripture in the liturgy that one of the loci of revelation was to be found in the worshipping community either at the Temple or at the Synagogue (although the conviction of the "Presence" of God was mainly

---

[191] As we noted earlier referring to A. M. Denis' research, this is a composite work. Cf. further A. R. C. Leaney, *op. cit.*, 113ff.

[192] This is further justified by the fact that parts of the document were certainly used as liturgical texts (in the narrower sense of the term) in the "rite for the entry into the Covenant" (1 QS 1:16-2:18). Cf. also the concluding hymn (1 QS 10:8b-11:22). Cf. above ch. VIII, # 3.

bound to the Temple). Just so the Qumran community had the conviction that the "Presence" of God was bound to the community.[193] It is not surprising therefore to find Scripture used as a mere language: the community itself was the locus of revelation. This is not to say that Scripture had an insignificant role: it provided the framework in which the "Presence" manifested itself. Yet precisely to fulfill this function, Scripture had to stay in the background. To put it in terms of the Sectarians' explicit understanding of Scripture, to use Scripture (to study it) was to "prepare the way of (the Lord)" (1 QS 8:15). The "Presence" of the Lord pushed into the background this preparation for His coming.

In this scroll, therefore, it is as if the Temple-community had preeminence over Scripture. We have only the remnant of the former use of Scripture, which led to the establishment of the liturgical identity of the community as the locus of revelation. Yet Scripture was also pointed out, specifically, as a locus of revelation which had to be kept in balance with the preceding one. As we indicated above (in our introduction to this chapter) the community defined itself as a community which studies and searches Scripture![194] Although this search of Scripture was quite different from that of classical Judaism, we find here an analogous balance between two loci of revelation: the community and Scripture itself.

---

[193] Cf. B. Gärtner, *op. cit.*, 16ff.

[194] Cf. 1 QS 5:7-12; 6:6-7, *passim*.

VI

THE USE OF SCRIPTURE IN THE SCROLL OF THE WAR OF THE SONS OF LIGHT AGAINST THE SONS OF DARKNESS (1 QM)

We need first to make two general remarks about this scroll concerning its title and its literary unity. The scroll has often been entitled "Rule of the war" (*inter alios* by Dupont-Sommer,[195] J. Carmignac,[196] and G. Vermès[197]). Such a title stresses the kinship of this scroll with the "Rule of the community" (1 QS). Although their contents are quite different, the two scrolls are indeed similar in type; both have the same "liturgical" function. 1 QM presents the regulations concerning the eschatological war between the Sons of Light and the Sons of Darkness, just as 1 QS presents the regulations for the life of the community. Yet such a title[198] should not hide the striking differences with the "Rule of the community": 1 QM describes the eschatological time (i.e., the eschatological war). It presents a closer kinship with the "Rule of all the congregation of Israel" (1 QSa) if one considers the latter, with G. Vermès,[199] as "the messianic rule", i.e., a description of the community at the eschatological time.

---

[195] In *The Essenes Writings from Qumran*, 164ff.

[196] *La Règle de la Guerre*, Paris, 1958, and in *Les Textes de Qumran*, vol. I, 81ff.

[197] In *The Dead Sea Scrolls in English*, Baltimore, 1962, 122ff.

[198] According to Carmignac this may have been the original title. Yet his conclusion is based on the reconstitution of the lacuna at the beginning of the scroll. This is necessarily hypothetical. Cf. Carmignac, *La Règle de la Guerre, ad loc.*, and *Textes de Qumran*, 83.

[199] *The Dead Sea Scrolls in English*, Baltimore, 1962, 118ff.

Concerning this scroll's literary unity, let us state that we do not think it necessary to see in it a composite work. 1 QM 15-19 indeed contains many repetitions of the regulations of 1 QM 2-14. Yet this does not necessarily mean that 1 QM 15-19 is a "rule annexe", as Dupont-Sommer contends.[200] Such repetitions can readily be understood if one sees in this passage the description of the last phase of the eschatological war in which these regulations were to be implemented.[201]

So assuming a literary unity for this scroll, we can see in it three major parts.[202]

- A. Introduction: The eschatological war: col.1:1-2:14.
- B. The Rule of the war: col. 2:15-14:15 (in which with Yadin we can distinguish a) the "*Battle Serkh series*," col.2:15-9:16, and b) the "*Ritual Serekh `series*," col. 9:17(?)-14:15).
- C. Description of a final phase of the war (col. 14:16-19:13).

We shall examine briefly the use of Scripture in these three parts.[203]

---

[200] *op. cit.*, 166.

[201] Cf. Yigael Yadin, *The Scroll of the War of the Sons of Light against the Sons of Darkness*, Oxford, 1962, 10ff., and *passim*. Another hypothesis for the composite nature of the document is given in J. van der Ploeg, *Le rouleau de la Guerre*, Leiden, 1959. The author suggests a two step redaction for our texts. Yet his argument is less convincing than Yadin's: the latter shows the inner logic of the structure of our document. But we do not exclude the possibility that the author may have used sources when composing his work.

[202] In this we follow Y. Yadin, *op. cit.*, 8-10.

[203] For this part we are indebted to J. Carmignac, "Les citations de l'Ancien Testament dans 'La guerre des Fils de Lumière contre les Fils de Ténèbres'", *R.B.* 63, 1956, 234-60 and 275-90.

A. Introduction: the Eschatological War
   (col. 1:1-2:14)

In a first section (1:1-7) the author describes the fighting forces and the general purpose and plan of the war. The use of Scripture can be characterized as *anthological*. The list of the traditional enemies of Israel (1:1-2) echoes one of the several biblical lists (cf. Isa. 11:14; II Kings 24:2; Dan. 11:41; II Sam. 8:12; I Chr. 18:11 and Ps. 83:7-9). Although it may do so only indirectly through the intermediary of the *Book of Jubilees* 37:6ff., Ps. 83:7-9 seems the most probable source, since it presents the same names in the same order. In the following lines the author seems to have Daniel ch. 11 in mind. Yet this text does not structure the passage. Several phrases are borrowed from it: "the offenders against the Covenant" (מרשיעי ברית) (1:2) from Dan. 11:32; "He shall go forth with great wrath" (יצא בחמה גדולה) (1:4) from Dan. 11:44. "To fight the Kings of the North" (1:4) is possibly an adaption of Dan. 11:11. Dan. 11:44 is used at the end of the line: "His anger to destroy" (אפו להשמיד). "And none shall help him" (ואין עוזר לו) (1:6) is borrowed from Dan. 11:45. "None shall escape" (1:6) is reminiscent of Dan. 11:42. Yet it appears that our text is not a mere interpretation of Dan. 11: other biblical phrases are used as well, from Ezek. 20:35, line 1:3; from Isa. 49:8, line 1:5; from Isa. 31:8, line 1:6; and from Esd. 9:14, line 1:6.[204]

We have therefore a good example of anthological style in this passage, which, quite clearly, does not attempt to be apologetic. As Yadin has pointed out,[205] the revelation about the eschatological war is presented as a "matter-of-fact". The circumstances of this revelation are not mentioned, nor is it attributed to an eminent biblical personage, as is done in Apocalyptic literature. The author presents the details of

---

[204] These are only the most obvious instances. For other suggested uses of Scripture in this passage see Y. Yadin, *op. cit.*, 256ff.

[205] *op. cit.*, 7.

the eschatological war as if they were self-evident for his
readers, as if this were the repetition of a well-known
doctrine. Here we have only traces of how this Apocalyptic
doctrine was reached, i.e., we have biblical phrases from some
of the texts which were used.

This passage is not yet properly speaking part of the
"rule of the war". But from the very way it presents the
eschatological war, we can already infer that this scroll used
Scripture in a way similar to that of the *Manual of
Discipline*: both make a "quasi-liturgical" use of Scripture
(that is, a use of Scripture similar to the liturgical texts
of the Synagogue). And indeed, here too Scripture was used
primarily as a language which enabled the community to express
its identity, this time as *depository of eschatological
revelation* (rather than its identity as the holy community of
the last generation, as in the *Manual of Discipline*).

The second section (1:8-15), which describes briefly the
violence of the last phase of the war (against the Kittim),
presents an anthological use of Scripture, although it is
weaker.[206] Likewise the third section (1:16(?)-2:14(?), which
deals with the calendar of the war, and which takes into
account the sabbatical years and the role of each group of the
congregation,[207] presents an anthological style.[208] Our
comments about 1:1-7 are valid for these two sections.

B. THE RULE OF THE WAR
   (2:15-14:15)

In this second part, the author spelled out the
regulations of the eschatological war. For this purpose he

---

[206] For the list of biblical phrases used therein see
Yadin and Carmignac, *ad loc*.

[207] This section could have been included as well in the
second part, since it deals already with a number of
regulations.

[208] Cf. Yadin and Carmignac, *ad loc*.

took into account at once Scripture and the science of war in his time. As Yadin and Dupont-Sommer have pointed out the author refers to the techniques of war of the Roman troups.

In what Yadin has called the "*Battle Serekh series*" (2:15-9:16) we find a weak anthological style. The author chiefly had in mind the techniques of war in his time, although he adapted them for the Sons of Light by making reference to the holy wars of Yahweh. Thus, for instance, the destruction of Jericho, Joshua ch. 6, seems to have been in the author's mind when writing 1 QM 7:12ff.

By contrast, in what Yadin has called the "*Ritual Serekh series*" (9:17(?)-14:15), we find a dense anthological style. There is even a number of explicit quotations (from Deut. 7:21-22 in 10:1-2; from Deut. 20:2-5 in 10:2-5; from Num. 10:9 in 10:6-8; from Num. 24:17-19 in 11:5-7; from Isa. 31:8 in 11:11-12).

The first three explicit quotations (Deut. 7:21-22; 20:2-5 and Num. 10:9) are contained in a passage[209] (10:1-8) which exhorts men to be brave in the war; the exhortation takes the form of a ritual which would have been enacted before the battle. To strengthen the courage of the holy warriors, the ritual reminds them of God's promises such as the one found in Deut. 20:4: "for your God goes with you, to fight for you against your enemies, to save you". The three explicit quotations were, as usual, completed by other biblical phrases. Yet no further interpretation of them was given.

The ritual continued (10:8-11:12) with a re-telling of the sacred history, that is, a re-telling of the mighty deeds of Yahweh introduced by the formula: "who is like Thee, O God" (מיא כמוכה אל). This is a phrase which is frequently found in the Psalms (cf. e.g., Pss. 35:10, 71:19). In this re-telling numerous biblical passages were used--Num. 24:17-19 is even explicitly quoted in order to explain that the

---

[209] We do not have its beginning, which disappeared with the end of col. 9.

valorous deeds of Israel must be attributed to Yahweh.[210] In the conclusion of this section, Isa. 31:8 is introduced by the comment: "From of old Thou hast announced to us the time appointed for the mighty deed of Thy hand against the Kittim, saying. . ."[211] This points out that the mighty deeds of God in the past (mentioned in the preceding lines) were taken as promises of the mighty deeds which God would perform in the final battle against the Kittim.[212] Thus here, as in the *Zadokite Documents*, the sacred history is seen as the promise of God's new mighty acts at history's end. The hortatory style of the passage demanded references to biblical proof texts; these hint therefore at the process by which one received this revelation. In its following part the ritual expresses confidence in God and his upcoming mighty deeds in the eschatological war (11:13-12:5). Here an anthological style is used.

The author expressed the same ideas in a hymnic form (12:7-16(?)). This passage presents an almost perfect mosaic of biblical passages[213] which are carefully tallied with each other. Here we have the same use of Scripture as the one we found in the *Hodayot*: pure anthological style. This hymn is repeated in col. 19.

The following part of the ritual (13:1-18(?)) consists of several strands. There is the blessing of the Sons of Light and cursing of the Sons of Darkness by the Priests and Levites; then, the Sons of Light bless God for his Covenant with them and for his help in the battle against the Sons of Darkness. Here we find a very weak anthological style. There

---

[210] Cf. J. Carmignac, "Les citations de l'Ancien Testament". *op. cit.*, 237ff.

[211] Yadin's translation.

[212] Incidentally this quotation of Isa. 31:8, which refers to Asshur and is applied to the Kittim, allows us to understand the phrase "the Kittim of Asshur" (1:5-6; 18:2-3, . . .) as an application of Isaiah's prophecies about the destruction of Sennacherib to the present enemies of the Sons of Light. Cf. Yadin, *op. cit.*, 312.

[213] For the texts used see J. Carmignac and Yadin, *ad loc*.

was no need for further proof of the revelation. The holy warriors expressed their identity as those with whom God was fulfilling the Covenant which he had made with the forefathers (13:7).

The last part of this ritual (14:2-17) is a thanksgiving hymn after the victory. Here we have a dense anthological style; the deliverances of the past are used as prophecies of that victory.[214]

C. DESCRIPTION OF A FINAL PHASE IN THE WAR (14:16-19:13)

Applying the preceding regulations for the war (i.e., its battle order and its ritual) this part presents as a whole an anthological style which is quite dense in certain parts (e.g., 15:7-12) and much weaker in others, depending upon the topics. The use of Scripture here presents, then, characteristics similar to those in the preceding part of the scroll, although new biblical phrases are added.

The brief examination of the Scroll of the War (1 QM) allows us to conclude that despite its more marked eschatological character the different uses of Scripture in it are similar to those we met either in the *Zadokite Documents*, or the *Hodayot* and the *Manual of Discipline*. Therefore the conclusions we drew about the use of Scripture in these different texts are valid for this scroll. Its use of Scripture cannot be looked on as mere speculation of an allegorical sort. We have here the prolongation of the lines of the sacred history even beyond the community into the future. In this way the revealed identity of the community, which is constantly assumed, appears as one stage of the sacred history. Like any other stage of this history, the community itself was looked on as a promise of God's future mighty deeds.

---

[214] For the list of biblical texts used therein and how they are tallied see Yadin, *ad loc.*, and mainly J. Carmignac, "Les citations de l'Ancien Testament", *op. cit.*, 376ff.

VII

THE USE OF SCRIPTURE IN THE "ANGELIC LITURGY" AND OTHER LITURGICAL TEXTS

The texts which can be properly described as liturgical show a use of Scripture similar to that of the *Hodayot*. We have reports that many fragments of such works have been discovered in Caves I and IV.[215] These fragments generally present an anthological use of Scripture.

Such is the case of one of the longer fragments: the liturgy of the "Sabbath burnt offering" or the "angelic liturgy", as it is aptly called (4 Q sl 39).[216] Ascribed to a specific Sabbath service, it is a kind of poem about the seven "chief Princes" (i.e., chief angels) and about the respective blessings which they give to the "perfect of way" (i.e., the Covenanters). We find here a relatively weak anthological style.

AN ALLEGORICAL INTERPRETATION: 4 Q SL 40

Another fragment (4 Q sl 40)[217] presents a quite different use of Scripture: it describes how the angels worship God, possibly in order to provide a model for the Covenanters. Yet no mention of the latter is made. Here the

---

[215] Cf. M. Baillet, "Psaumes, hymnes, cantiques et prieres dans les manuscrits de Qumran" in *Le Psautier. Ses origines. Ses problemes litteraires. Son influence*, Louvain, 1962, 394-99; Dupont-Sommer, *op. cit.*, 329ff.; Carmignac, *Les Textes de Qumran*, vol. II, 265ff. and 289ff.

[216] Cf. John Strugnell, "The Angelic Liturgy at Qumran. 4 Q *Serekh Sirot 'Olat Hassabbat*" in *Congress Volume. Oxford 1959*, Leiden, 1960, 318-45; Dupont-Sommer and Carmignac, *ad loc.*

[217] *Ibid.*

text is quite clearly structured on two biblical passages from Ezekiel ch. 1 and ch. 10: Ezekiel's visions. We get the feeling that there has been a mere transposition of biblical texts for the above mentioned purpose. We have here, actually, an early *Merkabah* allegorical interpretation. There is no mention of any historical element (either of salient history or of the history of cultural changes), nor do we find an allusion to the community. We have pure speculation about the angelic liturgy. This is no longer a typology but an allegorical interpretation. Although in many border cases it is difficult to make a clear-cut distinction between the two kinds of interpretation, the allegorical one appears scarce, as we emphasized when discussing the use of terms for "mystery". It is nevertheless clear from this passage, as well as from the fact that we have constant traces of speculations on the angels or other Apocalyptic themes,[218] that such speculation and allegorical interpretations had a place in the Covenanters' use of Scripture. We have noted already an embryo of allegorical interpretation in the *Zadokite Documents* 6:2ff. (in which the "well" was interpreted as Torah). A few other examples can be found in the *Zadokite Documents*, for instance in CD 7:14ff., which interprets Amos 5:26ff. Even 1 QS 8:14ff., which interprets Isa. 40:3, could be considered allegorical.[219] But it is clear that such interpretations are very rare. There is no attempt to develop fully the allegorical interpretation of biblical texts in the *Zadokite Documents* and in the *Manual of Discipline*. This is rather an expansion of the symbolism of the sect. The second fragment of the angelic liturgy (4 Q sl 40) is the only real exception.[220]

---

[218] Cf. for instance the fragments describing the New Jerusalem in *Discoveries*, Qumran Cave I 32, plate XXXI.

[219] Cf. on this Betz, *Offenbarung*, 176-81, who suggests few other instances.

[220] This does not mean that there were not several others in the lost documents.

4 Q DIBRE HAM-ME'OROT AND THE ORIGIN OF TYPOLOGY

Another liturgical text, entitled "The Words of the Heavenly Lights", (4 Q Dibre ham-Me'orot),[221] was made out of prayers and hymns, apparently for the different days of the week. Of these fragments the remains of seven columns are published.[222] This document presents two liturgical texts. In 7:4 begin the "Hymns for the Sabbath day", of which we have only a few lines. The preceding part of the document appears to be the end of a liturgical text, possibly intended for worship on Friday.

This first part (1:8-7:2) can be called a "long penitential prayer".[223] It is indeed similar to the biblical prayers of this type (for instance I Kings 8:15-61; Esdras 9:6-15; Neh. 9:5-37; Dan. 9:4-19). It is the re-telling of the sacred history which is understood here as the history of the sins of Israel, of the divine wrath, of Israel's repentance and of God's love for his people despite everything. By re-telling this sacred history the worshipping community identified itself with the Israel which lived this history. This was done in order to ask for divine help in present tribulations. God had manifested his love by forgiving the rebellious people in answer to Moses' prayer (2:7-12), by giving the Law to them (2:12-19?), by choosing the people of Israel as his "first-born son" rather than the Nations (3:2-4:4), by blessing David's and Solomon's reigns (4:4-14), by bringing Israel back from the Babylonian exile (5:2-6:4). On each occasion the worshipping community humbled

---

[221] This title remains mysterious: the fragment apparently read דברי המורות (words of instructions), then it was corrected by the scribe to דברי המארות, a reading which is still conjectural: cf. J. Carmignac, *Les Textes de Qumran*, vol. II, 299.

[222] Cf. M. Baillet, "Un recueil liturgique de Qumran, Grotte 4: 'les paroles des luminaires'", in *R.B.*, 1962, 195-250, and plates XXIX-XXVII.

[223] As G. Vermes remarks: cf. *The Dead Sea Scrolls in English*, Baltimore, 1962, 202.

itself before God and accepted the trials sent by God in order to expiate their sins and those of their forefathers. Now this community implored Him to deliver them (6:5-7:2). All is expressed in a dense anthological style.²²⁴ This re-telling of sacred history in an anthological style is quite similar to that which we found in the *Zadokite Documents* (2:14-3:20), yet now it is presented in what is clearly a liturgical context. Actually we have here the *origin* of the very use of Scripture which we pointed out in the *Zadokite Documents*. In such penitential prayers the community identified itself liturgically with the Israel of biblical sacred history. Up to this point, the Covenanters' use of Scripture was identical with that of any Jewish community. The worshipping community of classical Judaism discovered its identity as God's chosen people by identifying itself with the biblical Israel. Yet in classical Judaism this process was strictly limited to the specific context of the liturgical setting: the rest of life was the place to carry out the vocation which was implied in the liturgically discovered election.

By contrast the Covenanters did not limit the liturgical use of Scripture to a worship setting. This use of Scripture was rather applied to the community's entire life. Its whole history was interpreted in terms of liturgical prayers (as w e saw in studying the *Zadokite Documents*). The *Rule* (1 QS) which structured the community's life was expressed by making liturgical use of Scripture. This is confirmed by the Covenanters' use of the "Temple" symbolism which suggests that the whole of the community's life, as well as the whole of the community's history, was considered an all-inclusive liturgy. Just as in classical Judaism Torah "the way to carry out the vocation" was co-extensive with life, so the liturgy by means of which the community discovered its identity as a chosen community became co-extensive with life. The Covenanters' liturgy was no longer Synagogal; it was historical and even "cosmic", since it was also the angels' liturgy. No wonder

---

²²⁴For the specific biblical references see M. Baillet's footnotes. Cf. also J. Carmignac, *op. cit.*, 302-10.

therefore that the whole of history was reckoned according to a liturgical calendar.

Thus in liturgical texts like 4 Q *Dibre ham Me'orot* we have the origin of the Scriptural use which we found in the *Zadokite Documents*. We can even say that we have here the origin of any typological interpretation of Scripture. Such a typology was present in embryo in the context of the Synagogal use of Scripture: as we noted, it was practically limited to the framework of Scripture itself; it was applied to the worshipping community at the Synagogue. Otherwise it was only a "moral typology", not an actual one. Now for the Covenanters this typology could be applied to the whole of life, since the liturgy was now a historical and even cosmic liturgy. This allows us to understand the liturgical character of the use of Scripture in the different scrolls studied above.

VIII

THE USE OF SCRIPTURE
IN 4 Q TESTIMONIA

4 Q *Testimonia* presents a use of Scripture which is noteworthy. It is simply a collection of quotations. According to the editor[225] we have the whole document: a simple sheet of leather clearly divided into four sections.

The first section (1-8) is made out of quotations from Deut. 5:28-29 and 18:18-19. (The latter is the promise of a prophet like Moses). The second section (9-13) is made out of quotations from Num. 24:15-17, Balaam's oracle about the star from Jacob and the scepter from Israel. The third section (14-20) consists of quotations from Deut. 33:8-11, the blessing of Levi. The fourth section (21-30) is a quotation from an Apocryphal book attributed to Joshua, cited here in the same way as the biblical texts. Allegro has pointed out that fragments of this very passage have been found in Cave IV as part of what has been entitled 4 Q *Psalms of Joshua*. The latter quotation gives curses against a man and his two sons. The juxtaposition of this fourth section with the rest of the text should be a reminder that for the Covenanters Scripture was not necessarily limited to the canonical books.

Despite M. Treves,[226] who sees in 4 Q *Testimonia* a panegyric of John Hyrcanus, it is safer to see here a collection of messianic texts referring on the one hand, to the three messianic figures whose coming was expected (a prophet like Moses, a lay Messiah, and a priestly Messiah), and on the other hand, the Covenanters' enemies.[227]

---

[225] J. M. Allegro. "Messianic References in Qumran Literature", *J.B.L.* 75, 1956, 182-87 and plate.

[226] "The Meaning of the Qumran Testimonia", *R.Q.* II, 1960, 569-71.

[227] We follow here the interpretation given by, *inter alios*, Allegro, Dupont-Sommer, Betz and Carmignac.

Although this document does not allow us any specific conclusion about its use of Scripture, it is significant in another respect: it points out that certain texts were thought to contain prophecies which were particularly meaningful for the Covenanters. The fact that these prophecies were found in the Torah is also significant: despite the fact that we have *pesharim* only on the Books of the Prophets and on the Hagiographa, which were thought to contain prophecies concerning the end time, it appears that at least some parts of the Torah were considered in the same way. This is worth emphasizing, for in the Dead Sea Scrolls there is such stress on this use of the Prophets and Hagiographa that one could easily neglect this use of Torah. Yet it should be noted also that these quotations from the Pentateuch occur in a Prophetic style.

IX

THE USE OF SCRIPTURE
IN 4 Q FLORILEGIUM

4 Q *Florilegium* has been presented by J. M. Allegro[228] as belonging to the *testimonia* category, despite the fact that the biblical quotations are given together with their interpretations, not merely by themselves as in 4 Q *Testimonia*. Yet as William R. Lane has pointed out,[229] this text is actually closer in its use of Scripture to the *pesher* type than to the *testimonia* type. This is said despite the fact that it does not intend to interpret a whole biblical book. For indeed, if we consider the first column (which alone is well enough preserved to allow a study of the text's structure), and if we take into account the division of the text at the end of line 13, we have on the one hand an interpretation of II Sam. 7:10b-14a, and on the other hand of Ps. 1:1 and Ps. 2:2.

In lines 1-13, as Lane has shown, II Sam. 7:10b-11a is first quoted in lines 1-2, then it is interpreted with the help of Exod. 15:17-18 (line 3), which is used as a proof text, as the formula כאשר כתוב indicates. II Sam. 7:10b-11a is interpreted to express the promise that the community (the true "people of Israel" and "God's sanctuary") will be afflicted no longer by its enemies (lines 4-7a). Then II Sam. 7:11b is introduced and interpreted (lines 7b-9). It is followed by II Sam. 7:11c-14a. The latter with the help of the proof text Amos 9:11 (introduced in a similar way to Exod. 15:17-18), is interpreted as a prophecy about the coming of the Davidic Messiah, "who will arise with the Interpreter of the Law" (line 11). This use of Amos 9:11 comes about, it seems, mainly because the image צמח דויד (shoot of David) in

---

[228] J. M. Allegro, "Fragments of a Qumran Scroll of Eschatological Midrashim:, *J.B.L.* 77, 1958, 350-54.

[229] W. R. Lane, "A New Commentary Structure in 4 Q Florilegium", *J.B.L.* 78, 1959, 343ff.

II Sam. 7:12 is associated with סוֹכָה (branch) instead of סֻכָּה (M.T.: סֻכָּה) (tabernacle). Thus as L. H. Silberman notes[230] "he understands the verse from Amos to mean: 'And I will raise up the fallen branch (or shoot) of David'". As we said earlier, this a method of interpretation used in classical Judaism.

Similarly in lines 14-19 (introduced by מ- מדרש), a quotation of Ps. 1:1 is followed by the expression פשר הדבר (pesher hadabar). This interpretation is made with the help of two proof texts: Isa. 8:11 and Ezek. 44:10. The latter texts are applied to the community, which is presented as composed of those who do not walk "in the counsel of the wicked". Line 18 quotes Ps. 2:1 and is likewise followed by the phrase פשר הדבר (pesher hadabar). Unhappily the rest of the text has been lost. It is quite clear therefore that 4 Q *Florilegium* presents a use of Scripture similar to the one we found in some parts of the *Zadokite Documents*, i.e., a *pesher*-like style. Here the starting point is clearly Scripture. The Scriptural vectors are prolonged with the help of other biblical texts up to the community and its eschatological beliefs. This implies the unity of Scripture.

---

[230] L. H. Silberman, "A Note on 4 Q Florilegium", *J.B.L.* 78, 1959, 158ff.

X

THE USE OF SCRIPTURE
IN THE PESHARIM

The doctrine of Scripture of the Dead Sea Covenanters emphasized Scripture as locus of the new revelation: it was in an inspired search of Scripture that they expected to uncover the mysteries. Accordingly the mysteries of the contemporary history were not expressed in visionary texts as in the Apocalyptic literature, but in inspired biblical commentaries: the so-called pesharim.

The pesharim present the most characteristic use of Scripture by the Covenanters. First, quantitatively speaking, they are quite well-represented among the manuscripts. We have fragments of pesher on the Prophetic books of Isaiah, Hosea,[231] Micah,[232] Nahum,[231] Habakkuk,[233] Zephaniah,[232] as well as on a number of Psalms (namely on Pss. 37,[231] 68,[232] and possibly 57[232]). Furthermore, as we have pointed out, from time to time, the pesher interpretation is presupposed by several other uses of Scripture which we have found in the Dead Sea Scrolls.

Many scholars have emphasized the importance of the pesharim. Witness the great number of works devoted to their study.[234] It must be noted that most of these are focused on the historical information one can find in these texts. The pesharim are indeed useful in this respect, although they are often very frustrating. Their highly symbolic character puts difficulties in the way of any specific identification of

---

[231] Cf. J. M. Allegro, *Discoveries in the Judaean Desert of Jordan V, Qumran cave 4*, Oxford, 1968.

[232] Cf. D. Barthelemy, J. T. Milik, *Discoveries in the Judaean Desert. I. Qumran cave one*, Oxford, 1955, 77ff.

[233] Cf. M. Burrows, J. C. Trever, W. H. Brownlee, *The Dead Sea Scrolls of St. Mark's Monastery*, vol. I, plates LV-LXI, New Haven, 1950.

[234] Cf. for instance the partial bibliography (up to 1963) in J. Carmignac, *Les Textes de Qumran*, vol. II, 60-64.

either events or historical personages. These studies are not directly relevant for our purpose, yet they should be kept in mind. The pesharim interpret the prophetic texts (certain Psalms being considered as such) as referring to the salient history of their time. This is indeed a first striking characteristic of the pesharim.

Other studies have been devoted to the hermeneutic principles of the pesharim: among them those of W. H. Brownlee,[235] K. Elliger,[236] O. Betz,[237] L. H. Silberman,[238] and A. Finkel.[239] Following these scholars we shall attempt to expose the axioms which govern the use of Scripture in the pesharim.

Another striking characteristic of the pesharim is that they are running commentaries on complete biblical texts, as is clear in the well-preserved scroll of the pesher on Habakkuk. The pesharim are therefore systematic interpretations of prophetic texts. This is significant in itself, as it shows the particular "stance" or "attitude" which is taken toward these Scriptural texts.

"PESHER" AS THE INTERPRETATION OF SCRIPTURE AS DREAM

Before we investigate in detail how this interpretation was done and how it stands related to Midrashic interpretation, let us emphasize the meaning of the term

---

[235] W. H. Brownlee, "Biblical Interpretation Among the Sectaries of the Dead Sea Scrolls" in *Biblical Archaeologist*, 1951, 54-76.

[236] K. Elliger, *Studien zum Habakuk-Kommentar vom Toten Meer*, Tubingen, 1953.

[237] O. Betz, *Offenbarung*, *op. cit.*, 75ff. and *passim*.

[238] L. H. Silberman, "Unriddling the Riddle. A Study in the Structure and Language of the Habakkuk Pesher", *R.Q.* III, 1961, 323-64.

[239] A. Finkel, "The Pesher of Dreams and Scripture", *R.Q.* IV, 357-70.

"pesher"; it is constantly used in these "commentaries" to introduce the interpretation of a passage which has just been quoted.

Although the term "pesher" (פשר) is found once in the biblical Hebrew (Eccl. 8:1, where we read that the wise man has the capacity for interpretation), it is an Aramaic term used thirty times in the Book of Daniel[240] to designate exclusively the interpretation of dreams or visions. Its Hebrew equivalent פתר is likewise used in Gen. ch. 40 and 41. In the Old Testament the interpretation of dreams implies that the dream as a whole related to a given situation. Yet the interpretation is not limited to this general outline of the dream. Each detail of the dream is interpreted as related to a specific situation or event (e.g., the seven healthy cows are seven years of prosperity) or to a specific personage (e.g., the head of the god is the King in Dan. 2:37). This is to say that each element of the dream is interpreted in turn.

K. Elliger notes that "pesher" is a technical term in Daniel.[241] It is used to introduce the "unriddling of the riddle",[242] the riddle of the dream. It refers to a revealed interpretation. As Elliger points out, the use of the term "pesher" was transposed by the Qumran community from the revealed interpretation of a dream to the revealed interpretation of an earlier revelation, namely the prophetic texts. Yet Elliger fails to show why this transposition was possible, that is, why the prophetic text could be submitted to a treatment similar to that used for visions and dreams. Silberman shows the missing link.[243] He finds it in the *Sifre* on Num. 12:6, which reads: "God spoke to all the prophets except Moses בחלום וחזיון, in dreams and visions". In early

---

[240] Cf. Dan. ch. 2, 5 and 7.

[241] *Op. cit.*, 154-57.

[242] To use Silberman's excellent title.

[243] Silberman, *op. cit.*, 327-31.

Palestinian Judaism the prophetic books were thought to be the dreams and visions of the Prophets. This conclusion is easily understandable when we consider the amount of visionary material contained therein.

Such an understanding of the term pesher is confirmed by the interpretation of Habakkuk 2:1-2. This biblical passage ends, "Write down the vision and make it plain upon the tablets so that he may read it easily that reads it". 1 Qp Hab. 7:1-5 interprets as follows:

> "And God told Habakkuk to write down the things which will come to pass in the last generation, but the consummation of time He made not known to him. And as for that which He said, *That he may read it easily that reads it*, the explanation of this (פשרו) concerns the Teacher of Righteousness to whom God made known all the Mysteries (רזי) of the words of His servants the Prophets".(244)

Just as in Daniel the interpretation, or better unriddling (פשר) of the dream or vision is the uncovering of the vision's mystery (רז) (cf. Dan. 2:18f., 27, 29f., 47; 4:6) so the unriddling of the prophetic texts (their visions) was possible for the author because of the revelation of "all the Mysteries (רזי) of the words" of the Prophets.[245]

This understanding of the prophetic texts as visions did indeed govern the Covenanters' interpretation. It was based on the conviction that the prophetic "visions" concerned the Covenanters' situation. This was a consequence of their eschatological consciousness; they were "the last generation". This is explicitly stated in the passage quoted above. The dreams and visions used to be interpreted as referring to the immediate situation of both the dreamer and of the interpreter. Now, by contrast, the prophetic texts are interpreted as referring to the immediate situation (i.e., the contemporary salient history) of the interpreters of the last generation, and no longer as referring to the situation of the Prophet (dreamer) himself.

---

[244] A. Dupont-Sommer, G. Vermes' translation.

[245] We need not come back to the meaning of the term רז. We discussed it in our general remarks on "the eschatological community and Scripture".

The Hermeneutical Methods of the Pesher

This understanding of the prophetic texts as visions may explain also why the pesharim offer a systematic interpretation of these texts. Each element of the vision is *a priori* meaningful. Nothing must be left aside if one is to uncover the full meaning.[246] As visions the prophetic texts were furthermore considered riddles; each was a cryptogram which must be broken.[247] We ought not to be surprised therefore to find an interpretation akin to "allegorical" interpretation. We shall refrain nevertheless from using this term[248] and keep it for a Scriptural interpretation which, although similar in its methods, refers to spiritual realities rather than to concrete historical situations (present or future).

At first one wonders what is the actual relationship between the biblical text quoted and its interpretation. The author is giving us the results of his use of Scripture without emphasizing the process itself. Yet scholars from W. H. Brownlee to L. H. Silberman have combined their efforts to show this connection. For this a wide knowledge of the early Jewish interpretations of Scripture was essential. Silberman's work on the pesher Habakkuk is remarkable in this respect. For our purpose we need only summarize the conclusions of these scholars, which we shall illustrate by examples from the pesher on Habakkuk (1 Qp Hab.).

---

[246] This may also explain why in the *Zadokite Documents* a proof text is further interpreted in a pesher-like manner: the rest of it cannot be left veiled. Cf. above our remarks on the *Zadokite Documents*.

[247] As L. H. Silberman and A. Finkel have shown quite adequately.

[248] It is used for instance by W. H. Brownlee, O. Betz, and A. Finkel. Yet these scholars do not adopt Dupont-Sommer's extreme position. The latter states: "son exegese est purement et entierement allegorique", *Les Manuscrits de la Mer Morte*, 36.

As noted above the author's purpose in the pesher is to interpret the prophetic text as referring to the community and its history. As in most of the uses of Scripture which we have discussed, we find a twofold movement. The text is interpreted in terms of the historical situation and the historical situation in terms of the text.[249] Our earlier metaphor of two poles in tension applies here also. This is to say that the revelation cannot properly be said to be contained *in* the visions of the Prophets: revelation appears in the tension *between* the two poles.

By understanding the key words and phrases as metaphors, ciphers, the pesher made an atomistic interpretation. In textual or orthographic peculiarities of the prophetic text the interpreter saw a clue which allowed him to grasp its mysterious meaning. Such is the case in 1 Qp Hab. 3:12-14 on Hab. 1:9a. It has been rendered by Silberman as follows:

> "And in rage they gather together and in anger.
> and fury they speak with . . . for this is
> the meaning of the phrase 'In their presence
> a scorching wing'".

Such an interpretation is based on a peculiar reading of the prophetic text; קדים (East wind, the devastating sirocco) is read instead of קדימה of the M.T. (east-ward, forward). The Massoretic Text of Hab. 1:9a can be rendered literally: "For the sake of violence he comes, turning (מגנת,[250] a singular!) their face forward". The interpreter understands this text as follows:[251] "For the sake of violence he comes. In their presence a scorching (מגמה) (East) wind". This reading, which is also that of the Targum, is the basis of the interpretation. Although most of the details in the descriptions of the invaders are interpreted literally (e.g., the "horses" of the Chaldeans are interpreted simply as referring to the "horses" of the Kittim), קדים is taken to be a riddle, open therefore to further investigation. As the violent and hot east wind, the קדים allows associations with

---

[249] As L. H. Silberman emphasizes, *op. cit.*, 334.

[250] This word is of uncertain derivation and meaning.

[251] Silberman's translation, parentheses mine.

חרן אף (a burning anger) and זעף אפים (fury, with the
connotation of a storm).[252] Therefore this mention of the
"rage" of the Kittim is indeed, despite the reader's first
impression, drawn from the prophetic text. The interpreter
saw in the word קדים, a reading different from that of the
M.T., a riddle which he deciphered by means of the
associations just mentioned.

We find in the pesharim many other examples in which a
peculiar reading of the prophetic text serves as the
cornerstone of an interpretation.[253] This raises the
question: was the interpreter aware of the readings found in
the M.T.? Although we cannot give a positive answer with
certainty in each case, it is often quite clear that he was.
Indeed he assumed both readings in his interpretation, i.e.,
the one which he proposed in his quotation of the prophetic
text and also that of the M.T. Thus for instance the text of
Hab. 1:11, as the interpreter quotes it (1 Qp Hab. 4:9ff.), no
longer contains the mention of guilt. The verb expressing it
(אשם) in the M.T. has been replaced by ישם (to be desolate, to
be laid waste). Strikingly enough the interpretation refers
not only to devastation but also to the "guilt-ridden
Council". It also interprets, therefore, the reading of the
M.T. Gaster translates: "This refers to the rulers of the
Kittaeans. In their guilt-ridden Council House they keep
replacing those rulers one after another and each comes in
turn to destroy the earth" (1 Qp Hab. 4:10-13).[254] Other
examples of this may be found in 1 Qp Hab. 8:3ff. and 9:8ff.

From this two conclusions may be drawn. Either the
interpreter used a number of biblical texts containing variant
readings, or he transformed the prophetic text to fit his
interpretations. These alternatives do not necessarily
exclude each other. There are indeed variants in the Scroll

---

[252] On this see Silberman, *op. cit.*, 339.

[253] See the examples pointed out by Brownlee (*op. cit.*),
in the pesher Habakkuk, and by J. Carmignac, *op. cit.*, 65-128,
who points them out carefully in each of the pesharim.

[254] Gaster, *op. cit.*, 246.

of Isaiah.[255] Yet it is also clear that the interpreter did not hesitate to change the spelling of a word in order that it might fit his interpretation. For him this practice accorded with the view of the prophetic text as a riddle. It was as if the text's meaning were veiled sometimes by a change in the order of the letters of a word. Thus for instance היכל, Temple, of Hab. 2:20 was interpreted as יכלה: "he (God) will destroy". More often the interpreter proceeded simply to the substitution of letters (generally of similar shapes): thus for instance in 1 Qp Hab. 5:1ff., the word וצור (O Rock) of Hab. 1:12, was read יצור (will be distressed).[256] These methods of interpretation were not new. They had already been used in the Hebrew Bible itself, namely in the "etymological" interpretations of names (cf. for instance I Chr. 4:9). They were used also by the Rabbis, although for other purposes.

Another means of interpretation is that of breaking a word into parts. This was generally a prelude to other kinds of interpretation, especially considering the letters of a word as abbreviations (each letter representing a word). This practice is also found in classical Judaism. Thus, to continue with the same passage (1 Qp Hab. 5:1ff.), in the quotation of Hab. 1:12, we find למוכיחו "chastizer of him" (instead of להוכיח in the M.T.). This was interpreted as meaning למו כיא הוא "to them, for that". The interpretation reads as follows: ". . . because they have kept His commandments in the time of the distress *of them. For that* is what He said. . ."[257]

We find another good example of this in the much discussed text of 1 Qp Hab. 9:2ff. on Hab. 2:15. Gaster translates:

> *"Woe unto him that plies his neighbor with drink,*
> *that pours over his flask (hematho), yea, makes*
> *him drunk in order to gaze on their festivals.*
> This refers to the wicked priest, who chosed

---

[255] Cf. W. H. Brownlee, *The Meaning of the Qumran Scrolls for the Bible*, New York, 1964, 155-296.

[256] This reading is assisted by other variants: cf. Brownlee, "Biblical Interpretation", 65ff.

[257] Cf. Brownlee, *ibid.* Cf. also 69: likewise in the text of the interpreter himself we find that ערלת (uncircumcision) is written in 9:13 עור לח: which was understood according to the context as meaning עור לבו תועבה, i.e., "the skin of his heart is an abomination".

> after the true exponent of the Law, right to the
> house where he was dwelling in exile, in order
> to confuse him by a display of violent temper
> (*hamatho*), and who then, on the occasion of the
> rest-day of Atonement, appeared to them in full
> splendor in order to confuse them and trip them
> up on the day of the fast, the day of their
> sabbatical rest".

Without going into all the problems involved in the translation of this text, let us note how the word "their festivals" מועדיהם was interpreted as giving the actual date of the persecution. Apparently the word was first broken into two parts מועד יהם. The first part entered the interpretation as "festival", with the added connotation of "resting". Then יהם was interpreted as an abbreviation for יום הכפורים the Day of Atonement. Thus the interpreter believed that the prophetic text successfully predicted the very day on which the Teacher of Righteousness was persecuted by the wicked Priest.

The interpreter used other methods of interpretation as well. He made inferences from the analogies between the circumstances described by the prophetic text and those of the sect's historical situation. He discovered more than one meaning in the words of the Prophets. He unveiled the meaning of a word by means of a series of synonyms. And, of course, he used other Scriptural passages to illuminate the meaning of a phrase in the prophetic text. We are familiar now with all these methods of interpretation; we have pointed them out elsewhere in the Dead Sea Scrolls and in the literature of classical Judaism. Therefore, we need not give examples of this. Let us note simply that the preceeding example contains an illustration of the interpretation by means of a series of synonyms. The verb "to drink" (שקה) is equated with the verb "to swallow" (בלע), understood in its secondary meaning "to destroy" (cf. Isa. 25:7ff.; Ps. 21:10, etc.). The use of other Scriptural passages is difficult to show. Besides the references to the prophetic text itself, we have at best a very weak anthological style which reduces us to conjectures.[258] Yet it cannot be doubted that such use was

---

[258] Yet see on this J. Carmignac (*op. cit.*) who points to the few uses of biblical phrases and Silberman (*op. cit.*) who suggests many possible uses of other biblical passages.

made, at least occasionally, if for no other reason than that many of the symbols are interpreted according to a biblical way of thinking.

It is clear that many of the methods which were used for pesher-interpretation are similar to those we found in classical Judaism. This led several scholars to call the pesher a midrash, a peculiar kind of midrash certainly, but a midrash anyway. K. Stendhal designates it, "a special type of *Midrash*, *midrash pesher* parallel to the *midrash halakah* and *midrash haggadah*".[259] Yet although the hermeneutic rules may be similar to those found in classical Judaism, and although the external structure of the pesher is very close to the midrashic structure of the "*Petirah*"[260] one must recognize that the pesher interpretation of Scripture is structured very differently. As Silberman and Finkel have pointed out, the only exact parallel in Rabbinic literature is to be found in the interpretations of *dreams* and not of Scripture.[261] For the Covenanters the hermeneutical structure was not therefore that of a tension between Scripture and the history of cultural changes, but that of a tension between Scripture and the salient history. This hermeneutical structure is found in other Dead Sea Scrolls and Apocalyptic books. In addition to it the pesher involves a specific understanding of the Scriptural text (namely the prophetic text) as a dream or vision. As suggested above this understanding determines its genre. We have now to crystallize the results of this last part of our research by comparing the Covenanters' hermeneutic with that of classical Judaism.

---

[259] *The School of St. Matthew*, Uppsala, 1954, 183; cf. also V. H. Brownlee, "Biblical Interpretations", 60 *passim*.

[260] Cf. Silberman, *op. cit.*, 327-30.

[261] Cf. Silberman, *op. cit.* 362ff. and A. Finkel, *op. cit.*, 358ff. We could add that there are also similarities with the interpretation of a *bat qol*.

XI

CONCLUSIONS: CLASSICAL JUDAISM, DEAD SEA COVENANTERS AND SCRIPTURE

The use of Scripture in the Dead Sea Scrolls is quite similar to that in the Apocalyptic texts, as we might well have expected from the fact that several of the latter were found among the Scrolls. The conclusions which we reached concerning the uses of Scripture in the Apocalyptic literature are valid for the Dead Sea Scrolls. We do not need to repeat them. Yet our study of the writings of the Covenanters allows us to be more specific: it allows us to point out different levels in the uses of Scripture. A comparison with our conclusions about the hermeneutic practiced in classical Judaism will allow us to see more clearly the specific nature of the Covenanters' hermeneutic. In classical Judaism we found two levels in the uses of Scripture: 1) the haggadic or synagogal uses of Scripture, and 2) the halakic uses of Scripture. In the writings of the Covenanters this distinction does not apply, or rather their whole use of Scripture appears to have been integrated at the first level, which therefore received new dimensions. This integration was the result of a radically different hermeneutical structure.

CLASSICAL JUDAISM AND SCRIPTURE

A brief reminder of our conclusions about classical Judaism will be useful here: [262] we shall emphasize the elements necessary for a comparison with the Covenanters' hermeneutic. A. At a primary level (the haggadic level) Scripture gave the Jewish community its identity as the Chosen

---

[262] Cf. above, chapter VI.

People. Scripture was interpreted by Scripture, since the complete and final revelation of the election and of the vocation was contained in it. Scripture was used to *uncover* the community's revealed identity. Concurrently the worshipping community itself was a locus of revelation, for it *embodied* this revelation, which is to say, it embodied Scripture. Since the *Sitz im Leben* of such a use of Scripture was the Synagogue, we called it "*liturgical*". We use this term in a broad sense;[263] we call "liturgical" the use of Scripture found in the reading of Scripture, in the homily, in the Targum, as well as in the liturgical texts themselves.

For the comparison with the Covenanters' use of Scripture we need to emphasize the two functions of the "liturgy". First, the "liturgy" was the never ending process of *uncovering* the community's revealed identity. This was expressed in the reading of Scripture, the homily and the Targum. Here the emphasis was placed on Scripture in itself as the locus of revelation. Second, the "liturgy" was *embodying* of this revealed identity. We find such an embodiment in the liturgical prayers themselves. Here the emphasis was placed on the worshipping community as the locus of revelation. Yet since the revealed identity embodied in this way had been and was still uncovered by an interpretation of Scripture by Scripture, the Jewish community remained inside the boundaries of Scripture as a closed system of signs. B. At a secondary level (the halakic level)--which was present also in the Synagogue but had its primary *Sitz im Leben* in the School-- Scripture was used in tension with cultural changes in order to discover how *to carry out the vocation* in the concreteness of life. This is the halakic hermeneutic. In it the community assumed its own identity, which had resulted from the primary use of Scripture (the haggadic hermeneutic). In this secondary use, Scripture was open; the Oral Torah appeared in the tension between Scripture and cultural changes.

---

[263] When we use the terms liturgy and liturgical with such a broad sense, we shall write them between quotation marks: "liturgy", "liturgical".

Although at the liturgical-haggadic level revelation was understood as static (the complete and final revelation was contained in Scripture), at the halakic level revelation was understood as dynamic. How to carry out the community's revealed identity (i.e., how to be God's Chosen People) was to be discovered in each new cultural situation. The Scriptural commandments were therefore to be interpreted in terms of the cultural changes and vice-versa. As we saw, this halakic hermeneutical structure was demanded by one of the basic convictions of early Rabbinic Judaism: Torah was to be co-extensive with life. The Jewish community was to assume its revealed identity (and therefore also to carry out its vocation) in the whole of its life and not merely in certain parts of it. It was this conviction that their religious life should be all-encompassing which led the early Rabbinic Jews to affirm implicitly that there was a locus of revelation besides Scripture and the Scripturally-structured community.

THE DEAD SEA COVENANTERS AND SCRIPTURE

We note then two levels in classical Judaism's uses of Scripture. By contrast the Covenanters' hermeneutic was integrated at one level. Although the setting was no longer the Synagogue, nor even necessarily a worship service, these uses of Scripture can still be said to be "liturgical". It was by these uses of Scripture that the revealed identity of the community was *uncovered*, and *embodied*; such uncovering and embodiment belonged essentially to the role of "liturgy" in classical Judaism.

Let us deal first with the *uncovering* of the revealed identity. The "liturgy", i.e., that which allowed the *uncovering*, was not limited to the Covenanters' community worship. The "liturgical" setting in which the Covenanters apprehended their election and vocation was the whole of salient history, and no longer the Scripturally-structured Synagogal service. This conviction was combined with, and strengthened by, the Covenanters' eschatological consciousness. As a result, new acts of God and new signs of the community's election were to be discovered in the salient history, present and future. The biblical sacred history was seen as the *type* of contemporary and future sacred history. By this primary use of Scripture the community could discover its identity as the eschatological community of the "new Covenant".

We need here to come back to our definition of hermeneutic as the prolongation of the vectors of the text up to the reader. What are the vectors of Scripture? These are apprehended in the (implicit or explicit) exegesis, which is influenced by the reader's culture, that is, by the reader's self-understanding. In the case of the Covenanters this self-understanding was characterized by their eschatological consciousness, which led them to look at history as a whole, as part of a cosmic liturgy. From this perspective they apprehended the Scriptural vectors, i.e., the nature of Scripture. The events and personages of the biblical sacred history were therefore understood as types of the events and personages of their salient history. Biblical events were promises that God acted in their contemporary history. Likewise the prophetic texts (whereever they may be in Scripture) were taken as dreams and visions concerning their time. The Covenanters' hermeneutic was therefore a reading of Scripture in terms of the contemporary salient history: a *typology* and an interpretation of Scripture as dream, a *pesher*. In both cases, although the methods of interpretation differed, the hermeneutic structure was the same: revelation occurred in the tension between two loci, Scripture and contemporary salient history. Typology and pesher interpretation were complementary. Nevertheless the pesher style seems to have influenced the Covenanters more than typology.[264] Thus, Scripture was used in tension with contemporary salient history as a means of uncovering the revealed identity of the community. Although much widened, this may still be characterized as a "liturgical" use of Scripture. The salient history as a whole became the setting

---

[264] Yet this degree of influence varied from one group of the sect to another, as our study of the *Zadokite Documents* suggests.

of the first liturgical function: *the uncovering of the revealed identity*. Thus from the outset Scripture was open: it was interpreted in tension with the salient history. By contrast, in classical Judaism, a very different understanding of Scripture informs this first "liturgical" function, for there Scripture is "closed".

Now let us deal with the second function of the "liturgy", the *embodying* of the revealed identity. The liturgical prayers of classical Judaism were characterized by the anthological use of Scripture. In the same way we found that many passages of the Scrolls are characterized by the anthological style. The latter allowed the Covenanters to elaborate on the identity of the community (as in the *Manual of Discipline*), to express this identity further (as in the *Hodayot*), and to project into the end time their consciousness of themselves as the chosen community of the last generation (as in the *War Scroll*). In other words it allowed the community to embody its revealed identity, which was expressed, significantly enough, by a Temple symbolism.

Yet the two functions of the "liturgy" and the corresponding uses of Scripture cannot be completely separated. Both uses of Scripture are "liturgical". An excellent reminder of this is the structural use of Scripture: we find in the latter a border-line situation in which the two "liturgical" uses of Scripture are mingled together.

As will be apparent from the preceding remarks, we find that most of the Covenanters' texts function at the primary level in their uses of Scripture (the "liturgical" uncovering and embodying of the community's identity). This is noteworthy. Yet was there not a secondary level for them as well? Once the community embodied the revealed identity, a further use of Scripture was needed in order that it might discover how to carry out its vocation. Therefore the Covenanters made a halakic use of Scripture. Indeed their halakah was outwardly similar to that of classical Judaism. Yet it was different (above all, much stricter) because of the specific self-understanding of the community. For such an eschatological community the cultural changes were thought to have no meaning, or else indeed a negative connotation. And so *this "halakic" interpretation of Scripture was done exclusively in terms of the community's revealed identity*. It was therefore fundamentally different from that of classical Judaism. We even wonder if we can indeed speak of a second level in the Covenanters' uses of Scripture. Their halakah itself appears "liturgical": it is to be compared with the ritual parts in classical Judaism's halakah. This was to be expected: the Covenanters considered their community the substitute for the defiled Temple of Jerusalem.

POSTSCRIPT[*]

A PROPOSAL FOR THE NORMALIZATION OF TERMINOLOGY

Anyone who is familiar with the secondary literature on the early Jewish uses of Scripture would agree: there is an urgent need of a normalization of the terminology about this topic.[1] This is even more manifest in the works which attempt to qualify the New Testament uses of Scripture by means of such a vocabulary. Although it was not the primary goal of this study, we believe that we have set the ground on which such normalization can be made. The following proposal would like to sketch a number of categories which, we hope, will be helpful for this purpose.[2] In doing so we will attempt to remain as close as possible to the traditional uses of the terms in order to avoid a greater confusion.

The main difficulty comes from the fact that this vocabulary is used at three different levels to designate a) different hermeneutical methods, b) different literary genres,

---

[1] See for instance Addison G. Wright, *The Literary Genre Midrash*, Staten Island, 1967, and Roger Le Déaut's response in "A propos d'une définition du midrash", *Biblica* 50 (1969), 395-413 (reprinted in *Interpretation* 25, 1971, 259-82).

[2] Cf. G. Vermès, "Bible and Midrash: Early Old Testament Exegesis", in *The Cambridge History of the Bible*, ed. by P. R. Ackroyd and C. F. Evans, Cambridge, 1970, I, 199-231. Our proposal is akin to G. Vermès' very suggestive synthesis. Nevertheless our research allow us to propose additional distinctions.

[*] Written in May 1975.

and c) different hermeneutical axioms (or convictions) which govern the uses of Scripture. As the above research showed we cannot expect to distinguish between the early Rabbinic and Apocalyptic uses on the ground of the hermeneutical methods (middoth); basically the same are used in both literatures. The literary genres provide a sounder basis for such distinctions, yet even here we find quite a few overlaps. For instance what we called the anthological and structural styles are found in both classical Judaism and Apocalyptic Judaism. As one may expect as a result of our study, we believe that the ground on which the primary terminological distinctions should be made for such a topic is to be found at the level of the hermeneutical axioms.

We will therefore have to take into account that this terminology is to be used at two levels: a) at the *convictional level* where it will refer to the attitudes toward Scripture, i.e., the hermeneutical axioms; b) at the *"symbolic" level* where it will refer to literary genres. Together they will form the horizontal lines of the diagram which will allow us to define this vocabulary. To continue this metaphor: since the early Rabbinic and Apocalyptic hermeneutical axioms have radically different orientations they cannot belong to the same diagram: we have to envision two clearly separated terminologies. They are nevertheless related to each other by the very fact that they express different uses of the same Scripture.

The vertical lines of these diagrams are determined by the object of these terminologies: the hermeneutic of Scripture. As we stressed in our introduction, the hermeneutic of a text is based on its exegesis which points out a specific understanding of the nature of the text. In both forms of Judaism an explicit exegesis of Scripture points out a twofold nature of the text; Scripture is apprehended as being composed of "stories" and "laws". Furthermore the "stories" are apprehended as providing the setting which gives meaning to the "laws"; the terminology which we shall use will have to show this relationship.

Still at the exegetical level, although both forms of Judaism acknowledge that Scripture is twofold, each of them apprehends in its own way the specific natures of the Biblical texts. For classical Judaism the "stories" express the complete and final revelations of the election and vocation of Israel (haggadah). The "laws" express how to carry out this vocation (halakah). For classical Judaism we have therefore the following diagram in which the proper terminology will have to be set:

Scripture	as stories	as laws
convictional level: hermeneutical axioms	I	Ia
symbolic level: literary genres	I'	Ia'

For Apocalyptic Judaism the "stories" are "promises"[3] (either "types" or "dreams"); they point to new revelations of a new election and a new vocation for the faithful Israel. The "laws" express how to carry out this vocation. For Apocalyptic Judaism we have therefore the following diagram:

Scripture	as promises	as laws
convictional level: hermeneutical axioms	II	IIa
symbolic level: literary genres	II'	IIa'

---

[3] We opted for the term "promises" rather than "prophecies" because the latter in its specificity may lead one to overlook the typological understanding of sacred history.

We have therefore two sets of categories. It should be stressed here that they are not artificial constructions; each set of categories is, rather, an attempt to express the close inter-relationship of different elements of the same phenomenon.

a) The convictional level (attitudes toward Scripture) and the symbolic level (literary genres) are related to each other as conviction and symbols are. Without the symbols (literary genres) the convictional attitudes toward Scripture do not even exist; they need specific literary genres[4] in order to take life and emerge although these convictions are more than these literary genres can express. Conversely these literary genres are somehow molded by and consequently reflect the convictional attitudes toward Scripture; furthermore such convictions ascribe to these literary genres a specific function in the total hermeneutic process. This is why we have to consider the convictional level (attitudes toward Scripture) as primary.

b) The interpretations of Scripture as "stories" and those of Scripture as "laws" are related in the sense that the hermeneutical process is complete only when both are taken into consideration. And yet the interpretation of Scripture as "stories" (in the haggadah or in the typology) has to be considered as primary because it provides the setting for the interpretation of Scripture as "laws" (in the halakah).

Consequently the cornerstone of each terminology should be the term which designates the interpretation of the Scriptural "stories" at the convictional level. Each of the other levels of interpretation is related in its own way to this cornerstone: the terminology should express this relationship. We indicated this by the symbols I, I', Ia' Ia'; and II, II', IIa, IIa'.

One other concern governed our classification of the terminology. As already mentioned, in order to avoid additional confusion we shall attempt to stay as close as possible to the traditional use of this vocabulary. This led

---

[4] Or "oral expressions"; for instance the homily or the Targum were first of all orally expressed. Yet, of course, they reached us in literary forms.

us to a choice of vocabulary which sometimes appears to be in
conflict with the terminological hierarchy that we set above.
It is a fact that the traditional vocabulary designates
primarily the literary genres. In order to satisfy this last
criterion we shall have sometimes to use traditional terms to
designate the literary genres and their derivatives to
designate the convictional attitudes, and this despite the
fact that the fundamental characterizations are to be found in
the convictional attitudes.

A. THE BASIC TERMINOLOGY
FOR THE USES OF SCRIPTURE
IN CLASSICAL JUDAISM

I. In Classical Judaism the primary term to designate
the interpretation of the stories of Scripture should be, of
course, *"midrash"*. For the reasons listed above, we propose
to keep the term "midrash" to designate a literary genre. At
the convictional level we propose to use phrases like
midrashic attitude toward Scripture or better, *midrashic
hermeneutic*. The adjective *midrashic* without further
qualification will designate this convictional attitude. Let
us stress that, following the traditional usage, the phrase
midrashic hermeneutic will have to be understood as referring
to the interpretation of the stories of Scripture. A
midrashic hermeneutic can be characterized as an
interpretation which assumes that Scripture is the final and
complete revelation of the election and vocation of the
community; it allows the identification of the community with
the biblical Chosen People; it is furthermore characterized by
an interpretation of Scripture by Scripture and what we called
a "moral typology". For a fuller description of these
hermeneutical axioms see again Chapter V ; we can summarize it
by saying that such midrashic interpretation takes place in
between the two poles "Scripture" and the "worshipping
community".

I'.   Such *midrashic hermeneutic* is expressed in various literary genres. Thus we have several *midrashic* literary genres: first of all the Midrash itself, but also the Targum, the Homilies and various types of liturgical texts.[5] All of these are *midrashic* because as far as their use of Scripture is concerned, they are governed by *midrashic* hermeneutical axioms. Several of these literary genres are used with other hermeneutical axioms.

Of course one may want to speak of these literary genres as such, that is without reference to the hermeneutical axioms which govern these uses of Scripture. In such case no qualification is necessary. But then it is not possible to make any fundamental distinctions between a given literary genre in classical Judaism and in Apocalyptic Judaism or in the New Testament for instance. Yet if one wants to point out such distinctions one will have to take into account the hermeneutical axioms which somehow molded these literary genres and which ascribed to them specific functions. In such case one will have to speak for instance of a *midrashic* homily, or of a *midrashic* liturgical text; we saw that the liturgical texts do not have the same function in classical Judaism and in Apocalyptic Judaism.

Ia. Still in classical Judaism, turning now toward the interpretation of the Scripture as "laws" at the convictional level we have to express the relationship of this attitude toward Scripture to what we called the *midrashic hermeneutic*. A phrase is readily available: *midrashic halakah*. The *midrashic halakah* is the hermeneutic of the "laws" by means of which one determined how to carry out the vocation pointed out by the *midrashic hermeneutic*. The *midrashic halakah* is characterized by the conviction that the vocation has to be carried out in each and every concrete situation of life. It demands therefore unfolding Torah into an evergrowing Oral Torah by interpreting the "laws" in tension with cultural changes. All this has been developed above in Chapter IV ("Scripture at the School: Written and Oral Toroth"). We can

---

[5] This list does not pretend to be exhaustive.

summarize this hermeneutical process by saying that it takes place in between the two poles "Scripture" and the "history of cultural changes".

Ia'. Such *midrashic halakah* is expressed in two main literary genres: a) in the literary genre *midrash* or better, *halakic midrash* as for instance in the Sifre and Sifra, in such case the "pole" Scripture is manifest; b) in the literary genre *Mishnah*, in such case the "pole" Scripture is generally implicit. For the period under consideration, besides the Mishnah itself, such literary genre is found in the Tosephta. Later on it is found in the Talmud.

We can recapitulate our suggestions for the terminology about classical Judaism's hermeneutic in the following diagram which shows the inter-relationship of the different terms.

Scripture	as stories	as laws
Convictional level: hermeneutical axioms	Midrashic hermeneutic or Midrashic attitude toward Scripture	Midrashic halakah
Symbolic level: literary genres	Midrashic literary genres: they include Midrash, Targum, Homilies, and liturcal texts	a) halakic Midrash b) Mishnaic literary genres: Mishnah, Tosephta, later on Talmud

B. THE BASIC TERMINOLOGY FOR THE APOCALYPTIC USES OF SCRIPTURE

II. As cornerstone of the terminology for the Apocalyptic hermeneutic we propose to use the term "*typology*"; in such a hermeneutical process the Scriptural "promises" are brought in tension with the events of the salient history.

Through this process the truly Chosen People was pointed out and the specific and new vocation of the eschatological community was determined. These hermeneutical axioms were common to the Apocalyptists and the Covenanters. Yet these two Apocalyptic groups had slightly diverging exegeses. Although both of them considered the Scriptural stories as promises, the former saw in them primarily "types" and the latter "types" *and* "dreams". This gave rise to two closely related forms of typology that we can term *typological hermeneutic* (which was practiced by both the Apocalyptists and the Covenanters) and *pesher hermeneutic* (which was practiced only by the Covenanters).

In order to avoid an undue reductionism we shall keep the twofold designation *typological hermeneutic* and *pesher hermeneutic*. Yet we propose to use *typology* as the cornerstone of our terminology; because typology is a term which is used traditionally to refer to a hermeneutical attitude. By contrast pesher is generally used to refer to a literary genre. Thus typology will refer to the set of hermeneutical axioms which set in tension the two poles "Scripture" and the "salient history". *Typological hermeneutic* and *pesher hermeneutic* will refer to two specific forms of the typology.

II'. Such *typology* is expressed in various literary genres: in historical texts (for instance in parts of the Manual of Discipline and of the Zadokite Documents), in re-writings of Scripture (for instance the Book of Jubilees), in Pseudepigrapha (for instance the Testaments of the Twelve Patriarchs), in visionary texts, in liturgical texts, in hymns, etc. All these can be qualified as *typological literary genres* when one wants to point out the hermeneutical structure which they represent. The literary genre pesher (which has many similarities with the literary genre Midrash of classical Judaism) is also a typological genre albeit of a specific kind.[6]

---

[6] In order to avoid any confusion when using the adjective *pesher* one will have to specify if he is doing so at the convictional level (to refer to the *pesher hermeneutic*) or at the literary level (to refer to the literary genre *pesher*).

IIa. At the convictional level, in order to designate the hermeneutic of Scripture as halakah, we propose to use the phrase "*typological halakah*". It is an interpretation of the "laws" in the light of the new election and vocation discovered by means of the typological hermeneutic and the pesher hermeneutic. *Typological halakah* will refer therefore to the set of hermeneutical axioms which set in tension the two poles "Scripture" and "the results of typological hermeneutic".

IIa'. Since the *typological halakah* depends so much on the results of the *typological hermeneutic*, the *typological halakah* is generally integrated in the various *typological literary genres*. One may want to consider the Manual of Discipline as a literary genre expressing primarily *typological halakah*. The other few instances are quite similar either to the *mishnaic* literary genre or to the *halakic midrash* of classical Judaism.

We can recapitulate our suggestions for the terminology about Apocalyptic hermeneutic in the following scheme:

Scripture	as Promises	as laws
Convictional level: hermeneutical axioms	Typology: --typological hermeneutic --pesharic hermeneutic	Typological halakah
Symbolic level: literary genres	Typological literary genres: historical texts, re-writings of Scripture, Pseudepigrapha, visionary texts, liturgical texts, hymns ... and Pesher	--Manual of Discipline --Mishnaic literary genre --Literary genre halakic midrash

The specific terminology that we suffested is intended to be more illustrative than normative; it is clear that it does not pretend to be exhaustive. For indeed the weight of this proposal for a normalization of the terminology about the

early Jewish uses of Scripture lies in its distinction between
the convictional and symbolic levels. For instance when
comparing the use of Scripture in a given text of the New
Testament with early Jewish uses of Scripture one should be
aware of the level at which the comparison is made. Is it,
for instance, a comparison with the midrashic hermeneutic or
with a specific midrashic literary genre? Raising such
questions would clarify many issues which, at the present
time, are far from being clear. What is essential in this
proposal is the formulation of the two sets of categories;
this is the ground for the normalization of the terminology.
We hope to have demonstrated the validity and the usefulness
of such an approach in the main body of this work in which we
compared the distinct hermeneutics practiced in early
Palestinian Judaism.

BIBLIOGRAPHY

BOOKS

Abel, F. M. *Les livres des Maccabées*. Paris, 1963.

Abrahams, I. *Studies in Pharisaism and the Gospels*. 2 vols. Cambridge (Engl.): University Press, 1917-24.

Aicher, G. *Das Alte Testament in der Mischna*. Freiburg, 1906.

Allegro, J. M. *Qumrân cave 4*. Vol. V of *Discoveries in the Judaean Desert of Jordan*. Oxford: Clarendon Press, 1968.

Amusin, J. *The Qumran Commentaries and their Significance for the History of the Qumran Community*. Moscow, 1967.

Avigad, N. and Yadin, Y. *A Genesis Apocryphon. A Scroll from the Wilderness of Judaea*. Jerusalem: Magnes Press of the Hebrew University, 1956.

Bacher, Wilhelm. *Die älteste Terminologie der jüdischen Schriftauslegung: ein Wörterbuch der bibelexegetischen Kunstsprache der Tannaiten*. Leipzig: J. C. Hinrichs, 1899.

_____. *Die Proömien in der alten jüdischen Homilie*. Leipzig: J. C. Hinrichs, 1913.

Baron, S. W. *A Social and Religious History of the Jews*. New York: Columbia University Press and Philadelphia: Jewish Publication Society of America. Second edition, revised and enlarged, 1952-1958. Vol. I-VIII.

Barr, James. *The Semantics of Biblical Language*. London: Oxford University Press, 1961.

_____. *Biblical Words for Time*. Naperville, Ill.: A. R. Allenson, 1962.

Barthélemy, D., Milik, J. T., and Allegro, J. M. *Discoveries in the Judaean Desert*. Oxford: Clarendon Press, 1955-1968.

Barthes, Roland. *Le degré zéro de l'écriture*. Paris: Editions Gonthier, 1968.

Betz, Otto. *Offenbarung und Schriftforschung in der Qumransekte*. Tübingen: J. C. B. Mohr, 1960.

──────. *Der Paraklet: Fürsprecher im häretischen Spätjudentum, im Johannes--Evangelium und in den neugefundenen gnostichen Schriften*. Leiden: E. J. Brill, 1963.

──────. *What do we Know about Jesus?* Philadelphia: The Westminster Press, 1968.

Bible und Qumran. Beiträge zur Erforshung der Beziehungen zwischen Bibel und Qumranwissenschaft. Berlin: Evangelische Haupt- Bibel-Gesellschaft zu Berlin, 1968.

Black, M. *An Aramaic Approach to the Gospels and Acts*. Oxford: Clarendon Press, 1946.

Blackman, E. C. *Biblical Interpretation. The Old Difficulties and the New Opportunity*. London: Independent Press Ltd., 1957.

Blackman, Philip, F. C. S. *Mishnayoth*. Vol. 1-7. New York: The Judaica Press, Inc., 1964.

Boman, Thorleif. *Das hebräische Denken im Vergleich mit dem Griechischen*. Göttingen: Vanderhoeck und Ruprecht, 1952.

Bonsirven, Joseph. *Le Judaïsm Palestinien*. Paris: Beauchesne et ses fils, 1934-35. 2 vols.

──────. *Exégèse Rabbinique et Exégèse Paulinienne*. Paris: Beauchesne et ses fils, 1939.

──────. *Textes Rabbiniques des deux premiers Siècles Chrétiens*. Roma: Pontificio Istituto Biblico, 1955.

Bowker, John. *The Targums and Rabbinic Literature. An Introduction to Jewish Interpretations of Scripture*. New York: Cambridge University Press, 1969.

Brierre-Narbonne, J. J. *Exégèse Targumique des Prophéties Messianiques*. Paris: P. Geuthner, 1936.

Brownlee, William, Hugh. *The Text of Habakkuk in the Ancient Commentary from Qumran*. Vol. XI. Philadelphia: J. B. L. Monograph Series, 1959.

──────. *The Meaning of the Qumran Scrolls for the Bible*. New York: Oxford University Press, 1964.

Bruce, F. F. *Second Thoughts on the Dead Sea Scrolls*. Grand Rapids, Mich.: William B. Eerdmans Publishing Company, 1st ed., 1956. London: Patenoster Press, 2nd ed., 1961.

_____. *Biblical Exegesis in the Qumran Texts*. London: The Tyndale Press, 1959.

Bultmann, R. *Jesus and the Word*. New York: Charles Scribner's Sons, 1934.

Burrows, Millar. *The Dead Sea Scrolls*. New York: Viking Press, 1956.

Burrows, Millar; Trever, J. C.; Brownlee, W. H. *The Dead Sea Scrolls of St. Mark's Monastery*. Vol. I and II. New Haven: American Schools of Oriental Research, 1950-1951.

Carmignac, J. *La Règle de la Guerre*. Paris: Letouzey et Ané, 1958.

Carmignac, J., Cothenet, E., et Lignée, H. *Les Textes de Qumran, traduits et annotés*. Vol. II. Paris: Letouzey et Ané, 1963.

Carmignac, J., et Guilbert, P. *Les Textes de Qumran, traduits et annotés*. Vol. I. Paris: Letouzey et Ané, 1961.

Charles, R. H. *The Greek Versions of the Twelve Patriarchs*. Oxford: Clarendon Press, 1908.

_____. *The Apocrypha and Pseudepigrapha of the Old Testament*. Oxford: Clarendon Press, 1913.

_____. *Eschatology. The Doctrine of a Future Life in Israel, Judaism and Christianity*. Sec. ed., 1913. New York: Schocken, 1963.

Churgin, P. *Targum Jonathan to the Prophets*. New Haven: Yale University Press, 1927.

Colson, Francis Henry. *Philo Judaeus*. 10 volumes. London: Heinemann; New York: Putnam, 1929-62.

Coppens, J. *Les Harmonies des deux Testaments*. Tournai, Paris: Desclée, 1949.

Cross, Moore Frank. *The Ancient Library of Qumran and Modern Biblical Studies*. London, 1958. New York: revised edition, Doubleday & Company, 1961.

Cullmann, O. *Christ and Time*. English translation, London: SCM Press, 1951, and Philadelphia: The Westminster Press.

Danby, Herbert, D. D. *The Mishnah*. London: Oxford University Press, 1933.

Daniélou, J. *Sacramentum futuri. Etudes sur les origines de la typologie biblique*. Paris: Beauchesne, 1950.

Daube, David. *The New Testament and Rabbinic Judaism*. London: The Athlone Press, 1956.

_____. *The Exodus Pattern in the Bible.* London: Faber & Faber, 1963.

Delcor, M. *Essai sur le Midrash d'Habacuc.* Paris: Editions du Cerf, 1951.

_____. *Les Hymnes de Qumran.* Paris: Letouzey et Ané, 1962

Denis, A. M. *Les Thèmes de connaissance dans le Document de Damas.* Louvain: Publications Universitaires de Louvain, 1967.

Dhorme, Ed. *La Bible. L'Ancien Testament.* Vol. I and II. Paris: Gallimard. Vol. I, 1956. Vol. II, 1959.

Driver, G. R. *The Judaean Scrolls. The Problem and a Solution.* New York: Schocken, 1965.

Dupont-Sommer, A. *Le livre des Hymnes découvert près de la Mer Morte.* Paris: Semitica VII, 1957.

_____. *Les écrits esséniens découverts près de la Mer Morte.* Paris: Payot, 1959.

_____. *The Essene Writings from Qumran.* Trans. G. Vermès. Cleveland-New York: World Publishing Company, 1962.

Elbogen, Ismar. *Der jüdische-gottesdienst in seiner geschichtlichen entwicklung.* Leipzig: G. Fock, 1913.

Elliger, Karl. *Studien zum Habakuk-Kommentar vom Toten Meer.* Tübingen: J. C. B. Mohr, 1953.

Finkel, Asher. *The Pharisees and the Teacher of Nazareth.* Leiden: E. J. Brill, 1964.

Finkelstein, L. *The Pharisees: The Sociological Background of their Faith.* 2 vols. Philadelphia: The Jewish Publication Society of America.

Fitzmeyer, J. A. *The Genesis Apocryphon of Qumran. Cave I. A Commentary.* Rome: Pontificio Istituto Biblico, 1966.

Friedländer, Michael. *Synagoge und Kirche in ihren Anfängen.* Berlin, 1908.

Funk, Robert. *Language, Hermeneutic, and Word of God.* New York: Harper & Row, 1966.

Gärtner, B. *The Temple and the Community in Qumran and the New Testament.* New York: Cambridge University Press, 1965.

Gaster, Moses. *Studies and Texts in Folklore, Magic, Medieval Romance, Hebrew Apocrypha and Samaritan Archaeology.* London: Maggs Bros., 1925-28.

_____. *The Samaritans, Their History, Doctrines and Literature*. London: Oxford University Press, 1925.

_____. *Samaritan Oral Law and Ancient Tradition*. London: The Search Publishing Co., 1932.

Gaster, Theodor H. *The Dead Sea Scriptures*. Garden City, N.Y.: Doubleday & Company, 1964.

Gerhardsson, Birger. *Memory and Manuscript*. Lund: C. W. K. Gleerup, and Copenhagen, Ejnar Munksgaard, 1961.

Glatzer, Nahum N. *Hillel the Elder*. New York: Schocken, 1966.

Goppelt, L. *Typos. Die typologische Deutung des Alten Testaments im Neuen*. Gütersloh, 1939.

Goudoever, J. van. *Biblical Calendars*. Leiden: E. J. Brill, 1959.

Grätz. *Kohelet*. Leipzig, 1871.

Guilding, Aileen. *The Fourth Gospel and Jewish Worship; a study of the Relation of St. John's Gospel to the Ancient Jewish Lectionary System*. Oxford: Clarendon Press, 1960.

Gunkel, H., and Begrich, J. *Einleitung in die Psalmen*. Göttingen, 1933.

Habermann, A. M. *Megilloth Midbar Yehuda. The Scrolls from the Judaean Desert*. Jerusalem: Magnes Press of the Hebrew University, 1959.

Hartmann. *Prophecy Interpreted. The Formation of some Jewish Apocalyptic Texts and of the Eschatological Discourse of Mark*. Lund: C. W. K. Gleerup, 1966.

Harvey, Van A. *The Historian and the Believer*. New York: Macmillan, 1965.

Hoenig, Sidney, Benjamin. *The Great Sanhedrin. A Study of the Origin, Development, Composition, Functions of the Bet Din Ha-gadol during the second Jewish Commonwealth*. New York: Bloch Publishing Co., 1953.

Holm-Nielsen, S. *Hodayot Psalms from Qumran*. Aarhus, 1960.

Idelsohn, Abraham Z. *Jewish Liturgy and its Development*. New York: Schocken, 1st ed. 1932, 2nd ed. 1967.

The Interpreter's Dictionary of the Bible. ed. by George A. Buttrick. 4 vols. Nashville, Tenn.: Abingdon Press, 1962.

Jaubert, Annie. *La date de la Cène: calendrier biblique et liturgie chrétienne*. Paris: Gabalda, 1957.

_____. *La Notion d'Alliance dans le Judaïsme aux abords de l'ère chrétienne.* Paris: Le Seuil, 1963.

Jonge, M. de. *The Testaments of the Twelve Patriarchs.* Assen, Netherlands, 1953.

Kahle, Paul Ernst. *The Cairo Geniza.* Oxford (Engl.): Blackwell, 1959.

Koestler, Arthur. *The Act of Creation.* New York: Macmillan, 1964.

Kuhn, H. W. *Enderwartung und gegenwärtiges Heil. Untersuchungen zu den Gemeindeliedern von Qumran.* Göttingen: Vandenhoeck & Ruprecht, 1966.

Kuhn, Karl, Georg. *Konkordanz zu den Qumrantexten.* Göttingen: Vandenhoeck & Ruprecht, 1960.

Krauss, Samuel. *Synagogale Altertümer.* Berlin, 1922.

Lauterbach, J. Z. *Mekilta de Rabbi Ishmael.* 3 vols. Philadelphia: The Jewish Publication Society of America, 1933-35.

_____. *Rabbinic Essays.* Cincinnati: Hebrew Union College Press, 1951.

Leaney, A. R. C. *The Rule of Qumran and its Meaning.* Philadelphia: The Westminster Press, 1966.

Le Déaut, R. *La Nuit Pascale.* Rome: Pontificio Istituto Biblico, 1963.

_____. *Liturgie juive et Nouveau Testament.* Rome: Pontificio Istituto Biblico, 1965.

_____. *Introduction à la littérature targumique.* Rome: Pontificio Istituto Biblico, 1966.

Levi, Israel. *The Hebrew Text of the Book of Ecclesiasticus.* Leiden: E. J. Brill, 1904.

Lewis, J. P. *A Study of the Interpretation of Noah and the Flood in Jewish and Christian Literature.* Leiden: E. J. Brill, 1968.

Lieberman, Saul. *Hellenism in Jewish Palestine.* New York: The Jewish Theological Seminary of America, 1950.

Lohse, E. *Die Texte aus Qumran. Hebraïsch und deutsch.* München: Kösel-Verlag, 1964.

MacDonald, John. *The Theology of the Samaritans.* Philadelphia: The Westminster Press, 1964.

Macho, Diez. *Ms. Neophyti I.* Vol. I, *Genesis.* Barcelone, 1968.

McNamara, Martin. *The New Testament and the Palestinian Targum to the Pentateuch*. Rome: Pontificio Istituto Biblico, 1966.

Macquarrie, John. *The Scope of Demythologizing: Bultmann and his Critics*. New York: Harper & Row, 1960.

Mann, J. *The Bible as Read and Preached in the Old Synagogue*. Vol. I, 1940. Vol. II, ed. by I. Sonne. Cincinnati: Hebrew Union College, 1966.

Mansoor, M. *The Thanksgiving Hymns*. Grand Rapids, Mich.: Eerdmans, 1961.

Marcus, Ralph, ed. and tr. *Josephus*. London: Heinemann; New York: Putnam, 1926-65.

Merleau-Ponty, Maurice. *Signs*. Evanston: Northwestern University Press, 1964.

Mielziner, M. *Introduction to the Talmud*. Cincinnati and Chicago: American Hebrew Publishing House, 1894.

Milik, J. T. *Dix ans de découverte dans le Désert de Juda*. Paris, 1957. Engl. transl. *Ten Years of Discovering in the Wilderness of Judaea*. Translated by J. Strugnell. Naperville, Ill.: A. R. Allenson, 1959.

Montefiore, C. G., and Loewe, H. *Rabbinic Anthology*. London: Macmillan and Co., 1938.

Moore, George, Foot. *Judaism*. Cambridge, Mass.: Harvard University Press, vol. I and II, 1927, vol. III, 1930.

Morawe, G. *Aufbau und Abgrenzung der Loblieder von Qumran*. Berlin, 1961.

Neusner, Jacob. *The Way of Torah*. Belmont, Cal.: Dickenson, 1970.

_____. *A Life of Yohanan Ben Zakkai, ca. 1-80 C.E.* Leiden: E. J. Brill, 1970.

Nickels, P. *Targum and New Testament*. Rome: Pontificio Istituto Biblico, 1967.

Oesterley, W. O. F. *The Jewish Background of the Christian Liturgy*. Oxford: Clarendon Press, 1925.

Patte, Daniel. *L'athéisme d'un chrétien ou un chrétien à l'écoute de Sartre*. Paris: Nouvelles Editions Latines, 1965.

Pedersen, Johannes. *Israel: Its Life and Culture*. 2 vols. London: Oxford University Press, 1926.

Perrin, N. *Rediscovering the Teaching of Jesus*. New York: Harper & Row, 1967.

Philonento, M. *Les interpolations chrétiennes des Testaments des Douze Patriarches et les Manuscrits de Qoumrân.* Paris: Cah. Rev. Hist. Phil. Rel. 35, 1960.

Ploeg, J. van der. *Le rouleau de la Guerre.* Leiden: E. J. Brill, 1959.

Pritchard, James B. *Ancient Near Eastern Texts Relating to the Old Testament.* 3rd ed. Princeton, N.J.: Princeton University Press, 1969.

Rabin, C. *The Zadokite Documents.* 2nd ed. Oxford: Clarendon Press, 1958.

Ricoeur, Paul. *De l'interprétation. Essai sur Freud.* Paris: Editions du Seuil, 1965.

Ringgren, Helmer. *The Faith of Qumran, Theology of the Dead Sea Scrolls.* Philadelphia: Fortress Press, 1963.

Robinson, H. Wheeler. *Inspiration and Revelation in the Old Testament.* Oxford: Clarendon Press, 1946.

Robinson, James M. *New Frontiers in Theology.* Vol. II, *The New Hermeneutic.* J. M. Robinson and J. B. Cobb, Jr., eds. New York: Harper & Row, 1964.

Rowley, Harold, Henry. *The Relevance of Apocalyptic* London: J. Clarke & Co., 1947.

Russell, D. S. *The Method and Message of Jewish Apocalyptic.* Philadelphia: The Westminster Press, 1964.

Schechter, Solomon. *Aspects of Rabbinic Theology.* 1st ed., London: Macmillan Co., 1909. Paperback ed. New York: Schochen, 1961.

Schürer, E. *Geschichte des jüdischen Volkes im zeitalter Jesu Christi.* Vol. III. Leipzig, 1898.

Seeligmann, J. L. *The Septuagint Version of Isaiah.* Leiden: E. J. Brill, 1948.

Smith, Page. *The Historian and History.* New York: Knopt, 1964; 3rd ed., 1966.

Sperber, A. *The Bible in Aramaic.* Vol. I, *Pentateuch according to Onqelos.* Vol. II, III, *The Prophets according to Targum Jonathan.* Vol. IV, *The Hagiographa.* Leiden: E. J. Brill, 1959-68.

Stendhal, Krister. *The School of St. Matthew and its Use of the Old Testament.* 1st ed. Uppsala, 1954. 1st American ed. Philadelphia: Fortress Press, 1968.

Stenning, John, Frederick. *The Targum of Isaiah.* Oxford: Clarendon Press, 1949.

Strack, Hermann. L. *Introduction to the Talmud and Midrash*. 1st Engl. ed. Philadelphia: Jewish Publication Society of America, 1931. Paperback ed. New York: Harper & Row, 1965.

Sukenik, E. L. *The Ancient Synagogue of el-Hammed. An account of the Excavations Conducted on behalf of the Hebrew University*. Jerusalem: University Press, 1933.

———. *Ancient Synagogues in Palestine and Greece*. Schweich Lectures, 1930. London: published for the British Academy by H. Milford, 1934.

———. *The Dead Sea Scrolls of the Hebrew University*. Jerusalem: Magnes Press of the Hebrew University, 1954.

Testuz, Michel. *Les idées religieuses du livre des Jubilés*. Genève, Paris: Drouaz, 1960.

Thackeray, Henry St. John. *The Septuagint and Jewish Worship, a Study in Origins*. London: published for the British Academy by H. Milford, 1921.

Travers Herford, R. *The Pharisees*. New York: Macmillan Company, 1924.

Theological Dictionary of the New Testament. Engl. transl. of the *T.W.N.T.* eds. Kittel, Gerhard *et al*. Grand Rapids, Mich.: Eerdmans, vol. I to VI, 1964-68.

Vaux, R. de. *La Genèse*. Paris, 1962.

Vermès, Géza. *Les Manuscrits du Désert de Juda*. Tournai, Paris: Desclée, 1953.

———. *Discovery in the Judean Desert*. New York: Desclée Co., 1956.

———. *Scripture and Tradition in Judaism*. Leiden: E. J. Brill, 1961.

———. *The Dead Sea Scrolls in English*. Baltimore: Penguin Books, Inc., 1962.

Viteau, Joseph. *Les Psaumes de Salomon. Introduction, texte grec et traduction*. Paris, 1911.

Wernberg-Møller, P. *The Manual of Discipline*. Leiden: E. J. Brill, 1957.

Wieder, N. *The Judean Scroll and Karaism*. London: East and West Library, 1962.

Wright, Addison G. *The Literary Genre Midrash* . Staten Island, N.Y.: Alba House, 1967.

Yadin, Yigael. *The Scroll of the War of the Sons of Light against the Sons of Darkness*. Oxford: Clarendon Press, 1962.

Zucrow, Solomon. *Adjustment of Law to Life in Rabbinic Literature*. Boston: The Stratford Company, 1928.

ARTICLES

Allegro, J. M. "Messianic References in Qumran Literature". *J.B.L.* 75 (1956), 182-87.

———. "Further Messianic References in Qumran Literature". *J.B.L.* 75 (1956), 174-76.

———. "Fragments of a Qumran Scroll of Eschatological Midrashim". *J.B.L.* 77 (1958), 350-54.

———. "An Unpublished Fragment of Essene Halakkah (4 Q Ordinances)". *Journal of Semitic Studies* (1961), 71-73.

Bacher, W. "The Origin of the Word Haggada". *Jewish Quarterly Review*, IV (1892), 406-29.

Baillet, M. "Psaumes, hymnes, cantiques et prières dans les Manuscrits de Qumran". *Le Psautier. Ses Origines. Ses problèmes littéraires. Son influence.* (Louvain, 1962), 394-99.

———. "Un recueil liturgique de Qumrân, Grotte 4: 'les paroles des luminaires'". *R.B.* (1962), 195-250.

Bamberger, B. J. "Books of Adam". *I.D.B.*, vol. I, 44ff.

Bardtke, H. "Considérations sur les Cantiques de Qumran". *R.B.* (1956), 220-33.

Barzun, Jacques. "Cultural History as a Synthesis". *The Varieties of History*, ed. by Fritz Stern (Cleveland, Ohio, and New York: World Publishing Company (1956), 387ff.

Betz, Otto. "Die Geburt der Gemeinde durch den Lehrer". *N.T.S.* (1957), 314-26.

———. "Das Volk seiner Kraft: zur Auslegung der Qumran-hodajah III, 1-18". *N.T.S.* (1958), 67-75.

———. "Le ministère cultuel dans la secte de Qumran et dans le christianisme primitif". *La Secte de Qumran et les Origines du Christianisme* (Louvain, 1959), 163-202.

———. "The Eschatological Interpretation of the Sinai Tradition in Qumran and in the New Testament". *R.Q.* 6 (1963), 89-108.

Beyer. "Κανών". *T.W.N.T.*, vol. 3, Engl. tr. 596ff.

Blank, S. H. "The Dissident Laity in Early Judaism". *H.U.C.A.* XIX (1945-46), 1-42.

Blau, L. "Bath Qol". *J.E.*, 1st ed., vol. II, 588-92.

———. "Holy Spirit". *J.E.*, 1st ed., vol. VI, 447-50.

———. "Bible Canon". *J.E.*, 1st ed., vol. III, 140.

Block, Renée. "Ecriture et tradition dans le Judaïsme: aperçus sur l'origine du Midrash". *Cahiers Sioniens* (1954), 11.

———. "Moïse dans la Tradition rabbinique". *Cahiers Sioniens* VIII (1954), 214ff.

———. "Note méthodologique pour l'étude de la littérature rabbinique". *Recherches de Science Religieuse* (1955). 194-227.

———. "Midrash". *D.B.S.*, vol. V, 1253ff.

Bowker, J. W. "Speeches in Acts: A Study in Proem and Yalammedenu Form". *N.T.S.* XIV (1967), 96-111.

Bowman, John. "The Exegesis of the Pentateuch among the Samaritans and the Rabbis". *Oud testamentische Studien* (Leiden, 1950). 226ff.

Brownlee, W. H. "Biblical Interpretation among the Sectaries of the Dead Sea Scrolls". *Biblical Archaeologist* (1951), 54-76.

Bruce, F. F. "Holy Spirit in the Qumran Text". *Annual of Leeds University Oriental Society* (Leiden, 1969), 49-55.

Buchanan, G. W. "The Priestly Teacher of Righteousness". *R.Q.* 6, (1969), 553-58.

Büchler, A. "The Reading of the Law in a Triennial Cycle". *J.Q.R.* 5, (1893), 420-68, and 6 (1894), 1-73.

Carmignac, J. "Les citations de l'Ancien Testament et spécialement des Poèmes du Serviteur dans les Hymnes de Qumran". *R.Q.* 2, (1959-60), 357-94.

———. "Les citations de l'Ancien Testament dans 'La guerre des Fils de Lumière contre les Fils de Ténèbres'". *R.B.* 63, (1956), 234-60, and 375-90.

Chamberlain, J. V. "Another Qumran Thanksgiving Psalm". *Journal of Near Eastern Studies* (1955), 32-41.

———. "Further Elucidation of a Messianic Thanksgiving Psalm from Qumran". *Journal of Near Eastern Studies* (1955), 181-82.

Cornill, K. N. "Book of Ezechiel". *J.E.*, 1st ed., vol. V, 318ff.

Daube, David. "Rabbinic Methods of Interpretation and Hellenistic Rhetoric". *H.U.C.A.* 22 (1949), 239-64.

Dembitz, Lewis N. "Geullah". *J.E.*, 1st ed., vol. V, 648.

———. "Synagogue". *J.E.*, 1st ed., vol. XI, 619ff.

Delcor, M. "Un psaume messianique de Qumrân". *Mélanges Bibliques rédigés en l'honneur de André Robert* (Paris, 1957), 334-40.

Denis, A. M. "Evolution des structures dans la secte de Qumran". *Aux origines de l'Eglise.* Recherches Bibliques VII (Louvain, 1965).

Dobsevage, I. G. "Sidra". *J.E.*, 1st ed., vol. XI, 328ff.

Downing, C. "Typology and the literary Christ Figure". *J.A.A.R.* (1968), 13-20.

Dresde, M. J. "Mythology of Ancient Iran". *Mythologies of the Ancient World* (New York, 1961), 331ff.

Dupont-Sommer, A. "La mère du Messie et la mère de l'Aspic dans un hymne de Qoumrân". *Revue de l'Histoire des Religions* (1955), 174-88.

Eichrodt, W. "Heilserfahrung und Zeitverständnis im Alten Testament". *T.Z.* XII (1956), 103-25.

———. "Is Typological Exegesis an Appropriate Method?" *Essays on Old Testament Hermeneutics*, ed. by Claus Westermann (Richmond, Virginia, John Knox Press, 1963), 224-45.

Elbogen, I. "Review of J. Mann's the Bible as Read . . ." *J.Q.R.*, N.S. XXXI (1940-41).

———. "Bemer Kungen zur alten jüdischen liturgie". *Studies in Jewish Literature in honor of K. Kohler.* **159.**

Finkel, A. "The Pesher of Dreams and Scripture." *R.Q.* IV, 357-70.

Finkelstein, L. "The Book of Jubilees and the Rabbinic Halakah". *Harvard Theological Review* XVI (1922), 39-61.

———. "The Oldest Midrash". *Harvard Theological Review* XXXI (1938), 291-317.

———. "The Transmission of the Early Rabbinic Traditions". *H.U.C.A.* 16 (1941), 115-35.

Fitzmyer, J. A. "The Use of Explicit Old Testament Quotations in Qumran Literature and in the New Testament". *N.T.S.* 7 (1960-61), 296-333.

Frey, J. B. "Apocalyptique". *D.B.S.*, vol. I (1928), col. 350f.

Gärtner, B. "The Habakkuk Commentary and the Gospel of Matthew". *Stud. Theol.* 8 (1954), 1-24.

Ginsberg, Louis. "Cabala". *J.E.*, 1st ed., vol. III, 456-79.

Gray, G. B. "The Psalms of Solomon". *Apocrypha and Pseudepigrapha*, Charles, R. H., ed., vol. II, 625-52.

Greenstone, J. H. "Custom". *J.E.*, 1st ed., vol. IV, 395-98.

───── . "Gezerah". *J.E.*, 1st ed., vol. V, 648ff.

───── . "Prosbul". *J.E.*, 1st ed., vol. X, 219ff.

Grelot, P. "Remarques sur le second Targum du livre d'Esther". *R.B.* (1970), 230-39.

Haacker, K. "Assumptio Mosis - eine samaritanische Schrift?" *T.Z.* 25 (1969), 385-405.

Hinson, G. "Hodayot III, 6-18: In What Sense Messianic?" *R.Q.*, t. II, 183-204.

Hirsch, Emil G. "Shemoneh Esreh". *J.E.*, 1st ed., vol. XI, 270ff

Hoenig, S. B. "The Suppositions Temple-Synagogue". *J.Q.R.* 54 (1963).

───── . "Dorshe Halakot in the Pesher Nahum Scrolls". *J.B.L.* 83 (1964), 119-38.

Hruby, K. "La survivance de la langue hebraïque pendant la période post-exilienne". *Mémorial du Cinquantenaire de l'Ecole des Langues Orientales anciennes de l'Institut Catholique de Paris 1916-1964*. (Paris, 1964), 120.

───── . "La Synagogue dans la littérature rabbinique". *L'orient syrien* (1964), 474ff.

Humbert, P. "Le Messie dans le Targum des Prophètes".*Revue de Theologie et de Philosophie* 44 (1911), 5-46.

Jacobs, Joseph. "Halakah". *J.E.*, 1st ed., vol. VI, 163.

───── . "Trennial Cycle". *J.E.*, 1st ed., vol. XII.

Jaubert, Annie. "Le calendrier des Jubilés et de la secte de Qumran; ses origines bibliques". *V.T.* III (1953), 250-64.

_____. "Le calendrier des Jubilés et les jours liturgiques de la semaine". *V.T.* VII (1957), 35-61.

Jonge, M. de. "Christian Influence in the Testaments of the Twelve Patriarchs". *Nov. Test.* 4 (1960), 222ff.

Kinkel, A. "The Pesher of Dreams and Scripture". *R.Q.* 4 (1963) 357-70.

Kohler, Kaufman. "Ahabah Rabbah". *J.E.*, 1st ed., vol. I, 281.

_____. "Habdalah". *J.E.*, 1st ed., vol. VI, 119.

_____. "Pharisees". *J.E.*, 1st ed., vol. IX, 661-66.

_____. "Sadducees". *J.E.*, 1st ed. vol. X, 630-33.

Lacocque, A. "Tradition dans le Bas Judaisme". *R.H.Ph.R.* (1960), 3-16.

_____. Article in C.T.S. *Register*, 1968.

Lanchester. "The Sibylline Oracles". *Apocrypha and Pseudepigrapha*, Charles, R. H., ed., vol. II, 368-406.

Lane, William R. "A New Commentary Structure in 4 Q Florilegium". *J.B.L.* 78 (1959), 343ff.

Laperrousaz, E. M. "Le Testament de Moïse (généralement appelé 'Assomption de Moise')". *Semitica* 19 (1970), 1-134.

Lauterbach, J. Z. "The Ancient Jewish Allegorists in Talmud and Midrash". *J.Q.R.*, N.S. I (1910-11), 291ff. and 503ff.

_____. "Oral Law". *J.E.*, 1st ed., vol. IX, 423ff.

_____. "Sinaitic Commandments". *J.E.*, 1st ed., vol. XI, 383.

_____. "Talmud Hermeneutic". *J.E.*, 1st ed., vol. XII, 30-33.

Le Déaut, R. "Le titre de *Summus Sacerdos* donné à Melchisédech est-il d'origine juive?" *Recherches de Science Religieuse* 50 (1962), 224ff.

_____. "Une citation de Lévitique 26:45 dans le Document de Damas 1:4; 6:2". *R.Q.* 6 (1967), 289-92.

_____. "A propos d'une définition du Midrash". *Biblica* 50 (1969).

Lehmann. M. R. "I Q Genesis Apocryphon in the Light of Targumim and Midrashim". *R.Q.* 1, 249-63.

Lieberman, S. "The Discipline in the so-called Dead Sea Manual of Discipline". *J.B.L.* (1952), 199-206.

Macho, A. Diez. "The Recently Discovered Palestinian Targum. Its Antiquity and Relationship with the other Targums". *Supplements to Vetus Testamentum*, vol. VII (1959), 222-45.

McCown, C. C. "Hebrew and Egyptian Apocalyptic Literature". *Harvard Theological Review* 18 (1925), 357-411.

MacDonald, John. "Memar Marqah. The Teaching of Marqah". *B.Z.A.W.* 84 (Berlin, 1963).

Menasce, P. J. de. "Traditions juives sur Abraham". *Cahiers Sioniens* (1951), 188-95.

Michalson, Carl. Review of *The Scope of Demythologizing"* by John Macquarrie in *Interpretation* 15 (1961), 496.

Mihaly, E. "A Rabbinic Defense of the Election of Israel. An Analysis of Sifre Deuteronomy 32:9, Pisqa 312". *H.U.C.A.* 36 (1969), 103-63.

Morgenstern, J. "The Calendar of the Book of Jubilees, its Origin and its Character". *V.T.* V (1955), 34-76.

Mowinckel, S. "Oral Tradition". *I.D.B.* IV, 683ff.

Murphy O'Connor, J. "La Genèse littéraire de la Règle de la communauté. *R.B.* 76 (1969), 528-49.

Neusner, J. "Studies on the Taqqanot of Yavneh". *Harvard Theological Review* 63 (1970), 183-98.

Ochser, S. "Takkanah". *J.E.*, 1st ed., vol. XI, 669-76.

O'Del, J. "The Religious Background of the Psalms of Solomon". *R.Q.* 3 (1961), 241-58.

Parzen, H. "The Ruah Hakodesh in Tannaitic Literature". *J.Q.R.* (1929), 51-76.

Patte, Daniel. "Histoire et foi". *C.P.E.D.* (Paris, 1970), I-XIX.

Perrot, C. "La lecture synagogale d'Exode XXI-XXII". *A la Rencontre de Dieu. Mémorial Albert Gelin* (Le Puy, 1961), 229.

Ploeg, J. van der. "Un Targum du livre de Job: Nouvelle Découverte dans le desert de Juda". *Bible et Vie Chrétienne* 58 (1964), 79-87.

Rabin, Ch. "Notes on the Habakkuk Scroll and the Damasan Document". *V.T.* 5 (1955), 168-77.

Rabinowitz, L. I. "The Study of a Midrash". *J.Q.R.* 58 (1967), 147ff.

Rad, G. von. "Typological Interpretation of the Old Testament". *Essays on Old Testament Hermeneutics*, 17-39.

Reicke, Bo. "Remarques sur l'Histoire de la Forme (*Formgeschichte*) des textes de Qumran". *Les Manuscrits de la Mer Morte*, Colloque de Strasbourg (1955).

Ricoeur, Paul. "Problèmes actuels de l'interprétation". *C.P.E.D.* (Paris, Mars, 1970), 51-70.

Rist, M. "Enoch". *I.D.B.*, vol. II, 103ff.

_____. "Assumption of Moses". *I.D.B.*, vol. III, 450ff.

Robert, A. "Genres Littéraires". *D.B.S.*, vol. V, col. 411ff.

_____. "Les attaches littéraires bibliques de Prov. I-IX". *R.B.* 43 (1934), 47ff., 172ff., 374ff.; 44 (1935), 344ff., 502ff.

_____. Le sens du mot 'Loi' dans le Ps. CIX". *R.B.* 46 (1937), 182-206.

_____. "Le Psaume CIX et les Sapientiaux". *R.B.* 48 (1939), 5-20.

_____. "Le Yahwisme de Prov. X, 1-XXII, 16; XXV-XXIX". *Mémorial Lagrange* (Paris, 1940), 163-82.

_____. "Le genre littéraire du Cantique des Cantiques". *R.B.* 52 (1944), 192-213.

Roberts, B. J. "The Dead Sea Scrolls and the Old Testament Scriptures". *B.J.R.L.* 36 (1953), 75-96.

Silberman, L. H. "Language and Structure in the Hodayot (1 QH 3)". *J.B.L.* (1956), 96-106.

_____. "A Note on 4 Q Florilegium". *J.B.L.* 78 (1959), 158ff.

_____. "Unriddling the Riddle. A Study in the Structure and Language of the Habakkuk Pesher". *R.Q.* 3 (1961), 224-64.

Slomovic, E. "Toward an Understanding of the Exegesis in the Dead Sea Scrolls". *R.Q.* 7 (1969), 3-15.

Slonimsky, Henry. "The Philosophy Implicit in the Midrash". *Hebrew Union College Annual* (1956), 235ff.

Smith, M. "Testaments of the Twelve Patriarchs". *I.D.B.*, vol. IV, 575ff.

Sonne, I. "Synagogue". *I.D.B.*, vol. IV, 476-91.

Stendhal, K. "Contemporary Biblical Theology". *I.D.B.*, vol. I, 418ff.

Strugnell, John. "The Angelic Liturgy at Qumrân 4 Q". *Serekh Sîrôt 'Olat Hassabbôt. Congress Volume Oxford 1959* (Leiden, 1960). 318-45.

Talmon, S. "The Calendar Reckoning of the Sect from the Judaean Desert". *Scripta Hierosolymitana* IV, 187ff.

Tedesche, S. "Book of Jubilees". *I.D.B.*, vol. II, 1002ff.

Thomas, D. Winton. "The Dead Sea Scrolls: What May We Believe?" *Annual of Leeds University Oriental Society*, vol. VI (1969) 7-20.

Treves, M. "The Meaning of the Qumran Testimonia". *R.Q.* 2 (1960), 569-71.

Vermès, G. "Notes sur la formation de la Tradition juive". *Cahiers Sioniens* (1953), 320-42.

———. "Essenes-Therapeutai-Qumran". *Durham University Journal* (1960), 97ff.

———. "The Qumran Interpretation of Scripture in its Historical Setting". *Annual of Leeds University Oriental Society* (Leiden, 1969), 84-97.

Vogt, E. "'Mysteria' in Textibus Qumran". *Biblica*, 37 (1956), 247-57.

Wernberg-Møller, P. "Some Reflexions on the Biblical Material in the Manual of Discipline". *Stud. Theol.* 9 (1955), 40-66.

———. "An Inquiry into the Validity of the Text-Critical Argument for an Early Dating of the Recently Discovered Palestinian Targum". *Vet. Test.* 12 (1962), 312-31.

———. "The Nature of the Yadah according to the Manual of Discipline and related documents". *Annual of Leeds University Oriental Society*, vol. VI (Leiden, 1969), 56-81.

Wiesenberg, E. "The Jubilee of Jubilees". *R.Q.* 3 (1961), 3-40.

Winter, P. "Psalms of Solomon". *I.D.B.*, vol III, 958ff.

Wonde, A. S. van. "Le Maître de Justice et les deux Messies". *La Secte de Qumran et les origines du Christianisme* (Louvain, 1959), 127ff.

Wright, A. G. "The Literary Genre Midrash". *C.B.Q.* (1966), 105-38.

Zeitlin, S. "The Book of Jubilees, its Character and its Significance". *J.Q.R.* XXX (1939), 1-31.

———. "The Halaka: Introduction to Tannaitic Jurisprudence". *J.Q.R.* XXXIX (1948-49), 4ff.

———. "Midrash: A Historical Study". *J.Q.R.* XLIV (1953), 21-36.